A CHURCH HISTORY
OF SCOTLAND

A CHURCH HISTORY OF SCOTLAND

BY

J. H. S. BURLEIGH

Formerly Principal of New College and
Professor of Ecclesiastical History
in the University of
Edinburgh

LONDON
OXFORD UNIVERSITY PRESS
NEW YORK   TORONTO

Oxford University Press, Ely House, London W. 1

GLASGOW NEW YORK TORONTO MELBOURNE WELLINGTON
CAPE TOWN IBADAN NAIROBI DAR ES SALAAM LUSAKA ADDIS ABABA
DELHI BOMBAY CALCUTTA MADRAS KARACHI LAHORE DACCA
KUALA LUMPUR SINGAPORE HONG KONG TOKYO

ISBN 0 19 213921 5

© Oxford University Press 1960

First edition 1960
Third impression 1973

Printed in Great Britain
at the University Press, Oxford
by Vivian Ridler
Printer to the University

PREFACE

THERE has been in recent years a marked increase of interest in Scottish studies, in which Scottish ecclesiastical affairs have shared, and to which the celebration of the fourth centenary of the Reformation may be expected to contribute. There will be many and various appraisals of that tumultuous movement, which was a turning-point in the political and cultural no less than in the ecclesiastical history of Scotland. Some will hold that the Reformation brought about a complete breach with the past. This view can find support in the utterances of the Reformers. So possessed were they by the sense of the need to purge the Church of glaring and universally admitted corruptions that they cared little or not at all to preserve institutional continuity. Nevertheless, in their adherence to the Scriptures and the ancient creeds, in their teaching regarding the nature of the Church, and in their insistence on the primary importance of its pastoral function, they conserved essential elements of continuity even while they preferred to think of themselves as restoring the True Church according to the Word of God.

However this may be, the church history of Scotland did not begin with the Reformation. *Ecclesia Scoticana*—the Kirk of Scotland—goes back a long way even before the name appeared officially in a papal bull towards the end of the twelfth century and passed into common usage. The expression would be as familiar and as dear to Cardinal Beaton as to John Knox, however different might be the picture it would conjure up in their minds. To Beaton it would suggest an ancient and venerable institution whose properties and privileges, rights, liberties, and jurisdictions had been repeatedly guaranteed by kings and parliaments, and whose prelates ranked with the magnates of the kingdom. To Knox from his Biblicist point of view the picture would be of the Church of Christ Jesus 'showing its face' in Scotland wherever the Word of God was truly preached and the dominical

Sacraments were rightly administered, with or without, though preferably with, the encouragement and support of 'the regiment'. These two views, though seeming to contrast violently, are in reality complementary; but they must be held in tension if the ecclesiastical history of a people is to be the record of the impact of the Christian Revelation on its life and not merely a form of its cultural history. Such tension has been a distinctive mark of the church history of Scotland since the Reformation, and especially during the crucial period 1560–1688.

To trace the church history of Scotland through all its phases from Ninian and Columba down to the present day is a formidable undertaking unlikely to avoid being controversial. The choice of title presented difficulty. The Church of Scotland to most readers today is one denomination among others. Yet the name expresses an idea, born before denominations were thought of, which has always had a fascination for the Scottish mind, and still has a powerful appeal. To some extent it has determined the scope of this book, which devotes perhaps less attention than it should to bodies which have diverged from the main stream of religious faith and practice in Scotland. By comparison with England Scotland has proved an unfruitful field for the more individualistic and exclusive post-Reformation denominations. Independents, Baptists, Methodists, and many others have contributed valuable elements to the religious life of the nation, but have tended to remain small groups. Possibly a Presbyterian *Volkskirche* sufficiently satisfies the requirements of the *Gemeinde* principle. Certainly Presbyterianism has known much division, but normally the pattern has been preserved and the idea of a National Church has not been seriously questioned.

Two denominations, however, presently existing in Scotland have been competitors for the name Church of Scotland, and sometimes claim to be the rightful heirs. The Scottish Episcopal Church originated with those who refused to accept the Revolution Settlement of 1688, and suffered for its loyalty to the Stuart dynasty. Since 1792, when it made its peace with the government, it has developed an active church

life and has had an appeal on social but also on devotional
and liturgical grounds. But though influential it has remained numerically small. It prizes its roots in Scottish
history and resents the popular appellation 'The English
Church'. But in the eyes of many of its clergy, Anglo-
Catholics attracted from England by the liberty to be enjoyed in a 'free' Church, it appears rather as the Scottish
Province of the Anglican Communion.

The Roman Catholic Church survived the Reformation
and was able to maintain and expound its faith in the Highlands and Islands even under the penal laws. Its record up
to the date of Emancipation is one of obscure and patient
missionary activity and slowly developing organization.
Only in 1878, and then with considerable hesitation, was the
hierarchy restored, but by that time it had been reinforced
by a massive immigration of Irish labour into the industrial
towns, where its strength still lies. With two archbishoprics
and six bishoprics and some 700,000 adherents it is now the
second largest church in the country, wielding immense
political power and carrying on unceasing and confident
propaganda, but still to the mass of Scots a strange and alien
community.

As this book is addressed to the general reader and not to
the specialist its pages have not been overloaded with foot-
notes. Scottish terms have been explained and references
have been given, where they seemed to be specially called for,
to the sources from which information has been drawn. A
Bibliography has been added which is obviously only a guide
to the more important literature available for consultation.

J. H. S. B.

New College, Edinburgh
May 1960

CONTENTS

MAPS

PART I
THE BEGINNINGS

I

ROMAN BRITAIN AND THE
EARLY BRITISH CHURCH

FOR the beginnings of Christianity in the country we now call Scotland we must go back to Roman times before the Scots had begun to make their home there. The whole island was known as Britannia and its numerous Celtic (Brythonic) tribes were designated collectively Britanni. It was from the Church as it grew up in Roman Britain that the Gospel came to the peoples of the north and west, and this must be our starting-point.

In 54 B.C. Julius Caesar invaded Britannia, but not until the reign of Claudius (A.D. 41–54) was its conquest seriously undertaken and a Roman province of Britain established in the south-eastern part of the island. By A.D. 71 the conquest had been pressed as far north as York, and Agricola, imperial governor from 78 to 85, envisaged the annexation of the whole of Britannia and indeed of the neighbouring Hibernia as well. By the end of 83 he had established a line of forts between the Forth and the Clyde, and next year he penetrated north of the Tay and defeated a confederate army of Britanni under Calgacus at the Battle of Mons Graupius, probably in Angus, between Forfar and Brechin. His recall in 85 put an end to his ambitious project, and in 120 the frontier of Roman Britain was fixed by the Emperor Hadrian and fortified by a wall bearing his name and running from the Tyne to the Solway. The erection of the Antonine Wall from the Forth to the Clyde in 142–3 indicates that the security of the province was felt to demand the military occupation of the region between the walls. By 184 this was abandoned.

The troublesome tribes of the north were for a second time visited by a Roman army when the Emperor Septimius Severus led a punitive expedition as far as modern Aberdeenshire. He withdrew, however, to Hadrian's Wall, which he repaired (211). Towards the end of the century the frontier

was again threatened and Constantius Chlorus, father of
Constantine, had to undertake a campaign in the north
'against the Caledonians and other Picts'. Here a new name
appears in the history of Britain. Who were the Picts? Were
they a people recently arrived in north Britain? Or were
they, as is now generally believed, the descendants of the
unsubjugated Britanni of the north, regarded as savages by
their romanized kinsfolk of the province, and hated and
dreaded as dangerous foes? The Latin writers, Claudian and
Gildas, use the name in the sense of 'tattooed savages'. Certainly from their first appearance in history the Picts were
enemies of the Roman province, liable from time to time to
storm over the frontier and carry their plundering raids far
to the south. In the eighth century Bede knew them as the
most important people in north Britain, from the Forth to
the Orkney Islands. They merged with the Scots during the
period of the Viking invasions, and their name and almost
every trace of their existence had disappeared by the end of
the eleventh century.

About 367 another name appears in the Latin writers,
coined by the Romano-Britons to designate another hostile
people who harassed the province as marauders from Hibernia across the sea. The Scots, or the Gael as they called themselves, seem to have effected a settlement for a time on the
northern coast of what we now call Wales, from which they
were ejected *c.* 400, by a British chieftain Cunedda. He and
his tribe, Collingwood supposes, were transported from the
neighbourhood of Berwick-on-Tweed to undertake the defence of the province in the west.[1] Later (*c.* 450) the Scots
were more successful with their settlement in Argyll, which
became the cradle of modern Scotland.

Throughout the fourth century the central imperial government had done its best to protect the province from its enemies, but in 410 it was compelled to withdraw its forces for
more urgent duties nearer home, leaving the cities of Britain
to look after their own defence and government. Very soon
the Anglo-Saxons from the Continent, who had long troubled
the province with their piratical raids, came to stay. During

[1] R. G. Collingwood, *Roman Britain*, p. 289.

the fifth century they extinguished Roman civilization in the eastern parts of Britain and drove the romanized Britons northwards and westwards, and across the sea to Brittany.

The establishment of the Roman province of Britain in A.D. 50 opened the door to Roman civilization. Government officials and their staffs, merchants, and craftsmen arrived in the wake of the soldiers. Towns were built whose citizens were partly immigrants from the Continent, but partly also natives; and by the beginning of the second century teachers of literature and rhetoric were in demand to instruct the sons of the British chiefs. Among these civilian incomers there were possibly some Christians. At all events Tertullian of Carthage and Origen of Alexandria in the first half of the third century refer to the existence of Christians in Britain, though Tertullian doubtless exaggerates when he refers *c.* 211 to 'regions of the Britons inaccessible to the Romans but subject to Christ'. The British Church claimed to have produced three martyrs, including St. Alban, during the persecution of Diocletian (*c.* 300), and it sent three bishops (London, York, and ? Lincoln), a presbyter, and a deacon to the Council of Arles (314), to which the Emperor Constantine, now a Christian, had summoned representatives of the Churches in the western half of the Empire. Athanasius testifies to its steady support of the orthodox cause during the Arian controversy, and it was again represented by a number of bishops, certainly more than three, at the Council of Ariminum, 359. As by the Edict of Caracalla, 211, Britons acquired Roman citizenship and became *Romani*, so by the Edict of Theodosius (380) they became *Christiani*, at least officially. It is important to remember that in faith, worship, and institutions the Church in Britain was an integral part of the Catholic Church.

By 380 the Roman power in Britain was tottering, but shortly after that date the British Church produced three figures of historical importance. The first, Pelagius, does not concern us here. He left his native land at an early age, became a monk, possibly in the East, and was for some years resident in Rome as a respected teacher of the Christian way of life before, in 411, he became the unwilling cause of the

B

controversy that has since been known by his name. Of Patricius we shall have more to say later, but something must now be said of the somewhat shadowy Ninian. Here it is best to follow the succinct account given by Bede, derived probably from his friend Pechthelm, the contemporary Anglian Bishop of Candida Casa, and representing the local tradition of the place in the eighth century.

Ninian was a British Christian and presumably also a Roman citizen who, like Pelagius, went abroad to study. At Rome—where he must at least have heard of Jerome, Ambrose, and perhaps even the newly baptized Augustine—he was 'regularly instructed in the true faith and mysteries'. That is to say, he knew nothing of the aberrations of the Celtic Church which were troubling the contemporaries of Bede. Returning to Britain as a bishop he chose for the seat of his bishopric a place on the north shore of the Solway where 'he built a church of stone in a manner unusual among the Britons [of Bede's time] and dedicated it to St. Martin the bishop, and there he lies buried together with several saints'. The place of Ninian's settlement came to be known as *Ad Candidam Casam*, 'At the White House', now Whithorn. Moreover, Bede tells us—and this is the reason for introducing the account of Ninian—that at his preaching the Southern Picts, who were separated from their northern kinsmen by dreadful mountains, forsook idolatry and embraced the truth of the Gospel. Obviously Bede cannot here mean that there were Picts in Galloway. 'Picts of the Nith' are nowhere referred to in his History, and their existence is extremely doubtful. It appears that the claim is being made—a claim that has been revived in modern times—that the credit for the evangelization of the Picts must in part at least go to Ninian and not wholly to Columba.

The period of Ninian's activity at Whithorn may be dated 397–431, but it is not easy to estimate the nature and extent of his labours. It would be helpful if we could assume that his dedication of his church to St. Martin implies that he had learned his methods. Martin was Bishop of Tours in Gaul, 381–97, but he was much else besides. His fame is chiefly due to his being abbot of a great monastery and to his energetic evangelism throughout central Gaul. Ninian could have found neither a Roman *civitas* nor a Christian congregation at Whithorn to which he might minister as bishop in the ordinary sense. His original settlement must have been of the nature of a monastery and a monastic school, as it certainly was later. The people among whom he settled must have been Britons with only the slightest tincture of Roman ways, and his diocese, if we may use the word, might have corresponded to what was soon to become the British principality of Rheged, comprising Galloway, Dumfriesshire, and Cumberland. As for his mission to the Picts the evidence is scanty, consisting mainly of archaeological objects such as sculptured stones and church dedications at Glasgow, Stirling, Blairgowrie, Arbirlot, Dunnottar, and places farther north still. In any case Candida Casa remained after Ninian's death an important Christian centre. As a monastic school from 431 to 731 it attracted students from Hibernia. In the eighth century, when it passed into the possession of the Angles, it was the seat of an Anglian bishopric subject to York, and Ninian's tomb was held in special honour. To this period belong the Ruthwell Cross and other interesting examples of Northumbrian Christian art. After a long, dark, and troubled history Candida Casa emerges again in the eleventh century as the seat of a medieval bishopric, ecclesiastically subject to the Archbishop of York.

St. Patrick is fervently acclaimed today as the Apostle of Ireland, but with equal appropriateness he might be called the Apostle of the Scots, Ireland in his time being the land of the Scots. But here we are confronted with a problem. Patrick's name is unknown to Bede and seems to have fallen into oblivion for at least two centuries even in Ireland. Prosper of Aquitaine (died 463) in his *Chronicon*, under the year 431, says that 'Palladius was sent by Pope Celestine to the Scots who believed in Christ as their first bishop'. This must be the deacon Palladius who, according to Prosper, had two years earlier moved Pope Celestine to send Germanus of Auxerre and Lupus of Troyes to Britain as his vicars (*vice sua*) to confound the Pelagian heretics who were then troubling the Church in Britain. So, says Prosper in another work,

'Celestine took care to keep the Roman island Catholic and to make the barbarous island Christian'. This is the story of the beginning of the Church in Ireland as Bede knew it.

It need not surprise us to be told that there were communities of Christian Scots in Ireland in 431, or that Celestine sent them a bishop in the person of Palladius, who was conceivably in Rome as a delegate of the Church in Britain sent to solicit aid against Pelagianism. But of Palladius' work in Ireland there is not a trace, while the successful mission of Patrick to the still heathen Scots began in 432. It has been surmised that Palladius died soon after his arrival, or, more desperately, that he was in fact identical with Patrick. Happily we need not concern ourselves with this problem, for a fascinating figure is presented to us in two short writings which bear upon the face of them the marks of genuineness, the *Confession* of Patrick and Patrick's *Letter to Coroticus*. In these two documents the true beginning of the Church of the Scots is revealed.

Patrick's *Confession*, in spite of its brevity and simplicity, may be compared with the *Confessions* of St. Augustine. It is no less sincere, and its purpose is the same, to acknowledge the good hand of God upon the writer throughout his life. Patrick tells us he was born near the village of Banavem Taberniae, a place unidentified, but most likely situated in the lower Severn valley. The year of his birth, it has been calculated, would be 389. His father Calpornius, son of Potitus a presbyter, had a small estate (*villula*) close by and was a *decurio*, i.e. a member of the governing class in Roman provincial society, and a deacon of the Church. Patrick came, therefore, of a well-to-do Romano-British family that had long been Christian. Indeed for Patrick 'Roman' and 'Christian' are not distinguishable.[1] Nevertheless, he has to confess that as a boy he had been careless and had neglected not only his religious duties but also the opportunity offered him of a literary education. To the end of his life he laments that by his own fault he was illiterate and unlearned. His Latin writings, as he says, prove it.

[1] Cf. Third *Dictum* of Patrick: 'Ecclesia Scotorum, immo Romanorum, ut Christiani ita ut Romani sitis. . . .

In 405, when he was sixteen years old, Scots pirates from Ireland raided his father's estate and carried him and many of the estate workers into slavery, 'a due punishment for our sins', and for six years he served as a cattle-man in Ireland. His misfortunes led him to turn to religion, and in answer to his frequent and fervent prayers God mercifully enabled him to escape. Of the next long years of wandering by land and sea he gives a brief and very confused account, but at last he reached his home in Britain, where his kinsfolk received him as a son, and besought him to stay with them. But,

> Then I saw in the night visions a man whose name was Victoricus coming as it were from Ireland with countless letters, and he gave me one of them . . . entitled The Voice of the Irish, and while I was reading aloud the beginning of the letter I thought . . . I heard the voice of them who lived beside the wood of Foclut which is nigh unto the western sea. And then they cried as with one mouth, 'We beseech thee, holy youth, to come and walk among us once more.' . . .

Another night Christ appeared to him saying, 'He who laid down his life for thee, he it is who speaketh in thee.'

Nothing now could content him but to return to Ireland as a missionary, and in spite of the vehement opposition of his family, his friends, and 'the elders' on the ground of the dangerous nature of the project, his illiteracy, and general unfitness to undertake it, he at last achieved his purpose, and went to Ireland with the rank of bishop. He does not tell us where he got his training and ordination, but one of the Patrician *dicta* preserved in the Book of Armagh says, 'I had the fear of God as the guide of my journey through Gaul, Italy and in the islands of the Tyrrhene Sea.' This may be held to indicate a sojourn at Auxerre, whose Bishop Germanus was well known and influential in Britain, and at Lérins, an island monastery near Marseilles which had a long connexion with the British Church. He did not make good the deficiencies in his literary education but he received a grounding in Christian doctrine and acquired great proficiency in the Latin Bible.

Patrick's work in Ireland continued from 432 till his death

in 461. His labours were immense, and his life was often in danger. Not only did he live in exile and an alien among a barbarous people, but he had to face much hostility from native kings and chiefs. Once at least an army from Britain (Strathclyde) under Coroticus, who regarded himself as a Roman general, descended on Ireland and slew or enslaved many of Patrick's converts. In his letter of protest to Coroticus he upbraids him and his soldiers as unworthy of being called Romans, being but a pack of mercenaries, heathen Scots, and apostate Picts. The use of the word 'apostate' possibly corroborates the claim of Ninian to have evangelized the Picts. Nevertheless, Patrick's mission was attended with much success. He preached the Gospel where it had never been preached before. He baptized multitudes and ordained clergy for them, and many youths and maidens of noble families adopted the religious life, becoming monks and nuns, often in despite of their parents. To all this Patrick points in justification of his mission, and as evidence of the goodness of God to one who was but an ill-qualified evangelist.

The Christianity Patrick brought to Ireland was, of course, that of the Catholic Church in Britain and Gaul. The Church of the Scots was to be identical with the Church of the Romans (i.e. romanized Britons and Gauls) in creed, in liturgy, in life, and in organization. Even its ecclesiastical language was Latin. But to evangelize a barbarous people and organize its Church must have been a superhuman task for one man with only a few fellow labourers. If Patrick got support from some local kings, in the nature of things there could be no Irish Constantine. Not only does he dwell on his toil, but even hints that his success may be precarious. Often he used to desire exceedingly to withdraw to Britain, to his fatherland and kindred, or to Gaul to visit the brethren and behold the faces of the Lord's saints, but that would be disloyalty to the mission appointed to him by Christ, and 'I fear to lose the labour which I began'.[1] When he died in 461 the future of the Irish Church can hardly have seemed secure, and especially since already the Anglo-Saxons in Britain and the Franks in Gaul were driving a wedge of heathenism

[1] *Confessio*, ch. 43.

that more and more threatened to isolate the churches of Britain and Ireland from the Western Church on the Continent. It is interesting to note that these churches accepted the system of calculating Easter adopted by Leo the Great of Rome in 455, indicating that contact was still unbroken at that date. By 600 obstinate adherence to that system was to be one of the characteristic marks of the 'Celtic' churches.

Patrick, it may be assumed, endeavoured to reproduce in Ireland the pattern of the continental episcopate, with a provincial primacy at Armagh, where he is said to have fixed, in 444, his own episcopal seat. The political configuration in Ireland must have rendered this difficult, for there were no *civitates* and *provinciae* such as had provided the basis for the Church's territorial organization within the Roman Empire. But where a diocesan episcopate could not take root, monasticism could and did. In the sixth century in Ireland Christian leadership passed to a number of saintly abbots, each ruling a vast 'family' of monks. One illustration may be taken from the Life of St. Comgall of Bangor. From Bangor 'very many churches and monasteries were built not only in the region of the Ultonians but also throughout the other provinces of Ireland. . . . In these churches and monasteries there were 3,000 monks under the care of the holy father Comgall.' Precisely the same development had been taking place in what was left of Roman Britain, i.e. in Wales under the leadership of Illtud, Dewi, Gildas, and others. Gildas is said to have spent much time in Ireland, and it is recorded that the second order of Irish saints 'received a Mass from David the bishop, Gillas and Docus, who were Britons'. On the other hand several of the great Irish monastic leaders are said to have had part of their training in Britain, especially at Menevia (St. David's), e.g. Finnian of Clonard, and at Candida Casa, e.g. Finnian of Moville, Columba's teacher, and Brendan of Clonfert. In the sixth century, therefore, the relations of the churches in Britain and Ireland were very close. They developed certain common characteristics which distinguished them from the churches in other lands. In particular, in these Celtic churches, as we may now call them, monasticism prevailed over the form of church organization normal elsewhere. The ancient orders of bishops, presbyters, and deacons continued to perform their traditional ritual functions but within a monastic framework. Apart from their special functions they were primarily monks under the care of an abbot who might or might not be in episcopal orders. Columba and his successors as abbots of Iona were simple presbyters, to whom, as Bede notes with astonishment, even bishops were subject.

II

ST. COLUMBA AND IONA

OF the abbots of sixth-century Ireland two achieved more than local fame. Columba the younger, or St. Columbanus as he is usually called, was trained at the Irish Bangor under St. Comgall. About 590 he went to Gaul with twelve companions, penetrated to Burgundy and laboured there with such success that soon his 'family' came to embrace three monasteries, Annegray, Luxeuil, and Fontaines. Driven from Burgundy, where his reforming zeal made him powerful enemies, he worked for a time in the neighbourhood of Lake Constance with lasting effects. Finally he crossed the Alps into Italy and founded the great monastery of Bobbio where he ended his days (616), true to the last to the traditional practices of his native land. His extant writings, viz. his *Rule, Penitential*, and several *Epistles*— one addressed to Pope Gregory the Great—attest the vitality of the Scotic Church, and throw light on its relations with the Church on the Continent.

The fame of the elder St. Columba belongs entirely to the British Isles. No writings of his are preserved except some poems credibly attributed to him; but his *Life* by Adamnan is the most important source of information regarding the Scotic Church during its most flourishing period. Adamnan was the ninth abbot of Iona, and head of the community founded by St. Columba. He was therefore the proud guardian of the fame of *Noster Patronus*. His work is hagiography rather than biography. It is divided into three books which offer in a series of disconnected chapters illustrations of the gifts of prophecy, miracles (*virtutes*), and angelic visitations vouchsafed to the saint. Chronological order is neglected, and many questions of great importance from an historical point of view are left unanswered. Nevertheless, from innumerable casual hints a picture emerges of the man, his character and work.

St. Columba was born at Gartan in Donegal in 521, of
royal parentage on both sides, a fact of some importance for
his character and career. Early attracted to the religious life
he entered the monastic school of Moville (Maghbile),
County Down, under Abbot Finnian (Finbar). There in due
course he was ordained deacon. Passing south he spent some
time with an ancient bard, Gemman, cultivating his poetic
gift. Soon he is found at Clonard whose abbot was the other
Finnian, 'The Tutor of Erin's Saints', and had as his companions several men who were later to be ranked with him
among the Twelve Apostles of Ireland. A curious story tells
how he was sent by Abbot Finnian to St. Etchen of Clonfad
to be ordained bishop, and how the saint by mistake ordained him presbyter. St. Columba saw in this the will of
God for him and vowed never to seek the higher dignity.
This story would explain why as abbot of Iona Columba
retained the rank of presbyter merely, and why his successors were always presbyters, never bishops.

After paying visits to other famous monastic centres, St.
Columba returned in 543 to Ulster, where he founded his
first monastery at Derry (Londonderry), and for twenty years
thereafter he carried on his apostolate in other parts of Ireland. As his disciples multiplied Durrow and Kells were
added to Derry. Then in 563 he crossed to Britain and
founded the monastery of Iona with which his name henceforth has been chiefly associated. Of this move Adamnan says
quite simply, 'In the second year after the Battle of Culdrevne
in the forty-second year of his age he sailed away from
Scotia (Ireland) to Britannia, wishing to live as a pilgrim for
Christ's sake' (*peregrinari pro Christo*). From what follows it is
apparent that by *peregrinari* Adamnan means 'to live the
religious life', which is the normal meaning in monastic
Latin.

Perhaps, however, it was not so simple. Other ancient
writers offer other explanations. The Battle of Culdrevne was
fought by the O'Neills, Columba's clan, in alliance with the
men of Connaught, against Diarmid MacCerball, High King
of Ireland, and the cause of the dispute was a judgement of
the latter to the effect that Columba must give up a copy of

a psalter which he had made surreptitiously without the permission of the owner of the original. Stung by what he regarded as an injury the scion of kings had called his clansmen to arms, supported them by his prayers, and was thus responsible for the deaths of 3,000 men slain in the battle. His vengefulness called down upon him the censures of the Church, moved by which, or alternatively, by remorse, he resolved to go into exile. Adamnan says nothing of this, but he does record that a synod met at Teltown in order to excommunicate Columba 'for certain venial and excusable causes, not rightly as became clear afterwards'. But as Columba entered, St. Brendan of Birr rose and gave him an honourable greeting. Reproached by his colleagues Brendan related how God had shown him a column of light preceding Columba and angels accompanying him. 'I dare not spurn a man whom I see foreordained by God to bring many people to life.' 'At these words they dared not proceed to excommunicate the Saint, but on the contrary honoured him with much veneration.' At all events, St. Columba's connexion with Ireland was by no means broken. He continued to exercise supervision over the Churches he had founded there. He received visits from notable Irish churchmen and was able to return them, and he retained a great influence in Irish affairs both ecclesiastical and civil.

Since *c.* 450 Scots from Northern Ireland (Dalriada) had effected a settlement in modern Argyll and had set up a kingdom of Dalriada in Britain. In 559 they had been conquered and reduced to subjection by Brude MacMaelchon, King of the Picts. Iona may have been part of the kingdom of Dalriada, but permission to settle there had apparently to be obtained from Brude as overlord. St. Columba, therefore, undertook the long and arduous journey to Brude's castle near Inverness. We learn elsewhere that he was accompanied and supported by Comgall of Bangor and Cainech of Aghaboe, who already had some acquaintance with the Picts. Brude, a heathen much influenced by his Druids, refused to admit the saints. But at the sign of the Cross, made by Columba according to Adamnan, the doors of his fortress flew open, and Brude henceforth honoured the saint as was meet. Presumably this means that permission to settle in Iona was granted, possibly also permission to evangelize in Pictland, but, though he gives several instances of Columba's vanquishing the Druids, Adamnan nowhere suggests that he converted Brude, or his people as a whole, to Christianity.

Iona (the Iovan island, in Adamnan; Hy or I in Gaelic; later Icolmkil) is a sea-girt island, 3 by 1½ miles, separated from the Ross of Mull by a Sound 1 mile in width. The southern part is rough and boggy and the north is even wilder, rising to a height of 330 feet in Duni, the highest point in the island. Through the centre from east to west runs a broad plain, the Machair, suitable both for pasture and corn-growing. Lying under the shelter of Duni to the east, and sloping gently to the Sound and the harbour, there is a strip of flat land, and here, some 100 yards north of the present Abbey, Columba planted the monastery which was to be his home or headquarters for thirty-four years until his death in 597. The buildings included, in addition to the huts of the monks and the abbot's house which stood apart and overlooked the whole, a little oratory, a refectory, and a guest house or hospice, which was very much in use, also a barn, a mill, and a byre. All these would be simple structures and nothing now remains of them. Only the mill-pond and the course of the stream that turned the mill-wheel may still be traced. In a wild rocky glen some distance away there are the remains of an isolated circular hermit-cell, recalling a notable feature of Celtic monasticism.

St. Columba brought twelve monks with him from Ireland, but the number soon grew and included Britons and Saxons as well as Scots. The monks naturally took some vow, but we do not know its exact terms, and there must have been some kind of rule even if it was not so elaborate as that of St. Benedict. Adamnan makes no reference to any rule, but indicates that the abbot's will was law and instant obedience was demanded. But if his power over his 'family' was absolute, it was also tenderly paternal. As in Benedictine monasteries worship and work alternated. The Canonical Hours were observed on ordinary days, and the Eucharist was celebrated on Sundays and Holy Days, and on other occasions as commanded by the abbot. The work of the *seniores* was copying the Scriptures and illuminating manuscripts. Though Adamnan does not mention it, we may suppose that the art which was to blossom later in the beautiful Books of Durrow and Kells would not be unknown in Iona. Farm work and household duties about the monastery would employ the younger monks, and it would appear that the community was economically self-supporting. Of theological thought there is not a trace, and it would be difficult to justify from Adamnan the high claims to learning sometimes made on behalf of the Scotic monks. But Adamnan could write in flowing Latin, as in his other work *De Locis Sanctis*, when he was not hampered by names of men and places, 'in the base Scotic tongue'.

It is needless once again to gather together the details of the daily life of the Iona community. That has been admirably done by Reeves, Duke, and several others.[1] Here it will be sufficient to quote a well-known passage from Adamnan's Preface, in which he describes the monkish life as perfectly exemplified by St. Columba himself.

Dedicated from boyhood to the Christian service, and by the study of wisdom and the grace of God keeping his body clean and his mind pure, though placed on earth, he showed himself fit for heavenly ways. Angelic in look, graceful in speech, holy in work, with talents of the highest order, great in counsel; for 34 years he lived as a soldier of Christ upon an island (*insulanus miles*). He could not allow the space of even one hour to pass without busying himself with prayer or reading or writing or some other work. He was so engaged without intermission by day or night with indefatigable labours of fasts and vigils that the burden of each of these austerities might seem to be beyond human possibility. And in all these he was beloved by all, and, always showing cheerfulness on his holy countenance, in his inmost heart he joyed in the Holy Ghost.

Such virtues in Columba and his monks are amply illustrated by Adamnan, and we may well believe that the strange new life of which they were the expression would have an awe-inspiring impact upon contemporaries. But by themselves

[1] See Bibliography.

they would hardly lead us to expect the claim made for Iona by Columba in blessing the monastery a few days before he died. Standing on an eminence, he raised both hands in benediction, and said, 'On this place, small though it be and mean, not only the Kings of the Scots together with their peoples, but also the rulers of barbarous and foreign nations with their subjects will confer no ordinary honour; and by Saints of other Churches also it will be held in no ordinary veneration.' This prophecy was certainly fulfilled by Adamnan's time, and the 'Life' helps us to see why. Evidently Columba was more than *insulanus miles*.

Related as he was to the ruling families of Ireland, St. Columba was inevitably involved in their feuds, and sometimes showed an unchristian vindictiveness, but after his establishment in Iona his interventions were on the side of order, justice, and gentleness. Of his relations with Conall, King of Dalriada in Britain (560–74), we hear little. It may be that Conall granted him the island of Iona, and that the gift had to be confirmed by Brude. If so, we may well suppose that the transaction did something to mitigate the hostility of Pict and Scot. When Conall died in 574 St. Columba took the initiative in the selection of Aidan MacGabran as his successor, and 'ordained' him as king. Laying his hand on his head, he blessed him saying, 'Believe firmly, O Aidan, that none of your adversaries will be able to resist you unless you first deal falsely against me and my successors or my relatives in Ireland.' Next year St. Columba with a great retinue accompanied the new king to meet the High King of Ireland and other notables, and at a council at Drumceate an important if obscure agreement was reached between the two kings. At all events Aidan proved a vigorous king and during his reign (574–608) he succeeded in making his kingdom formidable. He was the founder of the Scottish monarchy which was destined in the course of history to bring under its rule and so to unify the territories now forming the kingdom of Scotland. To this result St. Columba in some measure contributed, though neither he nor anyone for centuries to come could have foreseen it.

St. Columba has owed his fame, however, not so much to

his contribution to the political history of Scotland, as to the belief that he was the Apostle of Scotland, and the founder of its Church. Of course in his day Scotia meant Ireland, and northern Britain was divided between four distinct and often warring peoples. The Angles of Northumbria had already penetrated to the Forth, and were disputing with the Britons of Strathclyde the possession of the western lowlands. North of the Forth and Clyde lay the lands of the Picts and Scots separated from each other by the mountain range that forms the boundary line today between Perthshire and Argyllshire —Drumalban or, in Adamnan, *Dorsum Brittaniae.*

It is a remarkable fact that missionary evangelism plays a very subordinate part among the activities of St. Columba according to Adamnan's account, even with regard to his Scotic compatriots. No doubt the Scots had brought their Christianity with them from Ireland, but before the coming of St. Columba to Iona we hear only of occasional and temporary sojourns of Irish saints in Dalriada. Columba, while continuing to direct his churches in Ireland, at least came to stay, and his 'family' soon spread beyond Iona. We hear of monasteries or of cells in Tiree, Mull, Islay, Elachnave (Hinba), Skye, and, on the mainland, in Kintyre, Morven, and, perhaps, near Loch Awe. Dr. Reeves has compiled a list[1] of some thirty churches of old dedicated to Columcille in Dalriada, the great majority in the islands. If Adamnan lays little stress on this expansion we must remember that his interest, as head of the Columban 'Order', was in its founder, and that the Scotic Church did not minister to its people through a territorial ministry. The word *parochia* had not acquired its modern significance, but was a synonym for an abbot's 'family', however widely scattered. The evidence seems to warrant the conclusion that the Iona community provided effective ministrations at least for the Scots of Dalriada.

Of the peoples to the south the English or 'Saxons' were heathen and hardly came within St. Columba's horizon, although two Saxon monks are mentioned as being with him in Iona. With his nearer neighbours, the Britons of Strathclyde,

[1] *Life of S. Columba*, Introduction, pp. lx–lxvii.

NORTHERN BRITANNIA

in the time of Bede
and Adamnan

ORKNEY

HIBERNIA

Moville
•Drumceate
•Armagh
Bangor

R. W. FORD

Tiree

SCIA
(Skye)

Apuorcrosan

ARDATHMURCOL

MORVEN

MALEA
(Mull)

Iona
(Hy)

Elachnave
(Hinba)

Coloso
(Colonsay)

ILEA
(Islay)

ARA
(Arran)

BUTE

Cinn-
garadh

Lismore

Rosemarkie

Brude's Castle
(Inverness)

Murthillauch
(Mortlach)

R. Spey

Aberdoboir
Deer

R. Dee

Dunnottar

Brechin

Restennet
ANGUS
Dunkeld
Dull
R. Tay

Dunnichen (Nechtansmere)
Arbirlot

Scone

Abernethy

Kilrymont
(St. Andrews)

Dunblane
Lochleven
R. Forth
Stirling

Isle of May

Inchkeith

Tyningham
Dunbar

Abercorn

MANAU

LOTHIAN

Coldingham

Lindisfarne
Bamburgh

Alcluith
(Dumbarton)

Glasgow
R. Clyde

Melrose

R. Tweed

R. Nith

Hodelme

Carlisle

R. Tyne
Hexham

Jarrow
Wearmouth

GALLOWAY
(RHEGED)

Candida Casa
(Whithorn)

Solway Firth

MILES 0 10 20 30 40 50

kinsmen of the Britons of Wales, he did have relations of a friendly nature. Adamnan tells how Rydderch, their king, whose stronghold was the Rock of Dumbarton, sent to St. Columba to inquire whether he would perish at the hands of his enemies and was assured that he would die peacefully in his bed. Rydderch was the patron of Kentigern of Glasgow (St. Mungo) and Kentigern's biographer gives an account of a meeting of the two saints and of the gift by St. Columba to Kentigern of a staff which was long venerated. There were also some Britons among the Iona monks. But as the Britons had long been Christian the question of a mission to them naturally did not arise. The British and the Scotic Churches held each other in mutual esteem.

The belief that St. Columba was the Apostle of the Picts goes back to Bede who says that he came to Britain 'to preach the word of God to the Northern Picts' (in contrast to the Southern Picts) and that 'he converted that nation to the Christian faith'. One might hazard the suggestion that Bede's distinction between the northern and southern Picts was simply an attempt to do justice to the competing claims of Whithorn and Iona to be the Mother Church of the Picts. Adamnan tells us of Columba's monasteries planted among the Picts and Scots and held in very high honour by both peoples. He claims that the immunity enjoyed by both peoples from the great plague of 664 that devastated western Europe, including Ireland and Northumbria, was due to the prayers of Columba in spite of the grievous sins and base ingratitude of both peoples. At the same time he has very little to say of a mission of Columba to the Picts. He does not claim that he converted King Brude, though he gives several instances of victorious contests with the Druids in the presence of the king. About six incidents are mentioned in connexion with journeys of Columba or sojourns of a few days 'beyond Drumalban'. Three times he is said to have preached to and converted and baptized a heathen Pict and his household, and on two of these occasions it is expressly said that he preached through an interpreter. Dr. Reeves has listed a number of church dedications to Columba in Pictland[1] but

---

[1] Op .cit., Introduction, pp. lxvii–lxxi.

he has included many that are now generally held to belong
not to St. Columba but to St. Colm, a later saint. Columba's
connexion with Dunkeld does not begin till his relics were
transferred there from Iona after 843. Perhaps we must con-
clude that the credit for the conversion of the Picts cannot
be given to any one man. The names of numberless saints
occur in legends and are found in ancient dedications all
over Pictland. But that Columba had an important part in
winning that people to Christ can hardly be doubted.

Adamnan closes with a moving account of St. Columba's
last days, death (597), and burial in Iona among his monks
who mourned him as a beloved father and cherished his
memory. Just before the end he had been transcribing the
Psalter and continued till he reached the words 'They that
seek the Lord shall want no manner of thing that is good.'
'Here', he said, 'I must stop. What follows let Baithen write',
thus designating his successor. Baithen was his cousin, and
had served for a time as 'provost' of the settlement in Tiree.
He held office for three years and was succeeded by Laisren.
The 'family' continued to be ruled by abbots, most of whom
belonged to the same stock, until in the ninth century Iona
was abandoned after repeated Viking devastations, when the
headship passed to Kells in Ireland and to Dunkeld in Alban,
as the united kingdom of Picts and Scots came to be called.

III

IONA AND LINDISFARNE

THE first contact of Scot and Sassenach occurred in
603 shortly after the death of St. Columba. The Angles
of Northumbria under King Ethelfrith had been for
some time extending their conquests over the Britons northwards to the Forth and westwards to the Irish Sea and the
Solway. Alarmed by their advance the King of Strathclyde
sought the help of Aidan, King of Dalriada, who came with
a mighty army but was defeated with great slaughter at Deg-
sastan (Dauston) in Dumfriesshire. 'From that time', says
Bede, 'no King of Scots dared to come into Britain to make
war on the English until this day.' Ethelfrith also defeated the
Britons of Wales in a great battle at Chester, so severing them
from their kinsmen of Strathclyde. But in 616 he was himself
defeated and slain by his cousin Edwin who succeeded him
as King of Northumbria.

The Northumbrians, unlike the Britons and Scots, were
heathen, but in 597 Augustine, the emissary of Pope Gregory
the Great, had begun his mission to the English and had
converted Ethelbehrt, King of Kent, whose queen, Bertha, a
Frankish princess from Paris, was already a Christian. Edwin
became a suitor for the hand of their daughter, and it was
stipulated that she should have freedom to practice her religion. She came north attended by a number of clerics from
Kent, including Bishop Paulinus, and armed with a letter to
Edwin from Pope Honorius I. In due course Edwin and his
Witan accepted Christianity and Paulinus began, we are
told, the wholesale baptism of the Northumbrians. Naturally
he made York, the old Roman Eboracum, his seat and there
built himself a temporary cathedral of wood. It looked as if
the plan of Pope Gregory for a second archbishopric in
Britain was about to be carried out, and an archiepiscopal
pallium for Paulinus was dispatched from Rome. Before it
arrived Edwin had been slain and Northumbria ravaged by

the Christian Cadwalla, king of Gwynedd, in what seemed to Bede unnatural and unholy alliance with Penda, the pagan king of Mercia. Of Cadwalla Bede writes,

> Though he had the name and profession of a Christian he was so barbarous in disposition and conduct that he spared neither women nor children . . . being determined to blot out the whole Anglian race from the borders of Britain. Nor did he pay any respect to the Christian religion which had sprung up among them, for until to-day it is the custom of the Britons to make light of the faith of the Angles.

Paulinus fled to Kent, leaving the deacon James to carry on his work at York as best he could.

Help, however, was at hand. During the reign of Edwin two of Ethelfrith's sons, Oswald and Oswiu, had lived in exile among the Scots of Dalriada, and Oswald had moreover spent some time in Iona where he fervently embraced the Christian faith and was baptized. On the death of Edwin he returned to Northumbria, gathered an army and, encouraged by a vision of Columba, attacked Cadwalla and slew him. Thus he became King of Northumbria and, according to Adamnan, 'Emperor of the whole of Britain'.

Oswald now sent to Iona, his spiritual home, for a missionary to evangelize his people. The first to be sent soon gave up the task in despair, but his successor, Aidan, undertook the mission more understandingly. He was a bishop of the Scotic type. He remained a member of the Iona 'family' subject to the abbot of Iona, and he founded a settlement on the Iona pattern on the island of Lindisfarne, contenting himself with the simplest arrangements. But he was also a missionary, for he went about on foot from place to place preaching the gospel and baptizing converts, and in everything he had the support of King Oswald, who, Bede says, acted as interpreter of the word to his captains and servants. Moreover, many Scots, 'mostly monks', came to preach and baptize and educate the Angles. For Aidan's work and Christian character Bede has unbounded admiration. The Northumbrian kingdom extended to the Forth, and Aidan's influence was felt north of the Tweed. At least two monasteries were early founded there, Coldingham and Melrose. To this region, later known as Lothian, Cuthbert belonged who made his monastic profession in Melrose in 651, the year in which Aidan died. But the influence of Lindisfarne penetrated far beyond Northumbria. Missionaries were trained there who carried the Gospel over central England. And the connexion with Iona was maintained, for Finan and Colman, who in turn succeeded Aidan at Lindisfarne, were both commissioned from Iona.

Under Finan the Lindisfarne mission reached its zenith, but now the Roman mission in the south, which for a time had languished, became more active. Oswiu, who succeeded Oswald as king in 642, married a daughter of Edwin who had been brought up in Kent accustomed to the Roman ways. Moreover some young men, educated in Lindisfarne, travelled south, or even visited Gaul. They came to know the customs of the Latin Church and returned dissatisfied with the simpler practices of the Scots. Notable among these was Wilfred whom we may regard as the first Anglo-Catholic. Earlier the leaders of the British Church had encountered the Roman mission in the person of Augustine, who had offended them by roughly ordering them to conform to the usages of the Catholic Church, but up till now Rome had remained honoured but remote and almost legendary to the Scots of Iona. In Northumbria the two missions met and clashed, most obviously over a point of external observance. To both parties Easter Day was the central feast of the Christian Year, but it was a movable feast requiring a rather intricate calculation to determine the date for its observance. The Celtic Churches had retained the cycle which they had learned from their early evangelists before the wedge of Anglo-Saxon heathendom had severed their contacts with the Continent and with Rome, while the Roman Church had since adopted a more accurate mode of reckoning. And so it happened that in Northumbria the king and his queen might celebrate Easter on different days as much as a fortnight apart. It was clearly intolerable. Argument arose within the Lindisfarne community, but Finan refused to be moved. The matter came to a head under his successor Colman.

King Oswiu summoned a convention of clergy in 664, commonly called the Synod of Whitby, at which Wilfred was spokesman for the Roman party and Colman for the Scots. Bede gives a detailed account of the debate, in which Colman proved no match for Wilfred, who was not only more learned but also represented a more imposing ecclesiastical system than was to be found in the 'rustic simplicity' of Iona and Lindisfarne. 'Even if your fathers were true saints, surely a small company on a corner of a remote island is not to be preferred to the universal Church of Christ which is found throughout the whole world.' *Securus judicat orbis terrarum!* The king gave judgement in favour of Wilfred, but on another ground. Christ had given the Keys of the Kingdom of Heaven to Peter, and Colman could make no such claim on behalf of Columba. Wilfred's biographer, Eddius, says that the king gave his judgement with a smile!

The decision at Whitby was, however, of the greatest importance immediately for the Church in Northumbria but ultimately for the Church in Britain. The points at issue— the date of Easter and the form of tonsure—may seem trivial, and we may perhaps assume that in the fundamental matters of faith and life the parties discovered no deep disagreement. Such indeed is the testimony of Bede, himself devoted to the Roman point of view. Wilfred's haughty spirit is unattractive, but he did represent, however arrogantly, a richer culture, more highly organized and stable ecclesiastical institutions, and in the last resort a Catholic unity that had been temporarily broken by the historical accident that had isolated the Celtic Churches. The work of the Iona mission was not lost. It continued to bear fruit and has received due honour in the pages of its historian.

After Whitby Colman and his supporters withdrew from Lindisfarne to Iona and finally to Ireland, but some of his English monks, who conformed, remained behind at Melrose under Abbot Eata, one of the earliest pupils of Aidan, with Cuthbert as prior.

Through Eata there passed to Cuthbert a living memory of the first Irish mission to Northumbria, and through Cuthbert its spirit survived for twenty years the defeat of the Celtic party at the Council of Whitby. In his cultivation of the ascetic life, and in the evangelistic journeys through which he impressed Christianity on the imagination of a barbarous people, Cuthbert belongs to the world of the ancient Irish saints.[1]

With the reorganization of the Northumbrian Church we are here concerned only in so far as it affects north Britain. The King of Northumbria claimed some sort of overlordship over the Picts and Scots, and Wilfred's ambition apparently was to be sole bishop in the king's dominions, with his seat at York. Indeed he secured papal endorsement of his pretensions. Like many another great ecclesiastic Wilfred tended to regard his own interests as identical with the interests of God. His high-handed actions were, however, resented by King Egfrith (671–85), who twice expelled him from the kingdom, and once imprisoned him for some months in the royal castle of Dunbar. The reorganization was mainly the work of Theodore of Tarsus, Archbishop of Canterbury, 668–90, who with Egfrith's support aimed at the multiplication of dioceses in the north. Lindisfarne became the seat of a bishop of the new style, and its simple church was rebuilt and dedicated to St. Peter. At Hexham a new bishopric was erected. About 681 a bishop of the Picts was appointed but he had his seat at Abercorn, in Anglian territory, from which he could at least see his diocese across the Forth, an arrangement which was of short duration for it came to an end in 685. Somewhat later, about 731, a diocese of Candida Casa (Whithorn) appears which continued into the ninth century. Finally in 735, the Bishop of York received the pallium, the insignia of archiepiscopal rank. Thus at length was completed the plan of Pope Gregory the Great, which Theodore had evaded, perhaps in the interests of the unity of the English Church.

Not less important than the diocesan reorganization was the introduction into Northumbria of the Benedictine Rule to replace the more flexible methods of Celtic monasticism. For this much of the credit belongs to Wilfred, who first brought it to Ripon. But soon the pre-eminence in this new

---

[1] Stenton, *Anglo-Saxon England*, p. 126.

order passed to Wearmouth (founded 674) and Jarrow (founded 681). These monasteries became the centres of Northumbrian learning, where Bede lived and laboured, and succeeded Lindisfarne as the points of contact between the English Church and the Churches of the Picts and Scots.

IV

THE EMERGENCE OF SCOTLAND
AND THE CHURCH OF SCOTLAND

FOR a time during the seventh century it looked as if the kings of Northumbria might succeed in uniting the peoples of Britain north of the Humber in one kingdom. Oswald, Oswiu, and Egfrith, son of Oswiu, all claimed and exercised some kind of overlordship over the Picts, Scots, and Strathclyde Britons. But disaster befell the war-like Egfrith. For some reason unknown he sent an army to Ireland which devastated a large part of the country, sparing neither churches nor monasteries and carrying off many captives into slavery. Retribution quickly followed. In 685 he attacked Pictland in person, and penetrated into Angus where his army was cut to pieces and he himself was slain at the battle of Nechtansmere. 'The hope and strength of the Angles began to ebb', says Bede, and the Picts, Scots, and Britons recovered their lands and liberty. Egfrith was succeeded by his half-brother Aldfrith, a scholar king, who had been educated in Ireland, and was for a time a pupil of Adamnan in Iona. 'He nobly retrieved the ruined state of the kingdom though within narrower bounds.' Under his protection and fostering care (685–705) began the astonishing efflorescence of Northumbrian Christian culture of which Bede was the outstanding ornament.

Nechtansmere put an end to Northumbrian dominance in the north, and also to hopes of the organization of an ecclesiastical province of north Britain with its metropolis at York. Nevertheless southern influence soon began to penetrate northwards. In 686, the year after Nechtansmere, Adamnan, ninth abbot of Iona, came to Northumbria to visit his friend King Aldfrith, and obtained from him the release of the Irish captives taken by Egfrith's men. Two years later he returned to Northumbria, and this time visited the monasteries of Wearmouth and Jarrow of which Ceolfrid had just become abbot. Bede was then at Jarrow, a boy of 14 or 15, and may have seen the celebrated head of the Columban 'family'. Impressed by the arguments with which Ceolfrid plied him regarding the tonsure and the date of Easter, but still more perhaps by his experience of Benedictine order, Adamnan returned to Iona a convert to the Roman ways. In spite, however, of his authority as abbot and successor to Columba, he could not persuade his monks to follow his example. Most of the rest of his life was spent in Ireland where he had greater success but not, it seems, within the Columban family. He died in Iona in 704 honoured but not obeyed. The controversy did nothing to abate his veneration for the founder and patron of his order, and has left hardly a trace in his Life of St. Columba, though it was written after 688. For a time there was schism in the Iona community, and even rival abbots. Finally the Roman usages triumphed, partly perhaps owing to pressure from Pictland, as we shall see, but mainly as a result of the influence of a saintly Englishman called Egbert. Educated in Ireland, and disappointed in his hopes of devoting himself to missionary labours on the Continent, Egbert settled in Iona as a simple monk in 716, and, before he died in 729, had by his learning, holiness, and gracious character persuaded at least the great majority of his brethren to adopt the Roman usage.

In Pictland events followed a very different course. Nechtan, King of the Picts, 706–24, convinced, according to Bede, 'by frequent meditation on the ecclesiastical scriptures' that his people were in error, wrote to Ceolfrid, abbot of Wearmouth, asking for a statement of the arguments by which he might more readily persuade them to accept the correct Easter reckoning and the Roman tonsure. He asked also for architects to be sent to build him a church of stone after the manner of the Romans, and declared his intention ever to follow the custom of the holy Roman and Apostolic Church as far as possible. Ceolfrid replied at great length repeating the arguments with which he had convinced Adamnan. His letter was read to an assembly of nobles and learned men in the presence of the king, who gave thanks to God 'that he had been found worthy to receive such a gift from the land of the

Angles'. By royal decree he established the Roman Easter reckoning throughout his kingdom and ordered all the clergy and monks to receive the crown-tonsure. 'Thus', Bede concludes, 'the nation was corrected and rejoiced in that it was subjected to a new discipleship, that of Peter the most blessed prince of the Apostles, and was commended to his protection.' This was in 710. But it seems that the decree met with resistance on the part of the Columban monks in Pictland, for an Irish annalist notes in 717: 'Expulsion of the community of Iona across the Ridge of Britain by King Nechtan.' He adds that in the following year 'the tonsure-crown was put upon the community of Iona', as if Nechtan's royal authority could be effective there too. The date of the submission of Iona is not certain. Indeed it is most likely to have been a gradual process, and we hear of dissatisfied monks withdrawing to Ireland, taking with them relics of St. Columba.

It seems unlikely that Nechtan's romanizing policy could have been limited to the two relatively trivial matters just mentioned. Bede does not tell us whether Ceolfrid's architects built a church of stone, or, if so, where. Presumably they did; and it has been surmised that it was at Restennet near Forfar where an ancient tower still stands, resembling in some features the tower at Jarrow, and possibly dating from the eighth century. But, we may ask, was not a church of stone to be a symbol of a more permanent form of ecclesiastical organization? Did Nechtan in fact introduce into Pictland a form of episcopacy like that then functioning in Northumbria? Some medieval writers speak of a bishopric at Abernethy which may belong to this period. At all events Abernethy was an ancient Pictish capital, and a church had been endowed there by an early predecessor of Nechtan. The interesting Round Tower of Abernethy, however, dates from the ninth century. Some light would be thrown on Nechtan's achievement by the legend of St. Boniface, if 'Boniface' is to be identified with the undoubtedly historical Curitan, 'bishop and abbot of Rosemarkie' as he is described in an Irish calendar, whose name is associated with the spread of the cult of St. Peter in Pictland.

Bede concludes his history in 731 on a tranquil note. Peace reigns in northern Britain. The Picts have a pact of peace with the Angles and rejoice to share catholic peace and truth with the universal church. The Scots of Dalriada remain within their own territory; and the Britons, though sworn enemies of the Angles and persisting in their rejection of the catholic usages, have no power to do ill. Unhappily there now ensues a Dark Age of more than three centuries regarding which only the merest scraps of information are available. Only the dimmest outline can be traced of the process by which Picts, Scots, Strathclyde Britons, and Angles of Lothian became one nation.

The victory at Nechtansmere left the Picts the most powerful people in north Britain, and they speedily and thoroughly subjugated Dalriada. But the inroads of the Northmen, beginning *c.* 800, seriously weakened the Pictish kingdom, and in 843 Kenneth MacAlpin, King of the Dalriadic Scots, seized the Pictish throne. The united kingdoms of Picts and Scots, commonly known as Alban, carried on a desperate resistance to the Northmen who not only harried the coast-lands but often carried fire and slaughter far inland. Meantime in south Britain the Anglo-Saxons under the royal house of Wessex subdued and absorbed the Danes, and so increased their power that they could claim sovereignty over all the kings of Britain. In 926, according to the Anglo-Saxon Chronicle, Constantine, King of Scots, among others, swore allegiance to Athelstan of England. Soon after, however, we find him in alliance with the Norse and Strathclyde Britons fighting against Athelstan, losing the bloody battle of Brunanburh in 937, and in despair withdrawing to the seclusion of a monastery. His successor, Malcolm I, made peace with England, and in 945 received from the English king, Edmund, a grant of 'Cumbria', 'on condition that he be his helper both by land and sea'. Malcolm's son, Kenneth, is named as one of eight kings who swore allegiance to Edgar of England at Chester in 973, and rowed him in a boat on the river Dee. This same Kenneth is said to have received Lothian from Edgar in return for homage rendered, but not until 1018, when Kenneth's son, Malcolm II, defeated at Carham a host gathered from all Northumbria between Tyne and Tweed, was Lothian securely gained. Northwards also Malcolm extended his authority to Ross, Sutherland, and Caithness, so that with the exception of Orkney, Shetland, and the Hebrides, which long remained in Norse possession, the King of Scots ruled over all that now forms Scotland. In Malcolm's reign the name is applied for the first time to North Britain. Malcolm II was succeeded by his grandson, Duncan, slain by Macbeth, who in turn was slain by Duncan's son, Malcolm III, in 1057. With his reign we emerge from the long Dark Age.

If the political history of the period is dark its ecclesiastical history is darker still, lit up by occasional stories of heroic Christian martyrdoms. For two centuries after their first invasions, the Northmen were savage heathen delighting in cruelty, plunder, and destruction, and the centres of Christian life and civilization were natural objects for their attacks. Of those mentioned by Bede, Whithorn, Melrose, and Colding-ham were completely destroyed, leaving only memories to be revived when gentler times returned. Iona was peculiarly exposed. In 802 we read 'Iona of Columcille was burned by the gentiles'. In fact it was repeatedly sacked and its monks massacred. Several times the relics of St. Columba were removed for safety to Ireland, and then brought back, until at last monastic life became impossible on Iona. They were finally deposited at Kells, in Ireland, which became the seat of the Co-arb or successor of Columba. Nevertheless Iona cannot have been wholly abandoned. We hear of abbots of Iona in the ninth century and even of bishops of Iona in the tenth, though they may have been merely titular. But Iona continued to be the burial-place of the kings of Alban, and of Scotland. Duncan was the last to be

> . . . carried to Colmekill,
> The sacred storehouse of his predecessors,
> And guardian of their bones.

All the relics of St. Columba, however, did not go to Kells. Soon after he became King of the Picts Kenneth MacAlpin bestowed some of them on the church of Dunkeld, recently

founded by a Pictish king. Thus Dunkeld, in the heart of
Alban, became part-heir of Iona. Its church was dedicated
to St. Columba, and presumably became the centre of a
Columban monastery peopled by Scotic monks—part of the
penetration of the Scots into Pictland. In 864 we read of the
'death of Tuathal, first (or chief) bishop of Fortriu and abbot
of Dunkeld'. Fortriu was a name for the Pictish kingdom or
for a part of it, so that Tuathal has a territorial title, and was
apparently a diocesan or tribal bishop as well as abbot. His
office, therefore, must have been more like that of Aidan in
Northumbria than that of a bishop of the older Celtic type,
if indeed we may make a distinction which Bede does not,
at least explicitly, make. At all events we hear no more of
a bishop of Fortriu, though abbots of Dunkeld continue.
Crinan, who married the daughter of Malcolm II and became the father of King Duncan, was Abbot of Dunkeld, and
the title was held for the last time by Ethelred, a son of
Malcolm III and Margaret.

Here we must refer to a portentous but enigmatic statement in the Chronicle of the Kings of Scotland. King Giric,
we are told, who reigned 878–89, 'was the first to give liberty
to *Ecclesia Scoticana*, which was in servitude up to that time
according to the custom and fashion of the Picts'. It is surprising to meet thus early the expression, *Ecclesia Scoticana*,
which does not occur again till 1192 in an official papal
document virtually constituting the Church of Scotland.
Most modern writers assume that by *Ecclesia Scoticana* is
meant the Church in Alban, and that Giric set it free from
the exactions and servitudes usual under Pictish custom. Mac-
Ewen[1] sees 'a larger and more important emancipation',
the conferring of something like the medieval 'Liberty of
Holy Kirk', as indeed does Fordun.[2] Might it not be simply
the revocation of the Edict of Nechtan banishing the Scotic
monks beyond Drumalban—a restoration of the 'Columban'
family and a revival in Pictland of the Columban system?
If this interpretation be correct, it would help us to understand the compact of 906 entered into by King Constantine

[1] MacEwen, *History of the Church in Scotland*, vol. i, p. 120.
[2] *Chronicles*, book iv, ch. 17.

II and Bishop Cellach at the Hill of Credulity near the royal city of Scone. They 'pledged themselves that the laws and disciplines of the faith, and the rights of the Churches and the Gospels should be preserved in terms of equality with the Scots'. This would mean that Pictish Churches were to enjoy the same rights and liberties as had been granted to Scotic Churches by Giric, and that the Pictish and Scotic Churches within the united kingdom were to be assimilated and united.

Bishop Cellach is supposed to have been connected with St. Andrews, and it is time now to look at the early history of that important ecclesiastical centre. A monastery is said to have been founded in the sixth century at Kilrymont in Fife by St. Cainech of Aghaboe, an Irish 'Pict', and a contemporary of St. Columba. There was certainly an abbot there before 747, for in that year is recorded the death of Tuathalan, abbot of Kilrymont. Nearly two centuries later King Constantine himself is said to have retired to this monastery after the Battle of Brunanburh in 937, and to have become its abbot. But by then it had received the name of St. Andrews and was believed to possess certain relics of the Apostle. Numerous legends 'explain' how this happened. Of these the most famous is that of Regulus (St. Rule) who was said to have brought the relics direct by sea from Constantinople, to have been welcomed by a Scottish King Angus, recently victorious in battle, and to have received from him the church of Kilrymont in which to deposit his precious cargo. By dating Angus's reign in the fourth century the legend also vindicates the claim that *Ecclesia Scoticana* was much older than the Church of England and owed nothing to the latter, a claim that had become very important in the twelfth and thirteenth centuries when the legend of St. Regulus took final shape. Now Angus was a Pictish not a Scotic king and he reigned *c.* 730. He dethroned Nechtan, of whom we spoke earlier, subjugated the Scots of Dalriada, and also fought against the Northumbrians. Nechtan had put himself and his people under the care of St. Peter; Angus invoked the aid of St. Andrew in his battles. However or whenever the supposed relics of the Apostle were brought to St. Andrews, it is certain that from 900 onwards the ecclesiastical importance of St. Andrews increased. Its ancient monastic community continued, but in addition it became the seat of bishops who were known as High Bishops or Chief Bishops of Alban. Cellach, who made his pact with Constantine II, may have been the first of them. The last was Fodan or Fothad II who married Malcolm III and Margaret in 1068 and died in 1093.

This chapter cannot close without a reference, however brief, to the enigmatic Culdees. The name, a corruption of Keledei (friends of God), is found in Ireland as well as in Alban. In the latter it appears for the first time in the tenth century, and continues in use, particularly at St. Andrews, till 1332. It is associated with many ecclesiastical sites from Iona to St. Andrews, and from Glasgow to Dornoch. In his Life of St. Kentigern, written *c.* 1190, Jocelyn uses this name to designate ideal monks, so that MacEwen may be right in saying 'Culdee was a popular name for the monastic clergy, who were the only ministers of the *Ecclesia Scoticana*', i.e. before the introduction of a parochial clergy.[1] Even before Jocelyn wrote, however, the Culdees seem to have abandoned regular monastic life, and became colleges of property-owning hereditary secular priests. At St. Andrews, where David I attempted to merge them in the new Augustinian priory founded in 1144, they maintained their separate existence as a college of secular canons down to the Reformation, while at Brechin they became the cathedral chapter.

Christianity had thus survived the troublous period of the Norse invasions and the unification of the different racial groups in north Britain, and had increased its hold upon the people. The Church had outgrown the missionary condition with which it began and was identified with the nation. *Ecclesia Scoticana* emerges with a bishop at its head, with its properties, rights and privileges recognized by the king, and ministering to the people from many centres. Of its relations with the churches of other lands those with Ireland were doubtless closest. In 816 the English Church at the Council of Chelsea decreed that no one of the race of the Scots should administer Baptism or Holy Communion in the English

[1] Op. cit., vol. i, p. 128.

Church 'since it is uncertain by whom they have been ordained or whether they have been ordained at all'. About the same time organizing bishops and councils on the Continent were also concerned with *episcopi vagantes* of Scottish race. But the reference is presumably to bishops of the earlier Celtic type, who gave no trouble in Alban as far as we know. Rome remained remote, though a chronicler records that Macbeth in 1050 'distributed money broadcast to the poor at Rome'! We can hardly accept the statement of Alexander I, in a letter to the Archbishop of Canterbury, that 'in ancient times the bishops of St. Andrews were wont to be consecrated by none save by the Roman Pontiff himself or the Archbishop of Canterbury'. Alexander was seeking to repudiate the claim of the Archbishop of York to be metropolitan of the bishops of Scotland. In these circumstances we might have expected serious aberrations of doctrine or practice to develop, but even the critical eye of so good a Catholic as Queen Margaret could detect only minor failings, as we may think them, however important they might seem to her. Nevertheless, the time had arrived for *Ecclesia Scoticana* to be more closely integrated with the Catholic Church.

D

PART II

THE MEDIEVAL CHURCH

I

THE KINGDOM OF SCOTLAND,
1057–1560

THE reign of Malcolm III (Canmore), 1057–93, forms the prelude to a new period in Scottish history in which Scotland emerged from isolation and became an integral part of Western Christendom. Malcolm was little more than a boy when his father, Duncan, was murdered, and he spent fifteen years as an exile in England while Macbeth reigned in Scotland. On his restoration to his father's throne, with English aid, his main ambition seems to have been to add the earldom of Northumbria to his kingdom. He invaded it several times in the early years of his reign, forgetful of the kindness he had received from the old Earl Siward. A new situation arose when in 1066 William the Conqueror seized the English throne. English exiles came to Scotland seeking Malcolm's aid, among them Edgar Atheling, the dispossessed heir of the Anglo-Saxon line, with his mother and two sisters, Margaret and Christina. Malcolm willingly became the Atheling's ally, and the alliance was cemented by his marrying Margaret. But the Conqueror marched into Scotland and at Abernethy-on-Tay received Malcolm's submission. He was compelled to give Duncan, his son by his first wife, Ingibiorg, as a hostage to William, and to expel the Atheling from Scotland. William henceforth left Malcolm in peace, and soon allowed Edgar to return to England to an estate provided for him.

It was his marriage with Margaret that gave to Malcolm's reign its importance for Scottish history, and we are fortunate in possessing an account of her life and character by one who all but claims to have been her confessor for a time. He is generally supposed to have been Turgot, a Benedictine monk of Durham, who became prior of Durham in 1087 and Bishop of St. Andrews in 1107.

THE CHURCH IN
MEDIEVAL SCOTLAND

showing dioceses

Detached areas of dioceses:

1. Brechin   4. Dunblane
2. St. Andrews   5. Glasgow
3. Dunkeld   6. Galloway

ORKNEY

CAITHNESS

LEWIS

ROSS

Dornoch

Rosemarkie   Kinloss   Elgin

Inverness   Mortlach

MORAY

Deer

SKYE

Monimusk

ABERDEEN

Aberdeen

Nigg

R. Spey

R. Dee

THE ISLES (SUDREYS)

Leven Kinlochleven

BRECHIN

Lismore

DUNKELD

Brechin Montrose

Iona

Dowally

Dunkeld Caputh Restennet

Cupar Angus

Arbroath (Aberbrothock)

DUNBLANE

Perth Scone Balmerino

Abernethy Lindores St. Andrews (Kilrymont)

Dunblane Lochleven Pittenweem

R. Forth Stirling Dunfermline

ISLAY

Bannockburn Inverkeithing Inchcolm Tyningham Dunbar

Falkirk Leith Edinburgh Haddington

ARGYLL

Paisley Linlithgow Ratho Liberton Holyrood Coldingham

Largs Glasgow Roslin Newbattle

LOTHIAN

Berwick-on-Tweed

GLASGOW R. Clyde STRATHCLYDE Lanark

Biggar THE MERSE Swinton Carham

Ayr KYLE R. Tweed Melrose Ednam Kelso Roxburgh

Selkirk R. Teviot

R. Nith Jedburgh (Jedworth)

R. Tyne

GALLOWAY Dumfries

IRELAND

Sweetheart (New Abbey)

Wigtown Kirkcudbright

Whithorn CUMBRIA

ENGLAND

R. W. FORD

MILES 0 10 20 30 40 5

Turgot describes Margaret's illustrious ancestry and lauds her virtues as queen. He tells us how she exerted a civilizing influence on her rough husband and his court, introducing dignity and ceremony, comforts, and even luxuries into the palace, though, of course, she cared for none of these things; how she sought to ensure that mercy was mingled with justice in the administration of the law; how she brought up her numerous family—six sons and two daughters—strictly and in the fear of the Lord. As three of her sons became Kings of Scots, and a daughter, Maud, married Henry I of England, their careful upbringing may be regarded as the most important part of Margaret's work. But it is her personal religion that Turgot chiefly stresses. Nurtured as a child in the intense piety of the court of St. Stephen, King of Hungary, who had protected her father during a long exile, and then at the equally pious court of Edward the Confessor, her ambition had been to devote herself wholly to the religious life. Only as a result of pressure on the part of her relatives did she consent to marry Malcolm; and Turgot has much to say of her fasts, vigils, prayers, Scripture study, alms-giving, and care of the poor and the captive, in all of which good works she engaged her husband too. When due allowance has been made for a monk's view of his royal patron there remains a convincing picture of a genuinely saintly queen.

Naturally Margaret would see much that was wrong in the practice of the Scottish Church as it had developed in isolation. Though Turgot makes no reference to it, it appears to be a fact that she turned to Lanfranc, whom William the Conqueror brought from the Continent to be Archbishop of Canterbury and reformer of the Church of England, seeking his advice and aid in some project she had in mind. What it was we are not informed, but Lanfranc sent three Benedictine monks from Canterbury, who may have been the 'very few supporters' referred to by Turgot in connexion with a great council in which Margaret 'contended with the sword of the Spirit, which is the Word of God, against the defenders of perverted custom'. At the council King Malcolm, who knew English as well as his native Gaelic, acted as her interpreter, 'fully prepared both to say and do whatever she might direct'. Five points in particular Turgot mentions as having been debated for three days: (1) the correct date for the commencement of Lent; (2) forbidden degrees in marriage; (3) the obligation of Sunday rest; (4) the duty and privilege of actually partaking of the Eucharistic elements at Easter; (5) a 'barbarous rite' used in celebrating Mass. Could this possibly be the use of the vernacular, as Dr. Maxwell suggests?[1] However important these matters may be held to be, and interesting as some of them are, what is even more remarkable is their remoteness not only from the old points of divergence between Celtic and Roman Christianity, but also from the issues that were agitating Europe at that very moment, for example the celibacy of the clergy and lay influence over ecclesiastical appointments. Gregory VII was Pope 1073–85, and in 1077 celebrated at Canossa his victory over the Emperor Henry IV.

Apart from these divergences from 'the holy customs of the Catholic Church' Turgot has little to say of the Scottish Church or of Margaret's relations with it. He tells us that she was deeply impressed by the holiness of certain hermits, and that she was a benefactress of the church of St. Andrews, presenting it with an 'elegant crucifix', and making pilgrimage to its shrine easier for the people of Lothian by instituting the Queen's Ferry. Curiously enough he never mentions Bishop Fothad of St. Andrews. He tells us that Margaret built a church at Dunfermline in the place where she had been married and enriched it with costly ornaments. This was presumably the church of which the foundations have recently been excavated beneath the floor of the Abbey Church built by her son King David. Another writer says she gave an endowment to Iona and restored the monks there, but Dunfermline now supplanted Iona as the burial-place of the Kings of Scots. It is on record that Malcolm and Margaret, like Macbeth and Gruoch before them, made a gift to the Culdees of Lochleven, and that their son, Ethelred, Earl of Fife, was also Abbot of Dunkeld. Whatever may have been the project on which she consulted Lanfranc it is clear that Margaret undertook no drastic reform of the Scottish Church.

[1] *Worship in the Church of Scotland*, p. 29.

King Malcolm lost his life in 1093 on his last campaign in Northumbria. The news was brought to Margaret as she lay on her deathbed in Edinburgh Castle, and she accepted it with saintly resignation. A few days later she too died and was buried in the church of the Holy Trinity at Dunfermline, by the altar. In 1250 when the great Abbey Church was completed she was canonized and her body translated to a place beneath the new high altar where she was venerated until the Reformation.

Meantime it seemed as if Margaret's influence was to be utterly lost. The death of Malcolm Canmore was the signal for what has been called a Celtic reaction. His younger brother, Donald Ban, in accordance with the Scottish mode of succession, made himself king and drove out Malcolm's family and their English connexions, who naturally took refuge in England. Donald maintained himself in power for four years, though for a brief period challenged by Malcolm's son, Duncan. Then in 1097 William Rufus sent his loyal subject, Edgar Atheling, with an army to restore the family of Malcolm, three of whom in succession reigned as Kings of Scots, Edgar 1097–1107, Alexander 1107–24, and David 1124–53.

Malcolm's sons and direct descendants ruled for nearly 200 years, from 1097 to the death of Alexander III in 1286. Gradually the kingdom acquired its present territorial bounds. After much dispute with England over Northumbria, in 1237 the southern boundary was stabilized much as we know it today, except that Berwick-on-Tweed was lost in 1333. Galloway was subjugated by Malcolm IV in 1160, and as a result of the Battle of Largs, 1266, the Norse relinquished their hold on the Western Isles. Orkney and Shetland, however, did not become Scottish till 1469.

Moreover, the kingdom ceased to be predominantly Celtic. Malcolm III may have been the last Gaelic-speaking king. His son David, at all events, was more Anglo-Norman than Scots. When quite young he had accompanied his sister Maud to the English court when she became queen in 1100. He was knighted by Henry I and created Earl of Huntingdon, and by his marriage to the heiress he acquired in addition the earldom of Northampton. When he became Earl of Lothian in 1107 and subsequently King of Scots in 1124 he brought many Norman friends with him to Scotland to be his counsellors, officers of State, and sheriffs, rewarding them with estates and lordships bestowed by charter. He thus reorganized his kingdom on the model of England, accomplishing what may be called a Norman Conquest of Scotland, and introducing the ideas and practices of feudalism. Commerce was furthered by the foundation of royal burghs whose inhabitants were also largely drawn from England or Flanders. During the twelfth century royal charters are usually addressed to the king's good subjects, French (i.e. Norman), English, Scots, and Galwegians. It was a motley host which David commanded at the Battle of the Standard in 1138, and is said to have contained even Islemen! By the end of the thirteenth century these diverse elements were consolidated into one Scottish nation. This is assumed in a declaration in favour of Robert Bruce drawn up by the clergy of Scotland in 1310 and in the still more famous Declaration of Arbroath attested by the seals of the barons of Scotland in 1320. But it must be remembered that the racial Scots, Gaelic-speaking and preserving the ancient Celtic ways, were relegated to the Highlands and Islands, and regarded as 'wild Scots' and almost as a different people from the more civilized 'Scots' of the lowlands.

The kings of Malcolm Canmore's line were closely related by marriage to the contemporary kings of England, so that for the most part their reigns were marked by peaceful relations with England. Nevertheless they had to be watchful for their independence, and they successfully maintained it except for a brief period from 1174 to 1189. But the English claim to feudal superiority was never wholly abandoned. Even when not obtruded it was held in reserve, and was reasserted strongly by Edward I when the death of the Maid of Norway occasioned a dispute about the succession and appeal was made to him to act as arbitrator (1286). Nine of the thirteen 'competitors' admitted the claim, including John Balliol to whom Edward awarded the crown. But Edward's high-handed actions provoked resistance which developed into a truly national War of Independence under the brilliant leadership of Robert the Bruce, victor of Bannockburn, 1314. In 1328, by the Treaty of Northampton, Edward III acknowledged Bruce as king of a free and independent nation, and next year the Pope, John XXII, who had long withheld recognition, and whose predecessors had twice excommunicated Bruce, hailed him as Illustrious King of Scotland and granted him the right to be crowned and anointed by the Bishop of St. Andrews.

Glorious though the War of Independence might be, and important in fostering a strong national consciousness, it impoverished the country and halted its steady development. Bruce was succeeded by his younger son, David II, a weak and incompetent ruler whose long reign, 1329–71, was full of troubles. The first two Stewart kings, Robert II and Robert III, were unable to make headway against the increasing lawlessness which reached its height under the governorship of Albany, who ruled in the name of James, Robert III's son, who had been taken captive and was detained in England from 1406 to 1424. The period was, however, marked by the emergence of a parliamentary system, representative of the Three Estates, the clergy, the nobility, and the burgesses. The Franco-Scottish alliance, initiated by John Balliol, was also strengthened as a bulwark against England and remained the corner-stone of Scottish foreign policy until 1560.

The return in 1424 of James I brought the promise of recovery in the life of the nation, frustrated by the fact that every succeeding reign began with a long minority. Of the five Jameses who reigned in succession from 1424 to 1542 the most successful was James IV. He was a vigorous and popular king, and under him the administration of justice was tightened up and the country became in consequence more peaceful and more prosperous. His marriage to Margaret Tudor, elder daughter of Henry VII of England, promised happier relations between the two kingdoms, and even the possibility some day of a united kingdom. Unhappily James aspired to play a part in European power politics, and at the request of the King of France invaded England. His death together with the flower of his nobility on the fatal field of Flodden, 1513, brought dire consequences upon Scotland, which was confronted with the ambitious and aggressive Henry VIII, and was weakened by another long minority. James V was barely two years old when his reign began, and for fifteen years the country was the prey of factions. His personal rule after 1528 was troubled and brief. When he died, a disappointed man after the disgrace of Solway Moss in 1542, he left to his infant daughter Mary a kingdom distracted by war and civil and religious strife.

Throughout the medieval period the Church in Scotland while sharing in and reflecting the life of the Western Church as a whole, was deeply involved in all the vicissitudes of the nation's fortunes. In the early formative period to 1286, backed by a powerful Papacy, it consolidated its position. It took its part in the national struggle for independence and suffered from the lawless anarchy that followed, being itself weakened by the Babylonish Captivity and the Great Papal Schism. It contributed to the national recovery under the Jameses, but by that time general decline and corruption had set in, and in the reign of James V it was challenged by the Reformation. The history of the medieval Church in Scotland, therefore, is not to be disentangled from that of the nation. Indeed it has little history of its own, no striking movements of thought or action. Our present purpose will be best served by tracing the origin, development, and decline of its institutions, and by seeking an understanding of their effectiveness in promoting the Christian good of the nation.

II

THE PARISH CHURCH

THE earliest sign of the great ecclesiastical changes that were to be effected by Margaret's sons is a document which was preserved in the archives of the priory of Durham and is now in the University Library there. Strangely enough it has to do with the foundation not of a bishopric or a monastery but of a humble parish church. It reads:

To all the sons of Holy Mother Church Thor Longus (wisheth) salvation in the Lord. Know that Edgar, my lord, King of Scots, gave me Aednahem, a waste-land, which with his help and my own capital I have caused to be inhabited. And I have built a Church in honour of St. Cuthbert. Which Church with a plough-gate of land I have given to God and St. Cuthbert and his monks to be possessed for ever. This donation I have made for the soul of my lord King Edgar, for the souls of his father and mother, for the salvation of his brothers and sisters, for the redemption of my dearest brother Leswin, and for my own salvation both temporal and spiritual. If any one should presume to take away this my gift from the said Saint and the monks who serve him by any violence or craft, may Almighty God take from him the life of the celestial Kingdom and may he endure eternal punishment with the devil and his angels. Amen.

Thor Longus was, we may suppose, an Anglo-Norman knight from Northumbria in the service of King Edgar, who received a grant, on the usual feudal terms, of unoccupied land in the valley of the river Eden. This he proceeded to develop as a manor, bringing in peasants from the south to inhabit and cultivate it. As part of the normal development he built a church which he naturally dedicated to the great Northumbrian saint, Cuthbert, and endowed it with a ploughgate of land, roughly 104 acres. Even from the strictest ecclesiastical point of view it would have been perfectly in order for him to have appointed a priest to serve in his church and minister to the spiritual needs of his household and tenants, but he chose to gift the church and its endowment to the distant monastery of Durham, so that by the prayers of the holy monks of St. Cuthbert there might be secured the temporal and eternal welfare of his lord, King Edgar, and other members of the royal family, and of Thor himself and his relatives. It may be taken as certain that Thor also paid to the monks of Durham the tithes of his estate. If he does not include these in his charter it may be because he regarded payment of tithe as obligatory under the law of God, and not therefore his to give.

The Ednam ploughgate was not the only landed property in Scotland gifted to Durham at this time. The family of Malcolm and Margaret regarded St. Cuthbert with special veneration, and to his monks at Durham King Edgar made several gifts of land in Berwickshire or the Merse, mostly lying in and around the modern parish of Coldingham, but also at Swinton and Lennel (Coldstream). By 1127 there were churches and chapels on these lands.

Gifts of land and of tithes would obviously be a welcome enrichment for the monks, but churches so remote from their own home, one would suppose, would be a serious liability. Their obligation was well understood. They must employ a priest to do the parish work, i.e. to say Mass daily in the church and administer the sacraments to the parishioners, paying him out of the revenues and 'appropriating' any surplus to their own uses. But they were confronted with a great temptation. Monks were universally regarded as the perfect representatives of religion. To apply revenues derived from a remote parish to their own uses would appear perfectly right and even laudable, so long as the care of the parishioners was entrusted to a priest, who need not differ educationally or socially from his neighbours except that he was ordained and could read his service-book. The effect undoubtedly was to lower the status and emoluments and consequently the attainments of those who exercised 'cure of souls'. We know that the monks of Durham appointed a priest to minister in Ednam, for a certain Orm, describing himself as 'presbyter of Ednam', witnesses an important document in 1127. That he should so describe himself implies, of course, that he was ordained but indicates that he was what would now be called a 'priest-in-charge' without title or security of tenure, removable at will by his employers. Such an arrangement was very common in the twelfth century in England and throughout the Western Church. We need not suppose that Thor Longus was in any way dissatisfied with it. But who merited the curse contained in the last clause of his charter? In 1147 a Benedictine priory dependent on Durham was established at Coldingham and about that time the church of Ednam was attached to it. After the War of Independence the relations between Scotland and England were normally hostile and the dependence of Coldingham on Durham raised a problem which sometimes became acute. It was solved in 1509 by the transference of rights over Coldingham and its churches from the priory of Durham to the abbey of Dunfermline.

In the days of King Edgar and his liegeman Thor, the bishopric of the Scots at St. Andrews was vacant and there was no sign of episcopal activity anywhere in Scotland. The priory of Durham alone had an interest in the ecclesiastical affairs of the Merse, and that was chiefly financial. In 1127 that interest was fully recognized by Robert, the first effective Bishop of St. Andrews. Perhaps his first act after his consecration was to declare at Roxburgh in the presence of King David, the Archbishop of York, the bishops of Durham and Glasgow and others, that the church of Coldingham and its dependent churches and chapels which belong to the priory of Durham shall in all time coming be free of all financial servitude to the bishops of St. Andrews or their diocesan officers, archdeacons, or deans. This he does at the request of the king and his brother bishops, 'and for the love of St. Cuthbert and the monks of Durham'. That such a declaration was asked for and made implies a recognition of the fact that the Bishop of St. Andrews had spiritual responsibility for these churches. Not until the thirteenth century, however, was it insisted on that monasteries should appoint to their appropriated churches vicars whom the bishop should approve as suitable, and who should enjoy a fixed minimum stipend and security of tenure of their vicarages.

A step was thus taken towards increasing the effectiveness of parochial ministrations, at a time when parish churches had been generally established throughout the country.

The church of Ednam has been taken as typical because its foundation charter is the earliest extant. But it may not, indeed cannot, have been the earliest local church in Scotland. In Strathclyde and north of the Forth and Clyde there must have been many churches much older, going back to Celtic times. A claim to great antiquity has been made for the church of St. Cuthbert beneath Edinburgh Castle. It was certainly in existence in 1127 when King David endowed it with a piece of land. In the following year he gave the church and its endowments, together with its dependent chapels at Liberton and Corstorphine, to the Augustinian abbey of Holyrood which he had recently founded. The origin of these early churches is of local interest. What is of general interest is the fact that in nearly every case the first recorded mention of a parish church occurs in a charter announcing that it has been given to some monastery near or far. By the middle of the thirteenth century each of the larger abbeys is found in possession of a considerable number of 'appropriated' churches, not all of them in its vicinity. Kelso had 37, Holyrood 27, Paisley 29, and Arbroath 33. Even Cistercian monasteries, in contravention of their rule, came to have dependent churches, though not in great numbers. Among the churches given to monasteries some were situated in burghs which at first were not much larger than villages but were destined to grow in importance. St. Mary's, Dundee, for example, was given to Lindores; St. John's, Perth, to Dunfermline; Falkirk to Holyrood, and Inverness to Arbroath. In 1419 the citizens of Edinburgh complained that the church of St. Giles had been long before surreptitiously appropriated by the Augustinians of Scone. Most astonishing of all is the charter of David I granting in perpetual alms to God and St. Andrew the Apostle, the church of Linlithgow with the chapels, lands, and all other rights pertaining to the said church, to provide lights for the cathedral of St. Andrews, any surplus to be used to maintain the ministers of the altar there. When the Augustinian priory of

St. Andrews was founded in 1144 the church of Linlithgow was appropriated to it.

Such appropriations of parochial revenues are hard to understand today and may even appear scandalous. They were to prove disastrous for the medieval Church. The situation of a church appropriated to an Augustinian house could be advantageous, especially if it was in the immediate vicinity of the appropriating community. Even if it were remote it was possible and even common for canons to be seconded to do a spell of parish work. But in general the parish church was, as has been said, the Cinderella of the ecclesiastical institutions of the Middle Ages, most of all in Scotland. Not until the Reformation was its importance for the religious life of the people fully understood.

III

THE NEW MONASTICISM

MONASTICISM was of course no new thing in Scotland, but the old Celtic monasticism had passed away, and the Culdee communities were no longer truly monastic. On the other hand there had been in France during the eleventh century a great revival of Benedictine monasticism associated at first with Cluny in Burgundy. The movement spread and blossomed into a variety of distinct orders of which the most illustrious in the twelfth century was the Cistercian order to which belonged St. Bernard of Clairvaux, a contemporary of King David. In addition to the Benedictines there also flourished the Order of St. Augustine whose rule was believed to be the rule observed by St. Augustine for his clergy in Hippo, but was actually a later composition consisting of excerpts from St. Augustine's ascetic writings. The Augustinians were called canons regular rather than monks. Like monks they lived in community under a rule, but their life was less strictly regulated, and they were thus serviceable for other church work as cathedral canons and even as parochial ministers. The Premonstratensians, a stricter order of Augustinians, were organized by Norbert of Prémontré in Normandy under the influence of the Cistercians.

The Augustinians were the first of the new orders to be introduced into Scotland, and they became more numerous there, relatively to Benedictines, than in any other country. Their first settlement in Scotland was at Scone whither Alexander I brought a colony from St. Oswald's, Nostell, Yorkshire, endowing it with lands, dues, and privileges in 1107. Soon his brother, Earl David, introduced another group from Beauvais in Normandy and settled them in Jedburgh. After his accession to the throne David further founded Holyrood and Cambuskenneth and in 1144 he gave his approval to the foundation of St. Andrew's Priory by Robert, Bishop of St. Andrews, who had been prior of Scone and as bishop wished to surround himself with people with whose ways he was familiar. King David intended the new Augustinians to swallow up the old Culdee community and he transferred to the Priory a number of Culdee houses, such as Lochleven, Pittenweem, and Monimusk. But the Culdees of St. Andrews refused to be suppressed, and though denuded of some of their properties and excluded from the new cathedral they continued as a college of secular canons till the Reformation. Other Augustinian foundations were Inchcolm and Inchaffray. The Premonstratensians were chiefly settled in Galloway, notably at Whithorn, but their most famous house in Scotland was Dryburgh, founded in 1141 by Hugo de Moreville, Lord of Lauderdale, a Norman noble in the service of King David. Towards the end of his life Hugo is said to have himself joined the community of Dryburgh as a simple canon.

David did not limit his favours to Augustinians. The various branches of the Benedictine order were also beneficiaries. Soon after his accession he brought Benedictines from Canterbury to Dunfermline, where he greatly enlarged his mother's church of the Holy Trinity, handsomely endowing it as an abbey. At the same time he founded Kelso Abbey for a colony of monks from Tiron in France. He had settled them first in Selkirk and later transferred them at their request to Kelso. Two other great Tironensian houses were founded by his grandsons, William the Lion and David, Earl of Huntingdon, at Arbroath and Lindores respectively. The Cluniacs had passed their prime before David's reign, but they came to be represented by Paisley, founded in 1163 by Walter the Stewart for a colony from Wenlock in Shropshire, where his English estate lay.

The outstanding Order of the twelfth century was, however, the Cistercian, a vigorously ascetic Order in which glowed the purest fire of Benedictine enthusiasm. Its noblest ornament was St. Bernard of Clairvaux, the deeply evangelical mystic and preacher, whose influence was such that he has been called the uncrowned king of Europe in his day. He fascinated all classes, not least the knightly class, whom he called into the service of Christ either as Crusaders vowed to rescue the Holy Places from the infidel, or as monks pledged to extreme self-abnegation. Among those who came under the influence of St. Bernard was Aelred, a young Northumbrian knight who had been educated with Prince David, and accompanied him north when he became King of Scots. Suddenly Aelred was converted and became a monk and later abbot of the Cistercian monastery of Rievaulx in Yorkshire. His interest being thus aroused, David founded a daughter-house at Melrose in 1136, settling a company of Rievaulx monks there with no less a person than his own stepson Waltheof as their abbot. In 1140 he planted another group of Cistercians at Newbattle, and later still, in 1156, founded Kinloss in Moray when he had reduced that turbulent province to submission. Further Cistercian monasteries were founded later, Cupar-Angus (1163), Balmerino (1227), and, latest of all the great abbeys, Sweetheart or New Abbey, founded (1275) by Devorgilla, widow of John Balliol, Lord of Galloway, mother of King John Balliol.

The Benedictine and Augustinian rules were new to Scotland and were no doubt an improvement on anything of the kind that had previously existed there. The original groups of monks and canons with their abbots were likewise imported from England or France, most of them being Anglo-Normans. They would bring with them the arts and crafts of a more advanced civilization, and they would also exercise a powerful influence by the example of their regular, disciplined and industrious communal life. Outside St. Andrews there is little evidence of resistance to their coming. But the Annals of Ulster record what looks like an attempt in 1164 to bring the monastery of Iona into association once more with the Columban family in Ireland. It is, moreover, a curious fact that even the Cistercians hardly penetrated into the Gaelic-speaking areas of the north and west.

Most of the larger Scottish monasteries were founded in the reign of David I, and indeed by the king himself. If in this way he aimed at improving his kingdom, his chief motive was certainly religious. He wanted to foster what at the time was the prevailing form of religious devotion, and he hoped to gain advantage from the prayers of holy men not only for his kingdom and government but for the souls of himself and his kindred and friends. His grandsons, Malcolm IV and William the Lion, continued his work, but after their time the foundation of new monasteries became rare, and gifts to old ones became fewer and smaller. It would appear that from *c.* 1300 monasticism ceased to hold its pre-eminent place among the objects of Christian esteem and liberality.

King David endowed his monasteries lavishly and, we might think, indiscriminately. He gave them landed estates with additional rights of pasturage, fishing, wood and peat cutting, tofts[1] in various burghs, and tithes of royal revenues of various kinds. To some he gave the privilege of administering baronial justice to their tenants or of erecting a burgh with the customary trading rights. The Abbey of Holyrood, for example, in its foundation charter, *c.* 1128, was granted the right to erect the burgh of Canongate, beside the royal burgh of Edinburgh, with full trading privileges like other burghs. Some of those properties may have been ecclesiastical properties before David's time, but most of them were gifts from his own crown lands and royal purse. They were given with the consent of the magnates of the kingdom, bishops, earls, and barons 'in pure free and perpetual alms', free, that is, of all secular dues and exactions. Three hundred years later James I is said to have complained that his ancestor David had been 'ane sair sanct to the crown'. But he could not dream of alienating the ancient monastic properties, and he showed his personal devotion by founding a Carthusian house in Perth, thereby bringing to Scotland a new and stricter Order.

We are bound to ask, What contribution did these well-endowed communities make to the life of the nation during the long period between their foundation and their suppression at the Reformation? The answer is hard to find. We must always remember that the monkish ideal was above all religious and otherworldly. St. Benedict visualized the monastery as a community of men under an abbot as father-in-God perfecting themselves in the personal Christian virtues

---

[1] i.e. sites for house and garden.

by a carefully regulated routine of worship, work, and study, their eyes ever fixed on the heavenly country. It is obviously impossible to say how far this ideal was realized in practice. We can know little of the interior life of the Scottish monasteries—they boasted of only one saint, Waltheof, first abbot of Melrose. We do not know how the monkish population was recruited, or what its numbers were throughout the period. We must suppose that the ideal was inculcated as often as the rule was read to novices, or appealed to in cases of discipline, and that many found the life of the cloister a satisfying mode of cultivating the spiritual life. Estimates of the monastic contribution to culture generally—to economic and social progress, to education, learning, and the arts—have varied greatly. No doubt the contribution was considerable especially in the twelfth and thirteenth centuries. The monks' best document, however, is to be found not in their chartularies or chronicles but in their churches, which even in their ruined state still have power to win admiration and to stir the romantic imagination. They vary in date from the early twelfth to the late fourteenth centuries and even beyond, and represent every style from Norman to late Gothic. They witness to the place which worship was supposed to hold in the lives of those for whose use they were built, and together with the quiet, orderly life of the communities of which they were the centres, must have exercised a powerful influence for good not only on the monks but also on their tenants and neighbours.

It seems clear, however, that a certain deterioration affected the monasteries from the fourteenth century onwards. In 1425 we find James I chiding abbots and priors for neglecting discipline to the ruin of religion, and the church councils which met from 1549 to 1559 in order by reform to stem the Reformation are outspoken in their criticism of monastic abuses. Even in the early period of enthusiasm there were occasional scandals under slack or incompetent abbots. A fair number were deposed for various and sometimes grave misdemeanours. But as the ideal became conventionalized and monasteries became property-owning institutions, or rather in fact lucrative benefices in possession of their abbots, abuses increased, and abolition seemed the only remedy.

Obviously the character and capacity of its abbot was all-important for a monastery. In theory the abbot was the father and leader of his monkish family, whose members were vowed to unquestioning obedience. In practice the miscellaneous nature of the monastic endowments must have compelled him to become above all an administrator. He had to collect the revenues, rents, tithes, &c., not always an easy matter, and then he was responsible for everything connected with the internal management of his monastery, the comfort of the monks, their food and quarters, the buildings and their maintenance against their natural enemies, damp, fire, civil commotion, and war. English invaders thought nothing of burning down an abbey or two. Good abbots defend the rights of their abbeys against encroaching neighbours, bad abbots fail to do so. Good abbots are careful for the comfort of the monks, bad ones are negligent. Good abbots add to the monastic buildings, and bring groups of masons to build and craftsmen to beautify and enrich the abbey church, bad ones allow the existing buildings to fall into ruin or sell the abbey treasures. Such are typical judgements passed on abbots by contemporaries, and go to show that there were required in abbots qualities rather different from those demanded of leaders in saintliness. Moreover, when it is remembered that abbots were often members of the King's Council, or employed by him in matters of State, and that when Parliament was developed they sat with bishops to form the First Estate, it is not surprising that an abbey should have come to be regarded as a feudal benefice, held by the abbot in person, subject to providing for the needs of his abbey, of which needs he was himself judge. The practice which became common in the fifteenth century of bestowing abbacies *in commendam* on persons who were 'to provide for the needs' of the abbey without residing in it may be held to be an extension of the idea of benefice, reasonable enough in cases where there had been negligence and disorder, but obviously opening the door wide to all kinds of abuse.

St. Benedict taught that, ideally, monks would elect their

own abbot, but he was aware of the danger that, left to themselves, they would elect an easy-going head. He therefore
suggested some supervision by a neighbouring bishop. When
the monasteries became wealthy and their abbots in consequence became powerful prelates, kings and lay magnates
were apt to take an interest in their appointment, not always
to the advancement of the religious good of the community.
The monastic revival beginning at Cluny led to an attempt
to exclude lay influence altogether. The abbot of Cluny
became the head of all the monasteries adhering to his Order.
The Cistercians had an elaborate system of supervision of
daughter-houses by mother-houses, in order to prevent abuses
which experience had shown were apt to occur. The Scottish
monasteries of the twelfth and thirteenth centuries were not
much troubled by lay interference in the appointment of
abbots. They put themselves and their properties under the
protection of the Pope, who favoured them in every way,
granting them exemption from all outside control whether
secular or episcopal, making them directly subject to himself. To many abbots he gave the right to wear the mitre.
Soon he began to take an interest in their appointment,
and Scots clergy and even monks began to look to the Pope,
or even go to Rome, for promotion. In the fourteenth century
papal appointment was extremely common, and for its
trouble the Papal Curia was wont to charge a fee, usually
one-third of the annual income of the benefice, payable if
and when the nominee secured 'peaceful possession'. James I
endeavoured to put a stop to 'impetration' of benefices by his
subjects at Rome, and to prevent the flow of money from the
country that it entailed. A long conflict between the Crown
and the Papacy ensued, until in 1487 James III received from
Pope Innocent VIII a bull announcing an agreement to
wait for eight months before 'providing' to a vacancy, in
order that the king might have time to make a nomination.
By this agreement the king virtually received the right to
nominate abbots, while the Pope made the appointment and
received the fee without further question. It is hard not to
regard this as a cynical bargain which took no account of
the religious good of the monasteries. At all events from this

date abbacies are bestowed *in commendam* on royal favourites, whether clerical or not. Arbroath was held in succession by the Beatons, James and David, archbishops of St. Andrews. Kelso, Melrose, Holyrood, and the great priory of St. Andrews, the premier monastic house in the kingdom, were held by royal bastards who were appointed by the Pope on the nomination of the king when they were mere boys. Under such commendators it is not surprising that the monastic ideal fell into discredit, even before the Reformers abolished the system and the nobles secularized the properties.

It would, however, be unfair to end this chapter without a reference to a good abbot of the sixteenth century. We are fortunate to have a full and glowing account of the life and work of Thomas Chrystall, abbot of Kinloss 1504 to 1529, who died in retirement in 1535. It was written by Ferrerius an Italian scholar from Piedmont who, it is interesting to note, lived and taught in Kinloss for five years, returning to Italy in 1537. Chrystall was born at Culross of good parentage of the burgess class. He was educated in and around the monastery there, distinguishing himself in literary studies and by his musical gifts. The abbots of Culross and Cupar were eager that he should join their monks, but they were overridden by the authority of the abbot of Kinloss, their superior in the Cistercian Order, who persuaded him to come to Kinloss. There after the usual year as a novice he made his profession at the age of 20. Having proved his capacity in administration, though still a junior, he was selected by the abbot to be his successor. Presumably the nomination had to be forwarded by the king to the Pope, who made the appointment on the obligation being undertaken on behalf of Chrystall to pay the customary fee of 200 gold florins of the Camera. Ferrerius is rather vague about this but indicates there was some hitch in the procedure, which was soon put right.

On becoming abbot, Chrystall hoped to return to his studies but was prevented by the administrative tasks that had to be performed. For some years he had to carry through a series of lawsuits against persons who had robbed the monastery of its rights. These fill half of the biography. As a result of them Ferrerius declares that his hero had like a prudent *pater familias* doubled the income of Kinloss. He was thus able to repair the church, which had fallen into dangerous decay, to extend the other buildings, and to purchase ornaments, chalices, vestments, and a mitre for himself. Moreover, he laboured by exhortation, example, and discipline to restore to decent order the religious life of the monks, which had sadly deteriorated. He increased their number from 14 to 20 without however reducing their rations, which were in fact increased. He took an interest in their education, sending first one and then another to the then famous University of Aberdeen, so that on their return they might instruct their brethren. In so doing he revived a practice that was largely discontinued. Towards the end of his life he presented the library with a number of biblical and patristic texts. A curious paragraph bears on monastic charity. Chrystall, says Ferrerius,

often gave most liberal alms to the brethren of the Dominican and Franciscan Orders; and was much more kind to men who had fallen into calamity and people of the lower sort. Towards his kinsfolk, those of them who were frugal and good, he was so munificent that he might not unjustly be compared to great bishops. Above all he took great pains so to dower virgins for marriage that they might pass an honourable life as wives of noble husbands.

As abbot of Kinloss Chrystall was obligated to visit and discipline the daughter-houses of Deer and Culross annually. On one occasion he had the authority of the king to visit the mother-house of Melrose and depose its abbot. James IV would gladly have made him abbot of Melrose or Bishop of Ross, but he preferred to remain as abbot of Kinloss. Finally as a crown to all his good works he had Robert Reid appointed as his successor. Reid was an important man, frequently employed by the king in political missions. He was made Bishop of Orkney in 1541, holding Kinloss and Beaulie *in commendam*, and in 1548 he became President of the Court of Session. He died at Dieppe in 1558 as he was returning from a mission to France in connexion with the marriage of Mary Queen of

Scots and the Dauphin. A legacy of 8,000 merks left by Reid for the foundation of a college for the study of law was long after used to found the University of Edinburgh. Ferrerius's account of Chrystall and Reid is very delightful, but how remote from the spirit of St. Bernard, and from the issues confronting the Church at the time!

IV

THE BISHOPRICS

IN the reign of Malcolm Canmore there was a bishop of the Scots or of St. Andrews, Fothad by name. He is said to have married Malcolm and Margaret, but beyond that and the fact that he died in 1093 we know little about him. He is not mentioned by Turgot and we do not know what his attitude was to Margaret's reforms or how she regarded him and his orders, except that for some reason she preferred the guidance of Lanfranc in a matter she had at heart. After Fothad's death the see remained vacant for many years until Alexander I at the beginning of his reign in 1107 resolved to fill it. Like his brothers, Alexander had close connexions with England. His sister was Queen of England and he had married Sibylla, a natural daughter of Henry I. He knew St. Anselm, Archbishop of Canterbury, who sent him his blessing and godly counsel on his accession. He therefore resolved to appoint a bishop who would introduce into the Scottish Church the new and stricter order which Lanfranc had brought to England from the Continent. Obviously such a bishop must be sought in England, and Alexander naturally chose Turgot, prior of Durham, his mother's erstwhile confessor and biographer. But under the new rules kings might not appoint bishops, and Alexander may have been astonished when Turgot suggested that his election should be not by the Culdees of St. Andrews but by the monks of Durham. Worse was to follow. A bishop-elect must have his election confirmed by his metropolitan who, if he found it satisfactory, must carry through his consecration with the assistance of at least two other bishops. In 1072 at a Council of Windsor, Lanfranc with the support of William the Conqueror had arranged that Canterbury should have the primacy over all the churches of Britain, that the Archbishop of York should take an oath of obedience to the Archbishop of Canterbury, but should have metropolitical jurisdiction over

all churches north of the Humber including Scotland. Archbishops of York commonly protested against subjection to
Canterbury, but for long claimed that Scottish bishops belonged to their province. It was held in York that this arrangement had been accepted by King Malcolm and Bishop
Fothad, but Alexander I denied it, and he was not prepared
to allow Turgot to seek consecration at York. At last in 1109,
through the good offices of Henry I, Turgot received consecration from Thomas, Archbishop of York, the rights of both
sees being reserved. Turgot died at Durham in 1115 and can
hardly be said to have been an effective Bishop of St.
Andrews.

Nevertheless Alexander resolved to try again. York was
vacant in 1115 and he wrote to an old friend Ralph, now
Archbishop of Canterbury, asking for help. Receiving no
reply he wrote again in 1120 saying that St. Andrews had
been long vacant to the peril of men's souls and asking that
the monk Eadmer might be released in order to accept the
bishopric. Eadmer was a most important man at Canterbury.
He had supported Anselm in all his conflicts with the kings
of England and the archbishops of York. Only because of
his great friendship for Alexander would Ralph let him go.
Eadmer himself tells the story of the next three years. He was
elected, he says, by the clergy and people with the consent of
the king, and after considerable dispute was allowed to take
his pastoral staff from off the altar as from the hand of God
'that so he might undertake the care of all souls in the entire
kingdom so far as possible'. But now the question of consecration arose. Ralph, anticipating trouble, had advised that
after his election Eadmer should be sent back to Canterbury
as quickly as possible to be consecrated 'for there are many
who would willingly hinder his consecration'. In fact Thurstan, the new Archbishop of York, induced both Henry I
and the Pope to intervene in the interests of his metropolitical
rights. Eadmer insisted that he must be consecrated by Canterbury and Alexander was adamant that neither York nor
Canterbury should have authority over the Bishop of St.
Andrews. Eadmer therefore went back to Canterbury com-
plaining that the king and his friends had unjustly deprived

him of his episcopal properties. Correspondence ensued in the course of which Eadmer protested that he had never meant to slight the honour of Alexander or his kingdom, and offered to return. He died, however, in 1123. Scotland therefore just missed having an Anselm on a lesser scale!

In his third attempt Alexander was more fortunate. Robert, prior of the recently founded House of Augustinian Canons at Scone, an Englishman who had become accustomed to Scottish ways, was willing to accept the bishopric on Alexander's terms. He had not been consecrated when Alexander died in 1124. Two or three years later, to please King David, Henry I ordered Thurstan to consecrate Robert without profession of canonical obedience, the rights of both sees being again reserved. Robert was bishop till his death in 1159. His charter acknowledging the rights of the priory of Durham over its churches in Lothian has been mentioned; also his founding in 1144 of the Augustinian priory at St. Andrews. It would seem that he built as his cathedral the church of St. Regulus, whose tower still stands, a notable landmark.

While King Alexander was wrestling with the difficulties of the new order at St. Andrews, his brother David, Earl of Lothian and Prince of Cumbria, was having similar difficulties with regard to Glasgow. Memories lingered of St. Kentigern who had once been bishop there, and David made careful inquiries with regard to ancient ecclesiastical properties in Strathclyde, Tweeddale, and Teviotdale, with a view to restoring the see. It would appear that the first bishop to be appointed was Michael a 'Briton', i.e. a Strathclyde Welshman, that he was sent to York to be consecrated, and that, having made profession of obedience to the archbishop in writing, he was not welcomed back to Glasgow. At all events 'Michael, Bishop of Glasgow' is recorded as performing episcopal functions in Westmorland, a part of the ancient Cumbria, but definitely annexed to England by William Rufus.

Glasgow reckoned as its first bishop John, a monk and formerly tutor of the young Prince David. Elected, the Glasgow account says, by David with the advice and help of his clergy, but terrified by the savagery and vices of the people, John set out on pilgrimage to Jerusalem, but was stopped by Pope Pascal II, consecrated against his will and sent back to Glasgow where he was welcomed by the prince and people and diffused the gospel through the Cumbrian *parochia*. It is certain that he was consecrated by Pope Pascal II, but, it was believed at Rome, only at the request of the church of York. It may be that John sought consecration at Rome in order to avoid having to make profession of obedience to York. It did not help him. Several papal mandates were sent to him commanding him to do so—one of them giving him thirty days in which to do it. But he never did. John continued Bishop of Glasgow until 1147, and built himself a cathedral, of which nothing now remains. Otherwise he was chiefly concerned with the ecclesiastical activities of his prince and king.

When David succeeded Alexander as King of Scots in 1124 there were in his kingdom at least two bishops of unquestionable canonical standing. There may have been others of less authentic type, for Pope Callixtus II in a letter to Alexander had ordered him not to allow bishops to carry through consecrations without recourse to their metropolitan at York. David at once sought to have the position rectified from the Scottish point of view. He sent John of Glasgow to Rome to ask the Pope to confer on St. Andrews metropolitan rank. As it happened both the English archbishops were in Rome and David's request set them disputing as to their respective rights. The Pope, therefore, sent a legate to investigate and report. He held a council at Roxburgh, and the nature of his report may be inferred from the fact that the Pope continued to order the Scottish bishops to obey York.

Nevertheless by the end of David's reign there were nine bishops in Scotland, as we learn chiefly from their signatures appended to royal charters. But their existence was recognized at Rome, for they and their sees are named in a Brief of Pope Adrian IV in 1155 ordering them to submit to York. The origin of the sees apart from St. Andrews and Glasgow is quite obscure. There is no record of their foundation or endowment or delimitation. Indeed the curiously intricate pattern of the dioceses in central Scotland suggests that they arose from historical accident rather than by deliberate act. Farther north one suspects that except for Aberdeen bishops were for a long time little more than titular.

Dunkeld had been of old a Columban monastery and for a time the seat of a bishop of Fortriu. A charter of Alexander's reign bears the signature, 'Cormac bishop', and another, a little later, 'Cormac bishop of Dunkeld'. His successor Gregory witnessed many charters and died in 1164 or 1169. He is named in Adrian's Brief. The diocese included a large part of Perthshire and the mainland of Argyll, until *c.* 1200 Argyll was detached at the request of Bishop John of Dunkeld on the ground that he did not speak Gaelic, and a new see was founded with its centre on the island of Lismore. Iona, however, long remained attached to Dunkeld. To the east and south the diocese of Dunkeld was oddly intertwined with those of St. Andrews and Dunblane, and included the abbey of Inchcolm and even the parishes of Cramond, Aberlady, and Bonkil south of the Forth.

Bishops of Dunblane and Brechin appear as witnesses to charters from *c.* 1150 and are mentioned in Adrian's Brief 1155. Both places were religious centres in Celtic times, and at Brechin it seems clear that a Culdee community transformed itself into a chapter of cathedral canons. The diocese, which was small and curiously shaped, included Montrose and Dundee but not Arbroath. Dunblane was overshadowed by the abbey of Inchaffray and had a rather undistinguished existence until 1237 when it was reorganized by Bishop Clement, a Dominican.

Aberdeen had no roots in the Celtic period. The story of the foundation of its church near the mouth of the Don by Macarius, a disciple of St. Columba, is pure fiction. Nevertheless there may be truth in another tradition that a bishopric of the old Celtic type had existed at Mortlach in Banffshire, a Celtic monastic centre, and was transferred to Aberdeen by King David and transformed into a bishopric of the new order. Certainly the properties of the defunct 'monastery' of Mortlach belonged to the bishopric of Aberdeen. To this extent David may be said to have founded this bishopric.

The first Bishop of Aberdeen was a somewhat shadowy Nechtan. An obviously Anglo-Norman Bishop Edward witnesses a charter in 1150, is named by Pope Adrian IV in 1155, and in 1157 received from the same Pope a bull taking under the protection of St. Peter the properties of the see.

Moray, embracing the three modern counties of Moray, Nairn, and Inverness except Lochaber, was a turbulent province whose rulers were often in rebellion against the King of Scots. A bishop of Moray, Gregory, witnesses a charter of Alexander I in 1124. By the end of David's reign the bishop is William, doubtless an Anglo-Norman and a man of some importance, but the bishops of Moray led wandering lives until 1224 when Elgin was chosen as their seat, and a cathedral was built.

Farther north the writ of the King of Scots hardly ran, so it is surprising to learn that in David's reign there were persons witnessing charters as bishops of Ross and Caithness. Rosemarkie had been the seat of Bishop Curitan, and he may have had successors. At all events a charter of King David c. 1130 in favour of Dunfermline Abbey is witnessed by Macbeth, Bishop of Rosemarkie. The first Bishop of Caithness was Andrew whose signature appears in 1146 and frequently thereafter till his death in 1184. His long life is no doubt accounted for by the fact that he stayed away from his diocese, though he did witness a charter of a Norse Earl of Orkney and Caithness granting the payment to the Roman curia of 'one penny yearly from every inhabited house in Caithness'. His successors attempted to organize the diocese but one, John, had his tongue cut out, and another, Adam, was burned alive. The first bishop to make progress was Gilbert of Moray, who founded the cathedral of Dornoch c. 1224.

Thus, by the end of David's reign there were nine bishoprics, to which Argyll was soon to be added. But reference must be made to three others equally ancient which were subsequently to become parts of the Scottish Church. Two were of Norse origin, Orkney, and the Isles or Sudreys. In 1152 both were made subject to the metropolitical jurisdiction of the newly created archbishopric of Niderös (Trondhjem) in Norway. Only in 1472 when St. Andrews also reached archiepiscopal rank did they become ecclesiastically Scottish. Before 1152 we hear of purely titular bishops of Orkney assisting the Archbishop of York. One of them, called Ralph, was on the English side at the Battle of the Standard in 1138. He exhorted the army to fight bravely and absolved from their sins all who should fall in the battle. The cathedral of the Isles was on the Isle of Man which passed into English hands under Edward I. Not until 1506 did the abbey church of Iona become the cathedral of the Scottish diocese of the Isles. The original name Sudreys survives in the name of a diocese of the Church of England today—Sodor and Man.

Candida Casa or Whithorn had no history since Bede's time until Fergus, Lord of Galloway, King David's contemporary, and imitator in the founding of monasteries, restored the see. The first bishop, Gilla-Aldan, was consecrated by Thurstan, Archbishop of York, and made profession of obedience. His successors until 1472 continued to be subject ecclesiastically to York, although from Malcolm IV's time they were politically subject to the kings of Scots and sometimes members of his great council. Their position must have been very ambiguous during and after the War of Independence.

V

THE FRIARS

THE organization so far described might seem to be ideally complete for the purpose of fostering Christianity in Scotland. The monasteries should have provided an opportunity for those who felt called to 'enter religion' and to live the contemplative life; the cathedrals cared for 'the worship of God' in the amplest liturgical manner; and the parish churches, under diocesan supervision, covering the whole country, should have brought the ordinances of religion to the people everywhere. The weakness of the system was that cathedrals and monasteries tended to draw to themselves too large a share of the ecclesiastical endowments, leaving the parochial ministry poor and ineffective. It seems clear that the 'cure of souls', the task of the parochial ministry, was seriously undervalued. Vicars formed a depressed class in the ecclesiastical hierarchy. It is true there seems to have been no shortage of manpower at this level. Indeed the problem was made intractable by the very fact that there was a superfluity of unbeneficed priests ready to do for a pittance the work of absentee rectors, canons, or monks. But it was a dead-end occupation not to be accepted by any one in search of higher preferment.

This situation was not peculiar to Scotland but pertained everywhere throughout the Western Church, in spite of repeated attempts to improve it on the part of the church authorities. In 1215 Innocent III, the greatest of the medieval popes, summoned the Fourth Lateran Council in order to legislate much needed reforms. For already the consciences of many genuine Christians were offended by obvious abuses in the Church. Some bolder spirits were pointing out the discrepancy between the Church as it was in the time of the Apostles and the Church now when it had become powerful and wealthy, and were demanding a return to the Evangelical Law, that is the precepts of the Gospel. In the more advanced lands of Western Europe—in France, Italy, South Germany, the Rhineland, and the Netherlands, especially in the towns, among the humbler social classes there was a proliferation of sects, some heretical like the dualist Albigensians, others merely anti-clerical like the Poor Men of Lyons who drew their inspiration from the preaching of Peter Waldo. All of them were critical of the Church, which sought to repress them by persecution and inquisition.

In such an age one great figure towers above all others, the humblest, tenderest, most attractive figure of the Middle Ages, comparable in the extent of his influence with St. Bernard of Clairvaux a century earlier. St. Francis of Assisi was neither heretical nor anti-clerical. He was a simple devoted son of the Church and utterly submissive to the clergy, but he was an enthusiast who had conceived a new form of knight-errantry. He would abandon home and every worldly interest and comfort to follow the example of Christ who had not where to lay his head and whose life was a mission of itinerant evangelism and beneficence towards the poor, the outcast, and the leper. Francis was sure of his divine call when he realized that he had overcome his repugnance for lepers and could find joy in caring for them. Having been joined by some like-minded friends he gave them a rule based upon the commands of Christ to the Apostles when He sent them out to preach and heal the sick (Matt. x. 7–19), and together in 1210 they sought the approval of Pope Innocent III for a mission to be carried out on these lines—bare approval, for they asked no privilege of any kind. We can understand the hesitation of Innocent and his cardinals. They tried to dissuade Francis from his enterprise, pointing out the extreme difficulty, even impossibility, of his proposed way of life, and suggested that he and his friends might enter one of the established religious orders. But when Francis was not to be moved, and was recognized to be utterly sincere in his devotion to the Church, Innocent gave some sort of verbal approval to the *Fratres Minores*. At the same time for safety he appointed as their 'Protector' Cardinal Hugolino, then Bishop of Ostia and the future Pope Gregory IX. Their numbers now increased rapidly and they developed an

extraordinary missionary activity even beyond the bounds of
Christendom to Morocco, Tunis, Egypt, and Syria. But their
chief success was in the Latin countries where the novelty of
their enterprise and their obvious sincerity won for them
attention and widespread popularity. St. Francis always insisted that his followers must seek the co-operation of the
clergy and the permission of the bishops to preach in their
dioceses. Nevertheless his movement contained an implicit
criticism of the worldliness and sloth of the ordinary clergy,
which exposed it to much hostility on their part, and even
suspicion of heresy. Hence Francis's unwilling acceptance of
curial 'protection' and guidance. Twice the rule was revised,
in 1221 and finally in 1223, to meet those practical difficulties.
The *Fratres Minores* were organized as an Order under a
Minister Generalis with settlements throughout Christendom
ruled by guardians (*custodes*) and grouped in provinces each
under a *Minister Provincialis*. These titles reflect the desire of
Francis that his friars should be 'subject to all'. Nevertheless the organization was not the work of St. Francis himself,
who accepted it not without a sense that his original purpose
was being obscured if not frustrated. Just before his death in
1226 he expressed his misgivings in his *Testament*, which
became a bone of contention within the order for two hundred
years. In 1230 Pope Gregory IX ruled that the *Testament* was
not to be regarded as of binding authority, to the lively discontent of a large minority who clung to the ideas of the
founder to whom any kind of privilege for the friars was ab-
horrent. In particular their poverty must be absolute. Even
as an Order they must not own any property, not even friaries
to live in, an impossibly idealistic demand, of course. In 1279
Pope Nicholas III laid it down that while the Order of
Minorites might not itself hold property it might enjoy the
use of property held for it in trust by the Pope. There were
still recalcitrants who would not accept this subtle compromise, and after long dispute the order divided into two sec-
tions, Conventuals and Observantines, not to mention a third
section of *Spirituales* who passed into open opposition to the
Church, and were condemned by Pope John XXII, who
further pronounced heretical the doctrine that Christ and the

Apostles possessed no property in common. This was finally
to condemn the basic idea of St. Francis. The Observantines
continued to maintain themselves in spite of much suspicion
and finally obtained recognition as a separate Order from the
Council of Constance in 1416.

Contemporary with St. Francis was the Spaniard St.
Dominic, founder of another important Order of Friars. At
the age of 25 he became a Canon-Regular of the Order of
St. Augustine, but on a journey through southern France he
became impressed with the need for the defence of orthodoxy
against the Albigensian heretics. He therefore conceived the
idea of an Order of Preachers. Meeting St. Francis and his
brethren in 1215, and observing the popularity of the ideal
of absolute poverty, he adopted it as an apologetic weapon.
He found Innocent III unsympathetic. Innocent's policy was
to consolidate and discipline existing church agencies. Feeling, perhaps, some misgivings over the recognition accorded
to Francis, he wanted no more 'religions' and suggested that
Dominic could do what he wanted to do within the Augustinian Order. In 1216, however, Dominic secured the approval of Pope Honorius III, and in 1220 the Dominicans
were organized as a Mendicant Order of Preachers under a
Magister Generalis, provincials, and priors of individual houses.

Friars must be distinguished from monks of the older
orders. They were forbidden even corporately to own lands
or tithes or benefices, and were required to beg for their
living from day to day, though they did receive small grants
from towns and from kings. St. Francis would have forbidden
the ownership of convents, and we have seen how this difficulty was surmounted. But the friars also came to have
churches of their own in which they administered the sacraments and heard confessions; and cemeteries in which to
bury the dead. These rights, conferred one by one by successive popes, encroached on the existing rights of rectors
and vicars, and led to disputes. Moreover, unlike the monks,
their work was the active work of ministry in the world,
not contemplation in the cloister. Hence their settlements
were placed in or just outside the towns which were to be
their mission fields. They were to be primarily preachers,

fulfilling a function that was neglected by the ordinary clergy. While St. Francis had in view what we would call now the lapsed masses, to be won back by sincere popular preaching, Dominic's aim was to preach to the more educated who were in danger of falling into heresy. Friars of both Orders early made their appearance in the universities, but with a different purpose in view. The Dominicans came to teach and defend the faith in those new homes of learning. The Franciscans were looking for recruits for their Order among the young students who congregated there, for Francis and his first followers cared nothing for learning. Nevertheless the Franciscans soon fell into line with their Dominican rivals and began to cultivate theology and philosophy. All the great scholastics of the thirteenth century belong to one or other of these Orders. Alexander of Hales, Bonaventure, Duns Scotus, and William of Occam were Franciscans, and Albertus Magnus and Thomas Aquinas were Dominicans. Indeed two schools of theology can be distinguished, the Franciscan— Scotist, nominalist, pelagianizing—and the Dominican— Thomist, realist, Augustinian. The Franciscan school won the scholastic battle in the later Middle Ages, but in modern times the Dominican theology of Thomas Aquinas has been officially declared to be the 'normal' theology of the Roman Catholic Church. It should be added that both Orders, but particularly the Dominican, had much to do with the trials of heretics.

In spite of its remoteness and relative backwardness Scotland soon came within the orbit of the Mendicant Orders, the Franciscans following on the heels of the Dominicans. We shall take the Franciscans or Greyfriars first, though their story is more complicated. In 1224, two years before St. Francis died, eight of his followers came from Paris to London where their preaching and mode of life made an immense impression on the populace. An English province was constituted and grew rapidly. In 1231 some of the friars crossed the Tweed and established themselves at Berwick, then in Scotland, and shortly afterwards at Roxburgh, an important town and burgh under the shelter of a royal castle. We are not informed as to their reception, but it must have been friendly, for by 1235 they had built themselves a church dedicated to St. Peter and had marked out a cemetery. But the parish church of Roxburgh, St. James's, was an appropriated church of the abbey of Kelso. Fearing that their interests were threatened, the monks appealed to the Pope who remitted the case to the Bishop of Glasgow in whose diocese Roxburgh was included. The bishop heard Abbot Herbert and Friar Martin, Guardian of the Friars Minor in Scotland, and decided that the friars should be permitted to have their cemetery in which to bury members of their own order but no one else. He then forthwith consecrated the cemetery with the proviso that the rights of the monks of Kelso over their churches should suffer no prejudice. This is just one instance of the difficulty of fitting the friars into the system of established interests. When they received the right to bury laymen too and to hear confessions, their church of St. Peter must have become a serious rival to the parish church.

The growth of the Franciscan Order in Scotland was slow, in spite of the favour of kings, particularly Alexander III, of nobles and of citizens and town councils. Before the War of Independence only three friaries were added to the original two, Haddington (1242), Dumfries (1262), and Dundee (1284). It was in the church of the Greyfriars in Dumfries that Robert Bruce slew his rival, Comyn, for which deed he was excommunicated by the Pope though he afterwards made handsome amends by supporting the friars and establishing them at Lanark in 1329. Two later settlements, Inverkeithing (1346) and Kirkcudbright (1455) complete the list of the Conventuals.

Concerning the work of these friars our information is scanty. It is clear that they were forceful preachers, useful in campaigns organized from Rome in support of the Crusades. They were also credited with being the most dangerous enemies of the English aggressors, putting heart into the Scottish resistance by their sermons. Robert Bruce in founding the Lanark friary declares that they suffered in the war more than the older orders, and yet it is certain that Edward I ordered that the customary royal grants should continue to be paid. In the affairs of the Order itself they contended mainly for the right to form an independent Scottish province with a *Minister Provincialis* of its own. This was granted after the political independence of Scotland had been secured. In the great controversy concerning Franciscan Observance they took no part. The Observantines came to Scotland from abroad.

James I, doubtless in pursuance of his policy of church reform, having heard of the Franciscans of the strict Observance, in 1436 invited a colony to settle in Scotland. Not until 1447 in the reign of James II did they arrive in Edinburgh from the Netherlands. Fine buildings had been prepared for them near the Grassmarket through the generosity of the citizens, but Father Cornelius, their leader, declined to take possession of them until the Pope, on the motion of the Bishop of St. Andrews, incorporated them into the patrimony of the Roman Church and, in spite of their objections, gave them to the friars to be occupied by them as strangers and pilgrims according to their rule. In 1467 a Scottish province was fully recognized.

Thanks to the Chronicle of Friar John Hay, written in exile in 1586, more is known of the Observantines. Their numbers grew rapidly and in 1458, at the invitation of Bishop Kennedy, Robert Keith, son of the Earl Marshall, doctor in theology, led a colony to St. Andrews 'where the flower of the youth of the sacred University [founded by Bishop Wardlaw in 1413] deserted the allurements of the world and became followers of that holy father in his profession'. The bishop delegated to the friars to hear the confessions of the students. Similar invitations to Glasgow and Aberdeen followed, as well as to Perth, Ayr, and Elgin. James IV, who had an Observant as his Father Confessor, built the Stirling friary, worshipped in it when resident in Stirling, and even withdrew to it from worldly cares during Holy Week. In a letter to the Pope vigorously protesting against any proposal to unite the Observantines with the less strict Conventuals he declares himself to be their 'son and protector' and claims that by them alone true religion is preserved in Scotland. Friar Hay speaks of the popularity of his Order, evidenced by the alms given to them to superfluity. He tells of their devotion to preaching and hearing confessions especially of those drawing near to death, and claims that such was their influence over the king and the nobles there were in Scotland 'few quarrels and no divorces'! And yet Archbishop Hamilton and his colleagues, at their wits' end to provide preachers in order to counteract the Reformers, did not think of utilizing the friars!

Of the Dominicans, or Blackfriars, there is less to be said. They came to Scotland before the Franciscans and they spread more widely, for they had priories from Wigtown to Inverness, and from Ayr to Aberdeen. Their first settlement was at Edinburgh in 1230, and within three years one of their number, Clement, was appointed Bishop of Dunblane with the task of reorganizing the see. They had an important place in the University of St. Andrews from its inception, and as soon as heresy began to appear in Scotland they were found among the Inquisitors. The Reforming Council of 1549 met in their priory of Edinburgh and they were represented by their provincial (who later joined the Reformers) and two friars, but, again, not to them did the archbishop look for aid.

It seems clear that at their inception the Mendicant Orders did represent a revival of religious life and activity, and held the spiritual leadership of Christendom during the thirteenth century. But they lost it quickly, owing partly to rivalries between the Orders, partly to their conservatism which was rigidly opposed to new ideas and new methods. Long before the Reformation the friars and particularly the Franciscans in England provoked the contempt of Chaucer and the ire of Wyclif. In Germany at the time of the Reformation the Dominicans were the butt of all scholars for their obscurantism.

VI

COLLEGES OR
COLLEGIATE CHURCHES

SOME reference must be made to a later type of ecclesiastical foundation which became common in Scotland as elsewhere from the fourteenth century onwards, the college or collegiate church. Of these there came to be no fewer than forty in Scotland and, though most of them were small and insignificant, and none, unless it be St. Giles, ranks with All Saints', Wittenberg, or the Great Minster of Zürich in historic importance, several of them have considerable interest still. A college had no necessary connexion with education, as the name might now suggest. It was an incorporated body of secular clergy under a provost or dean, governed by regulations laid down in its charter of foundation. In every case the primary function of the 'colleagues' was to sing masses for the soul of the founder, his family, his friends and his heirs in perpetuity, so that a college was basically a glorified chantry. But provision was also made for the usual daily services as in cathedrals but on a smaller scale. Occasionally other functions were added. Usually the founder reserved to himself and his heirs complete control of the foundation including the appointment of the provost and prebendaries, which perhaps suggests a certain distrust of purely clerical discipline.

Two of the Scottish collegiate churches, St. Mary's on the Rock at St. Andrews, and Abernethy, were very ancient, and seem to represent Celtic Culdee corporations under a new name and form. Of the others the earliest was founded at Dunbar in 1342 by Patrick, Earl of March, and the latest at Biggar by Malcolm, Lord Fleming, in 1546, but most of them were founded in the fifteenth century.

More than half of the entire number might be described as private chapels of local magnates. In such cases the church would usually be without nave as it was not intended for any parochial purpose, and the staff would be financed out of the rectorial income of such parishes as were within the power of the founder. Such colleges were often very small and poorly endowed. Roslin is well known today for its elaborate carved ornamentation, but the three prebendaries who served there were poorly paid chantry priests. Sometimes a college would be superimposed on an existing parish church, in which case the founder would enlarge the chancel for its new purposes. No change would be made in the arrangements for parochial work. In 1429 Sir John Forrester of Corstorphine founded a college there, improved and enlarged the existing church, and for the benefit of the new clergy, appropriated the rectorial revenues of Ratho in spite of the protests of the laird and parishioners.

Much more ambitious were the colleges founded by royalty. In 1460 Mary of Gueldres, widow of James II, founded Trinity College, Edinburgh, for a provost and a large number of prebendaries, but it was also a charitable foundation supporting fourteen poor bedesmen. When she died she was buried in the church and on the anniversaries of her death the whole staff were obligated to pray for her at her tomb. The whole scheme was financed by appropriating the revenues of fourteen parishes of which the queen was patron. The church she built is still in existence though transported to another site and her charitable bequest is now administered by Edinburgh Corporation as the Trinity Fund. Restalrig, begun by James III and completed by James IV, was quite exceptional. Two parishes were appropriated for its endowment but further endowments were added from the royal revenues. The dean was required to be a Doctor of Laws and, on the erection of the Court of Session, was commonly its president. Provision was also made for the encouragement of music. An organ was installed in the church and one of the prebendaries was required to be a Doctor of Music.

Two colleges founded by bishops are specially interesting, St. Salvator's in St. Andrews, founded by Bishop James Kennedy in 1451, and St. Mary's (now King's) College, Aberdeen, founded by Bishop Elphinstone in 1505. In both cases the usual religious duties came first, but the educational interest of the two founders is expressed in the qualifications demanded of the provosts and prebendaries. They must be qualified to teach theology or arts. These colleges are now purely educational institutions and integral parts of the universities of St. Andrews and Aberdeen.

A particular interest attaches to the small group of Collegiate churches founded by or on petition of 'the provost, bailies and community' of certain towns, of which the outstanding example is St. Giles, Edinburgh. St. Giles was an appropriated church of the abbey of Scone, served on the usual terms by a perpetual vicar. But the church grew with the growth of the town and came to house a multitude of altars, served by thirteen chaplains endowed by the bequests of pious citizens to say masses for their soul's weal. In 1419 the provost, bailies, and community of Edinburgh petitioned the Pope to grant collegiate status to their parish church, promising to contribute annually towards its support. Nothing came of this at the time, but in 1466 the petition was renewed with the backing of the king, James III, and papal sanction was given in 1468. The new staff was composed of a provost, a curate to be appointed by the provost for parochial work, sixteen canons or prebendaries, a sacristan, a beadle, a minister of the choir, and four choristers. The funds came from the old chantry endowments supplemented by grants from the king and from the town, and the appointments of provost and canons were to be made partly by the king and partly by the town council. Thus St. Giles was made worthy of its position as the church of the capital. The most famous provost was Gavin Douglas, poet and translator of Vergil's *Aeneid*, who held the office from 1502 to 1516 when he became Bishop of Dunkeld.

An Act of Parliament of 1471 which forbade annexations of parishes to monasteries and cathedrals, nevertheless allowed annexations to be made to 'secular colleges'. This no doubt was due to the fact that the lords, barons, and burgesses of that time were specially interested in this form of foundation. The Reformers of 1560 on the other hand had a special aversion to 'colleges'. They regarded them as temples of idolatry, in which the central act of Christian congregational worship was degraded into an almost mechanical means of escape from purgatorial penalties for those on whose behalf votive masses, often in great numbers, had been instituted and endowed. They proposed to divert their endowments to the support of schools and universities.

VII

ECCLESIA SCOTICANA

PAPAL Rome, following the pattern of Imperial Rome, subdivided its ecclesiastical empire into 'provinces' and 'cities'. In northern Europe 'city' and bishopric were not coextensive, but the term 'city' (*civitas*) was used to denote the place where the bishop resided. 'The vill of Auld Aberdeen' on the Dee became an episcopal city in King David's reign. But the 'province' was an important administrative unit at whose head stood the metropolitan or archbishop. Gregory the Great had instructed Augustine, his missionary to the English, to divide Britain into two provinces with their capitals at London and York respectively, and the arrangement stood except that Canterbury was substituted for London. Lanfranc in 1072 secured that York should be subject to the primacy of Canterbury, while remaining metropolis for Britain north of the Humber. We have seen that Alexander I and David I resisted this arrangement in the interests of their independence as kings. But Rome was slow to recognize kingdoms or nations, at any rate small ones, as having any significance for the ecclesiastical map of Christendom; and in fact the boundaries of kingdoms fluctuated for long and the idea of nationality was hardly born. Nevertheless in 1152 the Churches of Denmark, Sweden, and Norway were reorganized each under an archbishop of its own, and about the same time four archbishoprics were erected in Ireland. On the death of Robert of St. Andrews in 1159, therefore, Malcolm IV sent William of Moray to Rome to ask that St. Andrews might be raised to metropolitan rank. Adrian IV, who had vigorously maintained the ecclesiastical superiority of York over the Scottish bishops, had now been succeeded by Alexander III (1159–81), the most important Pope between Gregory VII and Innocent III. Alexander seems to have taken a special interest in Scotland or at least in the diocese of Glasgow. His reply to Malcolm's request is contained in a letter to the clergy of St. Andrews. He would gladly have acceded to the prayer of his dearest son, the illustrious King of Scots, if it could be done 'with God and with justice', but the existing vacancy at St. Andrews made it impossible. For the good of the said Church and of the king he has conferred upon William—what he had not asked—legatine powers to correct faults and lay down statutes within the kingdom. If the clergy of St. Andrews unanimously elect William as their bishop, and the king assents, the Pope will excuse William from the obligation to return to Rome to have his translation confirmed, and will allow him to continue to exercise his legatine powers as Bishop of St. Andrews. If, however, they elect another who is 'educated, suitable and honourable', Alexander will treat him honourably and confer legatine powers upon him when William's tenure of them has expired. Ernald, abbot of Kelso, was elected and William as papal legate carried through his consecration in 1160, perhaps the first entirely regular all-Scottish consecration. On William's death in 1164 the Pope fulfilled his promise by conferring legatine powers on Ernald which he exercised till his death two years later.

In 1165 Malcolm IV, the Maiden, was succeeded by his brother William the Lion, a much stronger ruler, who reigned till 1214. Malcolm had allowed his cousin Henry II of England, the most powerful and capable monarch of the time, to rob him of his rights in the northern counties of England. When Henry was embroiled with rebellious subjects in Normandy instigated by his own sons, William thought he saw an opportunity to recover those rights, and invaded Northumberland. He was captured near Alnwick and ignominiously conveyed through England and over to Normandy where he was kept a prisoner in the castle of Falaise until he agreed to do homage to Henry for his kingdom and promised to hand over certain castles to the King of England (1174). In 1175 at York William and many of his nobles did homage to Henry and took an oath of fealty to him. Some of the Scottish bishops and abbots also took the oath of fealty, but as became their condition as ecclesiastical persons were excused from doing homage. It seemed the end of Scottish independence, and the hesitation of Pope Alexander must have appeared to have been justified. Moreover Henry must have felt he had been wonderfully recompensed for the penance the Pope had imposed upon him for the murder of the Archbishop of Canterbury, Thomas à Becket.

The agreement of Falaise contained the stipulation that 'the Church of Scotia shall make such subjection to the Church of Anglia as it ought to make and was wont to make' in times past. For clarification Henry summoned William and his bishops to a council at Northampton in 1176. He claimed that as they had bound themselves by an oath of fealty to the King of England the bishops must also be subject to the Church of England. The Scottish bishops replied that their predecessors had never been so subject and that they owed no such subjection. Roger, Archbishop of York, an eager champion of the claims of his see, maintained that some, particularly the Bishop of Glasgow, had been subject to his Church and produced papal bulls to prove it. Whereupon the Bishop of Glasgow asserted that if at one time the Church of York had had jurisdiction over the Church of Glasgow, it had now ceased to have it as witness a bull recently received from Pope Alexander declaring the Church of Glasgow to be the 'special daughter' of the Roman Church exempt from all intermediary jurisdiction. Fordun has a story of a Scots cleric called Gilbert who passionately attacked the English for trying to impose their yoke by violence upon nations older and worthier than their own, and called Bede to witness that the Catholic Scotican Church was the mother of English Christianity and once held the primacy of all England north of the Thames! Some praised him, says Fordun, for his courage in thus boldly speaking for his country; others regarded him as an impetuous Scots firebrand. In the end the archbishops of Canterbury and York renewed their old dispute as to their respective rights over the Scottish Church, and no conclusion was reached. King Henry gave the Scots permission to withdraw, and when they reached home they appealed to the Pope, representing that King Henry had forced them to swear to obey the Anglican Church. Alexander took a high line. It was no business of kings or princes to

G

take order concerning churches or ecclesiastical persons. That would be 'to the injury of God and contempt of us, and the suppression of ecclesiastical liberty'. He therefore ordered the Archbishop of York to exercise no metropolitical jurisdiction over the Scottish bishops until the matter of right had been finally settled by the Roman pontiff. So the matter stood until 1189 when Henry's successor, Richard, in order to provide himself with funds to go on the Third Crusade, sold back to William for 10,000 silver merks the rights conceded to the King of England at Falaise.

It is interesting to note that in the agreement of Falaise there occurs, possibly for the first time, the expression *Ecclesia Scoticana*, Church of Scotland. Hitherto reference had been made only to the bishops and their sees individually. Soon the expression was to become official for in 1192 a bull of Pope Celestine III declared *Ecclesia Scoticana*, embracing the sees of St. Andrews, Dunblane, Glasgow, Dunkeld, Brechin, Aberdeen, Moray, Ross, and Caithness, to be the special daughter of the apostolic see, directly subject to the Pope or a legate specially sent from his side (*a latere*). No appeal might be taken to any other authority.

The action of Celestine was welcome for at least it settled the vexed question of the pretensions to jurisdiction on the part of the archbishops of York. They had to content themselves with petulant opposition to repeated requests from the kings of Scots to the popes for the right to be crowned and anointed by a Scottish bishop or a papal legate. But it also fitted in very well with the papal policy of centralization of ecclesiastical administration. On the other hand the Church in Scotland was not fully constituted as a province of the Catholic Church, for it was still without a metropolitan of its own. Episcopal elections had to be confirmed by the Pope who, if he found them valid and suitable, ordered the consecration of the elect by three Scottish bishops named by himself. This involved the sending to Rome of commissioners, normally three, to report an election and to bring back the mandate for consecration. It also gave to the Pope the opportunity to exercise influence in episcopal appointments. Moreover an appeal from the judgement of a bishop's court or a dispute between bishops had to be taken to Rome for decision. The relations, therefore, of the Church of Scotland and Rome were peculiarly close, and great numbers of Scots clerics were to be found there on various pretexts from 1192 onwards. In the third place there was no one in Scotland authorized to convene the Scottish bishops and preside over them in synod. Consequently they could not act together unless a papal legate came to summon them, and legates were unpopular. They were very important persons requiring to be sumptuously and expensively entertained, or they were not tactful in their attitude to Scottish susceptibilities; and their commission usually included the collection of money for papal schemes. All these consequences of the bull of 1192 must have detracted somewhat from the advantage of being the special daughter of the Roman Church, though this might not have been realized at the time.

In 1215 Pope Innocent III, the ablest and most successful of the Popes, summoned the Fourth Lateran Council to meet in Rome for the correction of abuses and the reformation of morals in the whole Church. Two thousand persons assembled —2 patriarchs, 27 archbishops, 412 bishops, and more than 800 abbots and priors. From Scotland came the bishops of St. Andrews, Glasgow, and Moray, proctors of the other bishops, and the abbot of Kelso. Many important canons were drawn up for the regulation of ecclesiastical discipline, and it was decreed that in every province the metropolitan should hold annually a provincial synod to publish the Lateran canons and take steps for their enforcement. For obvious reasons this canon could not be obeyed in Scotland. Representations were made at Rome and in 1225 Pope Honorius III granted authority to the Scottish bishops to hold a provincial synod or council even without a metropolitan. This was a most unusual arrangement. Why the Pope did not rather complete the Scottish hierarchy, and constitute a Scottish province by erecting an archbishopric is a puzzle. Possibly he had to reckon with English opposition, or it may be that the Scots did not desire it. They took immediate steps to make the most of the concession granted to them. Elaborate regulations were laid down for an annual meeting of a council. All bishops, abbots, and priors, and certain other clergy were to assemble in ceremonial vestments. A special liturgy was to be used and a sermon preached by one of the bishops or by a substitute. A president was to be appointed with the title of conservator 'who shall hold office from Council to Council, and shall punish open and notorious offenders against the Council or its decrees', and summon the next one. The office of 'Conservator of the Statutes of the Council' or 'of the privileges of the Church of Scotland', was to be held for one year by the bishops in rotation, beginning with the Bishop of St. Andrews. *Ecclesia Scoticana* was henceforth more than a name. It had now a constitution, albeit of a quite abnormal kind.

The provincial council was presumably the supreme governing body of the Church of Scotland from its institution in 1225 till the elevation of St. Andrews to archiepiscopal rank in 1472, a period of 247 years. It may have met annually, but references to its meeting and work are extraordinarily few, and suggest that its business was mainly of a routine administrative order. It certainly did not make history. It played no part in national affairs, e.g. during the War of Independence. It was no doubt overshadowed by Parliament when the latter was developed in the fourteenth century and included as the First Estate the bishops, abbots, and priors who were also the chief members of the council. It had nothing to do, so far as we can tell, with deciding which side the Scottish Church was to take in the papal schism of 1378, with the various union projects, with the controversies of the conciliar period or with the return of Scotland to the Roman obedience. But in 1401 an Act of Parliament laid down that during the schism all the king's lieges should have appeal from their bishop to the conservator and from the conservator to the provincial council, by whom cases should be determined, which looks like a temporary abrogation of papal appellate jurisdiction. In the storm occasioned by the erection of the archbishopric of St. Andrews the council as such took no part. It did, however, promulgate canons for the regulation of clerical life and work, which were no doubt necessary and useful, but show little originality. On a few occasions in the fifteenth century it took cognizance of cases of heresy.

The final step in the organization of the pre-Reformation Church of Scotland was taken towards the end of the fifteenth century. Patrick Graham, Bishop of Brechin, had been translated to St. Andrews in 1465. In 1472, without consulting anyone in Scotland, he procured from Sixtus IV a bull creating St. Andrews an archbishopric with metropolitical jurisdiction over all the Scottish sees, to which were now added Galloway, Orkney, and the Isles. Formal protests were made by the archbishops of York and Trondhjem who were thus deprived of suffragans, but this was nothing to the storm of protest that arose in Scotland itself. The king, James III, was incensed that such a thing could be done without his knowledge or consent, and the bishops of Glasgow, Aberdeen, and Moray all claimed and received exemption for life from the jurisdiction of St. Andrews. The papal bull sets forth very clearly and fully the inconveniences occasioned to the Church of Scotland through having no metropolitan, and it has been suggested that Graham was moved by the spirit of a reformer. His motives seem, however, to have been chiefly ambition and greed, for he also represented to the Pope that his new dignity required additional income to maintain it. He received the priory of Pittenweem *in commendam*, and in defiance of an Act of Parliament it was proposed to annex seven parish churches to his *mensa*. He did not long enjoy his gains for in 1476 various charges were brought against him. He was found guilty, deposed, and condemned to imprisonment in a monastery where he died in 1478. An archbishopric, however, St. Andrews remained.

The elevation of St. Andrews was followed twenty years later by the similar elevation of Glasgow, this time with the full support of the king, James IV, and his Parliament. The sees subordinated to Glasgow were Dunkeld, Dunblane, Galloway, and Argyll, but very soon Dunkeld and Dunblane returned to St. Andrews. Further, the example of Canterbury and York was followed and Glasgow was made subject to the primacy of St. Andrews, with consequent archiepiscopal disputes and even brawls over rights and precedence. It can hardly be said that the completion of the hierarchy was an enrichment of the spiritual life or efficiency of the Church. From 1497 till 1513 St. Andrews was held by two young princes of the royal house as 'Administrators'. Presumably it was intended that they would become real archbishops on attaining canonical age, but neither of them did so. The Beatons were engaged in pressing political duties. Not until 1549 under the last pre-Reformation archbishop was attention given to the rapidly deteriorating condition of the Church.

In acquiring a national name, and in becoming imbued with a national sentiment, the Church of Scotland did not cease to be essentially a part of the Universal Church. Its doctrine, liturgy, laws, institutions, organization, the very language it used for worship, for theology and for its canons, were all those of the Western Church. Above all in common with the Church in Western Europe generally it recognized the ecclesiastical supremacy of the Bishop of Rome. Relations with Rome were, it is true, not always easy. When, as often happened, kings and popes were at loggerheads, the Scottish clergy, or a substantial number of them, would take the side of the king. Nevertheless they normally looked to Rome as the source of all ecclesiastical authority and the final court of appeal in all matters of dispute. They early put themselves and their properties under the protection of the apostolic see, and submitted, though not without protest, to papal taxation of their benefices, systematized on the basis of a valuation carried out in 1275 by Boimund de Vicci and known as Bagimond's Roll. Moreover, from Rome they sought personal favours of various kinds, promotions, exemptions, indulgences, dispensations. The record of Scottish supplications to Rome makes astonishing reading, and the frequency with which influential persons were for a fee dispensed from obeying the laws of the Church must have encouraged every kind of what would now be regarded as abuses. It looks almost as if the Pope were regarded as a sort of benevolent and indulgent head of the clerical profession, ready to make comfortable careers possible for the favoured few. And yet, while the corruption and venality of the Papal Curia were often recognized and sometimes criticized in Scotland and its repeated demands for money were resented and resisted, the papal government of the Church was accepted without question. It represented a universal, ordered and in many ways efficient system of law and administration in glaring contrast to the feudal disorder which too often prevailed in Scotland. It thus gave support to churchmen contending with difficulties which they were not strong enough by themselves to overcome, and secured their freedom from oppressors nearer home. The Scottish Church might be described theologically as, in the words of Eadmer in a letter to Alexander I, 'The Church of God which sojourns (*peregrinatur*) in your kingdom', or, more realistically, as the Scottish province of the papal empire. Unhappily it is as the latter that it appears most clearly in our documents.

Long before it was recognized as in any sense a national Church, the Church in Scotland began, as we have seen, as a number of inter-related foundations of various types already familiar in Anglo-Norman England. They took root and were soon naturalized. Almost immediately, in accordance with the ideas of feudal society they were conceived of as benefices, large and small, the larger and more important being the bishoprics and abbacies. Bishops and abbots, as part of their benefices, held lands in 'free barony' and sometimes 'in regality' from which they drew rents, and over which they exercised temporal jurisdiction. For these they were subject to the king as their feudal superior, though by the terms of their tenure they were exempted from certain feudal obligations. Bishops, in virtue of their office, also drew revenues from tithes and had jurisdiction over their clergy in all matters, and over laymen in matters affecting their salvation, such as their beliefs, participation in the sacraments and other ecclesiastical obligations. Such jurisdiction, obviously, affected very closely the lives of all subjects of the king, so that there was room for much dispute between Church and State, should a masterful king endeavour to extend his powers, as happened in England under the Plantagenets. These disputes were not wholly settled when Magna Carta confirmed the rights and liberties of the Church of

England. In Scotland similar pledges were given by kings, and in the fifteenth century repeated Acts of Parliament guaranteed the 'freedome of Haly Kirk'. From time to time this was explained to mean, for example, protection of church lands against alienation, freedom of the clergy to 'set'[1] their lands and teinds without hindrance, enforcement of the judgement of church courts by the secular arm. Even so, there remained certain matters that gave rise to dispute. Bishops were, of course, celibate and the kings of Scots claimed as their heirs to take possession of their moveable goods when they died. Moreover the kings claimed to administer and enjoy the temporalities of bishoprics during vacancies, which they were sometimes tempted to prolong. Both of these claims were contested, but in 1450 a compromise was reached. In return for the king's abandonment of his claim to the moveable goods of deceased bishops, his claim to enjoy episcopal temporalities during vacancies was conceded by the clergy and confirmed by the provincial council.

Much more serious trouble was caused by the claim made by the king to the right of appointment during an episcopal vacancy to benefices normally in the gift of the bishop. Obviously such a claim trenched on the spirituality of the bishopric and besides it conflicted with the policy of Rome which sought to bring all kinds of benefices great and small under papal patronage. This policy has been defended on the ground that the Pope would be likely to make better appointments than local patrons or local electors because he could evaluate the merits of candidates without fear or favour. In many cases this was undoubtedly true, but on the other hand benefices even in a poor country like Scotland were sometimes bestowed on curial officers and papal favourites who had no intention of fulfilling the duties attached. Moreover, for every benefice provided an appropriate fee was charged in proportion to its value, and these fees formed an important source of papal revenue from the fourteenth century onwards. It seems that the majority of Scots clergy were not dissatisfied if we may judge from the number of those who supplicated by themselves or by their agents for benefices at

[1] i.e. to lease.

Rome, binding themselves to pay the fees for promotion, and very likely something more in order to secure the good will of some curial official.

Whether this situation was good for the Church may well be doubted. Certainly there were many who thought it detrimental to the national interest. Alleging the impoverishment of his kingdom through this traffic in benefices and the consequent export of money, James I, with the support of his Parliament and his chancellor, the Bishop of Glasgow, passed several Acts against the purchase of benefices at Rome, called 'barratry' in Scotland, prohibiting export of gold and silver, and unlicensed passing of clerics 'oute of the realme'. The Pope, Martin V, and his successor, Eugenius IV, called for the repeal of the Acts as opposed to the freedom of the Church, and James in reply acknowledged the authority of the anti-papal council then sitting at Basel. The murder of the king in 1437 put an end to the first phase in the struggle. It was renewed with even greater determination under James III. Parliament repeated and strengthened the Acts against 'barratry', and finally petitioned 'his Holiness' that before appointing to the larger benefices he should wait six months for the king to supplicate for the promotion of 'sic persons as is thankfull to his hienes so that their be na personis promovit to prelacies without avise of his hienes sen all the prelatis of his realme has the first vote in his parlment and of his secret counsale'. To this Innocent VIII replied in 1487, promising to postpone appointments to vacancies for at least eight months to allow time for the king's supplications 'so that we may be the better able to proceed to these provisions as we shall think expedient'. In practice this meant that the king nominated to all the greater benefices—bishoprics and abbacies—and the Pope 'provided' the king's nominee, and secured without question the fee for provision. This seems a purely political and financial bargain between the king and the Pope which completely neglected ecclesiastical freedom and the good of the Church. Two appointments[1] to the archiepiscopal see of St. Andrews on the nomination of James IV were particularly scandalous. With the coming of

---

[1] See p. 90.

the Reformation and particularly when England broke with
Rome in 1534, the bargaining power of the Pope declined
and that of the king increased. Under James V and on his
nomination the priory of St. Andrews and the abbeys of
Holyrood, Kelso, and Melrose were given to three of his
illegitimate children who held them as lay commendators.

The freedom of the Church so often guaranteed by kings
and parliaments was in fact the freedom of the clergy to enjoy
their chartered and customary rights, properties and privileges
within the kingdom. This was invaluable as securing to
them status and the material basis for their work, and
protection in carrying it out. It has little resemblance to
the freedom of the Church in matters spiritual which was
later to become a crucial issue in Scottish church history,
when it had to be contended for by appeal to the Christian
people now fully conscious of themselves as church members,
and not by recourse to an external authority which could
bargain with the civil power. The medieval doctrine of the
Two Swords never developed into the Melvillian doctrine of
the 'Twa Kings and Twa Kingdoms in Scotland'. It is true
the clergy as ecclesiastical persons stood apart from laymen,
subject only to the 'spiritual' authority. Their properties
could be taxed only by the Pope, or by themselves with his
permission. This seems to have been conceded even by James
V who took more from Churchmen for State purposes than
his predecessors had ever done. Nevertheless the presence in
Parliament of bishops, abbots, and priors representing the
clergy as the Spiritual Estate, while giving to the Church
great influence in government, so integrated it with the body-
politic as virtually to deny to the Church of Scotland an
organic life of its own, and to give to the king in Parliament
the right to legislate in Church matters, outside the recognized ecclesiastical freedom, and so to overshadow the
provincial council. Indeed the Church was too exclusively
clerical to be itself fully 'Church' in any theological sense of
the word. It remained one of the Estates of the realm.

VIII

THE EPISCOPATE IN ACTION

FROM the first the bishops were the chief vassals of the king, valued and indeed indispensable counsellors, and often employed in high governmental offices such as the chancellorship of the kingdom. It is in this secular capacity that they are most conspicuous in the history of Scotland, and increasingly from the War of Independence onwards. We are here concerned with their activities in their ecclesiastical character, and our information is surprisingly meagre. That it should be meagre for the twelfth century, a century that brought many changes to the Church in Scotland, is especially unfortunate. But the changes were perhaps not so revolutionary as has been supposed. The early bishops were in no sense missionaries of new and original ideas. They were simply imitators, reproducing so far as Scottish conditions would allow the familiar pattern of Anglo-Norman ecclesiastical organization, and working, so far as their dioceses were concerned, from the centre outwards.

As soon as the king's strong arm gave him security of tenure of his properties and the Pope had taken them under the protection of the apostolic see, the early bishop's first concern was to build himself a cathedral. Robert of St. Andrews built the church of St. Regulus. This seemed inadequate to his successor, Ernald, who, as abbot of Kelso, had been engaged in building Kelso Abbey. He laid the foundations of a new cathedral in the presence of Malcolm IV in 1160. Slowly but steadily his successors carried on the work until it was completed and dedicated in 1318 in the presence of Robert Bruce. The cathedral built by John of Glasgow was destroyed by fire, and his successor, Herbert, who had also been abbot of Kelso, laid the foundations of a new one. He received from Pope Alexander III a bull ordering all Christians in the diocese to visit their cathedral mother church once a year with filial devotion and reverence both in word and deed. 'For he who does not love and honour his Mother Church as is meet gravely offends the eyes of the Divine Majesty.' Herbert's cathedral was consecrated in 1197, but was then far from completion. Bishop William de Bondington, 1233–58, built the choir, with the aid of money collected in all the parishes of Scotland. To stimulate contributions indulgences were published. The cathedrals of St. Andrews and Glasgow were national undertakings, but with more limited resources the bishops of Aberdeen, Dunkeld, and Moray succeeded over the years in erecting churches of great interest and beauty. For the building and enriching of a cathedral was the work of many generations.

The cathedral was the bishop's principal kirk and mother church of the diocese. Its purpose was to provide for the worship of God on a magnificent scale at the canonical hours, necessitating a large staff of clergy and the appropriate vestments, ornaments, lights, and other accessories. Having built his cathedral, Bishop Robert writes in 1144 'It is not sufficient for the praise of the Lord's name to heap up stones unless we bring living stones together for the house of God.' So he brought a company of Augustinian canons from Scone and settled them under Prior Robert in St. Andrews to be his cathedral clergy, endowing the new priory out of the possessions of the see. Soon further endowments were acquired from other donors, notably King David, including some thirty parish churches, not all within the diocese. At Whithorn too the services of Augustinian canons of the stricter Premonstratensian Order were utilized. It was proposed in a time of financial difficulty in Dunblane that the seat of the bishop should be transferred to the abbey of Inchaffray, so that the Augustinian canons there might also serve the cathedral; but the plan was not adopted. With the exception of St. Andrews and Whithorn, cathedral clergy in Scotland were secular canons, i.e. priests who were not bound by conventual vows, but formed corporate bodies known as chapters, governed by their own regulations or statutes. Chapters were responsible to the bishops for the management of Cathedral affairs and the due observance of the daily liturgical services. The chapter acted also as an advisory council to the bishop, and, according to canon law, had the right of electing to the bishopric.

The chapter had as its head the dean, responsible generally for everything connected with the cathedral. Next there was the cantor or precentor whose special responsibility was the cathedral worship. The chancellor was secretary to the chapter and kept its official seal, while the treasurer looked after its possessions. Those four officials were known as the dignitaries. In addition there was a varying number of ordinary canons, a number which tended to grow throughout the medieval period. All these offices were technically sinecures in the sense that they implied no pastoral work or cure of souls. When, as at Aberdeen, the cathedral was also a parish church a priest was employed by the dean to do the parish duties, but was not a member of the chapter. For all members of the chapter manses were provided in the vicinity of the cathedral where the dignitaries were expected to reside more or less permanently. Ordinary canons were obliged to reside three months in the year, presumably not all at the same time. But in order that the daily services might be carried on regularly and uninterruptedly, each member of the chapter was obliged to provide and pay for a vicar, termed a vicar-choral, and these formed an important if inferior class of cathedral clergy. Non-residence of canons seems quite early to have become an acute problem, and the reason for it may be gathered from one example, admittedly late. John Balfour, Bishop of Brechin, 1465–88, was at the date of his appointment rector of Conveth (Laurencekirk), vicar of Linlithgow and canon of Caithness, Aberdeen, and Dunkeld! The stipends of dignitaries and canons, termed prebends, were drawn from the revenues of parish churches appropriated for this purpose, the spiritual needs of these parishes being cared for by vicars. Other parishes were similarly appropriated for the fabric of the cathedral, for lights, incense, and other accessories of worship, as also for the common fund of the chapter. The most amazing document in this connexion is the constitution of Bishop Gilbert of Caithness (1223–45) for his new cathedral at Dornoch, a poorly endowed one. It seems there were some twenty parish churches in the diocese, and all of them were appropriated either to the bishop as mensal churches or to members of the chapter as prebends or to the needs of the cathedral. One of the canonries (Kildonan) was always to be held by the abbot of Scone! Commenting on this constitution a modern idealizing writer[1] has said, 'A body of learned and dignified clergy, residing in a remote and semi-civilized region, cannot have failed to exert a humanizing influence over its inhabitants'! That they resided is an unlikely assumption. It might be more truly remarked on the other hand, that in Caithness as elsewhere the cathedral engrossed too large a share of the diocesan endowments to the impoverishment of parochial ministrations.

The tradition of the ancient Church was that bishops should be elected by their clergy and people, and this tradition may be said to have been continued and regularized when it was laid down that the cathedral chapter should be the electoral body. This was not unreasonable on the assumption that the chapter consisted of the leading clergy of the diocese. The procedure to be followed was carefully regulated by canon law. The chapter should meet in the chapter house and, after invoking the aid of the Holy Spirit, decide on one or other of three recognized methods of procedure. If one name commanded instant and unanimous assent election was said to have taken place by the inspiration of the Holy Spirit. Naturally this form of election was extremely rare. When there were several nominations the chapter might decide to take a direct vote, and he was elected who obtained the votes of 'the greater or wiser part'! But perhaps the commonest method was for the chapter to appoint, not necessarily from their own number, commissioners with power to select a new bishop. These regulations seem extremely reasonable, and freedom of capitular elections was, at least in theory, one of the most cherished of the Church's rights. It is guaranteed, for example, in the first article of Magna Carta.

At the same time, since bishops were his most important subjects and counsellors, the king had a great interest in

[1] R. M. Stewart, *The Church of Scotland from the time of Queen Margaret to the Reformation*, p. 133.

episcopal appointments. It was therefore recognized that his assent to an election must be obtained 'as of custom'. What this might involve became apparent in the reign of William the Lion. Several times chapters were summoned to hold an election in the vicinity of the court, and bishops were commonly selected from among the king's chaplains or officers of State. One case of resistance to his wishes led to ten years of embittered controversy. In 1178 the chapter of St. Andrews, without the knowledge of the king, elected as Bishop John, archdeacon of St. Andrews. John, called 'the Scot' though he was an Englishman, was an entirely worthy person. He had studied at Oxford and Paris before coming to St. Andrews where for his merit he was appointed archdeacon. William, so far as we can tell, had no personal animosity against him, and John for his part was most willing to be William's loyal and obedient subject. But when the king heard of his election by the chapter, surreptitious as he probably thought it, he swore by the arm of St. James that John would never be bishop. He drove him from the kingdom and compelled the chapter to elect Hugh, one of the royal chaplains, and forthwith had him consecrated. John took his case to the Pope, Alexander III, who supported him vigorously. He sent a legate to Scotland in 1180, who in spite of King William got as far as Holyrood where with the assistance of four Scottish bishops he excommunicated Hugh and carried through the consecration of John. Next year at the request of the Pope, Henry II of England, then William's feudal superior, intervened and a compromise was agreed to. Hugh was to retain St. Andrews and John was to have the next see to fall vacant. The Pope refused to accept the arrangement. Instead he excommunicated William and laid his kingdom under an Interdict. These sentences lapsed on the death of Pope Alexander which took place soon afterwards, and his successor, Lucius III, tried to make peace with William. In 1183 he 'provided' Hugh to St. Andrews and John to Dunkeld, then vacant. Even so the dispute continued until Hugh died in 1188. John remained Bishop of Dunkeld until 1203. His pastoral care for his people was manifested by his action in securing the erection of the see of Argyll which was disjoined from Dunkeld in his time. He also distinguished himself by his saintliness. On his deathbed in Newbattle Abbey he assumed the habit of a Cistercian monk.

This incident illustrates the advantage of free capitular election at its best. Hugh is a rather ambiguous character, and clearly from the point of view of religion the chapter of St. Andrews chose the better man. But in spite of papal support for the chapter King William in effect won his battle. On the death of Hugh in 1188 he caused the chapter to 'elect' Roger, son of the Earl of Leicester, William's own cousin, who held the see for nine years before he sought consecration or even ordination to the priesthood. Again in 1202 William procured the 'election' to Glasgow of his nephew, Florentius, son of his sister Ada and her husband, the Count of Holland. Florentius may never have visited Glasgow and certainly was never consecrated bishop, but he held the see for five years and was succeeded by a royal chaplain of dubious character.

Until the death of Alexander III in 1286 it is clear that chapter elections were never quite free from royal pressure. It may be that William's successors were happier in their selection of bishops, and the Pope was also officially in a position to confirm or refuse to confirm elections, for after 1192 they had to be reported to him. During the fourteenth century it was the popes who encroached on the freedom of chapters, by 'reserving' bishoprics to their own appointment, 'providing' bishops as and when they fell vacant, and charging a fee for 'provision' to the fortunate applicant. In the fifteenth century the kings began to reassert themselves and in 1487 came to an agreement with the Papacy as to the mode of episcopal appointment, which in practice gave the nomination to the king, and the 'provision', with fee, to the Pope. Chapter election was thus reduced to pure formality. It would be hard to say whether these alterations in the mode of appointment influenced seriously the character of the episcopate as a whole, but on the eve of the Reformation it seems to have reached a low moral and religious level.

We turn now to see the bishop in his diocese, the vast area for which he had responsibility as chief pastor. We have

seen already that the process of delimitation is quite unknown. It was not due to any specific action on the part of
the *Episcopus Scottorum* as the Bishop of St. Andrews continued
to style himself. Nor is there much evidence of an interest
on the part of the early bishops in what we should call today
church extension within their dioceses. Local churches were
founded chiefly by local lairds and endowed with glebe-
lands. Out of these emerged parish churches each with its
altar, font, and cemetery and a priest to administer the
sacraments to the parishioners. Moreover, the Church claimed
on the ground of Scripture, i.e. the Law of God, the tithe or
tenth part of the annual produce of the parish, grain, butter,
eggs, and the like, and this claim was enforced by royal
commands. Likewise offerings, oblations, were expected on
certain occasions, such as baptisms, marriages, funerals, and
the celebration of Mass especially on Easter Day. These were
supposed to be voluntary, but they became customary, and
custom came to have the force of law. Care was taken to explain that they were in no sense payments for the sacraments,
but the point was not always grasped by parishioners. The
income from all these sources together formed the parochial
benefice which might be held by a parson or rector appointed
by the founder or his heirs as patron. But as we have seen it
was usual in the twelfth century for the founder to hand over
his church to some favoured monastery, which thereby became permanent 'rector', appropriated the 'fruits' to its own
uses and appointed a priest to perform the parochial duties,
at a salary which was only a fraction of the parish revenue.

It is universally agreed that during the twelfth century at
least the monasteries were in fact as they were in contemporary esteem the main centres of Christian devotion and
moral leadership. They were favoured by the popes who
readily granted them exemption from all external jurisdiction secular or episcopal, recognized their rights over their
appropriated churches, and sometimes specifically allowed
them to find their parochial vicars wherever they liked, so
that they might not be dependent even for ordinations on the
local bishop. As the bishop was responsible for the cure of
souls within his diocese, and therefore for the parochial

H

ministrations, it was inevitable that sooner or later conflict should arise between bishops and abbots over this matter.

An early instance of conflict and the settlement reached is to be found among the documents relating to a council of clergy held at Perth in 1201, by the papal legate, Cardinal John of Salerno. Kelso Abbey held certain churches within the dioceses of St. Andrews and Glasgow and had apparently complained that the bishops made unreasonable difficulties about accepting the vicars appointed to them, and that in their visitations of these churches the bishops were too exacting in their demands for entertainment and expenses, technically known as procurations. An 'amicable and reasonable composition' was reached with the legate's aid. The monks would present fit priests to be perpetual vicars of their churches, and those vicars would receive cure of souls from the bishop unless he could show reasonable cause why they should not. If the bishop 'maliciously or arbitrarily' refused to admit a presentee, alleging his unfitness, the matter was to be referred to the arbitration of 'three good men' mutually agreed upon by the parties. During a vacancy the revenues of the church were to belong to the monks on condition that divine ordinances were properly maintained in the vacant parish. On the other hand the bishops were to be moderate in their demands for entertainment when visiting the churches. The salary to be paid to the perpetual vicars by the abbot of Kelso was to be at his discretion, but must take into account the bishop's procurations, and each presentee must declare himself satisfied with it. Similar agreements were made during the thirteenth century between the bishops of Aberdeen, Moray, and Brechin and monasteries holding appropriated churches in their dioceses, except that it became necessary to fix the salary to be paid to vicars to prevent their being exploited.

It would seem that from *c.* 1300 onwards the situation as thus stabilized was accepted by all parties. But that the problem was not solved will appear from a later and perhaps solitary protest. The Bishop of Moray was scandalized at the neglect by the monks of Arbroath of their church of Inverness, and proceeded to fine them and compel them to do their duty. They appealed to Rome and in 1370 he wrote his version of the case.

The monks have been neglecting their churches and other property. The Churches are devoid of the necessary ornaments and almost destitute of divine service and the sacraments. Their vicars complain. The parishioners murmur. Daily we see grievous scandal and peril to men's souls. When the ordinaries do their duty and demand reform the monks take refuge in appeals. The Abbey bailiffs oppress the people and defraud the vicars of their due salaries and refuse to provide the churches with ornaments. All of which is evident in this church of Inverness, which is a thriving and renowned township abounding in the fruits of the earth and frequented by many noble knights and other worthy men. The Abbot has failed to supply vestments or a decent missal in spite of the Bishop's insistence. Besides the roof is no sufficient defence to protect the high altar or the vestry from being ruined by the rains whensoever they fall.

This may have been an extreme case, or the bishop may have exaggerated, but his letter illustrates a problem that confronted conscientious bishops throughout the medieval period.

Easy-going bishops accepted the situation and indeed aggravated it by allowing parochial benefices to be annexed to cathedrals, moved, as they said 'by zeal to amplify the worship of God'. But others were not so easily satisfied. As the burghs grew and became prosperous we find them at odds with the monasteries which possessed their churches. For example after much litigation 'and very great discord contention and altercation' between the burgesses of Dundee and the abbot and convent of Lindores, being the 'religious rectors' of St. Mary's, the parish church, an agreement was reached in the presence of the Bishop of Brechin in 1424, whereby the town bought out the rectors and became responsible for its own church. And in 1471 Parliament intervened to prohibit annexations of benefices to bishoprics, abbeys, or priories and to declare null all annexations made since 1460. Even if the Act had been effective it came too late for most of the annexations had been made long before that date.

There can be no doubt that the practice of appropriation of parish churches to monasteries and cathedrals was an evil, even when the best possible arrangements were made for parochial ministrations. It encouraged the idea that an ecclesiastical benefice might be held by a person or persons who did not or could not perform the duties attached to it. Rectors of unappropriated parishes rarely did the parish work, and were not even obliged to be ordained to the priesthood. The only obligation was that a rector 'have in his parish a priest who is capable efficient and able to read' (*literatum*). Vicars were commonly badly paid and poorly educated, and in consequence the status of the parochial ministry was low. This proved to be the fatal weakness of the medieval Church, but it was not recognized as such until it was too late.

It would be interesting, if we could, to catch a glimpse of a bishop at work in his diocese, but unhappily that side of his activity is but rarely referred to. He was in duty bound to visit the parishes every year, and it was laid down that every parish should have a manse suitable to receive him and his retinue, limited by the Third Lateran Council to thirty horsemen! There was naturally a good deal of resistance to such an imposition, and ultimately the obligation to entertain the bishop on his visitations was commuted to an annual payment, called a procuration, payable sometimes by the rector, sometimes by the vicar. In all agreements with monasteries it was laid down who was responsible for the 'episcopal dues'. In his *Lives of the Bishops of Aberdeen* Hector Boece mentions devotion to the visitation of parishes as a virtue of certain bishops; notably Alexander de Kininmond (1329–44) who built himself four residences in different parts of the diocese, which he occupied when making his visitations. Boece says nothing of the institution of incumbents or of confirmation, but an Aberdeen statute of the thirteenth century ordains that parish priests when they hear that the bishop is coming are to warn parents to bring their children to him to be confirmed, and to explain to their people the meaning of the sacrament and its obligations.

Perhaps more is known of the diocesan work of David de Bernham, Bishop of St. Andrews (1239–53), than of any other Scottish medieval bishop. He made agreements on the usual terms with the abbots of Arbroath and Holyrood in respect of their appropriated churches within the diocese, and he 'gave' the church of Scoonie to the fabric of his cathedral. But a more unusual interest in his diocese is evidenced by the fact that his *Pontificale* or Book of Ceremonies,[1] which is preserved, contains a list of 140 churches from Berwick-on-Tweed to Nigg on the Dee, consecrated by him with elaborate ceremonial between 1240 and 1249. These were obviously not all newly founded churches for they include St. Giles' and St. Cuthbert's, Edinburgh, and St. John's, Perth, but the *Pontificale* enables us to trace the bishop's itinerary as he moved up and down his diocese, and to form an agreeable impression of episcopal diligence.

Bishop David also held diocesan synods of his clergy at which he promulgated statutes or constitutions to govern their conduct and work. A series of such constitutions promulgated in 1242 survives,[2] and its Preface runs:

To the office of Pastor [i.e. Bishop] it pertains, as concerns the state of the churches entrusted to him and the instruction of those under his charge, to take vigilant care that when called to account for the flock committed to him he may be able to render to the Lord interest on his talent. Therefore of the rules that have been made by the ancient fathers we now recall some to mind, adding new ones, lest we should appear to treat our office lightly.

Regulations are laid down for the decent keeping of churches and churchyards, and the safety of certain sacred articles. The life, dress, and good repute of the clergy are dealt with at some length, particular stress being laid on the obligation of strict celibacy. Rules are further laid down for the administration of sacraments, and for the ordination and residence of rectors or, failing them, of competent vicars. A copy of the statutes is to be available in every parish.

The diocese of St. Andrews was already highly organized. It was divided by the Forth into two great areas, the archdeaconries of St. Andrews and of Lothian, and the archdeacons had the duty of visiting all the parishes subject to

---

[1] ed. Chr. Wordsworth.
[2] D. Patrick, *Statutes of the Scottish Church*, pp. 57–67.

them and reporting to the bishop. The archdeaconries were subdivided into rural deaneries, whose deans, known as deans of Christianity, exercised authority under the archdeacon over the clergy of their deaneries, whom they might summon for certain purposes to ruri-diaconal chapters. The other dioceses had each one archdeacon, except the large diocese of Glasgow which had two, Glasgow and Teviotdale.[1] In most dioceses the division into rural deaneries is also found.

David de Bernham belongs to the period when Scotland was steadily progressing under its early kings. The death of Alexander III in 1286 was a disaster leading to more than a century of war and anarchy. James I, on his return from captivity in England in 1424, initiated a period of recovery which culminated in the reign of James IV. But the tragedy of Flodden left the country open to the intrigues of Henry VIII whose tortuous policies added to the difficulties of James V (1513–42). The fourteenth century was also calamitous for the Papacy. It lost its world-dominating position when Boniface VIII was successfully defied by the King of France. His immediate successors, all Frenchmen and dominated by French influence, forsook Rome and resided at Avignon from 1309 to 1378. The return to Rome led to the Great Schism, 1378–1415, when two and later three popes, each claiming to be the true Vicar of Christ, anathematized each other and contended for recognition. The scandal led to the summoning in 1415 of the Council of Constance to restore unity to the Church and to reform it in head and members. Unity was achieved but the cause of reform was lost in the struggle between curialism and conciliarism. The victory of curialism or papalism was secured but at the cost of a great reduction in the power and prestige of the Papacy. Successive popes, to maintain their position, were compelled to make concessions to the national kings, including the King of Scots, and their moral character seriously deteriorated.

The Scottish bishops certainly became more prominent after 1286 but their activities belong mainly to political

[1] The diocese of Orkney also was early divided into two archdeaconries, Orkney and Shetland.

history. Two of them, Fraser of St. Andrews and Wishart
of Glasgow, were among the six guardians of the kingdom
appointed in 1286. Wishart later distinguished himself as a
patriot by his support of Wallace and then of Bruce. Six times
compelled to take the oath of fealty to Edward I he as often
broke it and suffered long periods of imprisonment. From
1309 nearly all the bishops in spite of his condemnation by
the Pope supported Robert Bruce, and some of them were
excommunicated for doing so. From the standpoint of Avignon the national struggle against England must have seemed
a vain and hopeless disturbance of the peace of Britain which
the bishops wickedly abetted. They stood by the monarchy
in its darkest days and suffered from the anarchy to which
its weakness gave free reign, as, for example, when Alexander
Stewart, the Wolf of Badenoch, son of Robert II, burned the
cathedral of Elgin in 1390 to the great grief of the aged bishop.
They followed the lead of the government when for political
reasons it gave recognition to the anti-pope. In the fifteenth century Cameron of Glasgow as chancellor supported the legislation of James I against barratry, and from 1424 onwards the
bishops of Scotland were the chief buttress of the Crown—
Kennedy of St. Andrews, for example, under James II, Elphinstone of Aberdeen and Forman of Moray under James IV,
and above all the Beatons of St. Andrews under James V.

On the purely ecclesiastical side from a study of the papal
records of the period, both at Rome and at Avignon, one
might draw the conclusion that the fifteenth-century bishops
were simply the most successful of the great multitude of
benefice-hunters. Nearly all of them were pluralists on a
grand scale. Even 'the good Bishop Kennedy' profited not
a little from his papalism. But all this was so natural and
normal as to be accepted almost without remark or censure.
The scramble for benefices, however, is not the whole story,
as we can see from Alexander Myln's *Lives of the Bishops of
Dunkeld*,[1] and Hector Boece's *Lives of the Bishops of Aberdeen*.[2]
However inadequate these works may be from a biographical
point of view, the writers at least knew the qualities that go

[1] ed. Cosmo Innes for Bannatyne Club, 1831.
[2] ed. J. Moir for New Spalding Club, 1894.

to make a good bishop, and give evidence that they were not extinct in their time.

Alexander Myln became abbot (commendator?) of Cambuskenneth in 1516 and in 1532 first president of the Court of Session. He wrote the *Lives* before 1516 while he was still rural dean of Angus and intimately associated with the diocese of Dunkeld and with George Brown, its bishop. The *Life* of Brown, his patron and hero, occupies more than half of his book. George Brown was a native of Dundee, son of the town treasurer. Educated at Dundee Grammar School he continued his studies at St. Andrews and Paris, and on his return to his native land was appointed one of the four regents in St. Salvator's College St. Andrews, obtaining also the chancellorship of Aberdeen Cathedral, and the rectory of Tyningham in East Lothian. Sent to Rome by James III to secure the see of Glasgow for the king's nominee, he failed in his mission, but he attached himself to the household of Cardinal Rodrigo Borgia, afterwards the notorious Pope Alexander VI, who secured for him a papal 'provision' to Dunkeld in 1483. The king had his own nominee for Dunkeld, and refused to accept Brown, whom he denounced as a rebel and traitor in terms of repeated Acts of Parliament against barratry. For some years therefore Brown had difficulty in securing possession of his see, and spent so much in defending his rights that he entered on his episcopate under a heavy burden of debt—including 450 florins gold of the Camera due for his provision. His conflict with the king, no doubt, enabled him to hold aloof from politics and therefore to devote his energies to his diocese. To begin with he had to defend his episcopal lands from the encroachments of secular lords, and his difficulties were all the greater because of their proximity to the Highlands. He found it necessary to build and fortify a castle on an island in Loch Cluny some six miles from his palace of Dunkeld, and was able to boast that he could ride between the two places by four different routes all within his ecclesiastical properties. He also cared for the religious interests of his people. He divided the diocese into four rural deaneries which he entrusted to learned and virtuous deans, and over all he appointed an official as judge in his consistorial court, to try and punish offenders against the laws of the Church. As the Highland parts of the diocese were in sad disorder he employed Franciscans and Dominicans, acquainted with the Irish speech (Gaelic) to preach to the people, and as a result of their efforts public and secret sins were confessed, reproved and punished 'so that there were no more grave excesses'. He also did something for church extension, for he divided the large and scattered parish of Little Dunkeld into three, building new parish churches at Caputh and Dowally. Myln tells us how he visited the sick in time of pestilence and sent them holy water to drink in which a bone of St. Columba had been dipped. Those who drank the water recovered, but a profane person, who said he would have preferred a present of the bishop's best beer, died of the plague! Brown was generous to his cathedral and beloved by its staff from the dean down to the vicars-choral, all of whom, according to Myln, were exemplary persons. Finally towards the end of his life the bishop started to build a stone bridge over the Tay, and in his last illness was happy to watch its progress from his palace window. The disaster of Flodden in which he lost many relatives was a blow from which he never recovered and he died soon after in 1514, having been a good bishop for thirty-one years.

Bishop Elphinstone of Aberdeen is more famous owing to the eulogy of Hector Boece whom he brought from Paris to be the first principal and professor of the liberal arts in King's College. Born in Glasgow, the son of a cleric, he studied law there before proceeding to Paris and Orleans. In Paris his distinction was such that he rose to be Primarius Reader in canon law. On his return to Scotland he was appointed official of the Glasgow diocese, i.e. judge in the bishop's consistorial court, and was soon transferred to the more important post of official of Lothian. As such he sat in Parliament and was sent by James III on important embassies to England, France, and the emperor. In 1481 he was 'provided' to the see of Ross from which in 1483 he was translated to Aberdeen, in both cases doubtless with the goodwill or perhaps on the nomination of the king. His work in Aberdeen must have been greatly interrupted by his political duties, but he did much for the cathedral and for the amplification and ordering of its worship. He was responsible for the editing of the Aberdeen Breviary which, in addition to being a collection of church rituals, contains a number of Lives of ancient Celtic saints. It was one of the first books to be printed in Edinburgh (1509–10) and was ordered to be the official prayer book for the whole realm. Above all in 1495 he founded the University of Aberdeen obtaining a bull from Pope Alexander VI for that purpose, and soon after, in 1498, he founded, endowed and built King's College, over which Boece came to preside, with professors of theology, canon law, civil law, and medicine. Elphinstone opposed the war policy which ended in the disaster of Flodden, and like Brown he never recovered from the blow. There was indeed a move to transfer him to St. Andrews, vacant by the death at Flodden of the administrator, Alexander Stewart. Though an octogenarian, he apparently consented to the translation but died in 1514 and Forman of Moray became archbishop.

Andrew Forman is the outstanding Scottish example of the clerical diplomat and careerist. Having finished his education at St. Andrews in 1479 he attached himself to the household of the Earl of Angus. About 1490 he transferred to the service of James IV from whom he received the commendatorship of Pittenweem. In 1499 he was engaged in the negotiations which led in 1503 to the marriage of James IV to Margaret Tudor, daughter of Henry VII, and to the signing of a 'perpetual peace' between the two countries. For these services he received from James the bishopric of Moray and from Henry the rectory of Cottingham in England. He was in England again bearing the congratulations of his king to Henry VIII on his accession in 1509. In 1511 he became King James's ambassador at large, ostensibly promoting the peace of Christendom. In particular his task was to make peace between the King of France, Louis XII, and the warlike Pope Julius II, who, it has been said, made and broke more treaties than any other prince. The task proved impossible though Forman impressed the Pope as well as the French king with his ability and energy, and though his diplomacy failed he was amply rewarded for his efforts by all parties. From James he received the commendatorships of Kelso and Dryburgh in 1511, and from Louis the archbishopric of Bourges in 1513 in recognition of his services in connexion with a renewal by Scotland of the Franco-Scottish alliance in 1512. All these appointments were confirmed by the Pope, who also hinted at the possibility of a cardinalate. The renewal of the French alliance made war with England inevitable. Forman has been held responsible, unjustly perhaps, for the adoption of that disastrous policy. The real responsibility must rest with the impetuous king who loved to think of himself as a world figure.

At Flodden there fell fighting by the side of his royal father the youthful Alexander Stewart, titular Archbishop of St. Andrews, leaving vacant the primatial see of Scotland. The Pope, now Leo X, with incredible lack of tact, 'provided' to St. Andrews his own nephew, Cardinal Innocenzo Cibo, offering to receive the Scots back to the favour of the apostolic see which they had gravely offended by attacking its ally, Henry VIII. Other candidates were in the field. Gavin Douglas, provost of St. Giles, had the support of the queen mother. The St. Andrew chapter would gladly have had Elphinstone, but on his death elected their own prior, John Hepburn, guardedly praised by Boece as the founder of St. Leonard's College at St. Andrews. And James Beaton of Glasgow let it be known that he would welcome the appointment. After furious disputes in 1514 Leo 'provided' Forman, allowing him to retain all the benefices he already held, including the bishopric of Moray in case he did not secure St. Andrews, and adding the commendatorship of Dunfermline!

Forman's rule at St. Andrews was brief and troubled. He delayed his return to Scotland for some months, and for a year he failed to secure possession. Till his death in 1521 his rivals were thorns in his side. In spite of this, we know that he took energetic measures to restore order and discipline in his diocese, which had doubtless deteriorated in the general demoralization after Flodden. Moreover, St. Andrews had had only titular archbishops for twenty years. As soon as he had secure possession, Forman emulated the example of his predecessor, David de Bernham, by holding diocesan synods, one at Holyrood for the clergy south of the Forth, and one at St. Andrews for the northern archdeaconry, at which he promulgated statutes to be obeyed by the clergy on pain of fine or deprivation. For the most part they are simply repetitions of the older statutes dealing with clerical dress, residence, continence, and professional duties. Stress was laid on regularity and decency in public worship which parish clergy were to celebrate devoutly in clean surplices and in a clear, high and intelligible voice so that the people might be incited to devotion. Monasteries were enjoined to revive the old practice of financing one or more of their monks while they studied 'the sciences and virtues' at St. Andrews. Study at the university was also recognized as a valid excuse for non-residence in their cures by rectors. Many other administrative acts of Forman within his diocese are recorded, and most interesting is his licence to an un-named St. Andrews Dominican, to preach throughout the diocese, to hear confessions and pronounce absolution. Rectors are enjoined to summon their parishioners to hear the preacher.

From all this activity we learn that below the level of the careerists and benefice-hunters the proper work of the Church was expected to go on. In the absence of pluralist canons the vicars-choral continued to sing the cathedral services. Parish vicars administered the sacraments to their parishioners, and Franciscans and Dominicans occasionally conducted preaching missions even in country places. The church courts continued in spite of difficulty to judge causes appropriate to them; and the ravages of war were made good by the repair of church buildings. And yet no important reforms were undertaken or even visualized. The complacency of such as Alexander Myln and Hector Boece is truly hard to understand.

One special form of episcopal activity remains to be mentioned, the founding of the universities of St. Andrews, Glasgow, and Aberdeen. The first universities of Europe owe their origin to an intellectual awakening in the twelfth century especially in France which produced a number of famous teachers of philosophy and theology. Soon Paris became their chosen centre, and by the end of the century the community (*universitas*) of doctors, masters, and scholars of Paris became a chartered corporation, called a *studium generale*, with officers of its own and statutes governing the life of its members. In time it further organized itself into faculties, according to subjects taught, and into 'nations' very roughly corresponding to the political divisions of Europe. About the same time a similar institution took shape in Oxford, which during the thirteenth century attracted many Scots students. In 1282 Lady Devorgilla of Galloway founded Balliol College to provide some of them with board and lodging and moral discipline. In the fourteenth century, in spite of the fact that relations between Scotland and England were usually hostile, numbers of Scots students continued to go to Oxford, though many also made their way to Paris. It was now usual for bishops to have university degrees, commonly in arts and law, less commonly in theology.

Towards the end of the fourteenth century the academic world everywhere was agitated by two great questions with which interests not strictly theological were apt to be mixed up. In 1377 John Wycliffe, professor of theology at Oxford, was condemned as a heretic by Pope Gregory XI, but his tenets remained for a time a subject of controversy. His followers were driven out of Oxford in 1382, but in the University of Prague his admirers succeeded in getting the upper hand, while those who condemned him, chiefly Germans, withdrew. Then there was the question of the papal schism. As an international community the University of Paris tried to remain neutral, but was compelled by the King of France to acknowledge Clement VII, the anti-pope. Many members of the German and English 'nations' therefore withdrew, as their rulers at home adhered to the Roman Pope, Urban VI. Scotland also supported Clement, so that the position of Scots at Oxford, though they were tolerated, was difficult. When, after 1409, France and the University of Paris forsook Clement's successor, Benedict XIII, leaving Scotland isolated in its adherence to him, Paris also became difficult for Scots scholars. Some of them seem to have taken up residence in St. Andrews, for in 1411 Henry Wardlaw, Bishop of

St. Andrews, granted to 'the doctors masters bachelors and all scholars dwelling in our city of St. Andrews' a charter of privilege 'within our City and Regality', pending confirmation by the Apostolic See, i.e. by Benedict XIII then a prisoner in Peniscola and soon to be deposed. They were recognized as a university under a rector, whose jurisdiction *vis-à-vis* that of the magistrates was carefully defined, not without leaving room for contentions between town and gown such as were frequent in university towns. In cases of dispute the bishop, who was both head of the regality and chancellor of the university, was to have the last word. The subjects of study were to embrace 'Divine and human law, Medicine and the Liberal Arts', and in due course faculties of arts and theology at least were organized, and even a division into 'nations' was introduced. The only reference to finance is contained in a clause which reads:

Beneficed persons of our diocese actually regenting, studying or wishing to study, provided however they be teachable, having sought leave of us and our successors, although they have not obtained it, may not be compelled to reside personally in their benefices, provided they cause the same to be decently served in divine things during their absence, and may reap and enjoy the fruits of their said benefices.

Nothing is said in the charter with regard to academic premises, and it would appear that regents took students into their own hired dwellings for board and tuition. Not until 1430 did Wardlaw provide a site on which the Faculty of Arts undertook to build a 'Pedagogy', a sort of common hall. Wardlaw was moved, no doubt, by zeal for learning, but his own experience while a student in Oxford when Wycliffite influence was powerful is reflected in the consideration that 'the Catholic faith surrounded by an impregnable wall of doctors and masters is enabled to withstand heresies and errors and to grow strong'. In 1416 the meaning of this phrase was made clear when the congregation of the university imposed an oath on all masters of arts 'to defend the Church against the insult of the Lollards, and resist with all their might whosoever adheres to their sect'. By the fifteenth century the universities had become orthodoxy's Maginot Line.

In 1413 the bull of Benedict XIII confirming Wardlaw's charter and granting to the university the right of conferring degrees was received in St. Andrews amid rejoicing. In 1417 the university that Benedict had recognized took the lead in withdrawing Scotland from his allegiance and in acknowledging Martin V, who in return confirmed its privileges, as did King James I after some hesitation, in 1432.

Further developments took place in St. Andrews. In 1450 James Kennedy, Wardlaw's successor, founded the College of St. Salvator, himself building the chapel, furnishing it with costly ornaments, providing it with a piece of the True Cross, and procuring in 1460 from Pope Pius II, as a form of endowment, an indulgence of ten years for all who, 'confessed and contrite', visited St. Salvator's on the Feast of the Apparition of St. Michael. St. Salvator's was a dual-purpose college. It was an academic institution. The provost and the next two prebendaries were theologians and teachers of theology. Four were masters of arts in holy orders who were to teach arts subjects while studying for a theological degree. Six were 'poor clerks' fit to profit from an academic course. For the sustenance of those foundationers Kennedy annexed four rectories to his college. At the same time in addition to this academic staff numerous chaplains performed the daily canonical services in the chapel and celebrated masses for the soul of the founder after his death. Two further colleges were added at later dates, St. Leonard's by John Hepburn, prior of St. Andrews, and St. Mary's by Archbishop James Beaton.

It is unnecessary to enter into any detailed account of the other two universities, which followed similar lines to those indicated in St. Andrews. In 1451, the year of the erection of St. Salvator's, Bishop Turnbull of Glasgow received a bull from Pope Nicolas V creating a university in his 'city' which was intended in particular to specialize in the study of law; and in 1495 Elphinstone obtained a similar bull from Alexander VI privileging a university in Aberdeen, within which he himself founded King's College. Of this college and its colleagues we have a pleasantly enthusiastic account from its first principal, Hector Boece.[1]

[1] *Lives of the Bishops of Aberdeen*, pp. 89 ff.

Kennedy and Elphinstone professed to be specially interested in providing well trained pastors 'to sow the Word of God more abundantly in the hearts of the faithful'. Among the higher clergy many in fact graduated, mostly at St. Andrews, but it is impossible to check statistically, as has been done for some English dioceses, how far Scotland's three universities affected the standard of service of the parish vicars. Archbishop Hamilton's Catechism was a product of St. Andrews University, though its actual author is unknown. The fact that it could be produced apparently at short notice makes it evident that theological acumen and teaching capacity were to be found at St. Andrews on the eve of the Reformation, but the injunctions laid upon vicars for the use of the Catechism seem to show that no familiarity was expected on their part with its contents, nor even ability to read it intelligently or intelligibly to their congregations. The importance of Aberdeen 'doctors' in the history of the Scottish Church dates not from Elphinstone's foundation, but from the resuscitation of King's College by Bishop Patrick Forbes in the seventeenth century.

IX

OPPOSITION AND REFORM

By the beginning of the thirteenth century the Church on the Continent had begun to be troubled by opposition, some of it heretical, but most of it simply critical of clerical and ecclesiastical abuses. These early movements affected Scotland not at all. It is true that Pope John XXII in granting (in 1328) the request of Robert Bruce that the kings of Scots should be episcopally anointed and crowned had required them to take an oath diligently to drive from their kingdom all heretics branded as such by the Church. But the Pope envisages the continental rather than the Scottish situation at that time. Throughout the anarchic fourteenth century when discipline largely broke down and the Avignon popes steadily increased their claims to 'provide' to Scottish benefices and to tax them, no voice of protest was raised in Scotland. Over the border, the England of Edward III enacted the Statutes of Provisors and Premunire to counter papal encroachments, and towards the end of the century produced its first great heretic, 'the Morning Star of the Reformation'.

John Wyclif, professor of theology at Oxford, first became prominent c. 1370 as spokesman of the national political opposition to the Avignon Papacy, with the support and encouragement of Edward III and the whole nation. After 1378, when the papal schism began, Wyclif became more trenchant in his criticism of the Papacy, the clergy, and the friars. He taught that all authority in Church and State is founded in grace, and that, therefore, a priest or pope in mortal sin has no authority in the Church. The supreme authority is the Scripture which is the 'Law of God'. The Pope is antichrist. The worship of saints, relics, and images is unscriptural and to be rejected, along with ceremonies not prescribed in the Law of God. Transubstantiation is heresy. Though condemned at Rome and at Paris Wyclif continued to teach at Oxford with much support from the turbulent student-body. But he also undertook a popular mission of reform, and trained 'poor preachers' to proclaim how far the clergy had departed from the manner of life of the Apostles. The Peasants' Revolt of 1381, in which some of his preachers had a hand, proved his undoing. The following year, Courteney, Archbishop of Canterbury, presided over a council in London at which many of Wyclif's tenets were condemned as heretical. The archbishop then 'visited' Oxford, drove Wyclif out, and banned his teaching. The Reformer withdrew to his rectory of Lutterworth where he continued his work by writing vigorous polemical tracts in English unmolested till his death in 1384. Thereafter his preachers carried on a widespread and successful propaganda until 'Lollardy' was driven underground by the Act *De Haeretico Comburendo* passed by Parliament in 1401.

Many Scots students frequented Oxford and must have heard Wyclif, but so far as is known none of them brought his doctrines home to Scotland. Certainly Wyclifitism made no such stir in Scotland as it did in Bohemia. The evils Wyclif attacked were at least as patent in Scotland, but political conditions did not favour the emergence of a Scottish Hus. Nevertheless precautions were taken. In 1398 when the Duke of Rothesay, son and heir of the feeble King Robert III, was made regent he swore to restrain 'cursit men and heretics'. The next regent, Albany, was praised by Wyntoun for his hatred of Lollards and heretics, and early in his regency (1406 or 7) the first Lollard to suffer martyrdom in Scotland was condemned to the stake by a clerical council at Perth, for denying that an unholy Pope could be the Vicar of Christ. He was, perhaps significantly, an English priest, James Resby, 'held in much renown through his preaching to simple folk'. His accuser was Laurence of Lindores who held an office which may then have been new to Scotland, that of 'Inquisitor of Heretical Pravity'. Laurence was a scholastic philosopher of European reputation, soon to become a dominant figure in the University of St. Andrews, where his influence may be seen in the fact that in 1416 the university imposed an anti-Lollard oath on all graduands in arts.

Laurence, we are told, exerted himself mightily to give the heretics no rest, and he was encouraged by an Act of James I's second Parliament in 1425 'anentis heretikis and lollardis' requiring the bishops to make inquisition for heresy, and to have heretics punished 'as lawe of Haly kirk requiris', with the aid of the secular power, if necessary. But we hear of only one further victim, again not a native Scot but a Czech, Paul Craw or Crawar. He had been a graduate in arts of Paris and in medicine of Montpellier, had practised medicine in Poland, and had come to Scotland as an emissary of the Hussites of Prague to enlist support for their cause which was to be discussed at the Council of Basel. Crawar was 'incorporated' in the University of St. Andrews, but his heresies being detected he was condemned and burnt at the stake at St. Andrews in 1433.

The influence of Wyclif's teaching in Scotland is altogether obscure. Apart from the executions just mentioned and the letters of Quentin Folkhyrd—*Nova Scotiae* or news-letters from Scotland addressed to Bohemia, whose author is otherwise quite unknown—there is only the curious tale told by Knox of 'the Lollards of Kyle'. In 1494 some thirty persons, among them a few lairds, were summoned before James IV and his Great Council at the instance of Robert Blacader, Archbishop of Glasgow, charged with holding thirty-four heretical opinions, covering almost the whole of Wyclif's teaching and implying a complete breakaway from the doctrines and practices of the Church. Apparently they neither recanted nor were condemned but were dismissed with a jest. The whole story is quite extraordinary and very obscure. Can it be in any way linked with the fact that within sixty years Ayrshire was one of the strongholds of the Reformers? But the Reformation was a very different movement from that of Wyclif even though the effects on religious observances may on the surface appear to be similar. The fundamental religious principle was different. While Wyclif insisted on the obligatoriness of the Evangelical Law, i.e. the precepts of the Gospels, at any rate for clerics, the Reformation proclaimed the Pauline Evangelical faith. The profound change in the meaning of the word 'Evangelical' is significant.

In 1517 Luther challenged academic disputation on ninety-five theses touching the doctrine and practice of indulgences. The challenge was not accepted. Instead he was attacked for questioning the supreme spiritual power of the Papacy. In 1520 he published his Primary Works setting forth his new understanding of the Gospel and his consequent programme of evangelical reform, and burnt the papal bull that pronounced his condemnation. In 1521 he appeared before the Diet of the Empire at Worms, and his cause became a world-issue that was to shatter the unity of the Western Church.

During these years Scotland was occupied with the bitter aftermath of Flodden. James IV was succeeded by an infant of seventeen months, and until James V assumed personal rule in 1528 he was the pawn of factions ruling in his name. Apart from the ambitions and enmities of the nobles, the burning question of the day was whether Scotland should look for friendship to France or England. The campaign that ended at Flodden had been undertaken at the request of the King of France who had since cynically abandoned his ally, so that the French party might have been wholly discredited, but for the overweening policy of Henry VIII, and the folly of his sister Margaret, mother of King James. Only one man in Scotland seems to have pursued a truly Scottish policy, countering Henry's intrigues without allowing himself to become the tool of France. This was James Beaton, Archbishop of Glasgow, 1509–22, and of St. Andrews, 1522–39, Chancellor of Scotland 1513–24. But as Beaton belonged wholly to neither of the contending factions his political influence was small. To his honour be it said, unlike his predecessor and his successor, he held no French benefice.

It was during Beaton's tenure of the primacy that signs of an interest in Luther first appeared. Merchants trading between Scotland and the Low Countries were it seems bringing Lutheran books into Scottish ports, where discussion of Luther's 'dampnable opunyeounis' was taking place, not always 'to the confusion thairof'. In July 1525, therefore, Parliament passed an Act prohibiting the importation of such books into the realm 'under the pane of escheting of their schippis and gudis and putting of their persounis in presoun', the Act to be proclaimed at all ports and in all burghs.[1] In the same year in the name of King James a warrant was sent to the sheriffs of Aberdeen narrating that 'sundry strangers and others were possessed of Luther's books and favoured his errors' and charging them to make inquisition after such persons and confiscate their goods. Then in 1528 the first Scottish martyr was burnt at the stake at St. Andrews.

Patrick Hamilton belonged to the powerful Hamilton family, whose head, the Earl of Arran, was one of the leading nobles of Scotland. Destined for the Church, at the age of fourteen he received the commendatorship of the abbey of Ferne in Ross-shire to enable him to study in Paris, where he graduated master of arts in 1520. Passing to Louvain he came under the influence of Erasmus and the new Humanism and returned to Scotland in 1523 to teach at St. Andrews in the faculty of arts. There the celebrated John Major was also teaching, a native of Haddington, who had acquired fame as a doctor of scholastic philosophy and theology in Paris, before settling, at Archbishop Beaton's invitation, first at Glasgow and finally at St. Andrews. But Major represented the old learning while Hamilton represented the new. Becoming suspected of sympathy with Luther's teaching, Hamilton left St. Andrews and betook himself to Wittenberg to study with Luther and Melanchthon. An outbreak of the plague prevented his remaining there, and in 1527 he appears as one of the earliest members of the new University of Marburg established by the Landgraf Philip of Hesse, and presided over by Francis Lambert. At Marburg he drew up a series of theses to be publicly defended in the university, which were subsequently translated into English by John Frith under the title of *Patrick's Places*; 'which knowen', the translator says, 'ye have the pith of all Divinity'.[2] Certainly they contain the pure milk of the Lutheran word. Hamilton now felt an urgent call to preach in his native land the Gospel as he had come to understand it. Returning to his ancestral home at Kincavil near Linlithgow, he did so with some success in the

---

[1] *Acts of the Parliament of Scotland*, vol. ii, p. 295.
[2] See Peter Lorimer, *Patrick Hamilton* (1857).

neighbourhood, persuading among others his brother, now the laird, and his sister. Early in 1528, therefore, Archbishop Beaton summoned him 'to a conference' in St. Andrews. He was interrogated for several days, but was left at liberty, perhaps in the hope that he would again save himself by flight—for it might be dangerous to antagonise the Hamiltons. Instead, for a whole month he lectured in public and disputed in private, until at last he was brought to formal trial before Beaton and others and condemned to the stake as a heretic. What is noteworthy about Hamilton's teaching is that it was not at all concerned with ecclesiastical abuses or clerical scandals, but solely with the positive religious and evangelical core of Reformation doctrine, viz. justification by faith alone.

Patrick Hamilton was not more than twenty-four years old when he died, but by his noble birth and gracious character, by his teaching and above all by the manner of his death, his influence was great. In St. Andrews he made an impression on the younger men, notably on Alexander Alane (Alesius) a canon-regular, who became a Lutheran and fled abroad. St. Leonard's College, under Gavin Logy, acquired notoriety for open-mindedness. But beyond St. Andrews, Knox tells us, the spirit of inquiry was aroused.

Almost within the whole realm there was none found who began not to enquire; wherefore was Master Patrick Hamilton burned? And when his Articles were rehearsed, question was held if such Articles (sc. as he had denied) were necessary to be believed under pane of damnation. And so within a short space many began to call in doubt that which before they held for certain verity.

As a wit remarked to Beaton: 'The reek of Master Patrick Hamilton infected as many as it blew upon.' It is certain that his condemnation did give rise to question and controversy as appears from the charges laid against several of the persons brought to trial in the following years.

In 1528 King James V, now seventeen years of age, assumed personal rule. He drove into exile the Earl of Angus, head of the Douglas family, and all his adherents including

Gavin Douglas, the scholarly but violent and unscrupulous Bishop of Dunkeld. Angus was the leader of the English party, but James did not break with England. On the contrary he made a five years' peace with Henry VIII and devoted himself to restoring law and order within his own kingdom. But he was young, high-spirited, and inexperienced. His severity with law-breakers on the borders and in the highlands was resented, and he also gave offence to some of the greater nobles. Even with the higher clergy his relations were at times strained. In 1531, taking advantage of the straits in which Pope Clement VII found himself owing to the advance of the Reformation, James asked for a bull authorizing him to tax the prelates to the tune of £10,000 Scots[1] annually to finance a proposed college of justice for the better administration of the law. Clement perforce granted it on condition that James should remain loyal to Rome. Some of the bishops resisted, notably Beaton, and by 1535 agreement was reached on a much smaller annual sum. Beaton never enjoyed the confidence of the king, which was reserved for his rival, Gavin Dunbar, Archbishop of Glasgow and Chancellor of Scotland from 1528 to 1543.

In 1534 came Henry VIII's definitive breach with Rome followed two years later by his suppression of the English monasteries. Henry brought pressure to bear on his nephew to follow his example, but the young king was also courted by ambassadors from the King of France, the Pope, and even from the emperor, bringing him honours and flattery, gifts and promises. Moreover he realized that he could now dictate his own terms for his continuing loyalty to Rome and to the Church. More and more he sought support and counsel from the higher clergy who found a determined leader in David Beaton, nephew of the archbishop and, since 1524, commendator of Arbroath. Beaton had been long resident in France and, for services rendered and to be rendered, Francis I nominated him to the French bishopric of Mirepoix and pressed for his elevation to a cardinalate. It was Beaton

---

[1] In Clement's bull '10,000 ducats gold of the Camera', equivalent, it is said, to £10,000 Scots or about £2,500 sterling of that date: an enormous sum for the times, equal possibly to £200,000 sterling today (1959).

who negotiated James's marriage with Madeleine, the frail daughter of Francis, and, when she died within a few months of her arrival in Scotland, found him another bride in Mary of Lorraine, of the house of Guise. He was made in 1538 coadjutor to his uncle and succeeded him as Archbishop of St. Andrews early in the following year. The ascendancy of Beaton made it certain that James would follow in the old paths. He would remain loyal to the Church and maintain the French alliance even if it meant war with England. Beaton believed, no doubt sincerely, that only thus could James preserve the independence of his kingdom, and the overbearing conduct of Henry VIII may be held to justify his belief. Besides Beaton was a pillar of the Church of which Henry had become an enemy. He has been much praised as a patriot and statesman. Possibly, however, a purer patriotism and a wiser statesmanship would have realized that Scotland's need was for a *modus vivendi* with England, and a reform of the Church.

Beaton's policy had many opponents. It is said that he prepared a list of 360 nobles and gentry whose goods the king might lawfully confiscate on the ground that the owners were tainted with heresy. Their 'heresy' may have been at this stage no more than opposition to the cardinal's pro-French policy. The first name on the list was that of the Earl of Arran, second person in the realm! But there were also humbler opponents whose interests were more purely religious. These were chiefly friars, Augustinian canons, and lower clergy, who preached reform. About a score of them are known to have been burnt at the stake or to have fled to England between 1538 and 1539. Persecution of 'Lutherians' no less than the French alliance was an essential part of Beaton's patriotic statesmanship.

The demand for church reform was not confined to 'Lutherians'. Some loyal churchmen who entirely approved of the liquidation of heretics recognized the clamant need for reform. Hector Boece in 1526 lamented the degeneration that had set in since Bishop Elphinstone's day. John Major, stolidly orthodox as the Sorbonne from which he came, declared that the wealth of the Church had stifled its piety, and he even showed interest in parochial ministrations which he knew had been neglected. He suggested some redistribution of the Church's resources, but believed that the canon law if enforced by the bishops would be adequate for the remedy of abuses. Most striking of all is the description of the state of the Church due to the evil lives and ignorance of its clergy contained in Archibald Hay's panegyric on David Beaton on the occasion of the latter's elevation as Cardinal-Archbishop of St. Andrews.[1] Hay seems to have regarded Beaton as a possible reformer. If so it was a forlorn hope. Indeed Beaton in his own person represented all the vices that Hay decries. He held three rich and incompatible benefices. His private life was flagrantly immoral. His public life he devoted to diplomacy and politics rather than to religion, and his policies brought untold woe on his people. As a churchman his strife over precedence with his colleague of Glasgow, leading to an unseemly riot in Glasgow Cathedral, was unedifying, and his savage persecution of 'heretics' alienated sympathy. Boece, Major, and Hay were academic persons addressing limited circles in Latin, but what they have to say goes far to show that Lindsay's *Satire of the Three Estates*,[2] with its lurid exposure of clerical greed, imposture, sloth, and immorality, if a caricature, was at least recognizable.

James V, who found it possible to tap the wealth of the Church for both public and private purposes, was not blind to the failings of churchmen. When Sadler, the English ambassador, expatiated on the abominations committed by the monks, James is reported to have replied: 'The good may be suffered and the evil must be reformed; I shall help to see it reformed in Scotland, by God's grace, if I brook life.' Soon after, Lindsay's Satire was produced before the court at Linlithgow, and the king is said to have exhorted the clerics about him 'to reform their fashions and manners of living, saying that unless they did so he would send sex of the proudest of them to his uncle of England'. A series of Acts passed by Parliament in March 1541 seems to reflect the mind of the king. The old faith was to be upheld. The dishonouring

---

[1] See W. Murison, *Sir David Lindsay*, pp. 188–200.
[2] Ed. for Scottish Text Society.

of the sacraments and of the worship of the Virgin was forbidden. No person under pain of death and confiscation of goods was to impugn the Pope's authority. Conventicles for the discussion of Scripture were prohibited even in private houses, and informers, even if they had been themselves implicated in heresy, were to be rewarded. In the midst of these Acts stands one 'for reforming of Kirkis and Kirkmen'.[1]

Because the negligence of divine service, the grett unhoneste in the kirk throw not making of reparation to the honor of God Almychty and to the blissit sacrament of the altar the Virgine Mary and all the haly sanctis, and als the unhonestie and misreule of kirkmen baith in witt knawledge and maneris is the mater and cause that the kirk and kirkmen are lychtlyit and contemnit; for remeid hereof the King's grace exhorts and prayis oppinly all archbishoppis ordinaries and other prelatis and every kirkman in his awn degree to reform thare selfis, thare obediencaries and kirkmen under thame, in habit and maneris to God and man; and that thai cause in every kirk within thare diocy under thare jurisdictioun cure reule reparatioun and reparaling to be honestlie and substantiouslie maid and done to the honor of God Almychty the blissit sacrament and the divine service, every kirk efter the qualite and quantite of the rentis. And giff ony persoun allegiand thame exemit and will not obey nor obtemper to thare superior in that behalf the King's grace sall find remeid tharefor at the pape's halynes. And siklik aganis the saidis prelatis giff thai be negligent.

We might have expected Parliament to require a meeting of the provincial council to undertake these reforms. Certainly Cardinal Beaton, who was present in Parliament with five other bishops and eight abbots, had neither time nor inclination to further them. Instead he went to France to organize the powers of Europe against England. The failure of James V to fulfil a promise to meet Henry at York in 1542 gave the latter a pretext for a declaration of war. In Scotland divided counsels prevailed. The memory of Flodden perhaps dissuaded from a full-scale invasion of England. Instead a raiding army crossed the West March but was dispersed without a blow at Solway Moss. The king withdrew to his

[1] *Acts of the Parliament of Scotland*, vol. ii, p. 370.

palace of Falkland to die a broken-hearted man at the age of 31, leaving his kingdom to his infant daughter Mary, of whose birth he heard before he died. 'It cam wi' a lass', he murmured, referring to the royal Stewart line, 'and it'll gang wi' a lass.'

The death of King James and the birth of Mary gave Henry a new idea for the securing of Scotland. Mary should be betrothed to his heir, the young Prince Edward. He sent back to Scotland the Earl of Angus who had long been an exile in England, together with a number of nobles taken prisoner at Solway Moss, released under pledge to work for Henry's plan. Beaton, who had hoped to rule the country, was placed in ward, Arran was appointed governor, and negotiations were begun for a marriage treaty. In spite of a protest by Archbishop Dunbar permission was given 'to our sovereign lady's lieges' to have and read 'a gude and true translation' of the Scriptures in the vulgar tongue, but not to dispute about its contents. Protestant preachers appeared in the governor's entourage, and the populace of Dundee paid off old scores by sacking the friaries in the town and destroying the abbey of Lindores, with the connivance of the governor. It looked as if Scotland would go the way of England. But Henry was brutally over-bearing and Arran was weak. Under the influence of his half-brother, John Hamilton, commendator of Paisley, he was reconciled to Beaton and received absolution for his 'heresy', and by the end of 1543 the marriage treaty which had been drawn up and actually ratified by Arran was repudiated by the Estates. Henry took a dreadful revenge. The Merse and Teviotdale were mercilessly devastated in 1544 and again in 1545, and Edinburgh and Leith were burnt down. The leader of the resistance was Beaton who exerted himself to find money for the defence of the Church and Commonweal against the 'auld enemies' of England now 'declared heretics'. In 1543 he summoned a general provincial council to meet 'within our Metropolitan and Primatial Church of St. Andrews' to consult 'for the preservation maintenance and defence of the ecclesiastical liberty of the whole Scottish Church, and the privileges and immunities of the same' with special reference to the 'innumerable nefarious heresies that swarm on all hands'. No record of this council survives except the summons to the Archbishop of Glasgow to attend in person with his suffragan bishops and other prelates of his diocese and province, under pain of excommunication, suspension, and interdict in case of refusal. In all this there is no word of reform. On the contrary hierarchical claims are put forward in their most aggressive form. But Beaton's term of power was nearing its close.

Among the exiled preachers who returned to Scotland about this time was George Wishart. Son of an Angus laird, and educated at the University of Aberdeen he had been a teacher in Montrose, where he taught his pupils to read the New Testament in Greek. Threatened with a charge of heresy by the Bishop of Brechin, he fled in 1535 to Bristol where he worked under Latimer till 1539. The enforcement of Henry VIII's Six Articles drove him again into exile, this time to Strasburg, Basel, and Zürich, where he came into contact with the Swiss Reformers, who had been disowned by Luther, and whose confession, the First Helvetic, Wishart adopted. In 1542 he was again in England as a tutor in Corpus Christi College, Cambridge, and of his work and character we have a glowing account written by an admiring pupil.[1] In 1543/4 he returned to Scotland 'with divers of the nobility that had come for a treaty to King Henry', and for the next two years he was engaged in preaching in Dundee, Ayrshire, and finally in East Lothian, often to large audiences on whom he made a deep impression. He had supporters also among the nobility and gentry, naturally among those who were opposed to Beaton for various reasons. Some of them, indeed, were prepared with the approval and encouragement of Henry VIII to go to any length for the removal of the cardinal, by assassination if necessary. The fact that Wishart was arrested in the house of one of them has given colour to the view which identifies him with 'A Scottish man called Wysshart' mentioned in an English dispatch relating to a plot for the murder of Beaton. His activity as a preacher seems incompatible with the character and still more with the behaviour of a political

[1] Quoted in MacEwen, *History of the Church in Scotland*, vol. i, pp. 473–4.

plotter. His sermons as reported are quite remote from political concern, and the charges brought against him at his trial were entirely of a religious nature. Early in 1546 he was seized at Ormiston in East Lothian and handed over to Beaton who had him condemned as a heretic and burnt at the stake at St. Andrews (1 March 1546).

It seems likely that the sufferings caused by Hertford's invasions had undermined the popularity of Beaton, while the preaching of Wishart had done much to stimulate religious opposition among the people. At all events his death provoked a terrible retaliation. In the early hours of the morning of 29 May a party of Wishart's supporters, some of whom had personal reasons for enmity to the cardinal, made their way into his castle of St. Andrews, slew him in his room, and prepared to hold the fortress against all comers. Soon they were reinforced by others, including Sir David Lindsay, the poet and satirist, who felt themselves in danger because of their political or religious opinions. The citizens of St. Andrews, Beaton's immediate subjects, were deeply shocked by the crime, but elsewhere in Scotland there is little evidence of widespread grief or horror. The well-known words of Sir David Lindsay perhaps expressed the feelings of the people generally: 'Although the loon be well away the deed was foully done.'

Nevertheless matters had come to a crisis. The government had lost its strong man, and the governor, Arran, was at his wits' end. His hands were weakened by the fact that his son, who had been with Beaton, was captured and detained by the conspirators. He issued two proclamations, one warning against attacks on churchmen and their properties, as if he feared that the murder of Beaton might be the signal for a general outbreak of anti-clerical violence, the other forbidding the rendering of any assistance to the rebels. Slowly he prepared to lay siege to the castle, and did so towards the end of the year, not without negotiations for its surrender on easy terms. The 'Castilians', as they came to be called, appealed for aid to Henry VIII and Arran sought help from France. The death of Henry in January 1547 followed soon after by that of Francis prevented immediate action by either party, and for some months the 'Castilians' dominated St. Andrews. Their chaplain, an ex-Dominican, John Rough, preached to the people, and the clergy, led by John Winram, sub-prior of the Augustinians, and vicar-general of St. Andrews during the vacancy in the see, countered with non-controversial sermons. In April Rough was joined by John Knox, a devoted disciple of Wishart in the last days of his mission in East Lothian. For some years Knox had been in priest's orders but was unbeneficed and is first heard of as tutor to the sons of the laird of Longniddry. Not until he came to St. Andrews, and then only after much pressure from Rough, did he undertake the office of a preacher, which he exercised with polemical vigour in the parish church, un-dismayed by the presence of university doctors and digni-taries of the Church. Here too he engaged in his first formal controversy—with Friar Arbuckle, a Franciscan, on the sub-ject of the authority of the Church to ordain ceremonies not prescribed in Scripture. At the debate John Winram pre-sided, and gave signs of moderation if not of wavering in his attachment to the old Church.

This paradoxical situation could not continue. The new King of France, Henry II, came to Arran's aid and in July sent a fleet to St. Andrews which bombarded the 'Castilians' into surrender. Their lives were spared and they were taken to France. Those of noble birth were held in honourable captivity and an attempt was made to win them back from 'heresy'. The others, including Knox, were compelled to labour in the galleys, from which after a year and a half they were released.

The intervention of France provoked the intervention of England. Later in the same year (1547) Hertford, now Duke of Somerset and Protector of the Realm for the boy king Edward VI, invaded Scotland for the third time to enforce the implementation of the marriage treaty of 1543. He de-feated the Scots at Pinkie and occupied Haddington. But he did not gain possession of the young queen. Instead the Scots put themselves under the protection of Henry II, agreed to the betrothal of the queen to the dauphin and her immediate transportation to France for safety. Henry now sent a force

of French mercenaries to the aid of his Scottish ally. Haddington was recaptured, and by the treaty of Boulogne (1550)
England undertook to withdraw from Scotland. It looked as
if Henry II of France was to succeed where Henry VIII of
England had failed, and he could rely on the whole-hearted
support of the able queen dowager, Mary of Lorraine.

However hesitating Arran may have been in handling the
situation consequent on the murder of Beaton, he lost no
time in securing the primacy for his half-brother, John Hamilton. Born in 1512, Hamilton was early placed in the abbey
of Kilwinning of which James Beaton, then Archbishop of
Glasgow, was commendator. In 1525, at the age of 13, he
was made commendator of Paisley. As such he sat in Parliament in 1535 and again in 1540, but soon afterwards he left
Scotland to return in 1543 bringing with him the reputation
of an Anglophil and a favourer of the new opinions. Very
soon, however, Beaton won him over, and he had much to
do with the reconciliation of the cardinal and the governor
who contrived to have him promoted to Dunkeld in 1544,
in face of the opposition of a papal nominee. The latter had
to content himself with a pension from the revenues of Dunkeld until he later succeeded Hamilton in that see. By way of
compensation Hamilton was allowed to retain Paisley 'since
it was fitting that religion should be supported not only with
dignity but with substance and riches'. His translation to
St. Andrews was effected at Rome in 1547, but his enthronement was delayed till June 1549. Hamilton remains something of an enigma. His theological position is somewhat
indistinct and was perhaps mediating, but he died a professed Roman Catholic. His private morals were no better
than Beaton's, and yet his name is associated with a decade
of reforming activity. His consistent interest was the fortunes of the house of Hamilton, but he was also loyal to
Queen Mary and supported her cause to the end. Accused of
complicity in the assassination of the Regent Moray he was
executed in 1571.

Immediately after his enthronement as Archbishop, Hamilton presided over a general provincial council at Linlithgow,
presumably summoned by himself, and later in the same year

at a new or adjourned council in the church of the Black-friars in Edinburgh. We are fortunate in possessing the list of those who attended, some of whom were already distinguished, and others were to become so. The archbishopric of Glasgow was vacant, but among the bishops present were the notorious Patrick Hepburn of Moray, commendator of Scone, and the good and learned Robert Reid of Orkney, commendator of Kinloss. Also present were Quintin Kennedy, a future defender of the old Church and antagonist of Knox, Lord James Stewart, commendator of St. Andrews Priory, and future Regent Moray, and John Winram, sub-prior who was to join the Reformers. John Major, dean of the faculty of theology in St. Andrews, was excused personal attendance owing to age and infirmity. Unhappily nothing is preserved of the debates, which may have been lively, but sixty-seven canons attest the industry and thoroughness of the council.

Before it ended the council decreed that another should meet at Edinburgh or St. Andrews without further summons on 14 August 1550. In fact a number of clergy did meet in Edinburgh about that time and condemned Adam Wallace to be burnt as a heretic on the Castlehill. Whether it was a regular council or not, another met in Edinburgh in January 1552. It noted that the statutes of 1549 had not been carried into effect and ordered that there should be no further delay. It noted that 'the greatest neglect of the divine mysteries has prevailed among the subjects of the realm within these last few years, so that very few out of the most populous parishes deign to be present at the sacrifice of holy Mass on Sundays and festivals', and it approved a book submitted by the primate—Archbishop Hamilton's *Catechism*[1]—and enjoined parish clergy to read it to their people continuously Sunday by Sunday, with due care as to the proper enunciation of words and sentences, and with as intelligent and lively an interest as possible, lest the people should mock the reader.

But power was now passing from the Hamiltons. In 1553 Mary Tudor succeeded Edward VI and set about undoing

[1] See pp. 137–8.

the ecclesiastical changes of the two previous reigns. In the following year she married Philip II of Spain and, subordinating English interests to those of Spain, found herself at war with France. Henry II, intent on binding the Scots more closely to France, induced Arran to resign his governorship in favour of Mary of Lorraine (1554), compensating him with the French duchy of Châtelherault. The new regent's task was a difficult one, to keep the Scots united in hostility to England, and if possible to bring them into France's war. Moreover she was to secure their acceptance of Henry's terms for the marriage of her daughter to the dauphin. These, even as published, were exacting, but there were also secret undertakings which the young queen herself was made to sign at the time of the marriage, virtually disposing of her kingdom to the King of France in the event of her decease without heirs. Meantime the regent was provided with able French advisers, whom she promoted to offices of state, and an army of some six thousand French mercenaries ostensibly to carry on the war with the 'auld enemies' of England. Already in 1555 there were complaints about the influence of the French advisers and the insolence of the French soldiery. These complaints grew in volume when three of the Scots commissioners to Paris for the marriage of the queen died, of poison it was rumoured, on their way home, while the survivors presented a request for the Crown Matrimonial for the queen's husband. The regent had to use all her charm and diplomacy until Parliament met in December 1558, if there was to be any hope of obtaining this final symbol of political union with France.

A necessary part of her policy was temporarily to overlook the religious issue and to manifest a degree of toleration towards dissidents. Thus a number of preachers fleeing from the Marian persecution in England found refuge in Scotland. Strangely enough John Knox did not in 1553 return to his native land. Since his release from the galleys he had served as a preacher in Berwick-on-Tweed, and then at Newcastle, whence he was removed south to act as one of the chaplains of King Edward VI. On the accession of Mary he went into exile on the Continent, visiting Geneva, Zürich,

K

and Basel, before accepting a call to minister to a congregation of English exiles in Frankfurt-on-the-Main. As a result of bitter controversy over the use of Edward VI's Prayerbook he left to take up a similar position in Geneva, where he attached himself to Calvin, then at the height of his power. In 1555 he came back secretly to Berwick to marry Marjorie Bowes, and resolved to pay a brief visit to Scotland. He was astonished at the progress Protestantism had made in Edinburgh, and he stayed on for nine months visiting other parts of the country, notably Ayrshire and Angus, encouraging the Protestants to separate from the observances of the old Church, especially from the Mass. From this visit we may date the beginnings of the Reformed Church in Scotland and the general acceptance of Knox as its leader. In July 1556 he returned to his charge in Geneva, but was pressed by some Lords to come home in 1557, and got as far as Dieppe when he received news that his return would be premature. He wrote them a letter of stinging reproach, and as a result the First Covenant was signed by five powerful Lords who undertook 'to renounce the congregation of Sathan with all the superstitions, abominations and idolatry thereof' and 'to apply their whole power, substance and very lives to maintain and forward and establish the most blessed word of God and His Congregation'. The 'Lords of the Congregation' increased in number and became a political party to be reckoned with. Archbishop Hamilton's attempt to detach the Earl of Argyll was unavailing. The burning of Walter Myln, an aged priest, at St. Andrews in 1558 increased the bitterness, and the summoning of the preachers to Holyrood in July gave the Protestants an opportunity to show their strength. Iconoclastic riots occurred sporadically and ribald ballads attacking the clergy were in circulation in spite of all that could be done to suppress them. Petitions to the regent poured in with varied demands, and, with the question of the Crown Matrimonial to be settled, she had perforce to speak fair words to all. She persuaded the Lords to withhold the petition they had drawn up for presentation to Parliament (December 1558), and she prevented the recording of the *Protestation* they read, promising to remember what was protested and later at a more convenient time to put good order to all things that were at issue.

Meantime Mary of England died and the Protestant Elizabeth succeeded to her throne, to which Mary Queen of Scots and her husband the Dauphin of France laid claim as the legitimate heirs. Moreover by the treaty of Cateau Cambrésis (February 1559) France and Spain agreed to lay aside their rivalries and combine to crush Protestantism everywhere. In these cirumstances, and no doubt also in view of the increasing disorder in Scotland, the regent abandoned her policy of toleration and astonished the Protestant Lords who reminded her of her promises by saying that 'it became not subjects to burden their Princes with promises further than it pleaseth them to keep the same'. Nevertheless she did pay attention to certain 'Articles proponit to the Quene Regent be sum temporall Lordis and Barronis' who sought moderate reforms.[1] They took their stand on the Act of 1541 and the Conciliar Statutes of 1549-52 'of the quhilkis thar has followit nan or litill fruict as yitt, bot rather the Spirituale Estate is deteriorate, nor emends be ony sic persuasion as hes bene hidertils usit'.

The regent passed these *Articles* to the primate, 'piously and graciously' requesting him to summon a provincial council, which he accordingly did in the usual form. It is required 'For the tillage of the Lord's field . . . to reform deformities . . . to remove contentions . . . and to consider measures for the conservation, maintenance and defence of the ecclesiastical liberty of the whole Scotican kirk, and of her privileges and immunities' which 'Lutheranism, Calvinism and many other nefarious heresies, everywhere being propagated in the realm, strive to disturb, destroy and subvert.' The date appointed for meeting was 1 March 1559, but it was necessary to issue further mandates in order to secure a larger attendance by 6 April. The deliberations of the council were

assisted by the aid, co-operation and patronage of our most noble and most Christian Princess, Mary, Queen Dowager and Regent of the realm, whose pious goodwill we have experienced

[1] D. Patrick, *Statutes*, pp. 156 ff.

not only in the defence of this our realm from the fierce assaults of foreign enemies, but also in the administration of justice throughout the realm, as well as in the preservation, maintenance and advancement of true religion.

The names of those participating are not recorded, but the two archbishops were present together with their suffragans, also vicars-general, abbots, priors, commendators, deans, provosts, professors of Holy Scripture, rectors, and other learned churchmen representing the Church of Scotland. Among the records of the council are the *Articles* 'proponit be the lords', which were discussed, according to Bishop Lesley. Some of the suggestions were accepted and formulated as statutes, but two of them, ecclesiastical appointments and prayers in the 'vulgar toung' were pronounced to be *ultra vires* for the council, as no doubt they were. For the most part it contented itself with repeating and strengthening the earlier statutes. It was dissolved some time in April. On 2 May John Knox landed at Leith and soon 'the uproar for religion' began.

We may glance very briefly at the reforms undertaken by this series of councils. In 1549 the two causes of heresy were found to be 'the corruption of morals and profane obscenity of life in churchmen of almost all ranks, together with crass ignorance of literature and all the liberal arts'. The diagnosis is remarkable and unhappily was only too well founded. But so far as it can be taken as an act of sincere corporate repentance and represents a will to amendment it deserves respect. With regard to morals there was little that could be done except to reiterate older statutes that had been disregarded. The main evil was the result of the law of celibacy which made it impossible for a cleric to marry legally. If he lived with a woman who was his wife in all but name he was technically a *concubinarius*, and several members of the Council of 1549 were notorious *concubinarii*. Nevertheless, it was decreed that clerics must put away their concubines forthwith. They were forbidden to keep their offspring in their company or have them promoted in their churches or 'under any pretext marry their daughters to barons or make their sons barons out of the patrimony of Christ'. This was obviously

aimed at the higher clergy, and in token of sincerity the two
archbishops in 1559 submitted themselves to the scrutiny of
a committee, which, however, never reported on its diligence.

The evil of concubinage was found in all ranks of the
clergy and most conspicuously in the higher ranks. Crass
ignorance on the other hand becomes more evident as we
descend the clerical ladder, and prevailed especially among
vicars and curates. Again the remedy proposed was hardly
adequate, and was indeed harsh and unjust. Vicars and
curates were to be examined and if found insufficient for
their duties were to be compelled to resign. Rectors, who were
the real culprits, were more gently dealt with. They were
enjoined to preach in their churches four times a year, but
they might hire a substitute! No suggestion was made of any
educational standard to be required of ordinands, much less
a university degree.

It was clearly recognized that popular preaching was, next
after a reform of morals, the best method of church defence;
and it is surprising that no reference is made to the friars,
though preaching was held to be their special function, and
the Scottish provincials of the Mendicant Orders were present
in 1549. But a remarkable scheme was proposed for 'the
permanent establishment and maintenance of preachers
throughout the province'. Each bishop and abbot is 'to assign'
one of his appropriated benefices for the maintenance of a
preacher, and a list of benefices to be so assigned is appended
to the statute. Obviously this was a long-term project, and
completely visionary. No more is heard of it. But there is
every reason to believe that Archbishop Hamilton was
genuinely anxious to have Catholic truth taught to the people
of Scotland, and that he hoped within a few years to have a
sufficient number of able preachers. Meantime he must
make use of the available resources, the ordinary parish
clergy, and for them he supplied ready-made material. It is
unfortunate that we have no information as to the authorship
of what is known as Hamilton's *Catechism*,[1] which is admitted
on all hands to be an admirably clear and non-polemical

---

[1] *Catechism of John Hamilton, Archbishop of St. Andrews* (ed. T. G. Law).

exposition of the faith. Whoever the author was—and vague
tradition points to Winram—the Council of 1552 accepted
full responsibility. It was to be printed at the archbishop's
expense and circulated to rectors, vicars, and curates in all
dioceses, to be read by them to their congregations every
Sunday, when there was no preacher, for half-an-hour before
Mass. No questions or discussions were to be allowed, for
which the average parish priest might not be intellectually
equipped. Some scholars have pointed to features in the
Catechism which suggest a mediating document. No mention
is made of the power of the Pope, for example. Doctrinal
authority is repeatedly attributed to general councils, as if
the conciliar view, taught by John Major, was the accepted
one. And the doctrine of justification by faith is almost
implied, while certainly the Tridentine doctrine is not followed. It should be added that the Council of 1559 adopted
a suggestion of the Lords and authorized the production of
suitable exhortations to be used before the administration of
the sacraments. If these were actually prepared only that for
the Eucharist has been preserved, the so-called 'Twa-penny
Faith'.[1]

Perhaps it may be put down to the credit of the councils
that they concerned themselves so deeply with reforms affecting the clergy personally and the performance of their duties.
No doubt it was rather late in the day to be making statutes
about things so elementary, and it is not surprising that long
neglect brought its own nemesis. It is quite evident that the
action visualized by the councils could not have provided
in any measurable time an effective parochial ministry,
which was the urgent need of the moment. In any case the
parish priests were the victims of a system itself in dire need
of reform. Statutes dealing with reform of the institution there
are, less picturesque and more technical than the others, but
possibly even more important as closely affecting the every-
day life of ordinary people. Improvements in ecclesiastical
administration, by removing grievances widely felt, might
have done much to prevent or arrest alienation from the
church and clergy. But this was much more difficult because it

[1] Bannatyne Club *Miscellany*, vol. iii, pp. 313–20.

affected vested interests, many of them beyond the control of a provincial council.

Some abuses were dealt with in 1549, e.g. misappropriation of the funds of hospitals and endowments for the poor (a matter dealt with later more stridently in the *Beggars' Summons*); dilapidation of benefices through feuing or alienation of glebes and lands, leading to non-residence on the part of the parochial clergy; unions of benefices, the holding of incompatible benefices in plurality, and appropriations of parish revenues to cathedrals, monasteries, and latterly to colleges, all tending to deprive the parishes of their due ministrations. All these matters were to be carefully scrutinized, and abuses corrected where possible. Presumably members of the council knew how drastic an overhaul this would have meant for the whole ecclesiastical structure if anything remarkable was to be achieved, but they would also know how little conciliar decrees would avail against papal exemptions, privileges, and dispensations. In 1559 most of these matters came up again, including now the repair of dilapidated churches, which seems to have been a special interest of Hamilton's. The articles of the Temporal Lords called attention to others. The old grievance of the mortuary dues or offerings was dealt with in detail. They were not abolished, but the very poor were relieved entirely. The farming of teinds, which had met with considerable resistance 'during the last ten years' was made less vexatious for the peasantry, and the Easter offerings were so regulated that the appearance of their being payments for the Sacrament should be avoided. Above all proposals were made for the drastic curtailment of procedure in the consistorial courts. The Lords had asked for an improvement in clerical appointments, and it was pointed out to them, according to Bishop Lesley, that these lay with the patrons and, in the case of the higher offices, with the Crown. The council therefore had no power in the matter. Nevertheless in statute 279 it is laid down that no presentee is to be collated to a benefice unless he shall

after careful examination be found by the ordinary to be fit for the exercise and fulfilment of the duties attached to such benefice; [moreover that] our most serene lady, the Queen, be earnestly and humbly petitioned not to nominate present or suffer to be promoted to bishoprics, abbacies, prelacies or any other preferment appertaining to royal presentation, anyone unless in morals learning and age he shall be found fit and qualified to perform with honour to God and benefit to the people the duties incumbent on the holder of the said benefice. . . . Likewise the Council has thought it expedient that supplicatory letters should be sent to our most holy lord the Pope, praying him not to promote or suffer to be promoted to prelacies or any other preferments any one save such as are qualified in respect of age morals or learning.

This is to go to the heart of the matter. Since 1488 all bishops and abbots had been 'provided' by the Pope on the nomination of the Crown, by an arrangement entered into to serve the interests of both parties, which were not necessarily the interests of the spiritual life of the Church. The bishops and abbots of the council, who all owed their appointments to the operation of this arrangement, would be reluctant to call in question the astonishing judgement of the Council of Trent: 'It is not likely that unworthy persons can extort any privileges from the Apostolic See except by suppressing the truth or by uttering falsehood.' And they were, naturally, in no position to find fault with the concordat of 1488. In fact, even if a strong will had been present, the power of a provincial council to reform the ecclesiastical structure was extremely limited, at least without the co-operation of a strong and determined king. The Scottish councils barely touched the evils of the existing benefice-system, whereby the over-great wealth of the Church was concentrated in the hands of relatively few persons who had sufficient influence to secure high appointments, many of whom were not even in Holy Orders. They evaded the question partly because they could not solve it, but chiefly perhaps because they would not. It was left to the authors of the First Book of Discipline freely to imagine a scrapping of the whole system, and a redistribution of the patrimony of the Kirk in order to secure more effective ecclesiastical and education arrangements. The system, with the vested interests it had created, was too strong even for them and remained to create many a difficulty for the Reformed Church.

A decade of reforming legislation failed to save the old Church. Two diametrically opposite but perhaps complementary reasons were given by contemporaries for the failure. Knox's account of the work of the councils has been castigated as sheer misrepresentation. Obviously he did not write it in the spirit of an impartial historian and could hardly have been expected to do so. His point is that the councils were merely tinkering with the job and that the proposed reforms were utterly inadequate. On the other hand Bishop Lesley, himself a *concubinarius* in the good old days, says:[1]

They maid mony sharp statutes, and commandit all the bishoppis, abottis, prioris, deanes, archdeanes, and all the rest thair presentlie assembled, and utheris throche all the partis of the realme, to mak thame selfis able, and use thair awin offices according to thair fondationis and callingis, within the space of sax monethes, onder the pane of deprivation; quhilk was the principall caus that a gret nomber of younge abbottis, prioris, deanis and benefest men assisted to the interprice and practise devysed for the ourthrow of the Catholicke religeon . . . fearing themselves to be put at according to the Lawis and statutes.

In other words, the statutes were adequate but many of the kirkmen were insincere.

The reforming legislation may have been too little or too much. Certainly it was too late even in 1549. It could only have been rendered effective by determined leadership backed by a strong government, and both were lacking. Archbishop Spottiswoode tells a story[2] which, if true, sheds some light on Hamilton's policy. According to Spottiswoode, while the First Book of Discipline was being prepared Hamilton sent a message to Knox to say 'that albeit he had innovated many things and made reformation of the doctrine of the Church, whereof he could not deny but that there was some reason, yet he should do wisely to retain the old policy which had been the work of many ages, or then put a better in place thereof, before he did shake the other'. This sounds like the voice of Spottiswoode, but if there is any truth in it, Hamilton would seem to have been a moderate honestly seeking just

[1] *History of Scotland* (Bannatyne Club), p. 271.
[2] *History of the Church of Scotland*, vol. i, p. 371 (Bannatyne Club, 1847).

sufficient reformation to preserve the old structure. The fate of the First Book of Discipline shows that he was not without worldly wisdom. In that age ecclesiastics and preachers might propose but the politically powerful disposed. Hamilton failed because he had not the support of a strong government. The Reformers succeeded because their firm convictions enabled them to defy the powerful, and after long struggles to realize in a measure their ideal.

X

THE CRISIS OF THE CHURCH
1559–60

WHETHER the primate was or was not in earnest with his proposed reforms no opportunity was given him to put them into effect, for the adjournment of the provincial council (April 1559) was followed by a year of tumult and civil strife, the details of which were as confused as were the motives of the individuals and groups concerned in them. For some time there had been forming in various towns communities of convinced Protestants with regular meetings for worship, Scripture study, and the administration of the sacraments. As early as 1558 in Dundee and elsewhere elders were appointed to exercise church discipline 'to whom the whole Brethren promised obedience'. All this had been noted by the provincial council for condemnation and punishment, but it had the support with varying degrees of sincerity of some of the nobles and gentry especially in Fife, Angus, and Ayrshire. A very different form of opposition to the established system appears in a truculent document called the *Beggars' Summons* issued in January 1559 threatening the friars with eviction from their properties on the ground that these belonged to the genuine poor. Whoever may have been responsible for this placard, it was calculated to appeal to the cruder passions of the populace of the towns, who seem to have had a special grudge against the friars.

Fearing violence and disorder and naturally regarding the preachers as the ringleaders, the regent summoned them to appear before her at Stirling on 10 May. This was the signal for insurrection. The gentlemen of Angus assembled in Dundee intending to accompany Paul Methven and the preachers to Stirling. On 4 May they were joined by John Knox, recently arrived from France, and they proceeded to Perth where their forces were further strengthened. Here occurred the famous incident in which, after a vehement sermon from Knox, 'the rascal multitude' got out of hand, sacked the Dominican and Franciscan friaries, and wrecked and pillaged the rich Charterhouse in which was the tomb of King James I. In anger the regent vowed to take vengeance and ordered her army to march on Perth. But the arrival of a contingent of the congregation from the west compelled her to negotiate. Her ambassadors included the Earl of Argyll and Lord James Stewart, who, though professed Protestants, were still members of her council. It was agreed that she should be allowed to enter Perth unopposed on condition that no one would suffer for the recent riot, that liberty of worship would be allowed and that no garrison of French mercenaries would be placed in the town. When these conditions were broken, in the spirit if not in the letter, Argyll and the Lord James abandoned the regent, joined their associates of the Congregation and proceeded to St. Andrews 'for reformation to be made there'. With them went John Knox who, in defiance of the threats of the archbishop, preached after so many years in the church in which he had delivered his first sermon. In St. Andrews a more orderly procedure was followed than at Perth. There was no riot. By order of the magistrates the churches were stripped of the monuments of 'idolatry' which were solemnly burned on the spot where Myln had suffered two years before.

Meantime the regent's army had followed as far as Falkland, but learning that the insurgents had been reinforced and were strongly posted on Cupar Moor its French commander patched up a truce and withdrew across the Forth to Edinburgh. The army of the Congregation thereupon marched to Perth, which it liberated, and then by Stirling and Linlithgow to Edinburgh, whence the regent withdrew to Dunbar. In Edinburgh as elsewhere the populace attacked the friaries of their own accord, without any need of stimulus from Knox. It seemed that the victory of the insurgents was complete. On 29 June Knox preached for the first time in St. Giles, and soon after was chosen minister of Edinburgh.

But the end of the struggle was not yet. The unpaid feudal levies of the Lords of the Congregation began to disperse, and in July news reached Scotland that Henry II of France had died as the result of an accidental wound received in a tournament, and that Francis and Mary had succeeded as King and Queen of France. That meant that in France the chief power devolved on the Duke of Guise and the Cardinal of Lorraine, uncles of Queen Mary and brothers of the Regent of Scotland. The latter was now assured of adequate military support, and when reinforcements arrived towards the end of the year she took the offensive and reoccupied Edinburgh and Leith, fortifying the latter as a base of operations, and a port where troops and supplies from France might be received. The Lords with their diminished forces were in no condition to resist and were fain to accept terms and withdraw to Stirling. Knox alone refused to despair. At this time of defeat and failure, as at no other, was it true that 'the voice of one man is able in one hour to put more life in us than five hundred trumpets continually blustering in our ears'.[1] His strength was due to his firm conviction that the cause of the Reformation was the cause of God. 'As it is the eternal truth of the eternal God so it shall prevail, howsoever for a time it be impugned.'[2]

Nevertheless in its hour of defeat the Congregation had more mundane causes for hope. In the summer of 1559 Châtelherault had joined it, bringing with him the Hamilton interest and the prestige of a national figure. A still more important recruit was William Maitland of Lethington who brought consummate diplomatic ability to the cause which sadly needed it. Son of an East Lothian laird, he had been educated in Paris where he had inbibed something of the anti-clericalism of the Renaissance. In 1554 in spite of his religious opinions he became secretary of state to the regent, and later served as her representative at the negotiations leading to the treaty of Cateau Cambrésis. In 1556 he was one of a group of important persons invited by Erskine of Dun to meet Knox, and debate with him the duty of true believers to separate themselves from the established church observances. 'I see perfectly', said Lethington, 'that our shifts will serve nothing before God seeing that they stand us in so

---

[1] Letter of Randolph to Cecil (*Calendar of Scottish Papers*, vol. i, p. 1017).
[2] Knox, *History* (ed. Dickinson, vol. i, p. 270).

small stead before man.' We may well suspect sarcasm. In the Reformation movement Lethington stood at the opposite pole from Knox. For him religion was a secondary concern. He was 'a politic head' such as Knox abominated, who in return could have nothing but contempt for the passionate enthusiasm of Knox. Nevertheless he was needed if the movement was to survive and succeed. What was important was to secure the aid of Elizabeth of England, and for that purpose Knox was worse than useless. His *First Blast of the Trumpet against the Monstrous Regiment of Women*, written at Dieppe in 1556/7, was directed against Mary Tudor and Mary of Lorraine, but provoked in Elizabeth a lifelong resentment, which Knox's apologia, in terms not at all courtly or conciliatory, did nothing to remove.

As secretary to the regent Lethington had every opportunity to learn the secrets of French policy with regard to Scotland, and that he abandoned her service precisely when she appeared to be in a position to carry it out, is a credit to his patriotism. He put his knowledge to good purpose in winning over to the resistance a number of powerful nobles who were not in any sense Protestant and he was the perfect agent to treat with Elizabeth and her counsellors. Apart from her vehement dislike of Knox Elizabeth was unwilling to appear to give aid to rebels, and such the Lords of the Congregation were proclaimed to be by the regent. On the other hand Mary, Queen of France and Scotland, claimed to be also the rightful Queen of England. Lethington's plea was that the Lords were loyal subjects of their queen, and were in arms simply to defend the liberties of their country against French domination. Châtelherault's presence at the head of the party of the congregation made this plausible. The treaty of Berwick (February 1560) accordingly lays stress on his position as 'second person in the realm' and 'heir apparent to the Crown'. Elizabeth agreed to aid him and the Lords of his party to expel the French 'who aim at the conquest of Scotland and the suppression of its liberties'.

In April an English army entered Scotland and in May laid siege to Leith, which was simultaneously blockaded by an English fleet. The town was skilfully and bravely defended

while its provisions lasted. It surrendered on 11 June when
the death of the regent in Edinburgh Castle was announced
by the booming of cannons. On her deathbed she had sought
reconciliation with the leaders of the Congregation, professing that while she loved France she loved Scotland too and
had always sought its good. This might have been true although none of her contemporaries, least of all Knox, could
have believed it. She had been given as a bride to James V
in order to maintain an old alliance, and she might well
have believed that it was the fulfilment of destiny when the
marriage of her daughter to the heir of the French king promised the development of the alliance into a union of the
two countries under a common sovereign. It was her tragedy
to realize that her administration had led to the termination
of the traditional connexion. With regard to her treatment of
her Protestant subjects, the toleration of her earlier years may
have been merely a political expedient, similar to that used
by Charles V when he postponed his purpose to exterminate
Lutheranism until he had with the aid of the Lutherans
overcome his external foes. It may be that, as a devout
Romanist, she believed that faith need not be kept with
heretics, but it is undeniable that her later hostility to Protestantism was due in part to the violent proceedings of its
extremists. At all events with her was buried the French
alliance. We must be thankful that it ended as it did, and
that Scotland was spared the horrors that befell the Netherlands at the hand of their 'lawful' sovereign, Philip II of
Spain, to whom they were bound by nothing but an unnatural dynastic tie.

The fall of Leith determined the issue. Threatened with
internal religious war France could not continue the struggle
and sent ambassadors to treat for peace with England. After
much haggling terms were agreed to in the treaty of Edinburgh, 6 July 1560. All French and English troops were to
be evacuated from Scotland. Francis and Mary were henceforth to abstain from using the title or arms of the kingdom
of England, and were to show 'mercy and kindness' to the
nobility and people of Scotland in return for their obedience
and loyalty. The Scots were naturally not a party to the

treaty, but annexed to it was a series of 'Concessions to the Scots'. No more French soldiers were to be sent to Scotland, and no foreigner was to be appointed to any office under the Crown. The government was to be entrusted to a council of twelve, seven to be selected by the queen and five by the Estates. A general amnesty was to be proclaimed for all on both sides in the late troubles, and ecclesiastical persons who had suffered were to be indemnified, and to suffer no further injury or violence. Moreover Parliament was to be summoned to meet on 10 July and adjourned to 1 August, 'and this assembly shall be as valid in all respects as if it had been called and appointed by the express commandment of the King and Queen'. Those were to be summoned who were in use to be present, and there was to be no intimidation. Finally the religious question was to be remitted to the king and queen 'to understand their pleasure' in the matter.

The treaty of Edinburgh contained the provision that it should be ratified by Francis and Mary within sixty days, but on the evacuation of the French and English troops there seemed no reason to await their ratification, which in fact was never made. 'The Great Council of the Realm', a body appointed in the previous October by the Lords of the Congregation, set about convening the Estates. The ministers arranged a service of thanksgiving in St. Giles', and Knox resumed his interrupted ministry there, preaching from the words of the prophet Haggai concerning the restoration of the temple. So pointed were his applications that many murmured and their dissatisfaction was expressed by Lethington in a characteristic utterance: 'We must now forget ourselves, and bear the barrow to build the houses of God.'[1] Nevertheless there were some—barons, gentlemen, and burgesses—who were in earnest about Reformation. In July they made arrangements on paper, at any rate, for the distribution of the slender available ministerial manpower over the country. Ministers were appointed to eight of the larger towns and five superintendents were nominated to serve more extensive areas; and a Supplication was drawn up for submission to Parliament when it should meet. It complained

---

[1] Knox, *History* (ed. Dickinson, vol. i, p. 335).

of abuses in doctrine, the administration of the sacraments, and the exercise of ecclesiastical authority on the part of the hierarchy, and craved that the existing clergy 'be deamit unworthy of honour, authority, charge or cure within the Kirk of God and deprived of all voice in Parliament'.

On 1 August Parliament met and was presided over by Lethington. It was observed that some of the Spiritual and Temporal Lords contemptuously absented themselves. But there was a large representation of earls and 'the chief pillars of the Papistical Kirk' gave their presence, such as the bishops of St. Andrews, Dunblane, and Dunkeld. Beaton, Archbishop of Glasgow, was in Paris where he had gone on a diplomatic mission. Twenty-two burghs sent deputies, including Banff and Inverness. An unusually large number of lesser barons attended, 110 in fact. A statute of James I in 1427 gave them the right to be summoned, but that right had not been exercised for at least a century and might be held to have fallen into desuetude. Its exercise now raised a question as to the legality of the Parliament, as did the absence of the sovereign or her commissioner. This question was debated for a week, when it was decided in the affirmative by a majority vote. The next step was to appoint the committee known as the Lords of the Articles drawn from each of the three Estates. On this occasion the clerical members were chosen from among those known to favour reformation. The Supplication of the Protestants was then read, and after much debate it was decided to command the petitioners 'to draw, in plain and several heads, the sum of that doctrine which they would maintain, and would desire that present Parliament to establish as wholesome, true, and only necessary to be believed and to be received within that realm'. In four days Knox and his brethren produced the document now known as the Scots Confession which was read in Parliament. Objections were called for, and the ministers held themselves in readiness to make the necessary answers. Accounts of what then took place differ greatly. Some of the Temporal Lords demurred, and the prelates said little, which was remarked on by the Earl Marischal as an indication that they could not deny the truths contained

L

in the Confession. Clearly the majority of the Parliament were in favour, many of them enthusiastically so, and the prelates may have been restrained from speaking because they feared the consequences to themselves, or perhaps because they were sure that the legality of the proceedings would be called in question. For by the terms of the treaty of Edinburgh Parliament was expressly forbidden to handle matters of religion. Moreover they might rightly have protested that questions of doctrine were not properly to be debated in Parliament. At all events on 17 August the Confession received parliamentary sanction, and a few days later three further Acts were passed. The jurisdiction and authority of the Bishop of Rome, called the Pope, was abolished. The Acts of former Parliaments against heresy and for the maintenance of the rights, practices and privileges of the papal Church were annulled, and the saying or hearing of Mass was made a criminal offence, punishable for the first offence by confiscation of goods, for the second by banishment and for the third by death.

Such was the Protestant Revolution, carried out by the Estates in defiance of the 'pleasure' of the absentee sovereign, but its stability had still to be tested. Notwithstanding the Act against the Mass it continued to be said with impunity by Archbishop Hamilton and by many others. Apart from this ineffective prohibition laid on the performance of their functions the old clergy remained unaffected. It can only be matter for surprise that they made so little use of their opportunities to recover what they had lost unless indeed it is true that the old system was rotten to the core. On the other hand the Reformers had gained nothing from Parliament except the legalizing of their creed. A long struggle confronted them before their ideal of a Reformed Church could be realized.

PART III

REFORMATION

I

THE IDEALS OF THE REFORMERS

NEVER did the Scottish people stand in greater need of wise and strong leadership than in August 1560, after a year of tumult, confusion, and strife. Never was it less well served. At no time had the Crown possessed the power which the Tudors enjoyed in England, but now the queen was an absentee in France. Her interest in her ancestral kingdom was dynastic only, and her authority, though formally recognized, was but slight. The legality of the August Parliament was questionable, and among its more influential members there was no unanimity of faith or policy. A large majority of those present showed that they had no mind to leave ecclesiastical reform in the hands of Archbishop Hamilton and his provincial council whose statutes had proved ineffectual. So far as it was in their power they discharged the old clergy from performing their traditional functions, but otherwise left the clerical Estate intact. The creed of the Reformers received parliamentary sanction but their plans for reformation were not considered. These plans had already been formulated and were known to several of the great nobles, but only aroused their suspicion and dislike. What shape the Reformed Church of Scotland was to take was left an open question over which there was to be a long and bitter struggle. Not until 1689 can it be said to have been finally settled. With the history of that struggle, lasting for 130 years, we are now concerned.

In the first place we must make clear to ourselves the ideals of the Reformers, and particularly of John Knox. Of course Knox did not stand alone. There were others, among them some of higher birth and greater learning than were his. It is doubtful whether he had any university education, certainly he was not a graduate, but he had experience in England and on the Continent, above all in the Geneva of John Calvin which he held to be 'the most perfect school of Christ that ever was on earth since the days of the Apostles'. When he returned to his native land in 1559, at the age of 44, it was as undisputed leader of the movement for reform both in the troubled year of civil strife and in the attempts at reconstruction that followed. This is acknowledged in all contemporary documents, English and Scottish, friendly and hostile, and not only in his own account of the events in which he was involved. Knox's *History of the Reformation in Scotland*, apart from its value as history, is self-revelatory, but it reveals a religious type not commonly admired or even understood today. His judgements on his contemporaries, notably Mary of Lorraine, are often grossly unfair, and his severity with Queen Mary offends the romantic. His tacit assumption of the role of Old Testament prophet has made him to appear as a mere fanatic. But his forcefulness is without a trace of personal vanity, self-seeking, or self-exaltation, unless it be self-exaltation to believe with utter conviction that the cause he had at heart was the cause of the truth of God. His impassioned oratory was a source of strength to the movement when it seemed in danger of collapse, and if on occasion it provoked to destructive violence his positive preaching appealed to serious-minded people, and was the seed from which the Reformed Church was to grow. In the drafting of the *Scots Confession of Faith* and the *Book of Discipline* Knox had five collaborators, three of whom showed later that they had minds of their own, and yet his seems to have been the guiding hand. The *Book of Common Order* was wholly his own. To the study of these three important documents we must now turn.

THE SCOTS CONFESSION

However unusual and irregular it may have been for Parliament to receive, discuss, and sanction a doctrinal statement, it was natural that the Reformers should be eager to accept the opportunity to declare their faith publicly, and so to defend themselves against the charge of heresy commonly brought against them by their enemies both at home and abroad. No sooner was the *Confession* ratified and approved by Parliament than it was translated into Latin and transmitted in the name of the Estates of Scotland not only to their countrymen but 'to all other Realms and Nations, professing the same Lord Jesus with them'. Moreover since the Reformation claimed above all else to be a return to the pure Gospel and scriptural truth it was entirely appropriate that as the foundation of a Reformed Church there should be drawn up a Confession of Faith. Nevertheless the Reformers do not seem to have thought of the *Confession* as a constitutional document, to be used, for example, as a doctrinal test for ministers and office bearers, as was the *Westminster Confession* from 1690 onwards. It was not included in Knox's *Book of Common Order* which, instead, contains the Confession of Faith used in the English congregation at Geneva during Knox's ministry there. It was endorsed but not quoted in the so-called *Negative Confession* drawn up in 1581 by John Craig on the orders of King James, and signed by the king, his household, and privy councillors, and only to this extent is referred to in the National Covenant of 1638. In 1644 it was replaced by the *Westminster Confession*, a fuller and more carefully systematic document. But what it lacks in scholastic completeness is fully compensated for by its freshness and directness. Many today have preferred it to the later document in that it witnesses to a living faith confronted with a real and not an academic situation. As such it is still highly esteemed among the historic confessions of the Reformed Churches.

The *Scots Confession* contains twenty-five articles of which twelve treat of what may be called the basic doctrines of the Catholic faith: God and the Trinity (one Substance in three Persons); the Creation and Fall of man and the prophetic promises of redemption; the Incarnation (two Natures in one Person); the Passion, Resurrection, and Ascension of Christ, and His return to judge the earth; Atonement through the death of Christ and Sanctification through the Holy Ghost. All this, though there are traces in it of distinctively Calvinist emphases, is entirely orthodox and in accord with the Catholic creeds. The controversial note is first heard, but not stridently, in the articles which treat of good works. Any idea of merit or supererogatory virtue is ruled out. Good works are those done in faith and in obedience to God's commandments, but they are not done by man's free will. 'The spirit of the Lord Jesus dwelling in us by faith brings forth good works.' Among evil works are included not only contraventions of the moral law of God 'but those also that in matters of religion and worshipping of God have no assurance but the invention and opinion of man, which God from the beginning has ever rejected'. Thus briefly are dismissed the ceremonies of the Roman Church against which Knox battled from his first sermon to the end of his life, in accordance with the view of Calvin that in the worship of God nothing was permissible which had not express Scripture warrant.

More polemical in tone are the articles dealing with the Church and Sacraments. The Church is indefeasible,

a multitude of men chosen of God, who rightly worship and embrace Him by true faith in Christ Jesus who is the only Head of the Church, which also is the body and spouse of Christ Jesus: which Church is Catholic because it contains the Elect of all ages, realms, nations and tongues . . . who have communion and society with God the Father and with His Son, Christ Jesus, through the sanctification of His Holy Spirit . . . out of which Church there is neither life nor eternal felicity. . . . As without Christ Jesus there is neither life nor salvation, so shall there none be participant thereof but such as the Father has given unto His Son . . . and those that in time come to Him, avow His doctrine and believe into Him. . . . This Church is invisible known only to God, who alone knoweth whom He has chosen.

But the visible Church is Knox's real concern and is never long absent from his thoughts. There are certain notes by which the true can be discerned from the false Church. 'These Notes . . . we affirm are neither antiquity, title usurped, lineal descent, place appointed, nor multitude of men approving an error.' Where there is true preaching of the Word of God, right administration of the Sacraments of Christ Jesus, 'which must be annexed to the word and promise of God, to seal and confirm the same in our hearts', and ecclesiastical discipline uprightly ministered 'as God's word prescribes . . . there is the true Church of Christ . . . not the universal Church but the particular Church such as was in Corinth . . . and other places in which the ministry was planted by Paul'. 'Such Kirks we, the inhabitants of the Realm of Scotland, professors of Christ Jesus, confess us to have in our cities towns and places reformed; for the doctrine taught in our Kirks is contained in the written word of God . . . in which we affirm that all things necessary to be believed for the salvation of mankind are sufficiently expressed.' The stress laid on 'the particular Kirk' is not due simply to the historical situation at the time when the *Confession* was written, but to a fundamental principle of the Calvinist Reformation, according to which the Church shows its face where the Christian people gather for instruction and worship around the Word. Wider organization, national or ecumenical, may be helpful to refute heresies or declare the faith or 'for good order and policy' to be observed in the Church, but the life of the Church is in the local congregation, where Christ has promised to be present.

That the Church, whether particular or universal, is everywhere exclusively and absolutely subject to the word of God written is assumed throughout the *Confession*. To say that Scripture derives its authority from the Church is blasphemy against God and an insult to the true Church 'which always hears and obeys the voice of her own Spouse and Pastor, but takes not upon her to be mistress over the same'. Moreover the interpretation of Scripture pertains neither to private nor public persons nor to any Kirk for any pre-eminence or prerogative, personal or local, but pertains to the Spirit of God, by which also the Scripture was written. This is not, however, an appeal to 'the internal testimony of the Holy Spirit'—a phrase of Calvin which has sometimes been invoked as an antidote to fundamentalism—but simply an appeal from a difficult passage to a plainer clearer passage in Scripture itself. The authors of the *Confession* in their Preface protest 'that if any man will note in this our Confession any article or sentence repugning to God's holy word, that it would please him of his gentleness and for Christian charity's sake to admonish us of the same in writing; and we do promise him satisfaction from the mouth of God, that is from his holy Scriptures, or else reformation of that which he shall prove to be amiss'. In other words, they regard the *Confession* as strictly subordinate to Scripture, and hardly even claim that it is put forward as a standard of Scripture interpretation.

It is in the treatment of the Sacraments that the language of the *Confession* becomes most fiercely polemical, and the reason is that the Reformers took a 'high' view of the two Sacraments which they accepted as dominical. 'By Baptism we are ingrafted into Christ . . . and in the Supper, rightly used, Christ Jesus is so joined with us that he becomes the very nourishment and food of our souls. . . . The faithful . . . so do eat the body and drink the blood of the Lord Jesus, that he remaineth in them and they in Him . . . are made flesh of His flesh and bone of His bones . . . have such conjunction with Christ Jesus as the natural man cannot comprehend' even if 'they do not profit so much as they would at the very instant action of the Supper . . . for the Holy Spirit . . . will not frustrate the faithful of the fruit of that mystical action.' But, of course, 'all this comes by true faith, which apprehendeth Christ Jesus, who only makes his Sacraments effectual unto us'. This doctrine explains the indignation with which the assertion that 'we believe Sacraments to be only naked and bare signs' is repudiated as a slander. It explains the invective against the 'adulterated' Sacraments of the papistical Church and especially the Mass, as superstitious and idolatrous. It explains the reverence and glowing faith with which Knox himself regarded the Sacrament of the Lord's Supper, and which long remained in the Church of Scotland as a legacy from him.

On the other hand if the efficacy of the Sacraments depends on true faith it will be necessary for the minister and the participants to know their meaning and purpose and to fulfil the moral conditions of worthy participation. To some it has seemed that the *Confession* at this point comes dangerously near the error of Wyclif. It certainly raises the question of 'lawful ministry' which it denies to be in the papistical Kirk. 'We flee the society of the Papistical Kirk in participation of their Sacraments, first because their ministers are no minsters of Christ Jesus; yea they suffer women to baptise'(!) More seriously 'they have so adulterated both Sacraments by their inventions that no part of Christ's action abides in its original purity', and they have made of the Lord's Supper a propitiatory sacrifice, derogatory to the sufficiency of His only sacrifice, so perverting its true use and meaning. Lawful ministers are those 'who are appointed to the preaching of the word, or into whose mouths God has put some sermon of exhortation, they being men lawfully chosen thereto by some kirk'. They must follow Christ's institution as originally given, and explain its purpose and meaning as well as the moral conditions required of those who participate. This is to take a 'high' view of the Ministry of Word and Sacraments, but is at the same time to dismiss the question of validity in the technical sense, which in the Scottish Church has remained of doubtful relevance.

Only one other article in the *Confession* need be mentioned, that dealing with the civil magistrate. His office is affirmed to be ordained of God 'for the singular profit and commodity of mankind'. He is to be loved, honoured, feared, and held in reverent esteem. 'To Kings, Princes, Rulers and Magistrates chiefly and principally pertain the conservation and purgation of religion . . . not only are they appointed for civil policy but also for the maintenance of the true religion and for suppressing of idolatry and superstition.' This article has seemed to some writers to be so alien from the views of Knox that they have suggested that Maitland of Lethington had a hand in it. And yet it is pure Calvinism. Knox himself had petitioned Parliament to do this very thing, and was not yet disillusioned by his political allies. The relations of Church and State were to have a long and painful history in Scotland, but in 1560 it might well appear that the true religion would have the support of the civil magistrate, and the Acts of Parliament so far as they went would support that hope.

Doubtless Edward Irving was exaggerating when he described the *Scots Confession* as 'the banner of the Church in all her wrestlings and conflicts'. But it well expressed the conviction of the first Reformers, Knox above all, convictions which by their preaching and that of their successors have deeply influenced the traditional faith and practice of the Scottish Church ever since.

THE BOOK OF COMMON ORDER

What effect the Act of 1560 prohibiting the saying or hearing of Mass may have had in the cathedrals, abbeys, colleges, and parish churches up and down the kingdom is largely a matter for conjecture. No doubt the effect varied from place to place. Protestant commendators and patrons would see that in their respective spheres of influence the law was obeyed. But even when effective the Act was purely negative. There could in Scotland be no question of an Act of Uniformity such as accompanied and enforced the general use of the successive editions of the Book of Common Prayer in the England of Edward VI and Elizabeth. Not till the Black Acts of James VI in 1584 did the government intervene in matters of worship, and the attempt of Charles I in 1637 to impose upon the Church the use of what is generally known as Laud's Liturgy aggravated his troubles. By that time the Scottish Church had formed its own tradition which it was prepared to maintain and defend. Even before 1560 the beginnings of that tradition were apparent.

By 1556 groups of convinced Protestants had been forming here and there. Especially in the towns and largely under the influence of Knox they then began to give themselves at least a rudimentary organization under elected elders, 'for at that time we had no public ministers of the word'. Nevertheless worship was a regular feature of the life of these 'privy kirks'. 'It was concluded that the brethren in every town at certain times should assemble together to Common Prayers, to exercise and reading of the Scriptures, till it should please God to give the sermon of exhortation to some for comfort and instruction of the rest.' In a 'Letter of Wholesome Counsell', written in 1556 just before he left Scotland to return to his charge in Geneva, Knox described in some detail what should be done at these assemblies which he would wish to take place once a week. There should be confession of sins, invocation of the Spirit of the Lord Jesus, reading of passages from the Old and New Testaments, followed by exposition, thanksgiving, and intercession. This looks like the first 'directory' for Reformed worship in Scotland. Nothing is said about the Lord's Supper, no doubt because Knox is thinking of groups in which no recognized minister would be available, and such a minister was in his view indispensable for the ministration of the Sacraments. During his nine months' visit to Scotland Knox had himself in several places administered the Sacrament of the Lord's Supper according to the Reformed manner.

On the other hand the influence of England early made itself felt. In 1549, during the reign of Edward VI, a Book of Common Prayer in the English tongue, largely the work of Cranmer, had been issued and ordered to be read uniformly in the Church of England. In 1552 another edition, somewhat revised in a Protestant direction, had been issued, and it is likely that this 'Book of England' would be brought to Scotland by those preachers who had served in the Church of England under Edward VI, and who fled from the Marian persecution and worked in Scotland during the period of relative toleration under Mary of Lorraine. At all events the Lords who signed the First Covenant in December 1557 and those who joined them in consultation for a programme of reform, declare—'It is thought expedient, devised and ordained that in all parishes of this Realm the Common Prayers be read weekly on Sundays and other feast days publicly in the Parish Churches, with the Lessons of the New and Old Testaments, conform to the order of the Book of Common Prayer', presumably the Second Prayer Book of Edward VI. This was to be done by the parish clergy if they were capable; if not by 'the most qualified in the parish'! As the Lords of the Congregation became, after the accession of Elizabeth, increasingly dependent on English aid, and were deeply interested in the policy of amity between the two countries, it might have been expected that they would favour uniformity in worship after 1560. So indeed they probably did, but most of them were concerned with the political and financial aspects of the Reformation, and much less with the worship of the Reformed Church. Besides, Elizabeth's Prayer Book of 1559 was more 'catholicizing' than Edward's of 1552, in spite of the desires of most of her bishops and an increasing number of her subjects.

John Knox, like so many other Scots preachers, served in the Church of England under Edward VI, and enjoyed some influence in high quarters. A sermon he preached in the presence of the king is said to have been responsible for the insertion in the 1552 Prayer Book of the Black Rubric, explaining that to kneel when receiving the communion did not imply worshipping the elements. Though Knox did not entirely approve of the book, he recommended its use to his old congregation in Berwick in the interests of unity and peace and because of the order of the magistrates. The accession of Mary Tudor drove him into exile on the Continent and he became one of the ministers of the congregation of English exiles who had received the hospitality of the town of Frankfurt-on-the-Main. There he declared himself for a simpler form of service, and after much controversy, went with his sympathizers to Geneva where another congregation of English exiles had gathered, and where with the approval of Calvin and on Calvin's own lines he drew up the 'Book of Geneva'. This he brought to Scotland in 1559. It is mentioned several times in the *Book of Discipline* as 'the Book of our Common Order called the Order of Geneva'. It was printed in Edinburgh in 1562 and confirmed by the General Assembly in December of the same year as 'ane uniforme order to be keepit'. It was enlarged and reprinted with the addition of the Psalms in metre in 1564, and remained the standard of worship in the Scottish Church till it was replaced by the Westminster Directory in 1643.

The *Book of Common Order* contains the Confession of Faith of the Church of Geneva, forms for the election of superintendents, ministers, elders, and deacons, for public worship and the administration of Sacraments, for marriage and burial, for the visitation of the sick, for ecclesiastical discipline, e.g. excommunication, public repentance, and absolution, and for a General Fast. It professes to be simply a guide to ministers in the performance of their functions, though it was intended to be followed in substance if not in form of expression, and its use was prescribed for readers, whose office was precisely to read the Common Prayers in church. Whether it is to be properly called a liturgy or not has been matter of dispute. It certainly has neither the brevity nor the beauty of the English Prayer Book, but is strong in biblical and theological content. If it made no provision for the people's participation in the service in the way of responses, it allowed them to share in the worship by singing Psalms in metre to plain and noble tunes. Printed editions commonly included the Psalms in metre, sometimes with tunes, and the name Psalm Book by which it was popularly known seems to show that it was intended to be used by others besides ministers and readers. The Lord's Prayer and the Apostles' Creed, which with the Ten Commandments were regarded as essential elements of religious knowledge, were repeated at every service. The Lord's Supper, it is suggested, should be 'commonly used once a month or so oft as the Congregation shall think expedient', but it is unlikely that it was in fact 'used' so frequently. In the celebration the Lord's action in word and deed as recorded in 1 Cor. xi was to be closely followed. As 'the Sacraments are not ordained of God to be used in private corners as charms and sorceries, but left to the Congregation and necessarily annexed to God's Word as seals of the same', baptism is to be administered after the sermon in face of the congregation on the day appointed to common prayer and preaching.

Knox's Liturgy, if we may so call it, in its ruggedness bears the mark of its age but, even more than does the *Confession of Faith*, it affords a glimpse of the religious core of the Scottish Reformation, the ardent biblical faith that was its strength and inspiration.

THE BOOK OF DISCIPLINE

According to Knox's narrative,[1] on the dissolution of Parliament towards the end of August 'consultation was had how the Kirk might be established in a good and godly policy . . . Commission and charge was given to Mr. John

[1] *History* (ed. Dickinson, vol. i, p. 343).

Winram, Subprior of St. Andrews, Master John Spottiswoode, John Willock, Mr. John Douglas, Rector of St.
Andrews, Master John Row and John Knox, to draw in a
volume the Policy and Discipline of the Kirk, as well as they
had done the Doctrine.' Knox then proceeds to tell of the
fate at the hands of the nobility of the *Book of Discipline* thus
produced before inserting it in his *History* 'that posterity
may judge what the worldlings refused and what the godly
Ministers required'. In the copy so inserted however it is
stated that the commission was given on 29 April, and that
the book was completed and signed on 20 May. This would
mean that it had been composed before the victory of the
Protestants was assured, but if so it is strange that it was not
submitted to Parliament. The question of the date of composition must be left undecided. More important is it to
know the names of its authors, and here Knox could not have
been mistaken.

The committee charged with drafting a policy for the Kirk
is a remarkable one, including distinguished men of very
diverse antecedents. Only two of them, Knox and his close
friend Willock, had taken part as preachers in the troubles of
the previous year. Winram and Douglas had long held high
office in the old Church and were in good standing till the
summer of 1560, Winram as the most important ecclesiastic
in St. Andrews after the archbishop, and a doctor and professor of theology as well, with a seat in Parliament as prior
of Portmoak (St. Serf's, Lochleven); Douglas as provost of
St. Mary's College since 1547 and as rector of the university
since 1550. Both were much older men than Knox and were
presumably more conservative. John Row was a graduate of
St. Andrews and had been a noted pleader in the archbishop's
consistorial court. In 1550 he went to Rome as agent for the
Scottish clergy and especially for Archbishop Hamilton. He
found time to continue his legal studies for he became a
licentiate in laws of the University of Rome and a doctor of
laws of the University of Padua. In 1558 he returned to his
native land for reasons of health, bringing with him some
kind of papal commission in connexion with the suppression
of heresy. Disgusted, it is said, by a faked miracle staged by

the friars in Edinburgh he joined the Reformers in 1559. John Spottiswoode, of the family of Spottiswoode of that Ilk in Berwickshire, studied in Glasgow, but discovering Protestant sympathies went to England where he entered the household of Archbishop Cranmer and received ordination from him. Returning to Scotland in 1543 he became chaplain and tutor in the family of the Earl of Glencairn, an opponent of Beaton, and after some diplomatic employments of importance was in 1557 presented by Sir James Sandilands of Calder, a leading Protestant, to the rectory of Calder Comitis, which he held for the rest of his life. His son, later Archbishop of St. Andrews, more than hints that he was not always in agreement with the views of Knox.

Nevertheless, Knox with his Genevan experience was clearly the driving force in this group of distinguished men. The *Book of Discipline* shows traces of ideas borrowed from various sources but the Calvinist influence is apparent throughout, though, of course, Calvin's *Ecclesiastical Ordinances*, devised for a single purely urban community, were not directly applicable to a whole kingdom. The *Book of Ecclesiastical Discipline* adopted by the French Protestants in 1559 was not helpful either, for its purpose was to organize and regulate on a national scale the life of scattered congregations already formed, which had no expectation of ever becoming more than a minority of the nation. The Scottish *Book of Discipline* aims at a total 'Reformation of Religion in the whole Realm'. It claims to be advice tendered, on request, to the Great Council of Scotland, that is the acting government, as to the course it should follow with that end in view. Its tone is firm but respectful and it is assumed that with the council lies the responsibility and the opportunity of purging the commonwealth of superstition and furthering its moral, religious, and educational 'comfort and commodity'. Religion is the dominant concern, and it is realized that some of the proposals will seem strange to 'their Honours' at first sight and may offend many, but they are summoned to hear God calling who will reward their obedience and punish disobedience.

The *Book of Discipline* does not attempt to sketch an

ecclesiastical polity for Scotland in the accepted sense of that term. It is true that from time to time such expressions occur as 'the Superintendent and his Council' or 'the Council of the whole Kirk' which seem to adumbrate the later synod and General Assembly, but these are left wholly indeterminate. The word 'policy' is no doubt merely an older form of 'polity', but where it occurs in the *Book of Discipline*, in the ninth, and last, head, it is used rather in the modern sense, as if the book were designed to set forth a missionary policy felt to be urgent rather than a scheme of church organization. 'Policy we call an exercise of the Church in such things as may bring the rude and ignorant to knowledge, or also inflame the learned to greater fervency, or to retain the Church in good order.' Most of what is proposed under that head concerns matters of expediency, practical details which every particular kirk will have to be left to decide for itself—times for preaching, common prayers, and administration of the Sacraments (e.g. The Lord's Supper should be celebrated four times a year in towns, and less frequently in the country); practice in community psalm-singing; family prayers; exercise in Bible study in some convenient centre, and who may or even must attend; rules for marriages and funerals; repair of churches and the punishment due to those who presume to act as ministers without 'lawful calling'. Nevertheless, some matters of policy are 'utterly necessary; as that the Word be truly preached, the sacraments rightly administered, and common prayers publicly made; that children and rude persons be instructed in the chief points of religion, and that offences be corrected and punished. These things, we say, be so necessary that without the same there is no face of a visible Church.' These words express the controlling purpose of the whole book, and suggest that the primary concern of the Reformers was with the particular kirk or local congregation. This is borne out by an earlier passage, in which it is required that abbeys, monasteries, friaries, nunneries, chapels, chantries, cathedral kirks, canonries, colleges other than presently are parish kirks or schools, should be abolished as monuments of idolatry. It is the logical conclusion to be drawn from the doctrine of the 'notes' of the true Church. The Cinderella of the old system was to be raised from the ashes.

Two of the essential notes of the true Kirk, according to the *Confession of Faith*, were that the holy Evangel of Jesus Christ should be truly preached, and that His Holy Sacraments should be truly ministered, as seals and visible confirmations of the spiritual promises contained in the Word. This involves a Ministry of Word and Sacraments, and of that ministry the Reformers held a serious, even a 'high', view. This is clear in the *Book of Discipline*. 'In a Kirk Reformed or tending to reformation none may presume to preach or minister the Sacraments till orderly they be called to the same.' Ordinary vocation, i.e. as distinct from an extraordinary call of God evidenced by signs and wonders, consists in election, examination, and admission. Election pertains to the people of every several kirk, though if they cannot or will not exercise the right, a nomination may be made by others. Even in such a case the consent of the people must be sought that there be no violent intrusion. Examination is by competent persons, if possible neighbouring ministers, in Scripture exposition and in the topics of controversial theology, and searching inquiry must also be made into the character and conduct of the candidate. This is followed by a test of his ability to preach, before the congregation to which he is to minister, sermons dealing with the main articles of the faith. Finally he is to be admitted by those who examined him after a sermon by 'the chief minister' on the duties of the ministry, and charges given to both minister and people. 'Other ceremony than the public approbation of the people and the declaration of the chief minister that the person there present is appointed to serve that Kirk we cannot approve; for albeit the Apostles used the imposition of hands, yet seeing the miracle is ceased, the using of the ceremony we judge is not necessary.' The same form is prescribed for the admission of those ministers who as superintendents were entrusted with the charge not of particular kirks but of wider areas described as provinces or dioceses. It is abundantly clear that the particular kirk is not conceived as an independent congregation, however important it may be. It is part of a whole, though that whole is left inevitably indistinct and sketchy.

This elaborate procedure of admission to the ministry closely follows Calvin's. In 1560 it was manifestly unworkable in Scotland, but was intended to produce in time what the Reformers regarded as a 'lawful ministry'. It was designed to exclude persons, seemingly already in evidence, who took upon themselves without any kind of authorization to exercise a disorderly ministry to the profanation of God's holy ordinances. On the other hand the *Book of Discipline* sweeps aside all claim to lawfulness on the part of the old clergy in spite of the fact that its authors had all been in priest's orders in the old Church, except Spottiswoode who had Anglican ordination. 'The Papistical priests', it is declared, 'have neither power nor authority to minister the Sacraments of Christ Jesus' and the reasons given are (1) that they do not preach the word and (2) that they have defaced the true primitive form of the Sacraments by their unauthorized ceremonies, and have become in effect ministers of superstition. Soon Ninian Wingate was to press Knox with questions as to the lawfulness of his ministry, and of the ordinations he had carried through since he had renounced and esteemed null or rather wicked that ordination by which he was formerly called Sir John. These were and still are awkward questions, unanswerable unless it be assumed that, at any rate in 1560, validity of orders was a minor issue in comparison with the urgent need for reform, which Wingate acknowledged as heartily as did Knox. If Knox and his colleagues underestimated the ordinations of the old Church, they certainly laid a new and significant emphasis on the pastoral obligations implied in ordination, which had been scandalously neglected. Ordination became a solemn admission to the pastoral office in a particular charge which the ordained may not leave of his own pleasure, but only if the whole Kirk for good reasons shown decide to translate him to another.

The number of persons able and willing to qualify for the ministry in the manner described was obviously quite inadequate to supply the needs of all the parishes in Scotland, even if, as suggested, 'their Honours' could compel men with the necessary gifts to enter the ministry. Nevertheless it is insisted that the standard of character and attainment required was in no case to be lowered. To have no minister for a period was better than to have an inefficient one. The *Book of Discipline*, therefore, falls back on an English expedient. Where no minister may be had, someone able to read the Common Prayers and the Scriptures should be appointed, and such might be found among simple Protestants of long standing whose life and gifts might edify the people. These readers should be encouraged in every way to improve their gifts. After some experience they might be recognized as exhorters, and in time might be raised to the full status of ministers of the Word and Sacraments. The Exercise for Bible Study which was recommended to be held weekly in convenient centres, and which was to be regularly attended by ministers and readers within a radius of six miles, would offer to readers the opportunity to qualify for such advancement. Through the door thus opened many parochial vicars of the old Church found their way into the ministry of the new.

The situation of 1560 demanded, however, a still bolder expedient and this may have been suggested by the experience of the Lutheran churches. It was recognized as most important that 'chief towns especially where learning is exercised' should be served by resident ministers by whose labours young people might be trained for the service of the Reformed Church and commonwealth. But lest the greatest part of the realm should be destitute of all doctrine and return to its accustomed idolatry, certain ministers should be appointed superintendents of provinces or dioceses, as the ten great areas were called into which it was proposed to divide the whole country. Some of these corresponded roughly to the dioceses of the medieval Church. The duties of the superintendent were laid down with great care so as to distinguish him from 'yon idle Bishops heretofore'. He might not stay at home in his principal town for more than three or four months in the year. For the rest of the time he must be occupied in the assiduous visitation of his diocese, in preaching at least three times a week, in ensuring that the parishes were

provided with ministers or at least with readers, in super-
vising the work and behaviour of these, in promoting the
education of the young and the care of the poor. In short he
was a minister on a large scale. If he exercised supervision
over the ministers and kirks within his diocese, they also
exercised a sort of supervision over him and might complain
of his faults and negligence. The procedure in his election,
examination, and admission was the same as for ministers
generally, except that in his case the electors were not the
members of a single congregation but the inhabitants of the
diocese, gentlemen and burgesses. To begin with, it was conceded, 'their Honours' must make the appointments with the
consent of as many of the people as possible, but when the
Church had been established and three years had passed
stricter rules would be applied. This raises the question: Was
the office intended to be permanent? The *Book of Discipline*
does not directly answer, but the impression is distinctly
given that it was conceived as a missionary agency to meet
an urgent need of the moment, if the Reformation was to
be carried to the whole nation within a measurable time.
'Nothing desire we more earnestly than that Christ Jesus be
universally once preached throughout this Realm, which shall
not suddenly be' unless superintendents be appointed. 'Once'
clearly is intended to mean 'in the shortest possible time'.

Of the Notes of a True Kirk as defined in the *Confession of
Faith* two were the special care of the Ministry of Word and
Sacraments. The third, ecclesiastical discipline, aimed at
furthering the Christian life of the Kirk. Unhappily it was
conceived in a rather negative way. According to the *Book
of Discipline* its function was to reprove, correct, and punish
vices with which the civil magistrate did not normally deal,
but which brought disgrace upon the Church, e.g. drunkenness, brawling, swearing, licentious living, but also, be it
noted, oppression of the poor by exactions or by cheating
them with false weights and measures. Discipline is to be
exercised through private rebuke, public admonition, and, as
a last resort, in the case of heinous public offences, by excommunication involving penalties as terrible as the medieval
Church had known. It is explicitly claimed that the Reformed

Church must perform the duty which the papistical Kirk had notoriously neglected, without, however, closing the door irrevocably to the truly penitent. Moreover there is to be no respect of persons. All Estates of the realm must be subject to discipline, and especially ministers who as 'the eye and mouth of the Church' ought to be single and irreprehensible.

Who, then, is to exercise discipline? The answer is the Church, that is the local congregation, acting through its special organ the ministry, here used in a wider sense to include also elders and deacons, and thus we come to a characteristic feature of the Reformed Church of Scotland, the eldership. It is true that in the Genevan consistory as established by the *Ordinances* of 1541 laymen sat with ministers in the exercise of discipline, but the consistory was not, as Calvin wished, a purely ecclesiastical court. It was rather a special branch of the municipal government. In the *Institutes* Calvin found, chiefly in the Old Testament, scriptural warrant for a purely ecclesiastical office, that of seniors elected from the Christian people to join with the ministers in the government of the Church. However the idea came to Scotland, by 1558 at the latest Protestant groups in Dundee and Edinburgh, desiring to have the 'face of a Kirk' among them, elected elders 'to punish open crimes without respect of persons'. Obedience on the part of members of the group was purely voluntary, but this was the rudimentary beginning of a Reformed Church organization. The register of what came to be known as 'the Session of the City of St. Andrew' begins in October 1559. In its section on elders and deacons the *Book of Discipline* is simply regularizing a development already well established.

'Men of best knowledge in God's word, of cleanest life, faithful men, and of most honest conversation that can be found in the Kirk' are to be nominated publicly so that from their number elders (seniors) and deacons may be chosen by vote of the congregation. Election is to take place annually 'lest that by long continuance of such officers men presume upon the liberty of the Kirk'. But provided popular election is held annually there is no harm in anyone holding office for more than one year. There is no hint of any kind of ordination to the eldership, and no salary is proposed because elders hold office normally for one year only and are not so occupied with the affairs of the Church as to prevent them from attending to their private business. Nevertheless the duties assigned to them were varied and arduous. They are to assist the minister in all public affairs of the kirk, in judging and deciding cases of discipline, in admonishing the licentious, and in watching over the manners and conversation of all under their charge, not excluding the minister and his family! If the minister fails in his duty, even if he is merely 'light in his conversation', he is to be admonished. If he proves incorrigible his elders may complain of him to the 'ministry' of two adjacent kirks. Once every year they are to report on 'the life, manners, study and diligence' of their minister 'to the ministry of the Superintendent's Kirk'. Thus it was sought to prevent in the new Church the clerical indiscipline that had been a notorious feature of the old. Very high claims were made for the new Ministry of Word and Sacraments, but by giving to the Christian people, through their popularly elected representatives, an effective voice in the government and discipline of the Church the Reformers sought to abolish clericalism, and to restore to the Church its New Testament character. On the other hand Ninian Wingate was soon to complain, as Erastus did later, that the institution of the eldership was a usurpation of the powers of the civil magistrate. The boundary between the civil and the ecclesiastical jurisdictions has never been easy to fix. The *Book of Discipline* proceeds from a clear recognition that there is a dividing line, and the jurisdiction given to the eldership has to take cognizance only of personal behaviour of church members which brings slander upon the Church. If, however, the Church claims to be coextensive with the nation, and if the distinction between crime and sin is not clearly drawn, the relations of civil and ecclesiastical jurisdiction will be obscure.

Less important was the office of deacon, which was also a development of the Genevan pattern, so far as it was applicable in Scotland. The deacons were essentially church treasurers, appointed to collect the revenues of the Church

whether accruing from rents or from alms, to keep and distribute them as the minister and elders direct, but always in
accordance with the general policy of the Church as a whole,
which includes the payment of schoolmasters and maintenance of the genuine poor. But deacons might also assist in
judgement with the minister and elders, and might be admitted to read in the assembly if required and found able
thereto. Like the elders the deacons were to be elected annually, and on demitting office must hand over to their successors accounts audited by the superintendent and any
balance in coin or in kind. Church finance proved too complicated a business to be handled by the deacons as here
visualized, and the office virtually disappeared.

The *Book of Discipline* also contains a long section setting
forth in detail an elaborate scheme of national education,
which it insists should be compulsory, aimed at instilling
wisdom, learning, and virtue into the youth of the land, so
that the Church should not lack preachers nor the commonwealth its necessary officers. Every several kirk, it is proposed,
should have its school, though in rural parishes the minister
or reader may have to undertake the task of instructing the
children in 'the rudiments' as well as in 'the Catechism of
Geneva'—Calvin's Catechism which was issued with the *Book
of Common Order*. From beginning to end education is religious
education. Every sizeable town should have a schoolmaster
able to teach Latin and grammar, and every notable town
should have a college in which should be taught 'the tongues'
(i.e. Latin and Greek) and 'of the Arts at least Logic and
Rhetoric'. Those who at college showed themselves apt for
learning should proceed to a university. It is interesting to
notice that the reason given for the multiplication of what
we would now call high schools is to avoid the dangers in-
curred when children are too early removed from the care of
their homes. There is no proposal to add to the number of
the existing universities—two were added later, Edinburgh
in 1581 and Marischal College, Aberdeen, in 1593—but
changes were proposed in their organization and curricula.
The time to be spent in every stage in the educational career
was specified, as also were the qualifications required for

passing from one stage to the next. Those who qualified were to be compelled to proceed, even if the parents were unwilling, and bursaries were to be provided so that poverty should be no obstacle. The students at a university, it is assumed, would be drawn from all classes, from the families of earls, burgesses, and peasants. At the age of twenty-four students should be ready to enter the profession of their choice, law, medicine, or the ministry, unless they were retained at the university as teachers.

Some of the details in this scheme may suggest the hand of Douglas, but the spirit in which the whole is conceived is that of Knox, for whom education and Reformation are inseparably linked. Little enough was done for a long time towards the realization of his ideal, though the government from time to time showed an interest in the universities by appointing commissions of visitation. Indeed in 1574 the Regent Morton demanded that no one should be admitted as a minister who had not studied philosophy in one of the universities of the realm and had also graduated bachelor in theology. That was to go much further than the *Book of Discipline*, and comes surprisingly from the lips of Morton who was no friend to the ministers. In that same year Andrew Melville returned to Scotland, and became the leader of the opposition to the ecclesiastical policies which Morton initiated. But at least equally important was Melville's contribution to education. As principal of Glasgow University (1574–80) he revolutionized academic studies there, and his ideas had influence elsewhere in Scotland. In 1580 he was appointed principal of St. Mary's, or the New, College in St. Andrews which became a purely theological college for the training of ministers. It is to Andrew Melville that the Scottish Church owes its ideal of an academically educated ministry.

It is obvious that the proposals made in the *Book of Discipline*, if they were to be carried out in full, would be costly. It was not suggested that ministers should be pledged to poverty. On the contrary what must be regarded as generous provision for their needs is proposed, and that for two reasons. The first is economic, and has a strangely modern ring. It is not to be expected that men will dedicate themselves to God to serve His Kirk so wholeheartedly as to look for no worldly commodity. The second may sound almost cynically realistic today, certainly more in accord with the ideas of Archbishop Hamilton than with those of St. Francis. 'Human nature being cankered as it is, men esteem virtue when they see honour and profit annexed to it, and despise it when they see virtuous and godly men living without honour!' To find cynicism here would be grossly to misread the passage which, however crudely, foreshadows the extraordinary respect for the ministry as such, which long prevailed in Scotland, and may still be found perhaps in the West Highlands. Ministers were to have manses and glebes and adequate stipends. Their sons were to have bursaries to enable them to go to school and university if they were qualified. Their daughters were to have suitable dowries when they came to marriageable age, and their widows were to be provided for. Larger stipends were to be assigned to superintendents because their office required almost constant travelling. In addition provision must be made for the maintenance of schools and universities, and also for the relief of the genuine poor.

Where was the money to come from? As yet the voluntary principle of later times was hardly dreamt of. But there were the rents and patrimony of the Kirk, which, though, distributed very unevenly amongst a great number of individual benefice-holders, in the aggregate amounted to a very large part of the national income. The section of the *Book of Discipline* dealing with this matter is none too clear and reveals a problem of very great complexity. The Reformers evidently expected or at least hoped for the total expropriation of the old churchmen, the abolition of the medieval benefice system, and the creation from the existing ecclesiastical revenues of a national endowment for the ministry, education, and poor relief. In particular they claimed (1) that the rents of the church lands belonging to the bishoprics should be used for the maintenance of the universities and the superintendents; (2) that the true patrimony of the Kirk was the teinds. The peasantry were to be relieved of the more oppressive exactions of this nature, but the great teinds were to be retained as the normal endowment of the local kirks, and were to be collected and administered by the deacons on behalf of the minister, the schoolmaster, and the poor. And (3) that rents and annual subsidies paid to hospitals, chantries, chaplaincies, colleges (in the old sense), friaries, and nunneries were to be used to supplement the teinds, and rich burgesses who paid no teind were to contribute to the support of the kirk in their burghs. It is curious that no reference is made to abbey lands which were also extensive. This can hardly be due to a desire to placate the commendators. It can only mean that these properties were admittedly lost to the Kirk beyond recall. The financial proposals of the *Book of Discipline* were bold and hardly diplomatic. In the unstable political situation of 1560 they were impracticable, and some of them remained as matters of contention till 1690.

The three documents we have been considering are of the greatest historical importance, setting forth as they do both positively and negatively the faith and programme of the Reformers, above all of John Knox. In a period of confusion and uncertainty he alone knew his own mind and had the assurance that comes of strong conviction and disinterested zeal for his cause. He was never in his lifetime a national leader in the sense that he had the whole nation behind him. His convinced and faithful followers were found mainly in the east coast towns among the more earnest and active members of the burgess class. His policy was for a long time to be a matter of bitter controversy and party strife. Nevertheless, it is an indisputable fact that his ideas and ideals have coloured the main stream of Scottish religious and ecclesiastical history since his time. It is true, of course, but quite pointless, to say that Knox was not a Presbyterian since he did not insist on ministerial 'parity', or propose a system of church government by presbyteries. Those who, a generation later, introduced that system into the Scottish Church and proudly accepted the designation Presbyterian, rightly regarded themselves as his spiritual heirs and defenders of the inheritance of doctrine and practice they had received from him.

It is another question altogether whether Knox's leadership was wise or right. That will always remain a matter of opinion. It may be regretted that the negative side of his teaching is unduly emphasized even in documents which are primarily and in the main positive and constructive. Bitterly polemical expressions occur in the *Confession of Faith* and more frequently in the *Book of Discipline*, and they offend us today who expect sweet reasonableness even in theological and ecclesiastical discussion. The extreme anti-papalism of these documents savours of revolution rather than of reform. Continuity with the old Church is explicitly disowned. It was a synagogue of Satan, by its doctrinal, ceremonial, administrative and moral corruptions disfiguring the face of the true Church. *Écrasez l'infâme!* Not continuity but restoration is the operative principle. The true Church is to be restored by a return to scriptural purity in doctrine, worship, and discipline. The Word of God must be its absolute and unique norm, for the true Church always hears and obeys the voice of her Spouse. But if formal and external continuity is slighted, the essential continuity of faith is insisted on. The Reformed Church must hold fast the basic doctrines of the Christian faith—the Trinity, the Incarnation, and salvation through Christ alone—and, always subject to the Word of God, it must witness to the Gospel and the Christian life, and thus faithfully perform its function as the God-given means of salvation for men, the function which the old Church had professed to perform, but had notoriously neglected.

II

QUEEN MARY

As we have seen, the Parliament of August 1560 had accepted by an overwhelming majority the Reformed Confession of Faith submitted to it, but made no provision for a Reformed ministry to propagate it. Nevertheless the Reformers went on with their task. The ministers who had in July been allotted to the chief towns took up their appointed duties, supported presumably by their congregations and in some instances by the town councils. On 20 December there met in Edinburgh what is usually reckoned the first General Assembly. It consisted of six ministers and some lairds and representatives of towns to the number of 41 all told and resembled the less formal gathering which in July had prepared the petition for Reformation presented to Parliament in August. Among its activities was the drawing up of a list of thirty-one persons judged qualified for the ministry. Such persons were naturally most numerous in St. Andrews, with its ecclesiastical and academic institutions, but there were others found elsewhere. Many of these were placed in pastoral charges. The assembly enjoined the organization of local churches by the election of elders and deacons wherever practicable. It noted the names of persons who encouraged the saying of Mass in their houses or parish churches contrary to law, and demanded their punishment. Finally it required at least one commissioner from every kirk to come to Edinburgh on 15 January supplied with a roll of the local ecclesiastical revenues from all sources, in view of the fact that a parliament, or at least a convention of nobles, was to be held about that time.

To this convention the *Book of Discipline* was at last submitted, and Knox gives an account of its mixed reception. Some were in favour of giving legislative effect to its proposals, but the majority refused, saying that these were 'devote imaginationis'. Knox attributes this hostility, even on the part of professed Protestants, to avarice and the desire to obtain church lands or to retain those already seized or otherwise acquired. Doubtless this motive was present, but there would also be some realization of the immensity of the proposed changes in the traditional benefice system. On 27 January, however, the Privy Council gave approval to the book with certain notes and additions and the twenty-seven signatories promised

to set the same forward to the uttermost of our powers; providing that the Bishops, Abbots, Priors and other Prelates and beneficed men who have adjoined themselves to us continue to enjoy the revenues of their benefices for life, they sustaining and upholding the Ministry and Ministers, as is herein specified, for preaching of the Word and ministering of the Sacraments of God.

This was ostensibly to make the ministry a charge upon the benefices of those who had accepted the *Confession of Faith*, a rather severe test of their sincerity!

Nevertheless the Kirk proceeded with the policy as best it might. On 9 March Spottiswoode was admitted superintendent of Lothian, in the prescribed form, and on 20 April Winram was similarly admitted superintendent of Fife, Strathearn, and Perthshire. In due course Willock, Erskine of Dun, and Carswell were admitted superintendents of the 'West', Angus, and Argyll and the Isles respectively. No others were appointed although nominations were made later for Aberdeen and Jedburgh. As instances of beneficed men who joined the Reformers, Alexander Gordon, Bishop of Galloway and titular Archbishop of Athens, should be mentioned together with Adam Bothwell, Bishop of Orkney, and Robert Stewart, unconsecrated Bishop of Caithness. There was no suggestion that they might continue their order. At most they received partial and temporary commissions to plant and superintend kirks within their dioceses. Gordon and Stewart were not always satisfactory, but there is ample evidence that the other superintendents took their duties seriously. They are, it is true, often accused of negligence, perhaps because the impossible was expected of them. Erskine of Dun, for example, was charged with admitting too easily as readers

conforming vicars of the old order who were unqualified for
the office, but in what other way could he have readily
found any ministry for the parishes in which these vicars
held the manses and stipends? The St. Andrews Kirk Session
Register bears eloquent witness to the difficult and exacting
nature of the superintendent's work, and to Winram's diligence in performing it. Carswell, it is interesting to note,
published a Gaelic translation of the *Book of Common Order*
for the use of ministers and readers in his wild diocese. John
Knox, it should be added, would not accept appointment
as a superintendent. As minister of Edinburgh he occupied
a central and strategic position from which to watch over the
interests of the Church. He had there the support of a devoted
congregation among the citizens as well as of the town
council.

It was no part of Knox's teaching that there must be conflict between Church and State, but the claims he made on
behalf of the Church rendered such conflict inevitable. His
noble allies disappointed him, partly because of their selfish
greed for the spoils of the Church but partly also because
of their handling of an extraordinarily difficult political
situation. In 1560 Francis II and Mary, King and Queen of
France, were also the sovereigns of Scotland. It was necessary, therefore, to obtain their approval for the legislation of
Parliament. For this purpose Sir James Sandilands, Lord
St. John, was dispatched to the court of France, where, as
might have been expected, he was dismissed with scant
courtesy. Mary regarded her Scottish subjects, in spite of all
their protestations of love and loyalty, as little better than
rebels. She said so openly to the English ambassador when he
pressed for ratification of the treaty of Edinburgh. It would
be time enough for her to relinquish her claim to the English
Crown when the Scots had returned to the obedience due
to their queen. Her attitude suggested that France might
attempt a reconquest of Scotland and forced the Scottish
leaders to seek to strengthen their alliance with England.
They proposed that Elizabeth of England should marry the
Earl of Arran, son and heir of the Duke of Châtelherault!
Thus, they pointed out, would the two kingdoms forget old

enmities and live in amity to the increase of Elizabeth's power. Elizabeth's advisers and the English Protestants favoured the match, and to humour them she toyed for a time with the idea before finally rejecting it on 8 December. Three days earlier the death of Francis II had changed the political situation in France, and made the future of his young widow a major concern of European diplomacy.

Could Mary have been content to be merely Queen of Scots, she might have been a happier if less important woman. But was she not also the rightful Queen of England? She made that claim herself, or allowed it to be made on her behalf, when Mary Tudor died in 1558, and the challenge to Elizabeth of England became more serious when in 1570 the Pope excommunicated her as a heretic. Mary thus became in the eyes of Roman Catholics everywhere the hope of the Counter-Reformation in England. Fortunately for Elizabeth, France and Spain, the two chief Romanist powers, were irreconcilable political rivals. Their mutual jealousies and internal troubles prevented either of them from intervening during the earlier years of her reign when her throne was far from secure. By 1588 when the great Spanish Armada was launched the danger had greatly diminished.

In Scotland the death of King Francis with the consequent fall of the Guises from power in France brought a welcome relief from fear of invasion. But it meant also that Mary, their niece, would almost certainly return to her native land, which she had left as a child thirteen years before. Most Scots of all parties in fact desired her return, but with different objects in view. The Romanist prelates were confident that she would be able and willing to undo the Reformation and restore them to their lost estate. Beaton, Archbishop of Glasgow, had been with Mary in France since the summer of 1560. He would be able to inform her of the sufferings of his colleagues and to assure her of their support. Early in 1561 Lesley, a prominent cleric of the diocese of Aberdeen, came to say that if she would come to Aberdeen Huntly and the northern earls were prepared to put a force of 20,000 men at her disposal, so that she might crush her enemies and enter Edinburgh in triumph. Finally there came the Lord James

N

Stewart, her half-brother, representing the dominant Protestant party, and promising, most likely, their support for her claim to the throne of England, at least to the extent of attempting to persuade Elizabeth to acknowledge Mary as her successor. They had hopes that if Mary should come to Scotland she would realize that an English alliance was preferable to the French one which few Scots now desired, and might even come to see that the throne of England was worth a Prayer Book! With all these encouragements Mary therefore resolved to return.

Elizabeth, not unnaturally in view of the fact that the treaty of Edinburgh was still unratified, refused Mary permission to travel through England. Eventually she arrived by sea at Leith on a drizzly August day in 1561, and took up her abode at Holyrood amid surroundings very different from those to which she had been accustomed at the most refined and elegant court in Europe. Her grief at leaving France is understandable, but she was young—only nineteen—and gay, and with her Four Maries as ladies-in-waiting, and a retinue of French courtiers and domestics, she determined to make the best of it. Her dancings and banquetings caused the sober citizens of Edinburgh to shake their heads, but they won for her much popularity, and that was enhanced by her personal beauty and natural affability. Moreover she was well-educated in the school of the French Renaissance, and highly intelligent; but the problems that were to confront her in her turbulent kingdom were intricate and intractable.

The chief difficulty was that Mary, a convinced Roman Catholic, was called on to govern a people the majority of whom had recently declared for Protestantism. But the situation was still fluid, and had Mary's sole ambition been to reimpose Romanism on Scotland she might have achieved it by accepting the proferred aid of Huntly, the acknowledged champion of her faith. Strange as it must seem she chose to commit herself to the Protestant party whose ostensible leader was Lord James Stewart, her half-brother, behind whom stood Maitland of Lethington, the brain of the party. However much these men might differ from the queen in the matter of religion both of them were ardent supporters of her claim to the throne of England. Lord James she created Earl of Moray and under his guidance made triumphal progresses through various parts of her kingdom, accompanying him even on the campaign in which he overthrew the vast power of Huntly, 'the Cock o' the North', and so weakened the Romanist cause.

Moreover, in February 1562 Mary made at least a gesture in favour of the Reformed Church. With the advice of her Privy Council she laid a tax of one-third upon all ecclesiastical benefices to meet 'the needs of the Queen's Majesty, the common weal of the realm and the sustentation of the preachers and readers'. Machinery was set up to collect the tax, 'the Thirds' as it was called, and to allocate the proceeds as prescribed. It was enacted further that the revenues of chaplaincies and friaries erected within the towns should be taken over by the town councils to be applied for the maintenance of schools and hospitals. These enactments might be regarded as a modest first step towards implementing the programme of the *Book of Discipline*. But it soon became apparent that the needs of the queen and her government would have first claim upon the Thirds, leaving little for the sustentation of the ministry. There was besides a still deeper cause for dissatisfaction.

On the Sunday following Mary's arrival in Edinburgh arrangements were made for Mass to be celebrated by her French chaplains in her chapel at Holyrood. The news reached the town and a mob surged down to the palace and were only prevented by the intervention of the Lord James in person from breaking in and disturbing the service. Next day a proclamation was issued to the effect that no one was to attempt alteration or innovation of the state of religion then subsisting pending an early meeting of the Estates at which the queen hoped for a final settlement to the contentment of all. Further, her good and loving subjects were forbidden to molest persons of the court who had come with her from France. Nothing was said of the legality or otherwise of the parliamentary Acts of 1560, but it soon became evident that the Lords of the Council, all of them Protestants, were determined to guarantee to Mary and her court, at Holyrood and elsewhere, the free exercise of her religion in spite of the Act against saying and hearing Mass. To many of her subjects such toleration gave offence for they held the Mass to be illegal and, worse still, idolatrous. From his pulpit in St. Giles Knox declared that one Mass was more fearful to him than if ten thousand men were landed in the country on purpose to suppress the whole religion. He had in mind the Old Testament threatenings against a land polluted with idolatry. But he also believed he saw in their toleration of the queen's Mass a sign of weakening in their allegiance to the Reformation on the part of the nobles who had been his allies. And of course the queen's example encouraged others to follow it openly. He at once took issue with the Lords and his intransigence led to a rupture of relations with the Lord James who had been hitherto his best friend among the nobility and his most sincere and consistent supporter.

Between Queen Mary and John Knox there could be no understanding. Before she set foot in Scotland Mary had declared that he was the most dangerous man in her kingdom, which could not hold both of them, and Knox could never forget that she was a niece of the Guises, the mortal enemies of his brethren in France. Mary had strong views as to the obedience due from subjects to their princes, and Knox's views were equally strong on the duty of a preacher to declare the truth of God's Word and to rebuke sinners. Mary, naturally, did not 'attend sermon' in St. Giles, but some of Knox's sharper utterances were reported to her at Holyrood, e.g. his attack on her Mass, his denunciation of the dancing and fiddling at court, and worst of all his call to the nobility to resist her proposed Spanish marriage. Four times he was summoned to the royal presence on account of such utterances and in the Fourth Book of his *History* he has set down what took place. His behaviour has been and will be variously judged. On the first three occasions Mary does not seem to have felt aggrieved, though no doubt his plainness of speech was not what she had been accustomed to. But his attack on the Spanish marriage was another matter. She was furious, and wept tears of anger.

What have you to do with my marriage? Or what are you within this Commonwealth?

A subject, Madam, born within the same. And albeit I neither be Earl, Lord nor Baron within it, yet has God made me (how abject that ever I be in your eyes) a profitable member within the same: Yea, Madam, to me it pertains no less to forewarn of such things as may hurt it, if I foresee them, than it does to any of the Nobility.

It would be an anachronism to interpret this as the voice of democracy. It was the voice of the preacher conscious of his vocation 'to speak plainly and to flatter no flesh'. Mary was not long in finding an opportunity for an interview of a very different kind. One Sunday when Mass was to be said as usual in Holyrood, though the queen was not present, two members of Knox's flock entered the chapel with no friendly intent. They were arrested and a day fixed for their trial. Knox circulated a letter to his Protestant brethren in various parts of the country asking them to assemble in Edinburgh on the day of the trial, to take counsel together. The letter fell into the hands of the queen and she summoned Knox to answer before the Privy Council on a charge of treason. He defended himself at length and, to the bitter chagrin of Mary, was acquitted, with the concurrence of his worst enemy, Henry Sinclair, Bishop of Ross and president of the Court of Session.

In her interviews with Knox Mary made no secret of her adherence to the Church of Rome in which she had been brought up. She even entered into argument with him as to its authority. But there was another pressing subject of debate. Was Knox not the author of the First Blast against female rule, and did he not teach subjects to resist their princes? Mary always professed to be willing to tolerate his religion, and no Act of the reign belies that profession. When in 1565 the assembly petitioned 'that the papistical and blasphemous Masse, with all papistry and idolatry . . . be abolished through the haill realm, not only in the subjects, but also in the Queens Majesties awin person' she answered that 'Her Hienes is no-wayes yet persuaded in the said religion, nor yet that any impiety is in the Masse'. She prays 'all her loving subjects, seeing they have had experience of her goodness that she neither has in tymes bypast, nor means heirafter to press the conscience of any man, but that they may worship God in sick sort as they are persuaded to be best, that they also will not press her to offend her awin conscience'. It is true that in her correspondence with the Pope she professed eagerness to bring her kingdom back to the Roman allegiance, but, though repeatedly urged by papal letters and emissaries to emulate the example of Mary Tudor, she always refused to do so. It was on these professions of tolerance that the Protestant Lords, inspired by Lethington, based their hopes that she would, as they did, put political expediency before religion and become a Protestant at least after the fashion of Elizabeth. Lethington may have believed, as some of his modern admirers have done, that Knox was the sole obstacle to the realization of these hopes, and certainly Knox was as obnoxious to Elizabeth as to Mary. The real obstacle lay elsewhere. Elizabeth, for reasons which should have been obvious, would not declare Mary her successor; and Mary's heart was set on marriage with Don Carlos, heir of Philip II of Spain. Had that marriage taken place it would have aligned Mary irrevocably with the most determined power behind the Counter-Reformation, and would have presented the most dangerous threat to Elizabeth's security. Lethington at least toyed with the idea of the Spanish match as a counter in the diplomatic game though he must have known that it would have been fatal to his cherished purpose of amity between Scotland and England.

Lethington was of a spirit completely antipathetic to that of Knox. The encounters between the diplomat-politician and the forthright preacher were less picturesque than those between Knox and the queen, but more significant as opening a rift between the political and the religious forces which had acted together in 1560, a rift which, partially closed in 1567, in 1638, and 1690, has left an abiding mark on Scottish church history. Of the two debaters Lethington will almost certainly win the approval of the modern mind, yet it cannot be denied that his policy led him into endless 'shifts' and soon proved a dismal failure. By 1565 Mary was turning to other counsellors, and was confiding chiefly, not in her secretary of state, but in her private secretary, the Italian, David Rizzio, who had no interest but to do what she commanded. Her marriage to her cousin, Lord Darnley, in July 1565 shattered Lethington's party, and was the beginning of Mary's tragedy, which it is not necessary to set out in detail here; her estrangement from her vain and foolish husband; the murder of Rizzio at Darnley's instigation; Darnley's own murder contrived, it was suspected, by Bothwell, followed immediately by Mary's marriage to Bothwell; her surrender to her indignant subjects, her imprisonment, and forced abdication in Lochleven Castle; her escape and flight to England to the serious embarrassment of Elizabeth; the plots and intrigues of which she was the not unwilling centre; and finally her execution in 1587. It is a pitiful story out of which none of the actors emerges with credit. The sufferings of the Queen of Scots must evoke sympathy for her personally, even in those who can have no sympathy with the part she chose to play in history. On 23 July 1567, in the castle of Lochleven, she demitted the government in favour of her infant son, 'native prince of this our realm', who was destined to take up Lethington's controversy with the Kirk and in 1603 to realize his dream of a peaceful union of the Scottish and English Crowns on terms honourable to both kingdoms.

III

CHURCH AND STATE UNDER
JAMES VI, 1567–1625

IN abdicating in favour of her son, then little more than a
year old, Mary named her 'dearest brother', the Earl of
Moray, as regent until James should have completed his
seventeenth year. Moray was then absent in France, but on
his return he accepted office and was proclaimed regent.
There were some, of course, who thought Mary had been
hardly used, and there were others who on personal grounds
resented the promotion of Moray. The Hamiltons, for example, thought that the head of their family, old Châtelherault, should have had the regency. When in 1568 Mary
escaped from Lochleven her friends rallied to her side, but
they were speedily defeated at Langside, and Mary's only
course seemed to be to put herself under the protection of
Elizabeth. There remained, however, a queen's party in
Scotland who hoped for her restoration, and their numbers
grew when it became evident that she was no longer in-
fatuated with Bothwell. Among these later adherents were
the chivalrous Kirkaldy of Grange, made captain of Edinburgh Castle by Moray, and Knox's old antagonist, Lethington. The assassination of Moray by a Hamilton in 1570 was
the signal for the outbreak of civil war. Lennox, the father of
Darnley and grandfather of King James, succeeded Moray as
regent, but he was killed in 1571 in an encounter with a party
of the queen's men. His successor was the Earl of Mar who
formerly, as Lord Erskine, had held Edinburgh Castle for
Mary of Lorraine in 1559. He died in 1572, and was succeeded by the Earl of Morton, the strong man of the king's
party, and a stout upholder of the English alliance. In 1573
he persuaded Elizabeth to send him artillery and engineers,
with which aid he reduced Edinburgh Castle, the last stronghold of the queen's party. From then until 1580 he ruled

Scotland with a firm hand, giving the country a period of peace. Personally unpopular, Morton was known to be solidly Protestant, and he profited from the wave of horror that swept over the Protestant world when the news of the massacre of the French Huguenots on St. Bartholomew's Day 1572 was spread abroad.

Morton paid too little attention to the precocious young king, and allowed him, now fourteen years old, to be completely won by his kinsman, Esmé Stuart, Lord D'Aubigny, who came from France in 1579 ostensibly to congratulate him on his accession. But D'Augbigny was widely suspected of being an agent of the French government sent to break off the Anglo-Scottish alliance, and to bring the King of Scots back to the French alliance and to Romanism. To the alarm of Queen Elizabeth, James made him Lord High Chamberlain and a privy councillor, and created him Earl and then Duke of Lennox. Morton's downfall was speedily accomplished, and in 1581, in spite of Elizabeth's attempts to save him, he was executed on a charge of complicity in the murder of Darnley, the king's father. Lennox's power was of short duration. It was brought to an end by a group of Protestant Lords who seized the person of the king, and attempted to rule in his name. James escaped from the 'Ruthven Raiders' and for two years (1583–5) was guided principally by another Stuart, an associate of Lennox whom he created Earl of Arran. Arran was hostile to the Reformed Church and showed his hostility in what are known as the Black Acts. His fall in 1585 made way for wiser counsels. Sir John Maitland of Thirlestane, brother of Lethington, as chancellor, brought about an understanding with Elizabeth, and a treaty was made in 1586 on the basis of a common Protestantism, each country promising to come to the aid of the other should it be invaded. Almost as soon as it was signed the treaty was put to a severe test, for the English government proceeded to put Queen Mary on trial for her part in the Babington Plot, and she was executed on 8 February 1587. Popular sentiment in Scotland was outraged, but James contented himself with a protest.

The Anglo-Scottish 'Protestant League' of 1586 enabled

James to devote himself to the better government of his kingdom, and his achievement in this respect is remarkable. In 1587 Parliament was made more representative by the inclusion of commissioners of the shires, elected by the barons or lairds who had discovered a new interest in politics since the Reformation. 'Justice Aires' were re-established for the administration of justice throughout the kingdom, and new rules were adopted for securing competent judges in the Court of Session. Steps were taken for the pacification of the Highlands and Islands, including plans for colonization by lowlanders. Something also was done to bring to an end the feuds among the nobility which had been a continual source of dispeace. The lenient treatment accorded to the rebellious earls of Huntly and Errol was doubtless part of this policy. Though unattractive in person, undignified in speech and behaviour, timorous and pedantic, James was more successful than any of his predecessors in curbing feudal anarchy and in establishing law and order in his kingdom to its general well-being. His most intractable problem was the Reformed Kirk, but here too he was ultimately successful, partly by guile, and partly by adroit use of the extravagances of some of its ministers. He must be credited with giving to Scotland the strong government which it had lacked since the death of James IV at Flodden, and there was some justification for his boast, when at last he ascended the throne of England in 1603, 'Here I sit and govern Scotland by my pen, which others could not do by the sword.' James was immensely proud of his 'Kingcraft', and before he left Scotland he expounded its principles in a treatise written for the benefit of his eldest son, Prince Henry, and entitled *Basilicon Doron*. His doctrine might be described today as absolute monarchy, but he preferred to call it the Divine Right of Kings. It would be easy to charge him with hypocrisy or absurdity, but perhaps it would be fair to say that for James the doctrine of Divine Right expressed his consciousness of his divine calling as king over against the consciousness in Knox and Melville of their divine vocation as preachers. However that may be, conflict between the king and the Kirk was the outstanding feature of the long reign of James VI.

The appointment of Moray as regent must have been welcome to the Reformers. Moray had been prominent among them since 1559, a close friend and ally of Knox until their familiarity was broken by Moray's inclining to the policy of Lethington in connexion with the queen's Mass. The friendship was renewed when that policy broke down after the Darnley marriage. One of Moray's first acts as regent was to hold a Parliament in December 1567, in which the Acts of 1560 were re-enacted, so removing all question as to their legality for the future. Further legislation was passed in favour of the Reformed Church. The *Confession of Faith* was not merely reaffirmed but was made a test for all who should hold office under the Crown, or teach in schools and universities. A Coronation Oath was devised binding the sovereign to maintain the true Kirk and root out heretics and enemies to the true worship of God. The *Book of Discipline* was not given legislative sanction, and its financial proposals were not followed. The benefice system was untouched, save that the tax of a Third on benefices was continued, and its collection was put in the hands of collectors appointed by the Church and responsible to church authorities in the first instance. Ministerial stipends were to be regarded as having a first claim on the proceeds of the tax, so that they were now paid more regularly. This was declared to be a temporary expedient 'until the Kirk come to the full possession of their proper patrimony which is the teinds'. But the teinds proved a thorny problem which remained unsolved for a long time. It was enacted, however, that henceforth when a benefice became vacant the patron, who must in many cases have been an ecclesiastic of the old order, should present a qualified person to be examined by the superintendent or other commissioner of the Reformed Church and admitted by him if found satisfactory. In this way ministers of the Reformed faith would in time obtain possession of the parochial benefices, that is parsonages and vicarages. No reference was made to the greater benefices such as abbacies and bishoprics. In 1567 practically all the abbacies were in the hands of lay commendators, who were usually members of noble families, and the bishoprics, with the exception of four, were still held by prelates of the old Church. All these were subject to the deduction of the Third, unless the possessors compounded by undertaking responsibility for the support of the ministry in parishes annexed to their benefices.

The first bishopric to fall vacant was St. Andrews when in 1571 Archbishop Hamilton was captured in arms against the king's government and hanged for treason. The regent, Mar, acting for the crown as lawful patron since papal authority was abrogated, appointed as Archbishop John Douglas, provost of St. Mary's College and rector of the University of St. Andrews. There was an immediate outcry, although he was a prominent Protestant and joint author of the *Confession of Faith* and the *Book of Discipline*. He was an infirm old man, quite unfit for the arduous duties that the holder of that office might be expected to perform. Perhaps neither the regent nor Douglas anticipated that there would be properly ecclesiastical duties, the appointment being regarded as a mere device to keep the archiepiscopal benefice in being. Douglas was not required to surrender his academic appointments, and nothing was determined as to what were to be his relations with the superintendents of Fife, Lothian, and Angus, who had all been exercising ecclesiastical authority over areas that belonged to the ancient diocese of St. Andrews. Erskine of Dun, superintendent of Angus, at once protested to the regent. 'A greater offence or contempt of God and his kirk can no prince do, than to set up by his authority men in spiritual offices, or to create bishops and pastors of the Kirk: . . . for the Kirk cannot be without it have its own proper jurisdiction and liberty, with the ministration of such offices as God hath appointed.' Erskine had no objection to the word bishop which he held to be equivalent to superintendent; nor did he deny the right of the crown to present to bishoprics, but as Douglas had not been examined or admitted by any ecclesiastical authority, he regarded him as an intruder having neither office nor jurisdiction in the Kirk of God. The superintendents in office who had been 'orderly placed by the Kirk' must continue to exercise their functions in the areas assigned to them.

In view of this protest a Convention, or extraordinary

General Assembly of the Kirk, met in 1572 in Leith, Edinburgh still being controlled by the queen's party. Among other things it appointed a strong commission, including the superintendent of Angus, with full powers to confer with a committee of the Privy Council and come to an understanding. The result was what is commonly known as 'the Concordat of Leith'. For the first time the vexed question of the greater benefices was treated in a thorough-going way. It was agreed that the archbishoprics and bishoprics were to remain as they were, at least till the king attained his majority. Cathedral chapters were also to remain as they had been until the members died out, when they were to be replaced by chapters consisting of the ministers of important churches in the diocese. Meantime interim arrangements were made. For example at St. Andrews Winram and Spottiswoode were to act as archdeacons of St. Andrews and Lothian respectively. Nomination to vacant bishoprics was to be made by the king, and chapters were to examine and elect the royal nominee! After consecration the new bishop was to take an oath of allegiance to the king, renouncing all foreign jurisdiction and acknowledging the king as the only lawful and supreme governor of this realm, as well in things temporal as in the conservation and purgation of religion. Ecclesiastically the bishops were to have no more power than the superintendents had had, and like the latter were to be subject to the General Assembly. But, though it is not explicitly stated, it was doubtless intended that they would have seats in Parliament. Care to preserve the constitution by the restoration of the Spiritual Estate becomes more explicit in the article dealing with the abbacies. There was no question of retaining the old monastic system beyond the lifetime of surviving monks, but abbots and priors in some form were constitutionally necessary as members of Parliament and as senators of the College of Justice. They were therefore to be retained in the familiar form of lay commendators. In vacancies the king was to have the right of nomination, and the bishop of the diocese was to 'examine and admit', though the commendators were only in name clergy. It was not proposed to sever appropriated churches from the appropriating abbey or priory, but on appointment the commendator was to undertake the obligation to provide stipends for the ministers of these churches.

Other matters affecting lesser benefices were dealt with, such as nunneries, provostries, and canonries. Everywhere it is evident that there is tenderness towards vested interests and traditional institutions. It must be remembered that the country was in the throes of civil war, and the outcome was still in doubt. All the bishops in possession, including three of the Protestant ones, were on the queen's side; and while in St. Andrews practically all of the old clergy had conformed to the new order, in Glasgow only six of the thirty-two canons had entered the Reformed ministry. One paragraph however in the Leith Agreement declares that all who hold any kind of ecclesiastical benefice shall at least publicly assent to and subscribe the Articles of Religion set forth in the Confession of Faith received by Parliament and take an oath acknowledging the king's supreme authority. This was enacted by Parliament in 1573 when the war was over, and meant the ejection from their benefices of some who continued loyal to the Romanist faith.

The Earl of Morton had a hand in formulating the Articles of Leith, and they reflect his ideas. He wanted the Church of Scotland to be constituted as like the Church of England as possible, though as a concession he was prepared to allow that the bishops might be subject to the General Assembly. What was of primary importance was that the Church should be subject to the supreme power of the Crown, as in England. Without waiting for the assembly to consider the agreement, Morton following the forms there prescribed carried through the nomination and election of Douglas to St. Andrews. At his admission Knox preached a sermon in which he expressed misgivings; Winram 'admitted', using the form prescribed in the *Book of Common Order* for the admission of superintendents; and the Bishop of Caithness, Spottiswoode, superintendent of Lothian and David Lindsay, minister of Leith 'consecrated' with imposition of hands. Similar procedure was followed in Glasgow when James Boyd was made archbishop.

When the agreement came before the assembly in August 1572 the members seem to have been remarkably acquiescent. There was criticism of the revival of such titles as archbishop, dean, archdeacon, on the ground that they were unscriptural, sounded popish and were offensive to many of the brethren. These were reassured by the Church's own signatories to the agreement that there was no intention to reintroduce popery. Moreover the assembly received a letter from Knox, now in retirement at St. Andrews, urging that 'all bishoprics vacant be presented, and qualified persons nominated thereto . . . according to the order taken at Leith'. Whatever Knox may have thought of the appointment of the aged Douglas, he must have come to the conclusion that only in the way proposed at Leith was it possible financially to secure the appointment of bishops or superintendents for districts which hitherto had been inadequately supervised by temporary commissioners and visitors. But it is evident that he shared the widespread suspicion that the new order might be used as a device for diverting the revenues of the bishoprics into lay hands. It was whispered that Douglas had entered into an arrangement with Morton whereby the latter might enjoy a large part of the archbishop's 'rents'. Knox therefore further urged the assembly to ordain that 'all Bishops admitted by the order of the Kirk now received give account of their whole rents and intromissions therewith once in the year as the Kirk shall appoint'! Knox's work was now nearly done. He died on 24 November 1572 and was buried in the churchyard of St. Giles in the presence of Morton, who two days earlier had succeeded Mar as regent, and who said at the graveside of the Reformer: 'There lies one who neither feared nor flattered any flesh.'

As regent, Morton put the Articles of Leith into operation regardless of criticism and opposition. As destroyer of the queen's party and the champion of Protestantism he was in a strong position. The Reformed Kirk could not afford to quarrel with him. Within four years he had filled all the bishoprics with his own nominees. Strangely enough of the four experienced superintendents actually in office only one, Carswell, was made a bishop—of the Isles. With the other

three, Winram, Spottiswoode, and Erskine of Dun, Archbishop Douglas had jurisdictional disputes and Winram had
to be content with the title of superintendent of Strathearn.
Morton's bishops cannot have been very happy. None of
them was remarkable for character or zeal. Their benefices
were burdened with pensions to Morton's friends, and they
were popularly derided as 'Tulchans', the name given to
straw-stuffed calf skins which country folk used to induce
their cows to give milk more freely! By the General Assembly
they were handled as rigorously as the superintendents had
been. Perhaps the best of them was James Boyd of Glasgow
who was elected moderator of the General Assembly in
March 1574 and long retained the confidence of his brethren.
But a special interest attaches to Patrick Adamson who succeeded Douglas at St. Andrews in 1576. He was one of the
bright young graduates of St. Andrews whom the General
Assembly in 1560 judged 'qualified to minister', and he was
soon placed, perhaps against his will, as minister at Ceres in
Fife. Dissatisfied with his post he pressed for permission to
study abroad. This was refused, but he resigned in 1564, and
spent the next eight years in study and other more exciting
experiences in France and Geneva. In 1572 he returned to
Scotland with the reputation of a distinguished Latinist and
an eloquent preacher, and with hopes perhaps of nomination
to the archbishopric of St. Andrews. When Douglas was preferred Adamson had to be content for the time being to serve
as minister of Paisley, relieving the sense of disappointment
by a well-known quip: 'There be three sorts of Bishops. My
Lord Bishop was in the Papistry: My Lord's Bishop is now,
when my Lord gets the benefice and the Bishop serves for
nothing but to make his title sure: and The Lord's Bishop is
the true Minister of the Gospel.' Nevertheless Adamson in-
gratiated himself with the regent and on the death of Douglas obtained the coveted position. On Adamson fell the brunt
of the battle with the Melvilles.

The Concordat of Leith has been regarded as a severely
practical expedient to tide over the difficult period of the
king's minority. It sought to preserve intact the Ecclesiastical Estate in Parliament, a constitutional matter of great

importance, and from it the Church had much to gain without sacrificing any essential principle. But it soon became evident that Morton had other ends to serve. He was aiming at the enhancement of the royal authority over the Church, and possibly at the ultimate secularisation of the church lands. Some of his nominees to bishoprics did not inspire confidence, and the assembly claimed the right itself to examine them before their admission. The opposition found a leader when in 1574 Andrew Melville, after years of academic teaching in Beza's Geneva, returned to his native land and was appointed principal of the Glasgow College. His services to university education in Scotland have been referred to, but his fame today rests chiefly on his contribution to ecclesiastical politics. At his prompting, it is said, John Dury, one of the ministers of Edinburgh, propounded in the General Assembly, August 1575, the fateful question: Whether the bishops, as they are now in the Kirk of Scotland, have their function of the Word of God or not, or if the chapters appointed for creating them ought to be tolerated in this reformed Kirk. The question has, of course, nothing to do with their uncanonical consecration! The assembly appointed a committee of six including Andrew Melville and David Lindsay, one of the Leith signatories, to examine the question, and they reported at a later session. They declined to give a direct answer to the question, but they agreed that

the name of Bishop is common to all those that have a particular flock over which they have charge to preach the word, minister the sacraments and execute the ecclesiastical discipline with consent of the elders . . . but of this number may be chosen some to have power to oversee and visit such reasonable bounds besides their own flocks, as the General Kirk shall appoint . . . to appoint ministers with the consent of the Ministers of that province and the consent of the flock to whom they shall be appointed, to appoint Elders and Deacons where there are none, with the consent of the people, and to suspend ministers for reasonable causes.

In other words a bishop is essentially the pastor of one congregation, and any supervision he may exercise beyond his own congregation is a duty entrusted to him by a church authority in addition to his proper work. Morton's bishops were there-fore called upon to regularize their position by taking upon them each a particular kirk! Boyd of Glasgow was prepared to come half-way to meet this requirement.

In April 1576 the assembly again debated this report and approved it by a majority. It also with some encouragement from the regent appointed a strong committee to discuss the policy and proper jurisdiction of the Church and to submit draft proposals. This question had been mooted in 1564, and Knox had noted its urgency in 1572. It had a foremost place on the agenda of General Assemblies until in April 1578 what we now know as the second *Book of Discipline* was approved by the Church. Unhappily but inevitably, the Church had in the meantime quarrelled with the regent. In October 1576 the assembly was informed that Patrick Adam-son, now the regent's chaplain, had been nominated to the vacant archbishopric of St. Andrews, and it claimed the right to examine him prior to his admission. Adamson, in the regent's name, protested that this was not in the agreement, but was understood to say that he would obey the assembly. Before the next assembly met in April 1577 Adamson had been elected and admitted to St. Andrews. A committee, there-fore, was appointed to charge him with intrusion and usur-pation, and to prohibit him from performing his functions. The regent was furious. He questioned the right of the Kirk to convene the king's lieges without the royal consent, and he declared the country would never have peace until a dozen ministers were hanged! Morton was ready enough to hang his enemies; but Melville stood firm, supported by his old patron Beza who was consulted by the government on the points at issue. Under these circumstances it was unlikely that the second *Book of Discipline*, which was largely Melville's work, would receive the approval of the regent. The assembly could only engross it in its records *ad perpetuam rei memoriam*.[1]

Nevertheless the second *Book of Discipline* or *Heads and Con-clusions of the Policy of the Church* is important as setting forth the principles of what has come to be known as Presby-terianism, and its authority was recognized by a large party

[1] Excerpts in *Source Book of Scottish History*, vol. iii, pp. 22 ff.

in the Church of Scotland until it was superseded by the Westminster form of church government. In some ways it is a disappointing document, lacking the precision and clarity of the contemporary document of similar inspiration drawn up for England by Travers and Cartwright. It has been unfavourably contrasted with the first *Book of Discipline* on the ground of its more strictly limited scope. But conditions had greatly changed and the Reformed Church had passed from the first fervent missionary phase of its existence to one where organization had become the primary consideration. In particular an answer was required to the situation that was developing as a consequence of the Concordat of Leith. The liberty of the Kirk *vis-à-vis* the State seemed to be in danger.

The book opens with a clear-cut distinction between civil government and ecclesiastical government, the power of the sword and the power of the keys, and claims that the latter derives immediately from God in Christ. The Christian magistrate or godly prince may purge the Kirk when it is corrupt, but when the ministry is lawfully constituted and does its duty faithfully the magistrate or prince ought to assist to maintain and fortify it in its functions, jurisdictions, and patrimony and submit to its discipline if he transgress in matters of conscience and religion. Within the ministry in the broad sense there are four ordinary offices, (*a*) pastor, minister, or bishop; (*b*) doctor or teacher; (*c*) presbyter or elder; and (*d*) deacon. All of these function within their own particular flock, by whose consent they are elected, and it would seem that all of them are to be ordained with fasting, earnest prayer, and imposition of the hands of the 'eldership'. Pastors, under whatever name, are preachers of the Word, ministers of the Sacraments, and watchmen set over the manners of their flocks. Elders are associated with the pastors 'for establishing of good order and the execution of discipline'. Theirs is a spiritual office, and once lawfully called to it they may not leave it, although where there are many elders they may serve in rotation. In 1560 elders, though their functions are the same, were to be elected annually, so that there has been some enhancement in the status of the office. It is to some extent assimilated to the ministry of word and sacrament and yet clearly distinguished from it. The government of the Church is by assemblies in which pastors and elders equally take part. They are of four sorts, congregational, provincial, national, and ecumenical, all having power to meet at times and places determined by themselves. Their purpose is to keep religion and doctrine pure, to make rules to that effect and to discipline transgressors. They form a hierarchy of church courts in which the acts of the lower court are subject to review in the higher. The National or General Assembly, representative of the whole Kirk within the realm, overrules the congregational and provincial assemblies, and takes responsibility for all important matters that concern the welfare and good order of the national Church. It has often been pointed out that the presbytery as now known is nowhere clearly defined in the *Book of Discipline*, though the local 'eldership' is not limited to a single congregation, as is a modern kirk session, and the powers of ordination and of visitation assigned to it suggest that it is not a kirk session simply but a presbytery as now understood. The problem of the patrimony of the Kirk is briefly and drastically but unrealistically dealt with. The patrimony includes all endowments given or to be given to the Kirk, lands and rents as well as teinds and manses and the oblations of the faithful! It is the office of the deacons to collect all ecclesiastical revenues from every source and to distribute them for the maintenance of the ministry, the schools and the poor. The book concludes with a long list of abuses remaining in the Kirk for which Reformation is craved from the godly magistrate. All papistical titles should be abolished. Bishops should become the ministers of particular kirks, and should not usurp the office of visitation of other kirks nor any other function beyond those of other ministers, except so far as shall be committed to them by the Kirk. Nor should they sit and vote in Parliament. The General Assembly should be free to meet and determine ecclesiastical causes without appeal to any judge, civil or ecclesiastical, within the realm. The whole medieval system of patronage and presentations to benefices is a papal corruption and should be abolished, so that lawful election of pastors by their people should be restored.

The second *Book of Discipline* was in short a demand for a complete reversal of the ecclesiastical policy pursued by Morton since 1572, and successive General Assemblies sought to carry out the programme on their own authority. The bishops were summoned to submit, and in July 1580 it was declared that the office of bishop as understood within this realm was unlawful as having no warrant in the Word of God. Those who held it were ordered to demit it and to cease from using in any way the office of pastors until admitted anew by the General Assembly. In April of the following year it was proposed to group the 924 parishes in the country, reduced by unions to 600, in 50 presbyteries, of which 13 were to be immediately erected, viz. Edinburgh, St. Andrews, Dundee, Perth, Stirling, Glasgow, Ayr, Irvine, Haddington, Dunbar, Chirnside, Linlithgow, and Dunfermline. The office of reader was abolished in spite of the fact that there were not nearly enough ministers to supply the parishes, but this seems to have been prompted by the idea already expressed in the first *Book of Discipline*, that the readership might be too easy and cheap a method of filling charges with unqualified men. Whatever may be said of its policy, the assembly must be credited with a deliberate and legislative vitality contrasting strongly with the Parliament; and, though not one member of it would have called it democratic, the young king saw clearly enough that it held a challenge to his power.

Meantime Morton had fallen and D'Aubigny stood high in the king's favour, in spite of the suspicion with which he was universally regarded. To allay the suspicion he professed conversion to Protestantism and signed, with others of the king's household, a document condemning all the errors and abuses of Rome, commonly known as the *Negative Confession*. But he now came into collision with the Kirk by nominating Robert Montgomery, minister of Stirling, to the archbishopric of Glasgow in room of James Boyd, with reservation of a large part of the revenue to himself. The new presbyteries of Stirling and Edinburgh were at once in the

fray, and after an undignified struggle Montgomery was compelled to yield. A short sharp reaction drove D'Aubigny, or
Lennox as he now was, out of Scotland, but the Kirk had
to pay for its approval of the Ruthven Raid. Under the
administration of Arran a subservient Parliament passed
a series of laws called the Black Acts (1584). The king's
authority, spiritual and temporal, was asserted. His majesty's
subjects of whatever quality, spiritual or temporal, were
forbidden to convene for councils, conventions, or assemblies
to determine any matter, civil or ecclesiastical, without his
majesty's special command and licence. It was forbidden to
speak privately or publicly in sermons in contempt of his
majesty or to meddle with his affairs. Finally, Patrick, Archbishop of St. Andrews, and other bishops within this realm
' . . . shall put order to all matters and causes ecclesiastical
within their dioceses, visit the kirks, examine those presented
to benefices by the king and collate them if found qualified'.
By these measures the episcopate was given a greater authority
than it had before.

In 1585 another palace revolution turned the tables once
more. The synod of Fife excommunicated the archbishop for
his part in passing the Black Acts, and for claiming ecclesiastical superiority over his clergy, and several preachers gave
great offence to the king by attacking his policy in their sermons. Nevertheless he now judged it politic to come to terms
with the Kirk. A conference was held between royal councillors and representatives of the Kirk, and articles of accommodation were drawn up. When after a lapse of three years
an assembly met in May 1586, on the invitation of the king
it held its first session in Holyrood when he expressed his
goodwill. The assembly showed itself so far ready to humour
him as to annul the excommunication of Adamson and
order two of the offending preachers to apologize. The articles
of accommodation were lengthily discussed and at last grudg-
ingly accepted. A scheme for the organization of presbyteries
covering the whole country with the exception of Argyll and
the Isles was drawn up at least on paper, and it was agreed
that the bishops should be moderators of the presbyteries
within whose bounds they resided, and act as visitors of

churches at the appointment of the assembly. When in 1587
the bishopric of Caithness fell vacant the king announced to
the assembly his desire to nominate Robert Pont, then minister of St. Cuthbert's, Edinburgh, whose long career of dutiful
service to the Kirk in many capacities had endeared him to
his brethren. After consultation with Pont himself the assembly wrote to the king:

We praise God that your Majesty has such opinion and esti-
mation of such a person as we judge the said Mr. Robert to be,
whom we acknowledge to be already a Bishop according to the
doctrine of St. Paul, and qualified to use the function of a Pastor
or Minister at the Kirk of Dornoch or any other Kirk where he is
lawfully called . . . as also to have the office of a Commissioner
or Visitor in the bounds of Caithness if he be burdened therewith.
But as to that corrupt estate or office of them who have been
termed Bishops hertofore, we find it not agreeable to the Word of
God . . . neither is the said Mr. Robert willing to attempt the
same in that manner.

It seems likely that the king concluded that bishops of this
kind could not serve his purpose, for within a month of the
receipt of this letter, in July 1587, Parliament passed an
Act of Annexation appropriating to the Crown the temporalities, i.e. the landed properties, of bishoprics, abbeys,
and other prelacies, with the exception of such properties as
had already been erected into temporal lordships. The
bishops' residences and the manses and glebes of parish
ministers were also exempted. Thus the only source of revenue left to the Kirk would be that derived from the teinds.
The reason given for the Act of Annexation, no doubt the
true one, was the poverty of the Crown which could not
otherwise be relieved save by 'importable taxations'. Thus
was the episcopate crushed between the upper and nether
mill-stones.

In 1589 King James went to Denmark to marry his Danish
bride. He was accompanied by David Lindsay, minister of
Leith, who married the royal pair. Another minister, Robert
Bruce of Edinburgh, had been appointed on the Council
of Regency during the king's absence, and he was chosen to
crown the queen. At a thanksgiving service in St. Giles on

his return James promised to be a loving and faithful king
and to make better provision for the Kirk. At an assembly in
August 1590 he spoke of the Kirk of Scotland as 'the sin-
cerest Kirk in the world'. 'As for our neighbour Kirk in
England, it is an evil said Mass in English, wanting nothing
but the liftings', and he promised to maintain the Kirk 'so
long as I brook my life and crown'. In 1592 came the Act
which has been regarded as the Charter of Presbytery. It
confirms all liberties, privileges, immunities, and freedoms
given to the true and holy Kirk presently established within
the realm. It gives the General Assembly the right to meet
once a year or oftener *pro re nata*, in the presence of the king
or his commissioner who shall appoint the time and place
of the next meeting. If neither be present the assembly itself may do so. The government of the Church under the
assembly by synods, presbyteries, and particular sessions is
approved. Episcopal jurisdictions are abolished, and presbyteries shall receive presentations to benefices, give collation
and put order to all matters and causes ecclesiastical within
their bounds, as the bishops had formerly been empowered
to do.

The Act of 1592 seemed to so uncompromising a Presbyterian as James Melville to grant all that he desired, and it
might have been expected that the king and the Kirk would
now live in harmony. That hope was soon dispelled. Anti-
Romanist feeling had always been strong in the Kirk and it
was inflamed anew when Philip of Spain launched his attack
on England. The ignominious defeat of the Armada in 1588
did nothing to allay the feeling. When it became known that
the earls of Huntly, Errol, and Angus and other Romanist
nobles had entered into correspondence with Philip the excitement was intense. James had to take action. He drove the
earls into exile but refused to proceed to extremities. Indeed
he allowed them to return. His moderation aroused suspicion
as to his Protestantism and was sharply criticized in the
assembly of March 1596. It occasioned also the famous scene
in Falkland Palace in which Andrew Melville plucked King
James's sleeve, called him 'God's sillie vassal', and forcefully
reminded him that 'there are two kings and two kingdoms in

Scotland. There is Christ Jesus the King and His kingdom the Kirk, whose subject King James the Sixth is, and of whose kingdom not a king, nor a lord, nor a head, but a member.'[1] Meantime the pulpits rang with furious attacks on the king who understandably conceived a lasting antipathy to presbytery. It 'as well agreeth with a monarchy as God and the Devil. . . . No bishop no King'.[2] He determined to make a test case of David Black, minister of St. Andrews and a protégé of Andrew Melville. Black was summoned to appear before the Privy Council on a charge of preaching sedition. He declined its jurisdiction over pulpit utterances, and he was supported by a petition signed by many ministers. The council rejected Black's plea and the trial dragged on for months amidst intense popular excitement. A riot in Edinburgh gave the king his opportunity. By threatening to reduce its status as capital he compelled the town to make a complete submission and to banish its ministers. This marked the end of the Melvillian ascendency.

James now began to use very shrewdly the power given him in the Act of 1592 to fix the time and place for meetings of the assembly. By choosing such places as Perth, Dundee, and Montrose he could secure the attendance of north country ministers, into whom he could instil a certain enmity towards their brethren of Lothian and Fife who had dominated assemblies meeting in Edinburgh. By promises and flattering attentions he rendered them amenable to his will, so that an assembly at Dundee in May 1597 agreed to the appointment of a commission of fourteen with wide powers to confer with the king on all matters concerning the welfare of the Kirk. Before the end of the year the commission petitioned for representation of the Kirk in Parliament, where the Spiritual Estate was now represented mainly by lay commendators of abbeys and priories, in no sense churchmen. Parliament thereupon passed an Act that ministers whom his majesty should please to provide to the dignity of a bishop, abbot, or other prelate should have vote in Parliament, and that only actual ministers or persons who undertook to become ministers

[1] *Autobiography and Diary of James Melville* (ed. by Pitcairn for Wodrow Society), p. 370.   [2] King James at Hampton Court Conference, 1604.

should be so provided to prelacies as they fell vacant. The matter was hotly debated in the presence of the king at an assembly in Dundee, March 1598, when it was decided by a small majority 'that it is necessary and expedient for the weal of the Kirk that the Ministry, or Third Estate of this realm, in name of the Kirk, have vote in Parliament' to the number of fifty-one. Consideration of how they were to be appointed and on what conditions was remitted to synods. The next assembly at Montrose in March 1600, again in the presence of the king, heard the reports of synods and drew up a long list of caveats and suggestions as to tenure and title. Later in that year James nominated George Gledstanes, minister of St. Andrews, to Caithness, David Lindsay of Leith to Ross, and Peter Blackburn of Marischal College to Aberdeen, who took their seats in Parliament as bishops. They had, however, no ecclesiastical functions, except as visitors of districts, commissioned thereto by the assembly.

An assembly in November 1602 appointed another to meet in Aberdeen in July 1604, but in the meantime James had achieved his highest ambition. In 1603 he peacefully succeeded to the throne of England, and to his delight was welcomed on all hands. In taking leave of his Scottish subjects he vowed to bear them continued love, and promised to return to visit them every three years. They on their part expressed sorrow at his going mingled with patriotic pride in the high position to which their king had attained, with hopes also of profiting by it. In England James found a church which suited him admirably, the clergy of which surrounded him with a nauseating flattery in its own way as offensive to modern feeling as the ill-mannered attacks of the rough Scottish ministers. James's colossal vanity could stomach it all. And he was now in a position to bestow upon his ancient kingdom the benefits of the English ecclesiastical system. But he must proceed slowly and carefully. First he must reduce the power of General Assemblies. That fixed for 1604 was postponed for a year, but when a further postponement was ordered some nineteen ministers met in Aberdeen in July 1605 and adjourned to meet again in September. They were summoned by the Privy Council to answer for their conduct, and, declining its jurisdiction, were condemned for treason and exiled. In 1606 the two Melvilles and six other brethren were summoned to London and subjected to a course of sermons by eminent Anglican divines to prove to them the advantages of episcopacy. This had no effect. Andrew Melville lectured Bancroft, Archbishop of Canterbury, much as he had formerly lectured King James, and for a Latin lampoon deriding the worship he had witnessed in the chapel royal he was exiled and spent his last years teaching in the Huguenot seminary at Sedan. The bishoprics were now rapidly filled by royal nomination, and by an Act of Parliament rescinding the Act of Annexation of 1587 their temporalities were restored. Step by step, with or without the consent of specially packed assemblies, their ecclesiastical jurisdiction was restored. But the new bishops lacked consecration, and James summoned three of them to London in 1610 to receive it from Anglican hands. One of these was John Spottiswoode, Archbishop of Glasgow, son of the superintendent. He pointed out that such a proceeding might raise the old question of the claim of the Church of England to superiority over the Church of Scotland. James, however, had thought of that, and had arranged that the consecration should be, not by either of the English archbishops, but by the bishops of London, Ely, and Bath. More important was the question raised by Andrewes, Bishop of Ely. He held that the Scots must first be ordained presbyters since they had received no valid ordination. The Archbishop of Canterbury, Bancroft, however, ruled that that was not necessary 'seeing where bishops could not be had, the ordination given by presbyters must be esteemed lawful; otherwise it might be doubted if there were any lawful ordination in most of the Reformed Churches'. This reasoning prevailed. Whatever may be thought of it now, it at least had the merit of saving Spottiswoode and his colleagues from having to require all the ministers in Scotland to be re-ordained, and thus to evoke inevitable resistance. On their return to Scotland they consecrated the other bishops according to the Anglican rite.

In 1617 King James paid his only visit to his northern kingdom since his accession in England. A Parliament completed the reorganization of the Church, but the king's proposal virtually to abolish general assemblies had to be abandoned. He now turned his attention to a reform of Scottish worship. As an example he had his chapel at Holyrood fitted up for Anglican worship, and intimated to the bishops what changes they were to introduce. After a vain attempt to dissuade him from so directly challenging public opinion they obtained his permission to bring Five Articles devised by the king before an assembly to be held at Perth in 1618. These required (1) that the sacrament of the Body and Blood of Christ should be received kneeling, (2) that it might be administered to the sick privately, (3) that baptism might be administered in private houses when necessity should require, (4) that children eight years old should be presented to the bishop for confirmation, and (5) that the Birth, Passion, Resurrection, and Ascension of our Lord, and the sending of the Holy Ghost be commemorated on the days appointed. Surprise has often been expressed at the opposition which these articles encountered, but it ought to be realized that the first three were in direct contradiction to the sacramental doctrine and practice of the Reformed Churches. Strenuous preparations had to be made to secure their acceptance by the assembly. Spottiswoode, now Archbishop of St. Andrews, took the chair as moderator and was supported by three royal commissioners. Noblemen, barons, bishops, burgesses, and doctors sat round a central long table, while the ministers stood behind. A letter was read from the king claiming that he had power to determine such matters without consulting them at all. Members were threatened that their conduct would be reported to the king, and the vote was taken on the question whether the assembly would obey his Majesty in admitting the articles, or refuse them. Eighty-six voted for obedience and forty-nine, nearly all ministers, against. It was harder to secure obedience in the country at large, where the articles were frequently disregarded in spite of proceedings taken against recalcitrant ministers in the Court of High Commission. On the whole the bishops were not enthusiastic in enforcing them, hoping that in time they would come to be accepted peacefully.

In his conflict with the Kirk James had won a notable victory even before 1603, which his elevation to the throne of England enabled him to exploit. His reputation perhaps might have stood higher today had not fortune brought him into a situation far beyond his comprehension and capacity, for as King of England he found scope to demonstrate, both in home and foreign politics, the personal and intellectual weaknesses of 'the wisest fool in Christendom'. So far as Scotland was concerned, he had almost succeeded in introducing the ecclesiastical system of Henry VIII in which the king was pope. But his last endeavour, i.e. to impose the Five Articles of Perth, showed that the embers of opposition still glowed. His successor was to fan them into a conflagration.

IV

CHARLES I AND THE COVENANTS

IN 1625 James VI and I was succeeded by his son Charles I. Unlike his father in many ways, being handsome, courtly, and accomplished, Charles fully shared his father's belief in the divine right of kings. He was moreover a devout Anglo-Catholic with a pious detestation of puritanism and all its works. His queen, Henrietta Maria, daughter of Henry IV of France, exercised great influence over him and his court. She was a Roman Catholic, surrounded by Romanist chaplains whose propagandist activities aroused much suspicion. Thus a gulf was fixed between the king and the great mass of his subjects both in England and in Scotland, which he did nothing either to comprehend or to bridge. Convinced that he knew what was best for them in matters of religion, he was prepared to impose it upon them by his royal will and prerogative regardless of their wishes and conscientious scruples. He had been born in Scotland but from the age of three had been nurtured in England. Nevertheless his accession was hailed with expressions of joy and loyalty on the part of his Scottish subjects, whom he speedily disappointed. He made it clear at once that he had no sympathy with those who were dissatisfied with his father's ecclesiastical policy, and was determined to carry it further.

Early in his reign Charles determined, in the interests partly of the Crown and partly of the Church, to straighten out a major financial tangle left over since the Reformation. Accordingly in 1625 he issued a sweeping act of Revocation ostensibly resuming all Crown and church lands granted since 1542! This was doubtless intended, as later explained, to be a purely legal form to give the king an opportunity to review the problem. But it thoroughly alarmed the nobles, many of whom had, as Lords of Erection,[1] come into possession of the lands and other properties of the ancient abbeys. After

[1] i.e. holders of ancient spiritual properties erected into temporal lordships.

years of complicated and often irritating legal and parliamentary procedure the Lords of Erection were confirmed in their possession, subject to the feudal superiority of the Crown, of the abbey lands, but they were deprived, not without compensation, of their right to the teinds of parishes formerly appropriated to the *quondam* abbeys. Every heritor or landowner was, in the quaint language of the *First Book of Discipline*, 'to have his awin teind', subject to payment in money to the parish minister of a proportion of stipend fixed according to a new system of valuation. This was to replace the ancient, cumbrous and often oppressive mode of collection in kind. Up to a point effect was thus given to suggestions made in the *Book of Discipline*. This would have benefited both heritors and ministers. Charles's bold attempt to deal with the problem of the teinds was in fact an act of statesmanship long overdue and its beneficial effects have endured until today. But it was all very complicated. The king's high-handed methods bred suspicion as to his intentions among the nobles and landowners, and earned him the resentment of many and the gratitude of none.

Not until 1635 was Charles able to come to Scotland for his coronation, and then he was rapturously received by the citizens of Edinburgh. But in his train he brought William Laud, soon to become Archbishop of Canterbury, and already the king's chief adviser or minister for ecclesiastical affairs. The abbey church of Holyrood was furbished for the coronation with altar and candles under the direction of Laud, who took upon himself to see that all was done as he thought fitting. He is said to have rebuked the Archbishop of Glasgow for coming improperly dressed! On the Sunday following the king attended St. Giles when the English service was read by two of Laud's chaplains. But Edinburgh was to be signally honoured. Charles announced that, on a petition from John, Archbishop of St. Andrews, he had decided to disjoin the parts of the diocese of St. Andrews lying south of the Forth, and subject them to a new bishopric of Edinburgh to be endowed out of the properties, both spiritual and temporal, of the abbey of Holyrood and of New Abbey in Dumfriesshire. Edinburgh thereby became an episcopal city and the church of St. Giles a cathedral. The first bishop, who died within three months of his consecration, was William Forbes, a learned and distinguished man of the Laudian school of thought and piety. Laud's relations with the Church of Scotland were correct in the sense that, even when he became Archbishop of Canterbury, he never asserted hierarchical superiority over it. But as the king's chief adviser in ecclesiastical affairs he could exercise a dominating influence even in Scotland. To the older bishops who had served under James he sometimes wrote peremptory letters when they fell below his standard of churchmanship. Archbishop Spottiswoode dreaded the loss of the king's favour which resistance to Laud might entail, and some of the other bishops were pathetically submissive to the rebuke of one who, having the ear of the king, controlled the royal patronage. To vacancies as they occurred Laud could secure the nomination of men who shared his views. Doubtless there was in Scotland a movement parallel to the Anglo-Catholic movement of which Laud was the acknowledged leader, but it was small and, without his support, would have been helpless. This was the group to which Robert Baillie gave the name of 'the Canterburian faction'.

During his visit to Edinburgh Charles held a Parliament to confirm his financial policy and for other purposes. Its first business as usual was to appoint the Lords of the Articles, a committee of 32 representatives of the Estates which had the task of preparing measures to be submitted to Parliament. As Parliament normally had the right only to accept or reject what was proposed to it, the Lords of the Articles virtually controlled all legislation. Their election was therefore important, though the method of election was somewhat ill defined. In 1633 the procedure followed was that the nobles chose 8 from the Spiritual Estate. These in turn chose 8 nobles, and together these 16 chose 8 from the representatives of the shires and 8 from the burgess estate. As the Spiritual Estate in 1633 consisted exclusively of the bishops, all king's men, the Committee of the Articles would naturally be composed of persons belonging to the king's party. When their legislative proposals were brought before Parliament, including one to continue to Charles the right given to his father in 1609 to prescribe 'the apparel of kirkmen', it was observed that the king noted the names of all who spoke in opposition. Dissatisfaction expressed itself in a supplication couched in very submissive terms. But the king refused to read it and resented it as containing reflections upon his kingly honour. One of the supplicants, Lord Balmerino, was imprisoned and, after a trial lasting more than half a year, condemned on a charge of publishing a seditious document. The fact that he received the royal pardon did not pacify public opinion, which was further inflamed by the appointment in 1635 of the Archbishop of St. Andrews to the chancellorship, an office which no cleric had held since the Reformation. Thus was dissipated much of the goodwill with which Charles's accession had been greeted.

While he was in Scotland Charles must have had consultations with the Scottish bishops with regard to the matters in which the Church of Scotland seemed to be defective. It had no code of canons and it had no proper liturgy, for the *Book of Common Order* naturally could not satisfy the king's taste. Already in the reign of King James there had been attempts towards remedying both of these defects, but without result. Charles decided that action must now be taken. It seems that the bishops set to work and in due course sent to the king a draft *Book of Canons*, which he invited Laud to revise, taking care that the canons 'be well fitted for Church Government, and as near as conveniently may be to the Canons of the Church of England'. Accordingly in 1636 there appeared a book entitled '*Canons and Constitutions Ecclesiastical*, gathered and put in form for the Government of the Church of Scotland, ratified and approved by His Majesty's royal warrant, and ordained to be observed by the clergy and all others whom they concern'. The first chapter contains the rule that all are to suffer excommunication who deny the king's supremacy in causes ecclesiastical, and it is assumed throughout that the king has the right, without any ecclesiastical consent, to impose a constitution and rules upon the Church of Scotland. The canons, in the main, deal with the life and work of the clergy, and the conduct of

P

church services. The substance of the Five Articles of Perth is retained, and the regulations regarding the placing of fonts and communion tables in churches flatly defy the Reformed doctrine and practice of Baptism and the Lord's Supper. Extempore prayer in public worship is forbidden. If the book was not the work of Laud himself, at least it obeys the king's injunction and thoroughly assimilates the Church of Scotland to the Church of England. Its ministers are designated presbyters and deacons, and there is no reference to elders, kirk sessions, presbyteries, or General Assembly. But reference is made to two books which had not yet appeared, the use of which is nevertheless prescribed. Of one of these, the *Book of Ordination*, no copy seems to have survived, but the *Book of Common Prayer* was the spark that kindled a consuming fire.

The latter, commonly and not without reason known as Laud's Liturgy, claims to be the *Scottish Book of Common Prayer*. Charles and Laud had pressed the Scottish bishops to accept the English book without alteration, so that there might be uniformity of worship in token of unity of religion in the united kingdoms and a common front against the English Puritans. On the other hand the bishops urged that a book with some claim to be Scottish might have a better chance of peaceful acceptance in Scotland. There followed a great deal of correspondence between them and Laud. Maxwell, Bishop of Ross, made repeated journeys to London, and Wedderburn, Bishop of Dunblane, a protégé of Laud's, most of whose ministerial life had been spent in England, also took some part in the preparation. Whatever share the Scottish bishops had in the making of the Prayer Book, Laud was intimately concerned from the beginning and gave the final draft his blessing. In the main it was the English book. The concessions to Scottish or at least Presbyterian doctrine and practice were small indeed, and these were offset by certain seemingly catholicizing features upon which attention inevitably fixed among a people violently anti-papal. The publication of the Prayer Book in 1637 was followed by a royal proclamation made at the market crosses of the chief towns commanding 'all our subjects . . . to conform themselves to the said Public Form of Worship which is the only form which *We* (having taken the counsel of our Clergy) think fit to be used in God's Public Worship in this our Kingdom'. Contraveners were to be condignly censured and punished, and every parish was to provide itself with at least two copies of the Prayer Book before Easter when it was to come into general use.

King James had sought to bring the Church of Scotland into conformity with the pre-Laudian Church of England, or, as we might say today, to make it an integral part of the Anglican Communion; but knowing, as he put it, 'the stomach' of his people, he walked warily, step by step, and achieved considerable success. In time his ecclesiastical arrangements, including the Five Articles of Perth, would almost certainly have won acquiescence and even general acceptance. In 1637 the majority of ministers must have been ordained and admitted to their charges by bishops, and knew no other system. Some indeed liked it well, as for example Robert Baillie, minister of Kilwinning in Ayrshire, but above all the group known as the Aberdeen Doctors who cherished the inheritance of Bishop Patrick Forbes who died in 1635. To others the Perth Articles were at least lawful as having been authorized by a General Assembly and ratified by Parliament. But there were non-conformists, mostly older men who had voted against the articles at the Perth Assembly and continued to disregard them with the connivance of their bishops. And there were also some younger men steeped in the Melvillian tradition. There was Samuel Rutherford, for example, minister since 1627 of Anwoth by the Solway, who in 1636 had been deprived and exiled to Aberdeen, a vigorous controversialist, and George Gillespie still a probationer in 1637 when he wrote his 'Dispute concerning the English Popish Ceremonies obtruded upon the Church of Scotland', a reasoned attack on the Perth Articles. All these found a leader in the scholarly and statesmanlike Alexander Henderson, minister of Leuchars. He had been a strong upholder of episcopacy, but before 1618 had been converted to the other way for he spoke against the articles in the assembly at Perth, and in a pamphlet denounced the assembly itself as no true ecclesiastical body. These three were theologians who understood the points at issue, and were able to present the Presbyterian case with learning and dignity. Charles's attempt to impose upon the Church of Scotland what may fairly be called Laudian Anglo-Catholicism was fitted as nothing else could to cement an alliance between those men and the nobles whose discontent had been otherwise provoked by the king's autocratic methods.

The Proclamation of Charles aroused intense excitement, much of it due to the feeling among the populace that his aim was the reintroduction of popery. It must be remembered that the Thirty Years War was still in progress, and that it had been, to begin with, a religious war for the extirpation of Protestantism. Many Scots served in the army of Gustavus Adolphus, the Protestant champion who fell at Lützen in 1632. In the hope that the excitement would die down, the bishops, many of whom were not enamoured of the Prayer Book, decided to delay its introduction for some months. But an order came from the king appointing the third Sunday of July as the day on which the book was to be first used in St. Giles' Cathedral. On that day the Bishop of Edinburgh was present, and with him Spottiswoode, Archbishop of St. Andrews and Chancellor, members of the Privy Council, and of the town council. No sooner had Dean Hanna begun to read the service than he was interrupted by clamour. When the bishop intervened to secure order the turmoil grew worse, and missiles, including a folding stool, were hurled at his head. The rioters were soon removed from the church but they continued to demonstrate outside, and at the conclusion of the service they manhandled the bishop as he tried to make his way home. In these circumstances the council with the archbishop at its head resolved before another Sunday came round to suspend the book until the king's pleasure could be known.

Charles's difficulties in England were now multiplying, for in 1637 the famous ship money case had begun. Perhaps for that reason he was all the more obstinate. He rebuked the council for its timidity and insisted that he must be obeyed. Meantime resistance began to be organized. Meetings were

held in various parts of the Lowlands, and petitions largely
signed by noblemen, barons, burgesses, and ministers began
to pour in, praying that the religion and the form of worship
established by Parliament and National Assemblies and practised since the Reformation might not be disturbed in a way
'which this Kirk has never been acquainted with'. In October,
when it was believed the king's answer to the petition would
be given, the petitioners crowded into Edinburgh, and refused to obey a royal proclamation ordering them to leave
the city. Instead another petition was drawn up and signed
by many nobles, lairds, and ministers accusing the bishops
of deceiving the king and of being the authors of the mischief
by enforcing the Liturgy and the Canons, and demanding
their exclusion from the council as parties to the dispute. A
second and more serious riot took place, in which the provost
and magistrates were besieged in the city chambers and
several members of the Privy Council suffered injury and
indignity. It now became necessary to treat with the rioters,
and in order to induce them to disperse they were asked
to appoint commissioners, representative of the nobles, lairds,
burgesses, and ministers, to negotiate with the council. From
these commissioners were drawn later the members of a
powerful steering committee known as the Tables. For a
time the council endeavoured to find a means of splitting
the opposition, and failing to do so at last in desperation
sent the lord treasurer, Traquair, post haste to London
to explain the situation to the king. All he obtained
was yet another proclamation in which the king took full
responsibility for the Prayer Book, assured his subjects
that it was not intended as a step towards popery but as a
bulwark against it, and declared his will that it should
be used.

The opposition now had recourse to an old established
Scottish practice whereby nobles to maintain their own interests or sometimes a public cause, would enter into a 'band'
pledging mutual support. Authority was given to Alexander
Henderson and Archibald Johnston of Wariston, a young
advocate of extreme puritan principles, to draw up such a
'band', and they took care that it would have as wide an

appeal as possible to all classes in the community. The National Covenant is a lengthy document consisting of three parts. The first part is the Negative Confession of 1581 originally intended as a sort of supplement to the Confession of 1560, and even more explicitly listing and abjuring the errors of Rome. The choice of this Confession was due doubtless to its expected appeal to the No-popery feeling in the nation. But the fact was also stressed that it had been signed by James VI and his household, and later by persons of all classes by order of the Privy Council and the General Assembly. There follows an exhaustive list of the Acts of Parliament since the Reformation passed against the Roman Church or in favour of the Reformed Church and the true religion, evidently the work of the professional lawyer. Finally there are the obligations to be assumed by the signatories—noblemen, barons, gentlemen, burgesses, ministers, and commons—to resist the innovations and evils recently introduced into the Kirk 'to the ruin of the True Reformed Religion and of our Liberties, Laws and Estates', and to maintain and preserve the True Religion, the king's honour, and the public peace of the kingdom. 'We promise and swear that we shall to the utmost of our power stand to the defence of our dread Sovereign, the King's Majesty, his Person and Authority.' Thus the scruples of loyalty were met. The Covenant was produced and read over to a concourse of nobles and barons in Greyfriars Kirk in Edinburgh, and signed by them on 28 February 1638. The ministers, burgesses, and commons then in Edinburgh had an opportunity to sign next day in Greyfriars churchyard where scenes of extraordinary enthusiasm were witnessed. Soon copies were being carried to towns and villages throughout the country and offered for signature to all. Sometimes compulsion was used to obtain subscription but as the recent 'novations' were not specified and as certain reservations were allowed the Covenant was widely signed except in Aberdeen, where even the presence of the Earl of Montrose could not prevail upon the people to accept it. The Highland area, too, was quite unaffected. It is certain also that the Covenanters were not all of one mind, but the Covenant was as truly national as any such document can ever be.

King Charles was helpless and by his indecision alienated many who might have been his friends. For three months he did nothing, but at last he sent the Marquis of Hamilton to Scotland as his high commissioner with highly ambiguous instructions characteristic of the king-craft of which he was so proud. Hamilton had for some years been living in London as a courtier high in favour, but was hardly the man for the difficult task now entrusted to him. Twice he returned to court to report and seek fresh instructions, and finally in September Charles was persuaded to withdraw the Canons and the Prayer Book and to amend the Court of High Commission. He also agreed to the summoning, under certain conditions, of a free General Assembly to be followed later by a free Parliament. But how was a free General Assembly to be elected? Charles had stipulated that it should be a purely clerical body, and a considerable number of ministers would have welcomed this, but the more ardent Covenanters insisted that commissioners should be elected by presbyteries in which elders should have seats and voting rights along with ministers. By the bishops and the clergy who supported them the intrusion of 'laic elders' into the presbyteries, which had become purely clerical bodies, was resented, and the dominating influence of such elders in the election of the commissioners to the assembly was one of their main reasons for holding it to be unlawful and without authority. To look for strict constitutional propriety in 1638 would be absurd. King James since 1600 had packed assemblies to obtain his own ends, and since 1618 no assembly of any kind had met. That which met at Glasgow in the cathedral or high kirk in November 1638 was doubtless packed by the Tables who now exercised the power. Its membership could be challenged and was challenged by the king's commissioner on various grounds, and its policy was revolutionary in the sense that it aimed at undoing all that had been done ecclesiastically since 1600, and at restoring the position as it was in 1592. The recovery and production of the records of the older assemblies, which were believed to have perished, increased confidence; and the election of Alexander Henderson as moderator and Johnston of Wariston as clerk did something to ensure that even so tumultous and inexperienced a convention would be guided along a well thought-out course.

A month before the assembly met it was known that an attack would be made on the bishops personally, and six of them fled to England whence they sent an elaborate and ably argued declinature of the assembly's jurisdiction. Nevertheless it was decided to proceed with their trials. They were charged with having accepted and exercised an office which the Kirk had previously condemned or at least hedged about with limitations, as also with having taught Arminian heresy. In addition a number of moral offences were alleged against many of them—some so shocking as to be quite incredible today. That such charges were made was doubtless due to the fact that the bishops had no regard at all for the Sabbatarian principles and puritan conscientiousness of so many of their people, indeed held them to be obscurantist prejudices, and chose to ride over them rough-shod. On neither side was Christian forbearance and charity in evidence. When it became clear that the assembly was bent on nothing short of abolishing episcopacy itself the commissioner dissolved it in the king's name and published a proclamation declaring its continuance treasonable. Undismayed it sat on. Its entertaining of the scurrilous charges brought against the bishops and the harshness of the sentences pronounced upon them, modified in the case of eight who submitted, are indefensible, but otherwise its acts for the restoration of Presbyterianism, lacked neither thoroughness nor legislative skill. The ground was cleared by a decision taken on 4 December declaring the six 'pretended' assemblies held between 1606·and 1618 'to have been from the beginning unfree, unlawful and null assemblies, and never to have had, nor hereafter to have any ecclesiastical authority'. On 6 December the Prayer Book, Canons, Ordinal and Court of High Commission were condemned as having been introduced without authority from the Kirk and to the subversion of its doctrine, worship, and government. Two days later the assembly with one dissentient voted that 'all episcopacy different from that of a Pastor over a particular flock was abjured in this Kirk and to be removed out of it'. On 10 December the Five Articles of Perth were pronounced to be contrary to the Confession of Faith of the Kirk; and on 19 December an Act was passed declaring that while the Kirk or its ministers are obliged to give advice in accordance with the Word of God to the king, Parliament, council or members thereof on ecclesiastical matters or on questions of conscience 'it is inexpedient and unlawful in this Kirk for Pastors separate unto the Gospel to brook civil places and offices' as justices of the peace, members of council, session, or Parliament, or as judges or assessors in any civil judicatory. This Act manifestly raised anew a constitutional issue of great importance, implying as it did the abolition of the Spiritual Estate in Parliament. But it expresses both positively and negatively a basic principle of the Reformed Churches everywhere as to the relations of Church and State. The Church is a society or kingdom independent of the State with officers of its own who have authority to pronounce on questions of religion and morals and on public questions in so far as they imply religious and moral issues, but who may not be as it were merged in the State so as to become part and parcel of the civil government. Finally it was declared that 'this national kirk hath power and liberty to assemble and convene in her yearly General Assemblies and oftener . . . as occasion and necessity shall require', and the next General Assembly was appointed to meet in Edinburgh on the third Wednesday of July 1639, unless his Majesty should otherwise appoint. It must appear surprising that an assembly which so openly reversed all the plans and defied the commands of the king should nevertheless profess loyalty, and indeed seek King Charles's sanction for its Acts. The word rebellion had still an ugly sound to minds trained in the Reformed theology, even if passive obedience was never a Scottish virtue. Besides it was possible to excuse the king's actions as due to the deceptions of evil advisers, and to offer the assembly's acts as good advice tendered to him in accordance with the Word of God. Nor must this be regarded as hypocrisy. Few Scots apart from Charles's bishops would have subscribed to the doctrine of the Divine Right of Kings, but none had any sympathy with republicans.

In the eyes of King Charles the Covenanters were now rebels to be reduced to obedience by force of arms. In Scotland itself he had little support except in Aberdeenshire where the Huntly influence was strong. The Glasgow Assembly had included seven earls in its membership as well as lesser nobles and barons and a strong representation of the towns, and the Covenanters received a powerful recruit when the young Earl of Argyll forsook the government and joined their ranks. Learning that the king was assembling an army in England they prepared to resist, and soon they had a force of some 20,000 men, trained by officers who had gained experience in the continental wars, and commanded by Alexander Leslie, who had served under Gustavus Adolphus and had risen to the rank of field marshal. A detachment under Montrose was sent to the north-east where Aberdeen was taken and Huntly made prisoner, while the main body encamped on Duns Law awaiting the king's attack. His army, however, being ill trained and ill paid, was obviously unreliable, so Charles thought it best to negotiate. The first Bishops' War was terminated without serious fighting by the Pacification of Berwick, in terms of which the Covenanters agreed to disband their army in return for a promise from Charles to appoint an assembly to meet in Edinburgh in August 1639 to be immediately followed by a Parliament. Unwillingly he consented to the exclusion of the bishops from the assembly, but he encouraged them to hand in a new declinature, and he assured them of his intention to restore them when he could. Traquair, who was appointed commissioner, dealt more subtly with this assembly than Hamilton had done at Glasgow. It was agreed that the Glasgow Assembly which the king still held to have been rebellious was not to be mentioned, but its acts were renewed one by one with the consent, after argument, of the commissioner. It remained now for Parliament to ratify them, and it showed itself ready to do so. It was, therefore, prorogued again and again, for Charles had resolved to appeal to an English Parliament to finance a second Bishops' War against the Scots. The 'Short' Parliament proved intractable and was dissolved within a month. Taking advantage of the king's difficulties and weary of

repeated prorogations the Scots Parliament met in defiance
of the king and his commissioner, June 1640, ratified the acts
of the assembly, dispensed with the Committee of the Articles,
and enacted that henceforth as the Spiritual Estate was
abolished Parliament was complete and perfect without it.
In future the three estates were to be the nobles, barons, and
burgesses. In August a Covenanting army crossed the Tweed
and occupied Newcastle and Durham, so compelling the
king to summon the fateful 'Long' Parliament (November
1640). Strongly Puritan and Presbyterian in sympathy the
Long Parliament regarded the Scots as allies in its conflict
with King Charles, and was in no hurry to secure their withdrawal. Not until August 1641 when it had forced him to
abandon many of the powers he had claimed and exercised
and to sacrifice Strafford, his ablest and most energetic minister, did Parliament agree to pay £300,000 as indemnity to the
Scots, while Charles on his part undertook to ratify the Acts
of the Scots Parliament of 1640 including that abolishing
episcopacy in Scotland. On these terms the Covenanting army
returned home.

The treaty of August 1641 might well have been the end
of his troubles if Charles had felt himself free to accept the
position of a constitutional monarch ruling his several kingdoms 'by their own Laws and the Kirks in them by their own
Canons and Constitutions'. Unhappily he could not in conscience abandon his twin ideals of divine-right monarchy and
divine-right episcopacy. For these he engaged in dangerous
intrigues that led to his execution, or, as some have it, his
martyrdom. No sooner was the treaty signed than he came
to Edinburgh in the hope of detaching the Scots from the
English Parliamentarians. He granted all the demands of
the Covenanters, both ecclesiastical and constitutional, and
showered honours and titles on their leaders. Nevertheless
he could not win their trust, and the outbreak of an Irish
rebellion with its resultant massacre of Protestants aroused
the old dread of popery. Meantime events moved fast in
England. The Long Parliament in November 1641 passed
the Grand Remonstrance after furious debate and began its
attack on the English episcopate. In January 1642 while

Parliament was debating whether the king should have command of the army required to suppress the Irish revolt, Charles made an attempt to seize within the House of Commons itself five of its leading members. Civil war was now inevitable and it began when on 22 August the king raised his standard at Nottingham.

Could the Scots remain neutral in the English struggle? Certainly the Covenanting leaders could not have contemplated a royal victory without grave anxiety and this must have predisposed them to listen favourably to the parliamentarian appeal for aid in November 1642. Moreover the English Parliament's declared policy of undertaking a reformation of the Church of England agreeable to God's Word would be welcome. Among the Covenanters there were many who had come to cherish the belief that the peace and unity of the two kingdoms would best be maintained if the two Churches had a common Confession, and a common form of worship and church government. This had of course been King Charles's idea too, but he wanted to realize it on a High Anglican basis. He had professed to have abandoned that basis; might he not now agree to a reformation of the Church of England on Presbyterian lines? It seems an absurd suggestion, but the Scots continued to press it upon him and in his later difficulties he gave the impression of not being unwilling to try it at least for an experimental period. Meantime, however, it was the parliamentary party that was in straits. Faced with the possibility of defeat it turned to the Scots, seeking their aid and proposing a purely military alliance, but the Scots insisted on something more far reaching. After much negotiation the Solemn League and Covenant, drafted by Alexander Henderson and approved by a Scottish Assembly and a Convention of Estates, was accepted by the English Parliament in September 1643. Again the Covenant army marched into England, and their cavalry under David Leslie contributed materially to the Parliament victory on Marston Moor, July 1644. From that moment the tide of war began to turn against the king.

The Solemn League and Covenant hardly resembles a treaty between governments. Like the earlier Scottish

National Covenant it was a religious bond to be solemnly entered upon in the presence of God by individuals of all classes. Its subscribers pledged themselves to all endeavours for the extirpation of episcopacy in England and popery in Ireland; for the bringing of the Churches of God in the three kingdoms, now providentially living under one king,

to the nearest conjunction and uniformity in Religion, Confession of Faith, Form of Church government, Directory for Worship and Catechizing . . . according to the Word of God and the example of the best Reformed Churches; and for the preservation of the Rights and Privileges of the Parliaments and the Liberties of the Kingdoms, of the King's Majesty, Person and Authority, and of the blessings of a firm peace and union between these Kingdoms, denied in former times but now happily enjoyed.

Some months before the Solemn League and Covenant was finally sworn the English Parliament had resolved that a reformation of the doctrine, worship and government of the Church of England was necessary in a manner 'most agreeable to God's holy word and most apt to procure and preserve the peace of the Church at home and nearer agreement with the Church of Scotland and other reformed churches abroad'. It therefore nominated 121 ministers and 30 laymen from its own number to consult and advise on the steps to be taken. Those nominated represented several varieties of opinion but Anglicans absented themselves, fearing to disobey the command of the king. The great majority were Presbyterian in sympathy, but there were also five Independents who held that every local gathered congregation was itself a Church with no formal subjection to higher ecclesiastical authority. The Westminster Assembly was not an ecclesiastical body but a sort of parliamentary advisory commission, and Parliament reserved to itself the final word in all decisions. The assembly held its first meeting on 1 July 1643. Soon an invitation was extended to the General Assembly of the Church of Scotland to send representatives, and in August a strong team was appointed, including Alexander Henderson, Robert Baillie, Samuel Rutherford, and George Gillespie. The Scots were not members and had not the right to vote, but they took a prominent part in the debates and wielded an influence out of all proportion to their numbers because they could speak from experience of the working of the Presbyterian system, which as yet was unknown in England.

The first task of the assembly was the preparation of a Directory for the Public Worship of God to replace the English Prayer Book which had proved an offence to many of the godly at home and to the reformed Churches abroad. This would be a first step towards the uniformity desiderated in the Solemn League and Covenant. The directory which differed also in some important respects from the Scottish Book of Common Order was completed and submitted to Parliament in 1644. Much more time was required for the drawing up of a Confession of Faith and two Catechisms, a Shorter and a Larger, for popular use. These documents which set forth in the clearest terms a Calvinism more rigid than Calvin's were completed by 1647. The most troublesome task, however, was that of preparing a Form of Church Government, and here the Scots had to meet the opposition of the Independents who could find no Scripture warrant for presbyteries or for elders, or indeed for a national church as opposed to a series of local Churches. Moreover the lay representatives of the House of Commons would not hear of kirk sessions and presbyteries exercising discipline and jurisdiction outwith the law of the land. The most learned member of the assembly was the lawyer Selden, who was a thoroughgoing Erastian. Parliament did, however, accept the Form of Church Government when it was completed in 1645, but its efforts to put it into operation were half-hearted except in London. In England generally the sectaries—Independents and Baptists—were on the increase and were dominant in Cromwell's army. To the Scots these were enemies to be feared and detested even more than Episcopalians. The Westminster documents, as they were completed, were brought to Scotland and were approved and adopted by the General Assembly, not without demur, in the interests of a hoped-for uniformity. They have remained the official standards of the Church of Scotland ever since, and of its daughter

Churches throughout the English-speaking world, though today a good deal of freedom in their use and interpretation is allowed and exercised.

Meantime, however, a serious rift had taken place within the Covenanting ranks, and it is necessary to trace briefly the career of James Graham, Earl of Montrose. He was educated at the University of St. Andrews, and then, like many of the Scots nobles, spent some years in foreign travel. In 1636 he returned home a high-spirited and ambitious youth of 24. Passing through London he sought to offer his services to King Charles and was introduced at court by the Marquis of Hamilton, the royal favourite. Charles received him coldly, and for this Montrose blamed Hamilton for whom he conceived a violent antipathy. He was thus in the mood to enter with enthusiasm into the national movement of opposition to the king's policy for Scotland then being organized by the Earl of Rothes. He signed the National Covenant in 1638 and sat in the Glasgow Assembly as an elder representing the presbytery of Auchterarder. We have seen the active part he took in promoting the cause of the Covenant in the north-east. In the Parliament of August 1639, however, he opposed the constitutional changes that were proposed by the Earl of Argyll as tending to rob the king of his due authority, and, though still in 1640 foremost among the leaders of the Covenanting army which invaded England, he made no secret of his hostility to Argyll whom he was prepared to accuse of aiming at a dictatorship. For this he was confined within Edinburgh Castle, but not before he had written to King Charles urging him to come to his ancient and native kingdom to remedy its distresses. Montrose's letter contains some of the wisest counsels ever offered to Charles. It warns him against flatterers, 'Rehoboam's counsellors', who advise absolutism, which the Western peoples and the Scots above all cannot tolerate. It is a calumny to say that the Scots intend the overthrow of monarchical government. They are devoted to the throne, and have no other end but to preserve their religion in purity and their liberties entire. If they are satisfied on these points they will be loyal subjects. During Charles's brief visit to Edinburgh in 1641 Montrose was a prisoner and so precluded at a critical time from the councils of the helpless king who made concession after concession but in such a way that he failed to conciliate the Covenanters and alienated his potential supporters.

Montrose had signed the National Covenant and professed to the end of his life to adhere to it. It was, he said, the Solemn League and Covenant entered into with a party in England against the king that made him a convinced Royalist, eager to take up arms for his master. Even so the king repeatedly rejected his proposals for action and relied on the advice of the cautiously scheming favourite, Hamilton. At last, on 1 February 1644, a fortnight after the Covenant army entered England, Montrose received a royal commission to raise an army in Scotland. In August he took the field with a small force of Irish Roman Catholics and Highlanders animated less by loyalty to the king than by hatred of Argyll and the Campbell clan. Within a year Scotland, denuded as it was of its fighting men, seemed to be at his feet. Ever sanguine, he could write again to the king describing his victories, and assuring him that before the end of the summer (1645) he would be able to come to his Majesty's assistance with a brave army 'which backed with the justice of your Majesty's cause, will make the Rebels in England as well as in Scotland feel the just rewards of Rebellion'. This proved to be empty boasting. His army melted away and on 13 September he was surprised and defeated at Philiphaugh near Selkirk by David Leslie at the head of a superior force detached from the main Covenant army then serving in England. He himself escaped into exile abroad. Montrose was personally the most attractive of the Scottish noblemen of his period, loyal, courageous, and chivalrous. He was also something of a scholar and political theorist whose idealism was, however, pathetically remote from the realities of his time. His fame rests on his gifts as leader of a guerilla band. His brilliant but fruitless campaign, conducted mainly with the aid of the dreaded and hated 'Irish', merely increased the bitterness and fanaticism of his opponents, for which he must bear some of the responsibility.

Before the battle of Philiphaugh the Royalist cause in England had been irretrievably lost on the field of Naseby, June 1645. The war dragged on for another year, but the king was driven back to diplomacy. In May 1646 he rode into the Scottish camp seeking the assistance of the army then besieging Newark. He hoped to make something of the fact that the Scots were becoming disillusioned regarding their English allies. The sectarianism, radicalism and republicanism of Cromwell's army were repugnant to them, and it was becoming evident that no party in England seriously intended to implement the League and Covenant. But Charles was not yet ready to undertake to do so either. The Scots were fain, therefore, to accept from the English Parliament a large sum of money due to them as expenses and to march home leaving the king to face his English subjects. Then followed a breach between the Parliament and the army which Charles sought to turn to his own advantage by intriguing with both until the army seized him, kept him in durance and clamoured for his trial. This was too much for the Scots, and a wave of popular sympathy for the king encouraged a group of nobles to enter into an Engagement with him to restore him to freedom and authority by peaceful means if possible, and, if not, by force of arms. In return he now undertook in a free Parliament to confirm the Solemn League and Covenant, provided no one should be compelled to sign unwillingly, and to establish presbyterial government and worship for three years, provided he and his household were allowed their accustomed mode of worship. He also undertook to consult the Divines of Westminster with a view to a general ecclesiastical settlement, and to suppress all manner of heretics and schismatics. By the Engagement it was hoped to bring together all parties in Scotland in support of the king. Instead it divided the Covenanters into Engagers and anti-Engagers, and drove a wedge between the Estates and the Kirk. For while a majority in the Estates accepted the Engagement, the General Assembly refused to countenance it. With great difficulty an army was raised and under the incompetent command of Hamilton marched to destruction at the hands of Cromwell at Preston in 1648. This defeat put

Argyll and the fanatical anti-Engagers in power, and they passed the so-called Act of Classes which aimed at excluding from every public office as 'malignants' in varying degrees all who had taken part in the Engagement or in Montrose's campaign, or who had in the slightest degree approved of them or even failed to oppose them, unless they satisfied the discipline of the Kirk by undergoing a humiliating process of repentance. This drastic purge in the interests of the Covenanting extremists was to be the cause of many troubles.

Within a week of the passing of the Act of Classes Charles I was executed in Whitehall to the indignation of nearly all in Scotland. As soon as the news reached Edinburgh his son, then an exile in Holland, was proclaimed king as Charles II. Commissioners were sent to invite him to Scotland on condition that he would accept the Covenant and all that it implied. Naturally he hesitated. He had hopes that an Irish rising might bring about his restoration, but that was crushed by Cromwell with merciless severity. Next he turned to Montrose, also an exile, who was eager to venture on a new campaign in Scotland. Landing in Orkney Montrose gathered a small army, and marched south through Caithness and Sutherland without gaining a single recruit. At Carbisdale in Ross-shire he was utterly defeated, and taking to the western wilds he was handed over to the government by Macleod of Assynt and executed in Edinburgh without pity. Charles now had no alternative but to accept the terms offered him, and in June 1650 he solemnly subscribed the Covenant and arrived in Scotland amid the jubilation of the people, though there were many who doubted his sincerity. Their doubts were fully justified, but the indignities to which they subjected him are nowadays incredibly shocking.

To proclaim Charles as king was as good as a declaration of war on the English Commonwealth and Cromwell hastened north. On 3 September 1650 at Dunbar he met the Scots army, sadly weakened as a result of the Act of Classes, but confident in its sense of the righteousness of its cause, and over it he gained a resounding victory. It was evident to the Scottish leaders that the Act of Classes must go, if not all at once at least piecemeal, and modifying resolutions were accepted by an ever-growing number, known as Resolutioners. Against them a dwindling minority of Protesters or Remonstrants led by James Guthrie, minister of Stirling, kept up a virulent opposition, and the courts of the Church were rent by bitter strife. On 1 January 1651 Charles was crowned at Scone with all due solemnity. Once again an army was equipped, and slipping past Cromwell marched into England with King Charles at its head. Hopes of English Royalist support were unfulfilled, and on 3 September 1651 Cromwell at Worcester obtained his 'crowning mercy'. The Great Civil War was at an end. The king after exciting adventures as a fugitive eventually escaped to France, and Monk, the Commonwealth general, soon completed the conquest and military occupation of Scotland.

To begin with the Commonwealth government necessarily treated Scotland as conquered territory to be held by an English army of occupation and administered by English commissioners. The estates of Royalists were confiscated and a heavy burden of taxation had to be imposed to meet the expenses of the régime. Otherwise so far as the maintenance of order and the administration of justice were concerned nothing was lost by the suppression of the Privy Council, the Estates, and the Court of Session. With regard to the Church the policy was to further the preaching of the Gospel by encouraging and protecting faithful ministers in their pastoral work. But difficulty was encountered in the division which rent the Church in two. In spite of the altered circumstances and repeated attempts on the part of the Resolutioner-majority to conciliate the Protester-minority the schism continued and even increased in bitterness. Disputes over ministerial appointments and wrangles over technical procedures provoked the government to intervene and forcibly dissolve the General Assembly in 1653, forbidding it to meet again—no bad thing as even the ultra-Presbyterian Kirkton admitted. On one matter, however, both parties were agreed, and that was their abhorrence of the principle of toleration as then established in England. In granting protection and encouragement to ministers of the Church of Scotland and all that should voluntarily join them in worship the

Commonwealth government insisted also on toleration for all 'whose conscience was not satisfied with that form and bade them worship God in other Gospel ways'. Popery and prelacy were indeed excluded from toleration but the 'Sectaries' were quite as offensive to Presbyterians of all parties, not least to the Protesters. This opposition to toleration accounted in part for the unpopularity of Cromwell's enlightened plan for uniting the people of Scotland with the people of England in one commonwealth under one government, with thirty representatives in the united Parliament and free trade with England and its dominions. The union was carried into effect in 1656 but few Scots ever sat in the Westminster Parliament. Cromwell's rule in Scotland could never be other than military rule.

The Covenanting movement which began as almost a national movement thus broke down in dissension and strife. But it has left its mark on Scottish religion. For many still it is the heroic period in the history of the national church. It certainly gave to ecclesiology a central place in the mind and heart of the Scottish people.

V

FROM THE RESTORATION TO THE REVOLUTION

THE course of events which led to the restoration of the monarchy in the person of Charles II was initiated in Scotland, when in January 1660 General Monk resolved to march on London ostensibly to restore to Parliament—still the Long Parliament—the power that had been seized by the army. By February it had become apparent that public opinion in England demanded the recall of the king. In these circumstances a group of Edinburgh ministers belonging to the Resolutioner party commissioned James Sharp, minister of Crail and a tried member of the party, to go to London to watch over events and to safeguard the interests of the Church of Scotland. In London Sharp kept in close touch with the Presbyterian ministers there, and also with Monk and other influential politicians. On Monk's behalf he visited the king at Breda shortly before his return to England and took the opportunity also to inform him of the state of affairs in Scotland. He witnessed the ecstatic welcome accorded to Charles when he entered London on 29 May, and he had interviews with the many Scots nobles who came south to greet the king and seek favours from him. Of his activities he rendered a full and faithful account in a series of letters to Robert Douglas, the most influential of the Edinburgh ministers.[1] Sharp had early discerned and reported that, so far as England was concerned, the Solemn League and Covenant was dead. The prelatic Episcopalians were in the ascendant and full of confidence. The English Presbyterians were hoping at best for an Accommodation with a modified Episcopacy. Even among the Scots nobles in London there was talk of the advantages of an episcopal polity in Scotland as in England and Ireland. Nevertheless

[1] Wodrow, *History of the Sufferings of the Church of Scotland*, ed. Burns, vol. i, pp. 5–55.

as Lauderdale, a Presbyterian, had the ear of the king Sharp professed to hope that Charles might be persuaded to continue Presbyterianism at least in Scotland. In fact when he returned to Edinburgh towards the end of August he brought with him a royal letter addressed to Douglas to be communicated to the presbytery of Edinburgh and by it to the other presbyteries throughout the kingdom. In his letter the king expressed his satisfaction with the conduct of the generality of the ministers of Scotland, and his determination to

protect and preserve the government of the Church of Scotland, as it is settled by law, without violation; and to countenance, in the due exercise of their functions, all such ministers who shall behave themselves dutifully and peaceably as becomes men of their calling. We will also take care that the authority and acts of the General Assembly at St. Andrews and Dundee in the year 1651 be owned and stand in force until we shall call another General Assembly which we purpose to do as soon as our affairs will permit.

This letter seemed to promise all that the Resolutioners desired, and all that Sharp had been commissioned to secure, and it was received with expressions of joy and gratitude, not abated by the fact that at the same time a number of Protesters, who had met in Edinburgh to draw up a characteristic supplication to the king, were seized and imprisoned in the castle, from which, however, all, except Guthrie their leader, were soon released. On the strength of the king's letter several presbyteries in which the Resolutioners were in a majority proceeded to depose ministers who belonged to the Protester party, and who had made themselves specially objectionable.

In Scotland as in England the Restoration was welcomed with transports of joy. Very few, if any, Scots had regarded the Commonwealth régime as other than a usurpation, violently suppressing cherished national institutions. Even the Protesters were not republicans though they made no secret of their doubts as to whether Charles II was the truly Covenanted king of their ideal. On the other hand the bulk of the nation had been in greater or less degree implicated in the revolt against Charles I and were eager to gain the forgiveness of his son by extravagant demonstrations of loyalty. All awaited with some anxiety the meeting of the Estates summoned for 1 January 1661 to clean up the mess caused by 'the troubles' just ended. The appointment as Lord High Commissioner of General Middleton, now Earl of Middleton, could hardly give confidence, for he was a rough soldier of fortune who had risen from the ranks, and whose virtues were military rather than statesmanlike. The Earl of Lauderdale remained with the king at Whitehall as secretary of state and chief adviser on Scottish affairs.

The Estates met on 1 January and continued in session until 14 July during which time a vast mass of business of the most various kinds was dealt with. Much of it concerned the rights of individuals, guilds, trades, parishes, town councils, &c., arrears of ordinary judicial proceedings, one may suppose. Appeals by loyalists all over the country, nobles, lairds, ministers, who claimed to have suffered loss for their loyalty to the king, were entertained and restitution ordered. The forfeitures pronounced against Montrose, Huntly, and others who had died in the king's service were cancelled. Naturally punishments were meted out to some of the more prominent of the king's enemies. The Marquis of Argyll who had put the crown on the head of Charles II in 1651 went to London to greet him on his restoration. He was at once sent to the Tower whence he was transferred to Edinburgh Castle and during the sitting of the Estates was tried for treason, condemned, and beheaded. James Guthrie, minister of Stirling and leader of the Protesters, who had aroused the special hatred of Middleton, was another victim; and a third was Johnston of Wariston who had drawn up the National Covenant and been clerk of the Glasgow Assembly of 1638, and who had taken office under the Commonwealth and a seat in Cromwell's Parliament. He fled the country, but was executed on his return two years later, a broken man. Samuel Rutherford, principal of St. Mary's College, St. Andrews, was summoned for trial but was already on his death-bed awaiting summons to a higher tribunal. After his death his book *Lex Rex* was condemned to be burnt by the public hangman. From these acts of vengeance it is pleasant to turn to notice the reward made to Mrs. Granger, wife of the minister of Kinneff, who had smuggled the regalia out of the castle of Dunottar when it was besieged by the Commonwealth army, and had them buried beneath the floor of her husband's church, whence they were brought to Edinburgh to be used at the opening of Parliament.

But of course the most important issue was the constitutional one, and this was dealt with at the beginning of the session. All the woes which the country had suffered since 1638 were attributed to invasions of the royal prerogative, and this was now exalted as never before. The Committee of the Articles was revived, so reducing Parliament once more from a deliberative assembly to one which merely registered decisions already reached elsewhere. The right of the Crown to appoint the officers of State, judges, and members of the Privy Council, and to summon and dissolve Parliament was recognized. An oath of allegiance was imposed on members of Parliament and all holders of public office in terms of which the king was acknowledged to be 'supreme governor of this kingdom over all persons and in all causes'. All assemblies of subjects without royal permission were declared unlawful, and the Solemn League and Covenant with its obligation to intervene in the affairs of England and Ireland was abrogated. Then, on 28 March, a general Act Rescissory was passèd, apparently in haste, rescinding and annulling 'the pretended Parliaments keept' from 1640 to 1648, declaring all their acts and deeds 'to be henceforth null and voyd', but promising indemnity to all, with exceptions still to be specified, who had obeyed these Acts. This was to sweep away the legal basis of the existing Church which Charles had so recently promised to preserve inviolate; and it was followed by another Act in which the king promised

to maintain the true reformed protestant religion in its purity of doctrine and worship as it was established within this kingdom during the reigns of his royal father and grandfather of blessed memory . . . he will give all due countenance and protection to the ministers of the gospel, they containing themselves within the bounds and limits of their ministerial calling and behaving themselves with that submission and obedience to his majesty's authority and commands [that becomes good subjects]. And as to the government of the church his majesty will make it his care to settle and secure the same in such a frame as shall be most agreeable to the Word of God, most suitable to monarchical government and most complying with the public peace and quiet of the Kingdom. In the meantime his majesty doth allow the present administration by sessions, presbyteries and synods and that notwithstanding the preceding act rescissory of all pretended parliaments since the year 1633.

Thus notice was given that serious changes in church government were in contemplation.

At once all who valued the Presbyterian establishment were alarmed. The presbytery of Edinburgh feeling itself cruelly deceived sent a Remonstrance which the High Commissioner refused to receive. In April the synods held their normal spring meetings, and the southern synods drew up protests, the most violent being that of the synod of Galloway which was almost solidly Protester. The northern synods apparently acquiesced, and that of Aberdeen adopted a 'humble address' to the government expressing sorrow for the guilt of the nation and the individual penitence of its members so far as each was accessory to the affronts offered to Charles I and to his son. These are enumerated in great detail. The synod prays that his sacred Majesty

may be pleased in his wisdom and goodness to settle the government of this rent church according to the Word of God, the practice of the Ancient Primitive Church, in such a way as may be most consistent with Royal authority, may conduce most for godliness, for unity peace and order, for a learned godly peaceable and loyal ministry, and most apt to preserve the peace of the three nations.

The synod declares that it would have adopted this address of its own accord, but it admits that it had been reminded of its duty 'by the noble and worthy Lord the Earl Marischal who has great influence in this corner of the land'. Whatever may have been the case in Aberdeen the southern synods were undoubtedly muzzled by the local nobility, for the nobles now were all for law and order, having perhaps been the worst sufferers in 'the troubles'. Moreover most of them now believed that, as the king put it, Presbyterianism was no religion for a gentleman!

When Parliament adjourned in July 1661 a Scottish Council of State was held in Whitehall to decide on the next step to be taken. Middleton in soldierly fashion pointed out that by the Act Rescissory the restoration of episcopacy was an accomplished fact. But others were not so sure and believed that majority opinion in Scotland was hostile and must not be provoked. That Scottish opinion was sharply divided was clear. The episcopalian sentiments of the north-east contrasted violently with the Protester convictions of the south-west. Even within the Resolutioner party there were degrees of loyalty to Presbyterianism with general abhorrence of extremists. Possibly if all Presbyterians had been of one mind a moderate form of Presbyterianism might have been established anew. But Clarendon, Charles's English adviser, observed that if Presbyterianism was established in Scotland it might be difficult to maintain Episcopacy in England and Ireland. So once more the delusive idea of uniformity in the king's dominions in disregard of their historic diversity carried the day. Charles sent his Scottish ministers back with instructions to issue a proclamation setting forth that Presbyterianism was unsuitable to monarchy and had been responsible for the late disturbances in Church and State, and that for the glory of God, the interest of the Protestant religion, the order, peace, and unity of the Church, and its better harmony with the ecclesiastical government in England and Ireland 'he was resolved to restore the Church to its right government by bishops, as it was by law before the late troubles began, and as it now stood settled by law'. By some extraordinary official blunder or piece of cynical effrontery Charles professed thus to fulfil his promise to the presbytery of Edinburgh.

The proclamation was made in September and before the end of the year the king nominated bishops to the various sees. Of those who had held office prior to 1638 only one survived, Thomas Sydserf of Galloway. He was appointed to Orkney, but as he was over eighty years of age he never visited his distant diocese and died in 1663. Of the new bishops appointed only two, Mitchell of Aberdeen and Wishart of Edinburgh, were life-long Episcopalians of the Laudian school who had suffered deprivation and exile for that cause. The others belonged to the Resolutioner party, to its right wing if the expression may be used, and this may indicate an intention on the part of the government to conciliate moderate opinion. Two of them, of very diverse character and aims, may be taken as together representing the lower and the higher ideals of the Restoration Church, James Sharp of St. Andrews and Robert Leighton of Dunblane.

Sharp's acceptance of the primacy exposed him at the time to charges of self-seeking and base treachery, from which it is not easy wholly to absolve him. We must remember, however, that he was a north-country man, born in Banff in 1618 and educated in King's College, under the famous Aberdeen doctors. After graduation in 1637 he betook himself to England and so escaped the commotions of 1638 and the dispersal of the anti-covenanting group in Aberdeen. The outbreak of the Civil War in England drove him back to his native land, where he must have subscribed the Covenants for he was appointed a regent in St. Leonard's College, St. Andrews, in 1643. But he made no secret of his lukewarmness in the Covenanting cause and certainly earned the disapprobation of the fervent Covenanter, Samuel Rutherford, then principal of St. Mary's. Nevertheless in 1648 he was ordained by the presbytery of St. Andrews to the parish of Crail. In the Resolutioner-Protester controversy he took the side of the Resolutioners, and was selected in 1656 to go to London to counteract the influence of Guthrie and Wariston with Protector Cromwell. The Resolutioners were of course Royalist, but such was Sharp's dexterity in putting their case that Cromwell is said to have dubbed him 'Sharp of that Ilk', a dubious compliment! Certainly contempt and loathing of the Protesters was Sharp's dominating ecclesiastical passion. This is made apparent in the correspondence with Douglas in connexion with the important assignment of which an account has already been given. It appears also that he had something to do with the terms of the king's letter to the presbytery of Edinburgh, though whether that letter was intentionally fraudulent is perhaps questionable. At any rate when Middleton came to Edinburgh as High Commissioner Sharp associated with him in the capacity of chaplain, and took no part in any protest made against the Acts of Parliament. By this time he, who had never been an enthusiastic Presbyterian and had always been opposed to the extremists, may have returned to the views of his Aberdeen teachers, if he had ever really abandoned them, or at worst followed the course that must have seemed natural to a cautious and able diplomat and politician. To his old associates Sharp undoubtedly appeared a self-seeking apostate and double-dealer. The attacks made on his character and conduct are understandable, but we may be more charitable now in an age which knows how easily the motives of 'collaborators' are misunderstood.

Robert Leighton was a man of a very different stamp. He was born in London where his father, a Presbyterian minister, had been cruelly punished for a pamphlet attacking prelacy in the time of Laud. He was sent to be educated at Edinburgh University, and in 1641 was ordained minister of Newbattle by the presbytery of Dalkeith, and for a time he took part in the general church struggle. From 1648 he began to grow weary of it, and was glad of an opportunity to relinquish his charge in 1653 when the town council of Edinburgh offered him the principalship of its college. From 1653 to 1662 he held aloof from politics, ecclesiastical and other, and devoted himself to the congenial task of inculcating his otherworldly piety on the student body. Leighton's name was suggested to King Charles by his brother who had become a Roman Catholic in the service of the Duke of York, and he accepted with great reluctance and only in obedience to the royal command, stipulating that he should be appointed to Dunblane because it was a small and poorly endowed see. His hope was that he might be able to reconcile the conflicting parties and bring the truly devout together again. His attempt proved a failure, but today both Presbyterians and

Episcopalians reverence the name of a man deeply and truly religious who in his inmost soul was neither.

As in 1610 it was necessary to arrange for the consecration in England of the new Scottish bishops. Four of the royal nominees, Sharp of St. Andrews, Fairfoul of Glasgow, Hamilton of Galloway, and Leighton of Dunblane, were accordingly summoned to London for this purpose. Fairfoul and Hamilton had been episcopally ordained in Scotland before 1638. But Sharp and Leighton had only Presbyterian ordination, and this Sheldon, Archbishop of Canterbury, insisted was not sufficient. They must first proceed to the inferior orders. The saintly Leighton acquiesced without question, characteristically regarding such matters as of little importance. On the other hand Sharp, the ecclesiastic, made a decent protest, recalling the precedent of 1610. His objection was overruled and he and Leighton were privately ordained first deacons and then presbyters; and on 15 December were consecrated with their colleagues according to the Anglican Ordinal in Westminster Abbey. Four months later they set off together for Scotland in a magnificent coach with which Sharp had provided himself. When Leighton realized that their arrival was to be made the occasion of a public welcome he left the party at Morpeth and travelled alone. He took no part in the consecration of six of the new bishops in Holyrood Abbey on 7 May, nor was he one of the nine bishops who took their seats in Parliament on the following day and were added to the Lords of the Articles. He did, however, take some part in the session which continued from May to September 1662, attending when church matters were to be considered.

One further step required to be taken. On 17 May an Act was passed 'for the restitution and re-establishment of the ancient government of the Church by Archbishops and Bishops'.

Forasmuch as the ordering and disposal of the external government and policy of the church doth properly belong unto his majesty as an inherent right of the crown, by virtue of his royal prerogative and supremacy in causes ecclesiastical . . . Therefore his majesty, with advice and consent of his estates in Parliament, hath thought it necessary and accordingly doth hereby redintegrate the state of bishops to their ancient places and undoubted privileges in parliament and to all their other accustomed dignities privileges and jurisdictions; and doth hereby restore them to the exercise of their episcopal function, presidency in the Church, power of ordination, inflictions of censures.

All Acts in favour of presbyterial church government and especially that of 1592, the so-called charter of presbytery, were rescinded. Furthermore it was enacted that 'all meetings and conventicles in houses which under the pretence of religious exercises may tend to the prejudice of the public worship of God in the churches and to the alienating of the people from their lawful pastors and that duty and obedience they owe to Church and State' were forbidden, and no one was to preach or teach without the license of the ordinary of the diocese.

Armed with all the powers which king and Parliament could confer upon them the bishops had now to face their clergy, who so far had not been consulted. It had been deemed advisable, when the decision had been taken to restore Episcopacy, to withdraw the permission earlier given to kirk sessions, presbyteries, and synods to continue their functions. Now they were abolished by the Act just quoted until they should be authorized and ordered anew by the bishops. Immediately after the dissolution of Parliament, therefore, the Privy Council issued a proclamation stating that the bishops had resolved to hold diocesan synods on certain specified days in October and commanding 'all parsons [*sic*], vicars [*sic*], ministers in burgh and land' to repair to their respective diocesan synods with certification that whosoever shall presume not to give their presence and dutiful attendance at these assemblies and other meetings as shall be appointed by the respective archbishops and bishops 'shall be holden as contemners of his Majesty's authority, and incur the censures provided in such causes'. 'No other Church meetings may be held by any ministers who shall not submit to and own the ecclesiastic government by Archbishops and Bishops. Such meetings shall henceforth be held to be seditious.' The northern synods, as we might expect, were almost fully attended, but in Glasgow and Ayr, Argyll, and above all

Galloway, there were many abstentions. In Galloway, indeed, hardly any ministers put in an appearance. Sharp's Fifeshire brethren in the main stayed away. It is interesting to note that Leighton, greatly daring, broke the letter of the law by inviting the clergy of Dunblane to meet him in synod a month before the appointed day. It is recorded that 'very few were absent, of whom the most sent their excuses either by word or writ'. The diocese was not entirely free from 'nonconformists', one of whom had ultimately to be deposed, but Leighton showed himself forbearing and conciliatory, declaring 'that the Synod and each member of it hath now as full and free liberty of voting and declaring their assent and dissent in all things that occur as ever they had in the former times'. Conditions in Dunblane were exceptional.

The synods of October 1662 met not to deliberate and decide on anything, but to hear from the bishop who presided what the new order would require of them. There is a certain variety in the injunctions given, but in general they indicate an agreed policy. Except possibly in Aberdeen under Bishop Mitchell there was no demand that those who had been presbyterially ordained should be reordained. Nothing seems to have been said anywhere as regards doctrine. The Westminster Confession had of course ceased to be authoritative, and this might mean the reinstatement of the old Scots Confession. But the Restoration Church was hardly a Confessional Church beyond insisting upon the use of the Apostles' Creed in Baptism and in public worship. All of the bishops have something to say about public worship, but none of them, not even Mitchell, proposed to revive the Liturgy of 1637. Sharp was expressly opposed to anything that might stir up old disputes. The Book of Common Prayer was used here and there, but most of the injunctions are content to insist on the use of the Lord's Prayer at all services, and the Doxology at the conclusion of each portion of the metrical psalms. The Westminster Directory was of course forbidden, but the Liturgy of the old Psalm Book (Knox's Liturgy) was not excluded. Indeed it has been pointed out that the changes enjoined represented a return from the Directory to Knox's Book of Common Order.

Throughout the period there was in fact little difference between Episcopalian and Presbyterian worship, except that the bishops encouraged the reading of Scripture lessons in place of the lecturing that had tended to replace it, and stressed the need for shorter sermons, and for greater decorum on the part of congregations. Leighton laid his programme before his first synod meeting and was quietly and patiently insistent on the need for reverence and devoutness in public worship as for charity and holiness in the lives of his clergy. Even he seems to have allowed the Perth Articles of 1618 to fall into oblivion.

The great divergence between the new system and the old was in the matter of church government. The royal supremacy was declared to be absolute. The king was the supreme governor and he ruled through the bishops, to whom the diocesan synods were subservient. The presbyteries were continued though they were refashioned as purely clerical bodies, and their powers reduced. Their moderators were appointed by the bishop except in Dunblane where some freedom of election was allowed. Ministers were enjoined to associate with themselves a competent number of fit persons 'to oversee the manners of the people'. Leighton had no objection to calling these, in Calvin's phrase, *seniores plebis* or elders of the people. Kirk sessions were thus constituted, and performed their disciplinary functions as before. Finally, but not till 1663, the Church constitution was completed by an Act of Parliament for the establishment of a national synod to consist of the archbishops and bishops, deans, archdeacons, moderators of presbyteries, and one member from each presbytery, together with representatives from the four universities. The synod was to meet where and when the king was pleased to determine to consider matters of doctrine, worship, and discipline submitted to it by the king through the Archbishop of St. Andrews who was to preside. Its decisions also required the royal assent. No meeting was ever held. When some of his colleagues proposed that a synod should be summoned Sharp angrily opposed the suggestion. On the other hand in 1664 he did persuade the king to revive the Court of High Commission to deal with ecclesiastical offences, but its powers were soon allowed to lapse, and discipline was henceforth administered by the Privy Council itself.

The Restoration Ecclesiastical Establishment was indubitably 'most suitable to monarchical government' to the point of being thoroughly Erastian. As a remarkably moderate settlement after years of bitter strife it might well have seemed to its promoters to be 'most complying with the public peace and quiet of the Kingdom'. It has also been hailed as an interesting experiment in the fusion of episcopacy and presbytery, by the exclusion of Laudian and Melvillian dogmatisms alike. But for success it would have required years of patient tolerant administration to allow old passions to cool. Irritated by unexpectedly widespread resistance, the government with the support of Sharp and Fairfoul determined on a policy of repression, and a hasty act of Middleton, in his cups it is said, fanned the embers.

Among the Acts of the Parliament of 1649 was one which abolished patronage, followed by an Act of the General Assembly vesting the right of electing ministers in kirk sessions, and giving the congregation the power to complain to the presbytery if they were not satisfied. This gave some recognition to the right, claimed in the First Book of Discipline, of a congregation to call its own minister. But ministerial appointments became a matter of bitter dispute between Resolutioners and Protesters and the latter did not hesitate to invoke the aid of the Commonwealth military government to intrude ministers of their own party on congregations which favoured the other side. The Act Rescissory automatically restored patronage. What then was the position of ministers appointed to parishes since 1649? Were they or were they not covered by the indemnity included in the Act itself? Ostensibly to regularize their position, but no doubt for other reasons too, the Parliament of 1662 declared all livings filled since 1649 to be vacant, and, while confirming to their holders all stipends already paid or due, enacted that every such minister must before 20 September apply to the patron for a presentation and to the bishop for collation. It was further enacted that patrons and bishops must give

R

presentation and collation to present incumbents who applied for them before the appointed day. There was no question of ordination, but to seek collation from a bishop was to give recognition to the hierarchy. In the north and east acquiescence was general, but in Lanarkshire, Ayrshire, Dumfries, and Galloway few if any ministers made the necessary application. Informed of this by Archbishop Fairfoul, Middleton convened the Privy Council at Glasgow, and on 1 October issued an order that all ministers who had failed to apply for collation should remove from their parishes by 1 November. To Middleton's amazement and indignation the great majority of ministers in the south and west took him at his word, and the churches were closed. Sharp's wilier scheme to proceed against recalcitrants one by one was thus frustrated, and all he could do was to secure delay in the operation of the order till 1 February of the following year. Few took advantage of the postponement, and 270 ministers were deprived and their places filled by licentiates drawn from other parts of the country. Against these 'curates', as they were contemptuously called, charges of gross inefficiency and immorality have been brought, unjustifiably in most cases; but however learned eloquent or virtuous they might be, it would have been under the circumstances next to impossible for them to endear themselves to the flocks over which they had been placed.

The curates required and received all the support the law could give them. Their predecessors, the outed ministers, were forbidden to reside within twenty miles of their former charges, and ruinous fines were imposed by an Act of Parliament, known as the Bishops' Drag-net, on all who should absent themselves from their parish churches. Nevertheless the people refused to countenance the curates and open-air conventicles which had been made illegal began to be held in Galloway and Ayrshire. In order to prevent conventicles, which the government professed to regard as seed beds of sedition, and to collect the fines for non-church-going, troops were raised and sent into the west country under the command of Sir James Turner, a mercenary soldier of fortune. His exactions and oppressions provoked resistance, and in

November 1666 a handful of Galloway peasants captured him at Dumfries and sought to raise the standard of revolt in the counties of Ayr and Lanark. Their number never exceeded 3,000 men, and dwindled when it became evident that no support was forthcoming in Edinburgh or the Lothians. At Rullion Green in the Pentland Hills near Edinburgh they were attacked and scattered, and savage punishment was meted out to the captives with the hearty approval of Sharp and Burnet, now Archbishop of Glasgow in succession to Fairfoul.

Sickened by the government's policy of repression, as early as 1665 Leighton had gone to London with the intention of resigning his see, but was sent back by the king with the promise that milder measures were soon to be introduced. Not until 1667 were there signs of a change with the accession to power of the Earl of Lauderdale. Lauderdale had been a keen Covenanter, and one of the Scots assessors at the Westminster Assembly. He was credited with being no friend to bishops, least of all to Sharp for whom he had the greatest contempt, but his easy morals made him a favourite with the king, and he compounded for his questionable past by singular zeal in promoting royal absolutism. It is strange that such a man should have been regarded as the hope of moderate men, but they evidently expected him to curb the persecuting enthusiasms of Sharp and Burnet, and he encouraged Leighton to produce his famous scheme of Accommodation.

Briefly Leighton proposed that the government of the Church should be by presbyteries and synods, with the bishops acting simply as permanent moderators; no minister should be required to promise canonical obedience to the bishop, or to approve episcopacy, only to accept it in the interests of peace; ordinations should take place normally in the church where the ordinand was to serve, and were to be carried out by the presbytery, the bishop officiating as chief presbyter; synods of clergy of the two archiepiscopal provinces should meet triennially with power to censure bishops. These proposals received no support from Leighton's colleagues. The archbishops, Sharp and Burnet, were openly hostile, believing that they sacrificed too much of the prerogatives of the episcopal order. An unsuccessful attempt on the life of Sharp made impracticable an immediate conference with the Presbyterians, which Leighton desired. The scheme was further frustrated by the action of the government in issuing in June 1669 a royal Indulgence permitting ministers 'outed' in 1663, who had lived peaceably and orderly, to return to their parishes, if vacant, or to be appointed to other vacant parishes on conditions not necessarily involving complete submission to the hierarchy. This was an offer of peace on terms that fell short of the 'comprehension' sought by Leighton, and it was accepted by some forty ministers who might otherwise have agreed to Leighton's plan, and who now constituted an unassimilated element in the ministry.

Most of these ministers were placed in parishes in the diocese of Glasgow, and this provoked Burnet and his synod to adopt a Remonstrance against any tampering with the law. Lauderdale countered with an Act of Parliament asserting in extreme form the king's supremacy over all persons and in all causes ecclesiastical, and his right to issue such orders concerning the administration of the external government of the Church as he in his royal wisdom should think fit. Sharp and the bishops, after a feeble resistance, acquiesced. Burnet was deprived and Leighton put in his place, first as administrator and later as Archbishop of Glasgow, accepting appointment in the hope of furthering his plan of accommodation. He gathered round him a group of like-minded ministers whom he sent round the diocese to commend it to the people, and he himself held several conferences with representatives of the Presbyterian party in which he patiently tried to argue them out of what he personally regarded as ignorant prejudices, but which they held to be principles of conscience. All his efforts were unavailing and negotiations were broken off in 1671, not to be resumed until our own time, under happier political circumstances and with a sounder theological understanding of the issues involved. Three years later Leighton was permitted to demit his charge and withdraw to a private life of characteristic piety in the south of England. Burnet, now a pliant tool of Lauderdale, returned to Glasgow and succeeded Sharp at St. Andrews in 1679

The abandonment of the accommodation plan left Lauderdale to seek peace by his own method of clemency mingled with severity. A second Indulgence was issued in 1672 and was accepted by a further fifty or more of the ejected ministers. This was followed in 1674 by a proclamation of indemnity, relaxing penalties for past contraventions of the laws in favour of the Church establishment, and expressing the hope that for the future obedience would be forthcoming. On the other hand the laws against conventicles were made more stringent. The death penalty was imposed for field preaching, and threats of rigorous punishment were held over any who harboured or in any way countenanced the preachers. The ranks of the Presbyterians were thus divided, but among the remnant who scorned to accept the Indulgence conventicling became more widespread. An attempt was made to put upon lairds responsibility for the behaviour of their servants and tenants, but when those of the western countries declared that they could not control their dependents, a Highland host, 6,000 strong, was quartered on the people for a time in 1678, and in 1679 a Convention of Estates agreed to a tax or 'cess' for the purpose of maintaining regular troops to suppress conventicles. On 3 May Archbishop Sharp was murdered on Magus Moor near St. Andrews, and his assailants took refuge in the west where soon the expected rebellion broke out. James Graham of Claverhouse, commanding a troop of newly raised cavalry, rashly attacked a conventicle attended by many who had come armed, and suffered defeat at Drumclog. The rebels grew in number but were badly led, and were soon crushed at Bothwell Brig by an army under the Duke of Monmouth. Many prisoners were taken and after harsh detention in Greyfriars churchyard in Edinburgh most of them were released, on promising not to take up arms again, but 200 were condemned to be deported to the Barbados, and perished when their transport ship was wrecked among the Orkney Islands.

The rebellion put an end to Lauderdale's rule which had become more and more violent and corrupt. In his place as

High Commissioner came James, Duke of York, the king's brother and heir, a Papist whom for that reason a strong party in England were endeavouring to exclude from the English throne. The Scots Parliament was more subservient. In 1681 it recognized James's indefeasible hereditary right to the Scottish throne irrespective of difference in religion, and it passed a Test Act imposing an oath on all holders of public offices in Church and State, obliging them to maintain the Protestant religion as set forth in the old Scots Confession, to disown all popish and 'phanatical' doctrines and principles, to recognize the royal supremacy over all persons and in all causes, to abjure the Covenants, and not to endeavour any alteration in the government either in Church or State as now established by the laws of this kingdom. Burnet, the primate, was enthusiastic in support of the Test but some of his colleagues were repelled by its reference to the Scots Confession. A number of ministers were deprived for refusing to take it, and the Earl of Argyll was condemned for treason because he offered to do so with reservations. He saved himself for the time being by flight to Holland. The purpose of the Test was of course to secure, so far as a parliamentary Act could do so, the succession of James to absolute power in Scotland. He was himself explicitly exempted from taking the oath.

There remained the problem of pacifying the south-west. Lauderdale's policy had succeeded in splitting the Presbyterians and in sowing seeds of bitterness between the indulged and those who held them to have been guilty of defection from the Covenants and the true Church. The latter found a leader in Richard Cameron, a young field preacher trained in Holland, who demanded absolute separation from all who had anything to do with the Indulgence. His followers, the Society Folk, are more commonly known as the Cameronians, and their principles—Presbyterian church government *jure divino*, loyalty to the Covenants, anti-erastianism—are set forth in a document designated The Queensferry Paper. In pursuance of these principles Cameron with some companions rode into the town of Sanquhar, Dumfriesshire, on 22 June 1680, and at the market cross read a declaration renouncing allegiance to Charles Stuart, declaring war on all who aided and abetted him in his tyranny, and disowning as heir to the throne the Duke of York, 'that professed Papist'. This declaration of war was accepted as such by the government, and troops were sent into the affected areas, under commanders of whom Claverhouse acquired the chief notoriety for cruelty. Cameron himself was slain in 1680 in a skirmish at Ayrsmoss. His successor, Donald Cargill, was caught and executed in 1681 to be succeeded in turn by James Renwick, executed in 1688. In general the sufferers were humble people, peasants, or mechanics of independent minds, who could not or would not clear themselves of suspicion of having some degree of sympathy with the Cameronian doctrines. In many cases they were butchered without a legal trial. 'The Killing Time', as it has been called, lasted from 1680 to 1688, and has left its memorials in many a west country churchyard, and has made an indelible mark on the soul of Scotland. Doubtless the number and the sufferings of the martyrs have been exaggerated as is usual in such matters. The Cameronians gave the government every excuse to wage war on them and they themselves retaliated. They were extremists whose excesses were condemned by nearly all of their Presbyterian brethren at the time. Nevertheless, though they were but a remnant, their loyalty to convictions more widely shared, their constancy under persecution and their warm if narrow evangelical faith, must be recognized, and without their testimony the victory of Presbyterianism would have been impossible.

Charles II died on 6 February 1685 and four days later his brother was proclaimed in Edinburgh as King James VII. His accession was greeted with expressions of loyalty and that rebellion was far from the thoughts of his subjects was shown by the failure of the Earl of Argyll's expedition. A sincere Romanist, James had set his heart on the restoration of Roman Catholicism in both his kingdoms. In this he had the example and financial support of Louis XIV of France whose Revocation of the Edict of Nantes, November 1685, was the culmination of an almost successful campaign to exterminate the Huguenots. But James had seriously underestimated the strength of his peoples' Protestant convictions.

Even the usually subservient Scottish Parliament, invited in 1686 to repeal the penal laws against Romanists, administered a rebuff. The king therefore had recourse to other means. He had the chapel royal at Holyrood furnished for Roman Catholic worship, and introduced Jesuit teachers, literature, and a printing press to carry on propaganda from Holyrood. On various pretexts he dismissed Protestants from offices of State, the Privy Council, the judiciary, military commands, even town councils, and replaced them with Romanists dispensing them from the requirements of the Test Act. He thus alienated many powerful people. He alarmed the clergy by punishing some who preached against popery, and by depriving the Archbishop of Glasgow and the Bishop of Dunkeld for quite minor acts of opposition. Finally in 1687 by his own authority he issued two proclamations of Indulgence. In the first after a grudging permission to Presbyterians to worship in private houses only, he went on to suspend all laws against Romanists whose principles were, he said, to be good Christians and dutiful subjects. The second, three months later, was in appearance more generous. All penal and sanguinary laws made against any for nonconformity to the religion established by law were suspended, and leave was given to all to serve God in their own way in private houses, chapels or places hired or built for that purpose, provided no disloyalty be preached, and the preachers and places be intimated to the public authorities. The laws against conventicles, however, were to remain in full force. James also declared his will to protect the clergy of the established church, while obviously weakening their position. They on their part showed little sign of resistance. The Presbyterians on the other hand, with the exception of the Cameronians, welcomed their new-found liberty and proceeded to organize themselves as a dissenting body. But James's rule was near its end. His attack on the privileges of the Church of England was his undoing. By the end of 1688 he had fled to France, and William and Mary reigned in Whitehall in his stead.

In Scotland the news of James's fall was a signal for a riot in Edinburgh and an attack on Romanist chapels and institutions. In the south-west the peasantry 'rabbled' the episcopalian clergy out of their manses and parishes. The bishops sent Rose, Bishop of Edinburgh, to London to watch over their interests, but, though assured by the Bishop of London that William was not unfavourable to episcopacy, he could not promise that his colleagues would follow the example of most of the English bishops, and for himself offered only qualified service—'so far as law reason or conscience shall allow me'. William was disappointed for he had learned from the many Scottish nobles and gentry who were in London that the aristocracy at all events were episcopalian in sympathy, and he realised the advantage of unity of church government in keeping England and Scotland together. He acceded, however, to the request of the nobles to take over the government of Scotland provisionally and to summon a Convention of Estates.

The Convention met on 14 March 1689. The Jacobite minority soon withdrew, Claverhouse (Viscount Dundee) to the Highlands in an endeavour to repeat the exploits of Montrose. His death at Killiecrankie in July put an end to such hopes. The majority, protected by a regiment raised among the Cameronians, resolved that James had forfeited the crown and that his throne was vacant. It drew up a Claim of Right enumerating a long series of illegalities of which James had been guilty, expressing confidence in William who had come to deliver the nation from violation of its religion, laws and liberties, and declaring William and Mary to be King and Queen of Scotland. Articles of Grievances were also drawn up and an oath to be taken by the sovereigns on their acceptance of the Crown, binding them 'to be careful to root out all heretics and enemies to the true worship of God that shall be convicted by the true Kirk of God'. William took the oath but with the reservation that he would not bind himself to be a persecutor. Finally a proclamation was issued commanding all ministers to pray for William and Mary as king and queen on pain of deprivation. By the end of the year the number of deprivations is said to have reached a total of 182, nearly all in the southern lowlands and Fife. When to this number is added that of the 'rabbled curates' of the south-west the extent of the sufferings of the episcopalian (and Jacobite) clergy will be understood.

On 5 June the Convention was regularized as a Parliament, with the Duke of Hamilton as royal commissioner. In spite of his earnest entreaties and assurances the bishops absented themselves, and in July an Act was passed abolishing prelacy on grounds which had already been stated in the Claim of Right in language not to be found in any Presbyterian formulary. 'Prelacy and the superiority of any office in the Church above presbyters is and has been a great and insupportable grievance to this nation and contrary to the inclinations of the generality of the people, they having reformed from Popery by presbyters, and ought to be abolished.' Sundry Acts in favour of episcopacy were repealed 'and the King and Queens majesties do declare that they, with advice and consent of the estates of this parliament, will settle by law that church government in this kingdom which is most agreeable to the inclinations of the people'. The promised settlement had to wait, however, for nearly a year, by which time it had become clear that William's government in Scotland had nothing to hope for from the Episcopalians, who remained loyal to James. In 1690, therefore, the Act of Supremacy was repealed, and Presbyterianism was established. The Westminster Confession of Faith was approved as the public confession of the church. The government of the church by kirk sessions, presbyteries, provincial synods, and general assemblies as established in 1592 was confirmed. Ministers ejected in 1662 were restored to their parishes whether vacant or not. Those removed in 1689, whether by 'rabbling' or for refusal to pray for William and Mary, were held to be deprived, and those who had irregularly taken their places were recognized; and a general assembly consisting of representatives of the restored Presbyterian ministers and elders associated with them was appointed to meet on the third Thursday of October 1690 'to try and purge out all insufficient negligent scandalous and erroneous ministers'. A petition from the Episcopalian synod of Aberdeen for a more fully representative assembly was ignored. Finally with much hesitation William consented to the abolition of patronage except in the case of town councils. When a rural parish fell vacant the heritors, being protestant, and the elders were to nominate a minister to the congregation for approval or disapproval, and reasons for disapproval were to be given in to the presbytery of the bounds, which should have the final decision.

Such was the Revolution Settlement which brought to an end the long, bitter, and complicated struggle between Church and Crown begun with Knox at the Reformation in 1560, and continued by Andrew Melville and the Covenanters. To extreme Covenanters the settlement appeared a compromise which they could not accept, but the government of the Church of Scotland was recognized by law to be Presbyterian and so it has remained. The conflict inevitably involved loss as well as gain. It must have retarded the economic development of Scotland, and still more its cultural development, literary, artistic and intellectual. If it kept religious issues dominant in the minds of the people, even from a religious point of view the passions aroused undoubtedly led to a neglect of the gentler Christian virtues and graces, notably charity. So thought the saintly Robert Leighton. Another attractive example of this way of thinking was Henry Scougal, professor of divinity in King's College, Aberdeen, 1674–8, who died at the early age of 28, and whose book *The Life of God in the Soul of Man* became a religious classic. Such men had little interest in ecclesiastical polity and found in Christian mysticism a refuge from the storm. Some conformed to episcopacy in 1662 and to presbytery in 1690, not all of them 'Vicars of Bray'. Laurence Charteris certainly was not. Ordained Presbyterian minister of St. Bathans (Yester) in 1654, he accepted episcopal collation in 1662. He was a friend of Leighton and one of the preachers chosen to advocate the Accommodation. Becoming professor of Divinity in Edinburgh University he resigned rather than take the Test in 1681, and was episcopally instituted to Dirleton in 1688. In 1690 he conformed to presbytery but refused to regard the introduction of prelacy as a national defection. 'The defection has not been from the truth or from the fundamental doctrine of the Christian faith, but from the life of God and the power of religion.'

These men had no monopoly of personal piety. On the other side in ordinary covenanting folk, even in the fiercest of the field preachers, there glowed a warmth of devotion to Christ Jesus the Redeemer, and a fervent loyalty to His Crown and Kingdom, to the Kirk of which He was the only King and Head. Both the Reformers and the Covenanters held a 'high' doctrine of the Church and its Christ-given authority which brought them into collision with royal claims to supremacy. Political historians have denounced their dogmatism and fanaticism, and their preposterous claim in the name of Christ to domineer over the civil State. Up to a point we may agree. Political liberty was not their ideal. Nevertheless they contributed not a little to its ultimate attainment. Their testimony was inevitably dogmatic and theological, but on no other basis could resistance have been offered to absolute monarchy whether of the Renaissance or of the Lutheran-Anglican Divine-Right type. It was the seed, moreover, from which has grown the spiritual freedom enjoyed by the Church of Scotland today, which is admired and coveted by other Churches.

From the beginning the Scottish Reformers recognized that the organizing of congregations or 'the planting of Kirks' was an urgent task. And Calvin had taught them what to aim at. In every congregation there must be a qualified and recognized minister of the Word of God and the Sacraments, elders representative of the people associated with him in the exercise of ecclesiastical discipline, and deacons to take charge of its financial and temporal affairs. Congregations would thus have a corporate existence exhibiting the essential notes of the true Kirk of God. In 1560 fully organized congregations were necessarily few but they multiplied with fair rapidity and gave to the Reformed Church a solid base and enduring strength for its long struggle with episcopacy and sectarianism. The preservation of the distinctively Reformed type of parochial ministry and congregational organization, which the Church of Scotland still enjoys, must be accounted gain.

During the struggle, and as a consequence of it, from 1574 onwards the Presbyterian system of church government was developed. Congregations were closely knit through graded ecclesiastical courts into one national Church whose judicial and legislative powers were focused in a General Assembly meeting annually or oftener as required. The assembly was an ecclesiastical but not an exclusively clerical body, for it consisted theoretically of ministers and elders in equal numbers, representative of the whole Church or ideally of the nation ecclesiastically organized. Such a body could not easily be fitted into the traditional constitution of the kingdom and threatened to be a rival to the civil power which had no such effective organ. Even Parliament was not. There might have been interesting developments if the Stuart kings had continued to rule only over their 'ancient Kingdom'. The General Assembly which they strove to suppress outlived them and continues to be a distinctive institutional expression of the corporate life of the Church of Scotland. Indeed, since the union of the Parliaments in 1707 it has been the most impressive reminder of Scotland's former independence as a nation.

The Covenanting struggle led to a hardening of presbytery and episcopacy into two antagonistic systems with a wide gulf between them which shows little sign of narrowing. But if the Church of Scotland was thus separated from the Anglican communion it was destined to become the honoured mother of large and flourishing Presbyterian churches throughout the English-speaking world, and since the founding of the Presbyterian Alliance in 1875 has occupied a central position in the communion of Reformed Churches.

PART IV

THE CHURCH BY LAW ESTABLISHED

I

THE RE-ESTABLISHMENT OF PRESBYTERIANISM

THE historical task of William of Orange was the organization of resistance to the domination of France in Europe. Success required the adhesion of England, and this was secured by the removal of the chief impediment, James II. But England must be united and prosperous, and for this the greatest possible toleration of minorities was imperative as a political expedient. But, it should be said, William believed in toleration for its own sake and public opinion in England in the main was with him. Scotland with its recent agonising history presented a more difficult problem, and King William was fortunate in having throughout his reign the wise counsel of a like-minded Scot, William Carstares. Son of John Carstares, Protester minister of the High Church of Glasgow 'outed' in 1663, William graduated M.A. at Edinburgh University in 1667, and soon after went to Holland, as did many refugees from persecution at home. While a student of theology at Utrecht he was introduced to the Prince of Orange. Between 1672 and 1685 he made several journeys to Britain on errands mainly political. Twice he was arrested and imprisoned. On the second occasion a deposition wrung from him by torture was used in evidence against his friend Baillie of Jerviswood who was alleged to have been implicated in the Rye House Plot. In 1688 he came with William's expedition to England and throughout his reign acted as his chaplain and adviser on Scottish affairs, both civil and ecclesiastical. Such was his influence at court that the Jacobites dubbed him 'Cardinal' Carstares. On the accession of Queen Anne he returned to Scotland as principal of Edinburgh University, and one of the ministers of the town. Four times he was elected moderator of the General Assembly, and by his moderation and kindly sagacity so guided his brethren in anxious times, that he may be said to have been the architect of the Church by Law Established.

The refusal of the Scottish bishops to follow the example of their English colleagues in accepting the Revolution compelled King William to turn to the Presbyterians, but the 60 ministers and 120 elders who formed the assembly of 1690 might have appeared most unlikely to advance the king's policy urged upon them in the royal missive. 'A calm and peaceable procedure will be no less pleasing to us than it becometh you. We could never be of the mind that violence was suited to the advancing of true religion, nor do we intend that our authority should ever be a tool to the irregular passions of any party. Moderation is what religion enjoins, neighbouring churches expect of you and we recommend to you.' They were all men with bitter memories of persecution, suffered for convictions which they could not easily abandon, and of which they were being sharply reminded by some, more extreme than themselves, with whose principles they were in full sympathy. The problem was posed by a petition presented by three Cameronian ministers, Lining, Shields, and Boyd, for admission to the Church, and again when a national fast as an act of penitence for national defections was proposed. The three ministers were admitted and placed in charges, but their people, the Society Folk, held aloof scorning an Erastian Establishment and ready to make the most of every weak compliance with the demands of an un-Covenanted government. Such reproaches touched a tender spot. Later assemblies would fain have passed an Act declaratory of the Church's intrinsic powers, 'derived from Jesus Christ, the Only Head and King of His Church, from Whom it has received its order and presbyterian government, which is a better foundation than the inclinations of the people or the laws of men'. A statement in these terms was issued by the Commission of Assembly in 1698, but a movement to embody it in an Act in 1703 was scotched by the commissioner who dissolved the assembly in Queen Anne's name. The idea was never abandoned but tended to fall into the background. The societies continued their independent life until having been joined by two presbyterially ordained ministers they were able in 1743 to constitute the Reformed Presbyterian Church, claiming to be the true Kirk of the Covenants. In 1876 the majority joined the Free Church of Scotland, leaving a remnant, who, however, have connexions with larger similar bodies in Ireland and the United States.

In spite of his disappointment with the bishops' failure to co-operate William hoped that it would be possible to include in the Establishment those of the parochial clergy who had escaped the 'rabblings' and civil deprivations of 1689, and were still in possession of practically all the parishes north of the Tay. He demanded only that they should take the prescribed oath of allegiance. The assembly of 1690 in accordance with the powers entrusted to it appointed two commissions to visit the areas north and south of the Tay respectively 'to purge out all insufficient negligent scandalous and erroneous ministers'. The northern Commission could make little headway owing to the opposition of the gentry and people, but elsewhere the purge was carried out with much harshness. At the same time commissions were appointed by the Privy Council to purge the four universities, and this was done with thoroughness in St. Andrews, Glasgow, and Edinburgh. Aberdeen alone escaped. Those who were thus ejected won a great deal of sympathy in England, and two of them carried their complaints to William in person. The king was indignant. He wrote letters to the Privy Council and to the commissions ordering the purges to cease. When the assembly met in 1692 he pointed out that it was not truly representative of the ministry as a whole, but only of a minority, and demanded that all should be admitted who took the oath of allegiance, promised to submit to and concur with presbyterial church government and subscribe the Westminster Confession 'as containing the doctrine of the Protestant religion professed in this kingdom'. Petitions for admission on those terms began to come in from some of the episcopal clergy, but the assembly was resentful of the king's interference in spiritual matters and took no action. It was therefore dissolved by the commissioner but the members refused to disperse until the moderator named a day in August 1693 for the next assembly to meet.

Meantime Parliament intervened. In view of Jacobite intrigues the simple oath of allegiance to William and Mary was expanded by an additional assurance, to be given by all office-holders including parish ministers. They were to undertake to acknowledge William and Mary 'as the only lawful and undoubted sovereigns of the realm *de jure* as well as *de facto*', and 'to defend their title and government against the late King James and his adherents who either by open or secret attempts shall disturb or disquiet their majesties in the possession and exercise thereof'. All episcopal ministers who should take the oath and give the assurance were to be protected in their livings until, having subscribed the Confession of Faith and acknowledged the Presbyterian government as the only government of the Church in Scotland, they should be received into the church courts by an assembly to be summoned by their Majesties for this purpose. Presbyterians should, it might be supposed, have found no difficulty in giving the assurance, but such was their abhorrence of Erastianism, that when the assembly met on 29 March 1694 it seemed that there must be a rupture of relations between Church and Crown. It is said that disaster was prevented by a dramatic intervention of Carstares, who succeeded in persuading William to recall his order demanding subscription to the assurance on the part of Presbyterian ministers. In gratitude for this gesture the assembly appointed a commission to receive episcopal ministers who qualified in terms of the parliamentary Act. In the following year Parliament took a further step. All Episcopalians still holding livings who would take the oaths of allegiance and assurance before 1 September 1695 were to have his Majesty's protection in retaining their benefices and exercising their ministry within their parishes but without a seat in the church courts 'unless they be first duly assumed by a competent church judicatory'. More than 100 took the oaths without seeking admission to the church courts, and many more continued in their parishes without even taking the oaths, especially in the north where these were not rigorously exacted. It is said that in 1707 there were still as many as 165 parish ministers in Scotland who held aloof from the established church government, and spoke of the General Assembly as the Assembly of the Presbyterians. The last of these must have been Archibald Lundie minister of Saltoun in East Lothian, 1696 till 1759. Of him we are told that 'he had been bred an old Scotch Episcopalian and was averse to the Confession of Faith. The presbytery showed lenity towards him, so he did not sign it to his dying day, for which reason he never could be a member of Assembly.' In addition there were many who had been ejected from their livings, but who 'intruded' either in their former parishes or else-where, preaching, administering baptism and solemnizing marriages clandestinely to the indignation of the Presbyterian ministers. All this diversity made the organization of a Scot-tish Episcopal Church difficult, apart from the fact that up to 1715 at least hopes were entertained that episcopacy might be re-established. A vigorous, not to say virulent, pamphlet propaganda was carried on with this end in view.

Certainly no leadership was offered by the pre-Revolution bishops. Deprived of their incomes and parliamentary privi-leges in 1689 they withdrew into retirement, so avoiding the necessity of swearing allegiance to William or breaking their oath to James. One of them, Cairncross, accepted a see in Ireland. Another, Gordon of Galloway, followed James into exile and finally into the Roman Church. Those who remained in Scotland seem to have regarded their diocesan jurisdic-tion as suspended while the lawful king from whom they had received it no longer reigned in fact. At most we find some of them endeavouring to enlist English sympathy and support for the dispossessed clergy. Non-jurors themselves, they must have been out of sympathy with those who took the oaths prescribed in 1693, which divided Episcopalians into Jaco-bites and non-Jacobites. Not until 1705 did the surviving bishops decide that it was possible to hand on the succession without infringing the prerogatives of the Crown, now legiti-mately represented in their view by the Old Pretender, James VIII and III. They secretly consecrated two new bishops while explicitly denying to them diocesan title or jurisdic-tion. Others were added on the same terms from time to time, consent being solemnly sought and obtained from 'the

King over the water'. In 1720, however, Bishop Fullarton was appointed Bishop of Edinburgh with the approval of the Pretender who also made him one of his trustees in Scotland. Their Jacobitism, honourable and romantic though it may be held to be, was the strength and weakness of the Episcopalians throughout the eighteenth century, and a real hindrance to their ecclesiastical development.

Though severely hampered by difficulties of many kinds 'the Church by law established' was acutely conscious of its position and responsibility as the national Church. Successive assemblies energetically pressed on with the task of restoring the full Presbyterian organization. Presbyteries and synods had continued to exercise certain limited functions during the episcopal period. In the south they resumed their old constitution and powers with comparative ease. In the north where there were extremely few Presbyterian ministers and the non-conforming clergy in the main retained possession of their parishes the problem was much more difficult. It was necessary at first to entrust large areas to what may be called 'skeleton' presbyteries, and later to divide these and rearrange their bounds as ministers became more plentiful. This process was not completed till 1730 or thereby. Presbyteries, it was enacted, should be represented in the General Assembly by commissioners, ministers, and elders, in proportion to their numerical strength. Further powers were given to them in 1697 when what is known as the Barrier Act was passed. It laid down that legislation proposed to and approved by a General Assembly must be sent down to presbyteries for their judgement, and only with the approval of the majority of presbyteries could be enacted by a later assembly. This was and is an invaluable check on hasty legislation, and ensures to the whole Church an opportunity for mature deliberation.

The chief difficulty of course was the shortage of Presbyterian ministers. Even the southern presbyteries were for many years understaffed, and the situation was much worse in the north. In 1695 the assembly made arrangements for some forty-two ministers to be sent to work in northern parishes for three months in the year, and enjoined that twenty-two of them should be settled there permanently if they found the people willing to call them. But not all who were appointed to go, even for three months only, obeyed, for they knew that their mission would be unwelcome and might be hazardous. Those who failed to go without valid excuse were censured. Attempted settlements in northern parishes which were frustrated by violence are recorded. Nevertheless some settlements were effected, and the presbyteries were thereby strengthened. It is interesting to note the special interest taken by general assemblies in the Gaelic-speaking areas. Even in 1690 arrangements were made for the distribution of Bibles and Catechisms in the 'Irish' language, and a few years later Gaelic-speaking ministers settled in the Lowlands were enjoined to seek charges in the Highlands, while Gaelic-speaking probationers were forbidden to accept settlement in the south. The progress was slow at first, but after the failure of the Rebellion of 1715, within a single generation even Wester Ross, which had been solidly Jacobite-Episcopalian, admitting no Presbyterian minister at all, had become the cradle of ultra-Presbyterianism, as it still is. While all allowance must be made for favourable political circumstances it is none the less clear that the Revolution Church was imbued with a real missionary enthusiasm.

In the outward forms of public worship Presbyterianism brought little change. During the episcopal period worship had been generally non-liturgical except that place was given in it to the Lord's Prayer, the Doxology, and the Apostles' Creed. These came to be, wrongly, regarded as badges of prelacy and were discontinued by the Presbyterians, but not by all of them. Sir Hugh Campbell of Cawdor contended for the retention of the Lord's Prayer at least, not without considerable support, and he might be said to have won his point when the assembly of 1705 seriously recommended to all ministers within the national Church the due observance of the Westminster Directory. The Lord's Prayer is of course recommended in the Directory as 'not only a pattern of prayer, but itself a most comprehensive prayer'. The Act of 1705 is, however, in rather general terms. More astonishing is the apparently universal departure from the Directory in the matter of reading from the Scriptures of the Old and New Testaments and the substitution of a lecture on a Scripture passage, often very brief. There can be no doubt that the intention was to make the people well acquainted with Holy Scripture, as liturgical reading might fail to do. It must seem to us now that public worship was unduly didactic, but that may have been more necessary than we are apt to think it is today. At all events as conducted by evangelicals like Thomas Boston it was also tinged with warm emotion, and nourished deep and fervent piety in the people. In spite of the efforts of Leighton the celebration of Holy Communion was of infrequent occurrence during the episcopal period and the post-Revolution Church was satisfied with its celebration once a year. But the Protesters had started a custom that gained popularity from its association with the work of the field preachers in the persecuting time. The minister of a parish in which communion was to be celebrated would be assisted by three or more, often many more, of his colleagues from other parishes whose people would gather in vast concourses for 'The Occasion'. From Saturday to Monday many sermons would be preached each day in the open air, and throughout Sunday communicants would be served in relays sitting at a table in the church. In this way Holy Communion acquired a distinctive place in the life of the Church which in spite of change it has retained.

In the lowland dioceses, at least, kirk sessions existed throughout the episcopal period, and exercised along with the minister oversight over the morals of the people. With the return of Presbyterianism the eldership would be more thoroughly integrated into the constitution of the Church, and, on the abolition of patronage, elders were given some say in ministerial appointments. But in matters of discipline Presbyterianism introduced nothing substantially different from what had gone before, unless possibly in some places the new discipline tended to be more severely puritanical than the old. The basic document is *The Form of Process in the Judicatories of the Church of Scotland with relation to Scandals and Censures* approved by Act of the General Assembly in 1707. The scandals to be dealt with are swearing, cursing, profaning of the Lord's Day, drunkenness, and sexual sins. The procedure to be adopted is carefully regulated with an eye to the reclaiming of the sinner and to edification; and the treatment varies from private admonition, through suspensions from the benefit of sealing ordinances, i.e. the Sacraments, to excommunication lesser or greater, from which absolution can only be obtained by public repentance before the congregation. In the last resort where offenders prove recalcitrant appeal is to be made to the civil magistrate 'who ought to use his coercive power for the suppressing of all such offences, and vindicating the discipline of the church from contempt'. All this is so repugnant to modern feeling that it is hard to do any kind of justice to the moral purpose which inspired it. We sympathize with Milton's protest against the whole disciplinary system of kirk sessions when it was being pressed upon England by the Scots at the Westminster Assembly—'New Presbyter is but old Priest writ large.' The worst that can be said of its operation in Scotland may be read in Henry Grey Graham's *Scotland in the Eighteenth Century*, with ample illustration from the records of kirk sessions and presbyteries. To obtain a more complete and balanced view, however, it is necessary to take account of the kind of men who actually operated it, many of them earnest but withal kindly men, respected and beloved by their people. A good example, well known from his fascinating and in its way attractive *Memoirs*, is Thomas Boston, minister successively of Simprin, Berwickshire (1699–1707), and Ettrick (1707–32), who realized to a high degree the ideal of the post-Revolution Presbyterian minister. An utterly sincere, godly, deeply exercised man, he watched over the moral and spiritual welfare of his people with entire devotion and genuine love. Men of his type were perhaps exceptional, but both in the Lowlands and the Highlands their influence had much to do with the shaping of the religious life of Scotland.

Dutch William, wholly engrossed in his continental commitments, never found time to visit Scotland or to take much interest in Scottish affairs. He had lost the traditional means of controlling its Parliament through the bishops and the

Committee of Articles, and he had sometimes reason to complain of the acts of his ministers. The pacification of the Highlands, after the Claverhouse campaign, had been proceeding happily enough, but William's Scottish advisers decided to teach the Highlanders a sharp lesson. Taking advantage of the fact that the chief of the MacDonalds of Glencoe had failed to take the oath of allegiance before the appointed day, they got William to sign an order for the 'extirpation of that sect of thieves'. On 13 February 1692 a massacre took place in circumstances of treachery and brutality. Widespread indignation was aroused which the Jacobites took care to foment to the king's discredit.

The Massacre of Glencoe was a local incident reminiscent of the past. The Darien adventure affected the whole nation and though disastrous in its immediate result pointed to the future. Scottish commerce since the Restoration had been hampered by English protectionist legislation, and by the wars with Holland and France. In 1695, therefore, the Scottish Parliament decided to grant a charter to 'The Company of Scotland trading to Africa and the Indies'. It soon transpired that this company was to be largely financed by English merchants who sought in this way to circumvent the monopolist English East India Company. That powerful body was able to compel the withdrawal of English subscribers, and to put obstacles in the way of support looked for from continental countries. National pride was aroused and the Scots determined to carry on alone. All classes subscribed. The enormous sum of over £200,000 was gathered in, and it was decided to plant a Scottish colony, New Caledonia, among the swamps of Darien, in the heart of the Spanish American empire (1698). Three expeditions were equipped and dispatched amid tremendous enthusiasm, and one after another they came to grief, with loss of lives and treasure that Scotland could ill afford. Worst of all King William's European policy at that time required the good will of Spain, and he felt compelled to order the governors of the English plantations on the American continent not to give any support to the Scots colonists. The angry feelings engendered by the disaster threatened a rupture between the two kingdoms.

William himself saw plainly that the only remedy was a closer union, which he pressed upon the English Parliament without success. His last message sent from his deathbed in 1702 urged that 'nothing can contribute more to the present and future peace security and happiness of England and Scotland than a firm and entire union between them'. The accession of Queen Anne helped matters not at all. Her known partiality for the episcopal clergy encouraged them to believe that episcopacy might be restored, and the Presbyterians were correspondingly alarmed. The two Parliaments recklessly widened the breach, and the Crown was powerless. In 1704 it was made clear that Scotland was prepared to have a separate sovereign on the queen's death without an heir. It was stipulated that the said sovereign must always be 'of the Royal Line of Scotland and of the true Protestant Religion', but there were many who hoped it might be, despite his Romanism, the Old Pretender whom France had recognized as James III and VIII.

The English statesmen now saw that it was necessary to come to terms. In 1705 both Parliaments agreed to the appointment by the queen of commissioners to treat for union, ecclesiastical questions being expressly excluded, on the Scottish side, from their deliberations. Early in the following year the commissioners met and drew up a series of agreed articles to be submitted to the respective Parliaments. The two kingdoms were to be united in one kingdom by the name of Great Britain, under one sovereign, after Queen Anne, of the House of Hanover who must be neither a papist nor married to a papist. There was to be one Parliament in which Scotland was to be represented by sixteen elected peers and forty-five members in the House of Commons. The Scottish legal system was to be preserved entire, and no appeal was to lie to English courts of law. There was to be free trade within the United Kingdom, its dominions and plantations, common taxation and a common currency. Finally England was to pay to Scotland a large sum, called the Equivalent, most of which was to go to liquidate the Darien Company.

In neither country was the idea of a union popular. It demanded sacrifices from both sides—from England mainly commercial privilege, and from Scotland long cherished national independence. Would this not be 'the end o' an auld sang?' Moreover, the Darien wounds were still smarting so that in Scotland much opposition was to be expected. Two determined groups of opponents were at once in the field. The Cameronians declared that the contemplated union with prelatic England was a further defection from the Covenants. The Jacobites, foreseeing the ruin of their hopes for a restoration of the old dynasty, flooded the country with a pamphlet literature appealing to every emotion from sentimental patriotism down to the meanest material interest. For a short time it seemed as if those incompatible groups might even make common cause. The Jacobite propaganda succeeded in stirring up a riot in Edinburgh during the sitting of Parliament, and in persuading some counties and burghs, and even three presbyteries, to send in anti-union petitions. Much depended on the attitude of the national church. The General Assembly of 1706 was in session when the commissioners for union began their conferences, but the only reference to the question that was giving rise to so much heart-burning is contained in its concluding Act appointing a Solemn National Fast. Prayers were to be offered for the queen and her counsellors, for her forces and those of her allies then at war with France 'in defence of the Reformed Protestant Religion and the just liberation of Europe', finally for those 'commissioned both in this Kingdom and the Kingdom of England for treating about a union of both Kingdoms, that all may be done to the glory of God and the good of this Church'. Many ministers used the occasion of the fast to inveigh against the union, and William Carstares in the name of the Commission of Assembly—a body appointed by each assembly to watch over the interests of the Church until the meeting of the next—sent letters to several presbyteries urging them to discountenance activities that would bring reproach upon the Church. In the commission itself, when the agreed articles were made public, complaint was made that in the legislature of the United Kingdom twenty-six English bishops would have seats in the House of Lords, contrary to the principles of the Church of Scotland, and also that under the English Test Act none but members of the Church of England might hold public office. The Earl of Marchmont, who was as an elder a member of the commission, retorted that such matters might be left to himself and others who as members of Parliament should be trusted to look after the interests of the Church. In fact Parliament did pass an Act for securing the Protestant religion and Presbyterian church government presently established by law 'as the only government of the Church within the Kingdom of Scotland'. The Act also laid down that all principals and professors in the universities should subscribe the Westminster Confession of Faith and conform to Presbyterian worship and church government; and that succeeding sovereigns in all time coming should on accession swear to maintain and preserve inviolably the right and privilege of the Church as established. This Act was to be inserted in any Act of Union, and expressly declared to be 'a fundamental and essential condition of any Treaty or union in all time coming'—an entrenched clause as it were. When this guarantee had been given, opposition on the part of the Church died away. The name of William Carstares appears but seldom in the official documents of the time, but from the tributes paid to him by the queen and her counsellors it is clear that in their view it was owing to his skilful and patient leadership of his brethren that they laid aside their hostility to the Union project and quietly acquiesced.

For three and a half months the Scottish Parliament debated the articles. The Jacobites offered a stubborn but dwindling resistance. On 16 January 1707 the Act of Union was passed. Soon after it was ratified by the English Parliament which added a further Act securing the Church of England in England; and on 1 May Union was effected. Whatever Scotland may have lost she certainly gained in political stability and economic opportunity, and was soon to produce their fruits in intellectual culture. To the Church and the law it was left to preserve her national identity.

The Union necessitated a number of adjustments in government administration, and the inhabitants of what was now officially 'that part of the United Kingdom called Scotland' soon discovered that their traditional usages would meet with scant respect from English lawyers or the British Parliament. At Westminster the Scottish members were in a minority, and, being unfamiliar with English parliamentary procedure, were seldom able to exert much influence. The abolition of the Scottish Privy Council, the extension to Scotland of the English law of treason and the reorganization of tax collection, all reasonable enough, were nevertheless carried out in so high-handed a manner as to give opportunity to opponents of the Union to point out that the safeguards contained in the treaty were illusory. So long, however, as the statesmen who brought about the Union retained power the Church had nothing to complain of. But in England the Tories had been growing restive. A court quarrel, and the impeachment at the instance of the government of the high churchman, Sacheverell, for a sermon attacking the Revolution Settlement and its toleration of Dissenters, brought matters to a head. A general election in 1710 gave the Tories a large majority in the new parliament. The Scottish representatives were also in the main Tories or even Jacobites led by Lockhart of Carnwath, the bitterest enemy of the Revolution, the Union and the church establishment. The Church had now some reason to tremble for its security.

The first alarm was caused by the judgement of the House of Lords in the Greenshields case, 1711. James Greenshields, said to have been the son of a 'curate' outed in 1689, was ordained by Ramsay, Bishop of Ross, after his deprivation. Proceeding to Ireland he served for many years in the Church of Ireland which was of course entirely loyal to King William, victor at the Battle of the Boyne! In 1709 he returned to Scotland, and found that there were now in consequence of the Union a considerable number of English people, soldiers and civil servants, resident there and desirous of having the worship they had been accustomed to at home. Greenshields was invited to minister to them. He therefore took the oath of allegiance and began to hold services in Edinburgh using the English Book of Common Prayer. He had no relations with Rose, the deprived Bishop of Edinburgh, and was an ecclesiastical freelance. The presbytery of Edinburgh, however, summoned him to answer for his conduct. He compeared, produced evidence of his ordination and good character and good standing in the eyes of the law, but declined the jurisdiction of the presbytery. The presbytery forbade him to exercise his ministry, and, as he paid no attention, appealed to the magistrates, who put him in prison. His appeal to the Court of Session was dismissed on the questionable ground that ordination by an 'exauctorate' bishop was no true ordination. He then appealed to the House of Lords, a proceeding not at least explicitly ruled out by the Treaty of Union, though on this occasion inconvenient as it raised thorny ecclesiastical issues. The Lords in 1711 reversed the judgement of the Court of Session and found the Edinburgh magistrates liable in costs. Episcopalians in Scotland were naturally jubilant, and were confident that this was but the first step towards their reinstatement. Many of them began to use the English liturgy even in the parish churches of which they retained or took possession, including the cathedrals of Brechin and Aberdeen, but it was said that they either omitted the prayers for the queen or so modified them as to include the Pretender.

Episcopalians soon had further cause for elation and Presbyterians for alarm when early in 1712 the government presented to Parliament a Bill 'to prevent the disturbing those of the episcopal communion in Scotland in the exercise of their Religious Worship and in the use of the Liturgy of the Church of England, and for repealing an Act (of the Scottish Parliament) against irregular Baptisms and Marriages' (viz. by ministers not belonging to the Established Church). Episcopal Dissenters were to have liberty to meet for worship according to their own manner, and establish congregations where they should think fit. Their pastors might preach and administer sacraments, provided they produced to a justice of the peace letters showing that they had received episcopal ordination. They were further exempted from the established church judicatories by a curious clause smacking of ignorance or contempt, to the effect that 'the Presbyterian clergy may continue to inflict ecclesiastical censures on those of their own communion'. No reference was made to episcopal church government. It is possible that the Bill was intended simply to cover cases like that of Greenshields, but to Presbyterians in Scotland a blow seemed to be aimed at their treasured conception of a national Church, uniform in faith, worship, and discipline. The Commission of Assembly at once dispatched to the queen 'a humble Representation and Petition' appealing to the Act of Security which it held to have been infringed. It also sent Carstares and two colleagues to London to oppose the Bill. They had little success, but they did secure some amendments before it was passed into an Act. Episcopal ordination must be at the hands of a Protestant bishop, and the clause relative to ecclesiastical censures was amended to read that civil magistrates should not compel any man to submit to the sentences of the church judicatories.

It would have been entirely reasonable to have required from episcopal clergymen in return for toleration some kind of acceptance of the political order, or oath of allegiance. None was prescribed in the Bill as drafted and there was much contention in Parliament on this question. To whom should allegiance be promised? To the queen, of course. But there was also the English Act of Settlement of 1701 which provided for the Hanoverian succession and required the monarch to be always a member of the Church of England. That Act was buttressed by an oath of Abjuration to be taken by all holders of public office. On pressure from Carstares, it was alleged, but more likely from the Whig opposition, the oath of Abjuration was now required by a clause added to the Toleration Act. Such an oath must have been repugnant to Scottish Episcopalians most of whom were Jacobite at heart; and Lockhart, the leader of the Jacobite Episcopalians, took his revenge by persuading Parliament to make the oath obligatory for Presbyterian ministers too. They were all, of course, eager and willing to abjure the Pretender and to welcome the Protestant Hanoverian succession. Most of them were 'clear' that they could conscientiously take the Abjuration oath in that sense. But some 'scrupled' to bind themselves to the principle that the monarch must always belong to the prelatical Church of England. A few even showed signs of seceding to the Cameronians. The assembly annually protested against the imposition of the unnecessary and divisive oath and exhorted ministers to live and work together in unity notwithstanding diversity of opinion with regard to it. In 1719 the terms of the oath were amended and the offence removed in recognition of the complete loyalty of the Presbyterians to the Hanoverian king during the Rebellion of 1715.

Apart from the question of the oath the Toleration Act must be regarded as a measure of justice, although it must be pointed out, as was done at the time, that zeal for toleration was anything but characteristic of the Parliament that passed it, for it went on to restrict the liberties of non-Anglican dissenters in England, as for example by the Schisms Act aimed at depriving nonconformists of their schools. In Scotland episcopal congregations were formed using the English liturgy, but the main body of Scottish Episcopalians remained constant in their Jacobitism. For this they suffered disastrously after the Rebellion of 1715, and still worse after the Forty-Five, being reduced to a mere remnant. They had also internal troubles, administrative and liturgical, but by 1766 they had overcome these and organized themselves territorially as the Scottish Episcopal Church. In 1784 three of their bishops quietly consecrated Samuel Seabury as Bishop for Anglicans in the revolted American colonies, and in 1792, finally, they made their peace with the government of George III.

Whatever may be said of Queen Anne's Toleration Act, the Act to restore the ancient patronages which followed immediately was to have baneful consequences for the Church of Scotland for a century and a half to come. King William in 1690 had unwillingly agreed to the abolition of patronage. The right to nominate a minister for a vacant parish was vested in the heritors, being Protestant, and the elders. The congregation might then approve or disapprove, and the presbytery had the final say. In the event of no nomination being made within six months the presbytery might itself appoint *tanquam jure devoluto*. The system could hardly be expected to work smoothly. Over much of the country

T

the heritors, i.e. the landowning gentry, when Protestant, were in the main episcopalian, and in country parishes, if there were elders at all they would tend to belong to a humbler class and often would be submissive to their 'betters'. Until a nomination was made a congregation had no voice. Thomas Boston is an example of a minister with popular gifts who pleased congregations but had difficulty in being nominated because he either positively offended heritors by his style of preaching or refused to court their favour. For many years following the Revolution there were many vacant parishes and few ministers to fill them. The right of appointment consequently frequently lapsed to the presbyteries, and at the assembly of 1711 careful proposals were drafted for their guidance in filling vacancies. The document containing them, which was to be sent down to presbyteries for comment under the Barrier Act, is most illuminating. It indicates the various difficulties that might arise, including 'heat and division in a parish about the call of a minister' and suggests the steps to be taken to overcome them. The presbytery is to make every effort to secure a peaceful settlement satisfactory to all parties, heritors, elders and people, and the interests of the congregation are to be jealously guarded. If the presbytery is baffled reference is to be made to the synod or even to the General Assembly. Such concern about the appointment of parish ministers is an indication of the importance attached to their office.

Before the presbyteries could deal with these proposals the Bill to restore patronage as it had been in 1592 was introduced in Parliament. No pretence was made of consulting the Church in any way. As originally drafted the Bill did not even provide that patrons must present licentiates of the Church. That omission, intentional or inadvertent, was rectified on the insistence of the Duke of Argyll. Nevertheless the Church was thoroughly alarmed by what it conceived to be a violation of its guaranteed security instigated by its avowed enemies. Once again the Commission of Assembly made strong representations. Carstares and his colleagues were still in London, and wore themselves out with lobbying at Westminster. They interviewed the Prime Minister, Lord Oxford, who was as usual charming and noncommittal. They even saw the queen, who received them coldly. The party in power was determined to have its way, and before the assembly met in May the Patronage Act as well as the Toleration Act was on the Statute Book. To the queen's assurance of her firm purpose to maintain Presbyterian church government the assembly replied deploring the recent legislation as 'grievous and prejudicial to this Church', and announcing that they had instructed their commission to use all proper and dutiful means to have the Patronage Act repealed. This remained a standing annual instruction to the commission until 1784.

Patrons seem to have been in no hurry to exercise their newly recovered right, perhaps because they knew that to do so would have raised a storm. In any case a presentation had to be made to the appropriate presbytery which had the duty to judge of the qualifications of the presentee and to ordain and induct him to the charge if found qualified. Presbyteries inclined to regard the call or at least the consent of the congregation as a necessary requirement, and most probationers would be likely to take this view. There is, it seems, only one example of a probationer who defied the church courts and was stripped of his licence. Moreover there was still a shortage of ministers, so that as before the right to appoint often lapsed to presbyteries on the expiry of six months after the vacancy occurred. Complaint was indeed made that some patrons eluded the *jus devolutum* by making out a presentation in favour of some eminent minister who was certain not to accept it, and repeating the ruse within the prescribed six months, so prolonging the vacancy. This abuse was rectified by an Act of Parliament in 1719. But for twenty years after 1712 there was much uncertainty and some confusion. It was not always clear to whom the right of patronage belonged. Presbyteries varied in their manner of proceeding, and sometimes when a presbytery refused to induct a presentee, the synod, or the assembly, or the Commission of Assembly would appoint a 'riding' committee to carry through an unpopular settlement. A notorious case occurred at Kinross. A vacancy occurred in 1726 and lasted

for six years. The people desired to call Ebenezer Erskine—
the popular minister of the neighbouring country parish of
Portmoak—whom many congregations desired to have as
their minister before he was translated to Stirling in 1731.
The patron, however, presented a certain Robert Stark who
was ordained by a 'riding' committee in 1732, but not in the
Church, access to which was barred by the people. The presbytery (Dunfermline) took no part in the ordination and
refused to recognize Stark or to enrol him as a member of
presbytery. This they were ordered to do by the assembly
of 1732, and again peremptorily in 1733, when they were
severely censured for their obduracy.

Clearly such a situation was intolerable and in 1731 an
attempt was made to remedy it. An overture was sent down
to presbyteries with the warning that if they neglected to
declare their opinion the assembly of 1732 would be asked
to pass it into an Act. The overture had to do primarily with
the procedure to be adopted when the right of appointment
to a vacant parish lapsed to the presbytery. No reference was
made to patronage save to say that with the consent of the
patron the procedure might be adopted on the occurrence
of the vacancy. Roughly the 1711 proposals were followed,
except that the right 'to elect and call' a minister was more
explicitly stated to lie with the Protestant heritors and elders
or, in royal burghs, with the magistrates, town council and
kirk session, and less stress is laid on the rights of the people.
As before, the congregation might approve or disapprove and
final determination was to be in the hands of the presbytery.
When the assembly met in 1732 it was found that 18 presbyteries had approved generally of the overture, 31 had dis-
approved, and 18 expressed no opinion. It was nevertheless
moved to pass it as an Act. The leader of the opposition in
the assembly was Ebenezer Erskine, now of Stirling, who contended for the right of the congregation of Christian people
to choose their own minister in accordance with the teaching
of the Books of Discipline. 'What difference', he cried, 'does
a piece of land make between man and man in the affairs of
Christ's Kingdom?'

Defeated in the assembly, Erskine fulminated from his

own pulpit against the assembly's Act, and again in the autumn as retiring moderator of the synod of Perth and Stirling. The synod took him to task for some abusive expressions he had used and he appealed to the assembly of 1733. In spite of an able defence he was not unnaturally censured for certain expressions found to be 'offensive and tending to disturb the peace and good order of this Church'. He then tabled a written protest claiming the right to maintain his views and to testify against any defections in the Church. Similar protests were also handed in by three of his friends. There the matter might have rested, had not the assembly in a passion of indignation instructed its commission to require the four brethren to withdraw their protest and express sorrow for having made it; if they refused, to suspend them from their ministerial functions, and if need be to proceed to a yet severer censure. In August they were suspended and as they disregarded the sentence in November the commission decided by a majority to remove them from their charges. Again they refused to accept the sentence. They were obliged, they said, to seccde from ministerial communion but would continue to fulfil their ministerial duties in their charges, and they appealed 'to the first free faithful and reforming General Assembly of the Church of Scotland'.

The threatened secession was widely felt to be a dire calamity, endangering the unity of the national Church when it appeared to be coming into its own. In contending for the rights of congregations the four brethren by no means stood alone. Many, perhaps most, ministers entirely agreed with them. They were highly esteemed for their character and gifts. They had the support of their own congregations, and had many admirers throughout the country. The assembly of 1734 sought to make amends. It repealed the Act of 1732 that had caused the dispute on the ground that it had been passed without due regard to the provisions of the Barrier Act. It rescinded an earlier Act against the recording of protests and acknowledged ministerial freedom to testify against defections. It empowered the synod of Perth and Stirling to take all steps to affect a reconciliation with the protesting brethren. The assembly of 1736 went further. It declared it to be and to have been since the Reformation the principle of this Church that no minister shall be intruded into any parish contrary to the will of the congregation, and recommended all judicatories to have a due regard to the said principle in planting vacant congregations. But it also recognized reality when it urged presbyteries to be at pains to bring about harmony and unanimity in congregations and to avoid everything that might excite or encourage unreasonable exceptions 'in people against a worthy person that may be proposed to be their minister'. Presentees were not always objected to for faults of their own! All efforts at reconciliation were unavailing. The four brethren had constituted themselves into a presbytery and by 1737 they were joined by four others, including Ralph Erskine of Dunfermline, Ebenezer's brother. They had also appointed one of their number, Wilson of Perth, as professor of Divinity to teach young men aspiring to the ministry, and they produced a 'Judicial Testimony' in which they declaimed against the errors and defections of the post-Revolution Church. 'There is a difference', said Erskine, 'to be made betwixt the Established Church of Scotland and the Church of Christ in Scotland, for I reckon that the last is in a great measure driven into the wilderness by the first.' Nevertheless while withdrawing from the 'corrupt judicatories' of the national Church, and reviling it in their sermons, they profited by its patience, for they retained possession of their churches, manses, and stipends for some years. Not until 1740 were they deposed and the schism made definitive.

The great majority of ministers still held strongly that patronage was a grievance and part of the effort to keep the Seceders within the Church had been to send deputations to London to secure the repeal of the obnoxious Patronage Act. They were completely unsuccessful. Instead, patrons were becoming more insistent on their legal rights and had begun to take action in the civil courts. In two cases ministers inducted ŏn the call of the people without a presentation were 'decerned' to have no title to the stipend. Even the Crown, which had the patronage of at least one-third of the parishes, in spite of the often warmly acknowledged sense of the loyalty of the Church and its ministers, was unco-operative. Between 1740 and 1750 it has been estimated that there were more than fifty disputed settlements in which presbyteries on conscientious grounds had refused to act, and inductions had been carried through by 'riding' committees appointed for the purpose by the assembly or its commission. It was, of course, easier for strangers than for local ministers to perform a disagreeable task. But the situation was clearly absurd and a growing number of younger ministers had come to the conclusion that it must be rectified. So long as the law of patronage stood it must be obeyed and presbyteries must do their duty. This was, doubtless, a reasonable view, but how to implement it as a policy was a difficulty. Presbyteries had been censured on occasion, but that had had little effect. The method actually adopted is quite indefensible, but it did prove effective.

A certain Andrew Richardson was presented to Inverkeithing in 1751. He was, as his subsequent record shows, a worthy man, but his settlement was opposed by the town council, the kirk session and the mass of the people. The presbytery of Dunfermline, therefore, refused to induct him in spite of a peremptory instruction from the Commission of Assembly to do so. The matter came before the assembly in 1752. On the motion of William Robertson, the young minister of Gladsmuir, later to become famous as principal of Edinburgh University and a noted historian, the presbytery of Dunfermline was enjoined to meet at Inverkeithing while the assembly was still in session, five members instead of the normal three to be a *quorum*, to induct Mr. Richardson to the charge, and to appear at the bar of the assembly on the following day to report what they had done. Three of them reported that they had duly turned up at the appointed hour, and had waited in vain for two hours for others to come to complete the *quorum*. Two said they had gone to Inverkeithing in the morning and endeavoured to persuade the people to abandon their opposition, but failing to do so they had gone home. Six members gave in a 'Humble Representation' in vindication of their abstention, quoting the Act of 1736 against intrusion of ministers contrary to the wishes of congregations.

The assembly then decided by 93 votes to 65 to make an example by deposing one of these six. They were recalled one by one on the next day, and given an opportunity further to defend themselves. Five of them added nothing, but Thomas Gillespie, minister of Carnock, made a further statement, and he was accordingly selected to be the victim. He accepted the sentence of deposition without bitterness, and perhaps hoped, as many certainly did, that a later assembly would reverse the iniquitous decision. He at once surrendered his church and manse, but continued preaching in the open air till a meeting-house was built for him in Dunfermline. In 1761, together with two like-minded brethren, he constituted the Presbytery of Relief 'for Christians oppressed in their Church privileges'. The new ecclesiastical body was free of the rancorous animosity towards the Established Church which marked the older Secession, and to begin with at any rate conceived of itself as an ally rather than an enemy of the national Church.

Soon after the deposition of Gillespie the presbytery of Dunfermline carried through the induction of Richardson, but three of its members who continued obdurate were suspended from their judicial functions and confined to the work of their parishes. Henceforth presbyteries did not venture to resist the ruling of the General Assembly, and found means to settle ministers on the presentation of patrons even though a call from the parishioners was signed by few or none at all. William Robertson and his friends might claim that one of the fundamental principles of Presbyterian church government had been vindicated by the drastic action of 1752. The inferior courts now acknowledged their subordination to the superior courts. But it was at a heavy price, as many friends of the national Church sorrowfully confessed. Disputed settlements continued to occur, but the dissatisfied could now resort to one or other of the dissenting, but still Presbyterian, bodies which had between them, it is said in 1766, as many as 120 places of worship attended by 100,000 persons. The assembly of that year refused to appoint a committee to consider the whole question of schism and by consultation with patrons, heritors and others, to try to find a remedy by consent. That of 1784 decided by a majority after long debate to discontinue the instruction given annually since 1712 by each assembly to its commission 'to make due application to the King and Parliament for redress of the grievance of patronage'. The instruction had indeed become a mere formality under the régime of Moderatism.

II

MODERATISM

WHILE the national Church—or the Established Church as its enemies preferred to style it—expanded its structure over the whole country and tightened its discipline, its ethos gradually changed under the impact of the movement commonly called the Enlightenment. Throughout Western Europe, beginning about the middle of the seventeenth century, there were signs of the rise of a purely secular culture. Natural science and history began to displace theology in the interest of educated people. Many weary of confessional strife and ecclesiastical pretension turned away from authority and sought to make reason the norm of all truth, even of religious truth. In this movement England took the lead with the Cambridge Platonists, soon followed by a larger group of Latitudinarians. In place of dogma Locke and Shaftesbury advocated natural religion or the religion of reason, and in the eighteenth century more radical thinkers expounded Deism and Unitarianism. All this came to have repercussions in Scotland which in the course of the eighteenth century produced Moderatism within the Church.

In 1690 this development could hardly have been foreseen. The Act establishing Presbyterian church government included the *Westminster Confession of Faith*, which it ratified as 'the public and avowed confession of this Church'. Those into whose hands the government of the Church was entrusted had all suffered for loyalty to the Covenants, and still cherished the ideas and ideals of the period of persecution. Only very slowly were people of a different type admitted to office in the Church, and emphasis was laid on purity of doctrine as the Church's primary concern. The Act of Security declared the Act of 1690 to be a fundamental and essential condition of any treaty of union, and it added the requirement that all university teachers should subscribe the

Westminster Confession as the confession of their own personal faith. In 1711 the questions to be put to persons seeking licence as probationers or ordination as ministers were carefully formulated, and they included one which required such persons to 'own sincerely and believe the whole doctrine contained in the Confession to be founded upon the Word of God, and to acknowledge it as the confession of their own faith'. The *Westminster Confession* was of course held to be subordinate to Scripture and to derive its authority from Scripture. But it was also held to be the perfect compend of Scripture doctrine, and therefore the perfect norm for the correct interpretation of Scripture, which the Church must uphold at all costs. To do this might have seemed a simple enough task, for the *Confession* was a carefully balanced formulation of Calvinism in its later scholastic phase. It answered the questions that were being urgently debated when it was composed, perhaps too conclusively and comprehensively, leaving little room for diversities of theological opinion. Nevertheless a series of acute theological controversies shook the whole Church from 1714 to 1730; for it was in the church courts—and in the pulpits—not in the schools that they were carried on.

In 1708 a certain John Simson was appointed professor of divinity at Glasgow, where students for the ministry from the west country and also from Ulster received their theological training. Simson belonged to an influential ministerial family. His father, Patrick Simson, minister of Renfrew, had been outed in 1662 and restored in 1690, and lived on till 1715, the last survivor of the pre-Restoration ministers or Antediluvians as they came to be called. His wife was the daughter of a leading Glasgow minister and niece of the principal of Glasgow College. His nephew, Robert Simson, was soon to become a famous professor of mathematics in Glasgow. He was himself, however, a rather colourless person and owes his fame entirely to his having been the object of two heresy hunts, the earlier being the first of its kind in Scotland. In 1715 Simson was charged with teaching Arminianism and the assembly appointed a committee on purity of doctrine to investigate the charge. Its report was

not given in till 1717. Simson had admitted using questionable modes of expression but had declared that he had never
intended to deviate from the teaching of the Church's Confession. He was therefore acquitted with a warning 'not to
attribute too much to natural reason and the power of corrupt nature to the disparagement of revelation and efficacious
free grace'.

On the very day on which this judgement was pronounced
the assembly had to deal with what looks like the precisely
opposite error. A certain William Craig appealed against the
action of the presbytery of Auchterarder, who after having
licensed him as a preacher refused to give him an extract of
his licence because he failed to satisfy them by his answers
to supplementary questions put to him. In particular he had
hesitated to assent to the proposition: 'It is not sound and
orthodox to teach that we must forsake sin in order to our
coming to Christ and instating us in covenant with God.'
The presbytery had obviously acted irregularly. They were
instructed to give Craig his certificate, and presbyteries were
forbidden to ask of those applying for licence other than the
prescribed questions. That should have been sufficient, but
the assembly went on to declare its abhorrence of the Auchterarder 'Creed' as unsound and most detestable, tending 'to
encourage sloth in Christians and slacken people's obligation
to Gospel holiness'. They ordered the presbytery to appear
before their commission and explain what they meant by it.
Their explanation was accepted but the assembly of 1718
forbade the use of such dangerous expressions for the future.
Arminianism and Antinomianism had alike been ruled out,
but it was noted by some that the latter had been repudiated
with more vigour than the former.

The Auchterarder incident, however, led to a more serious
controversy. During his Simprin ministry Thomas Boston
had picked up in a cottage in his parish a copy of an old
Puritan book, *The Marrow of Modern Divinity*, originally published by Edward Fisher of Oxford in 1646. It dealt in dia-
logue form with the relations of law and grace under the
Gospel, and laid strong emphasis on the part of grace in the
saving of men. Boston had found the volume full of spiritual

comfort and profit, and during the Auchterarder debate in the assembly he praised it to a neighbour as a book that handled the problem fully and admirably. In 1718 Thomas Hog of Carnock, one of Boston's friends, published a new edition of part I of *The Marrow* with a highly commendatory preface. This brought Principal James Hadow of St. Mary's College, St. Andrews, into the field. In a sermon preached before the synod of Fife and subsequently printed, he pointed out the Antinomian tendencies of the book, and tabulated passages in which its teaching deviated from that of the *Confession of Faith*. The assembly of 1719 instructed its commission to take note of books or pamphlets appearing contrary to the *Confession*, and next year the commission submitted a lengthy report singling out five distinct heresies in *The Marrow* and a number of clearly Antinomian statements. The assembly received the report, forbade ministers to use or commend the book, and enjoined them to warn their parishioners against it.

Hurt by this decision a group of twelve ministers including Boston, Hog, and the two Erskines drew up a strongly worded representation in which they challenged the report, pointing out that its quotations from *The Marrow* were highly selective, and urged that the assembly's decision should be reversed. They alleged that in receiving the report and also in another Act passed by the assembly of 1720 encouragement had been given to the preaching of 'mere morality without religion'. The assembly of 1721 had to be dissolved soon after it met owing to the commissioner's being unable to attend through indisposition, but it appointed its commission, and remitted to it consideration of the representation of the Marrow men, who were ordered to attend. On the commission Hadow took a leading part, and brow-beat the representers. They were all country ministers but they maintained their case ably if rather acrimoniously. A long report was submitted to the assembly in 1722 in which the representation was answered paragraph by paragraph, and its framers were charged with casting 'injurious reflections' on the proceedings of the assembly of 1720. Their request to have its decision reversed was refused, and they themselves were appointed

to be rebuked and admonished by the moderator and reminded that their offence deserved a higher censure. They
protested against the sentence, but fortunately no further
official action was taken and the controversy died down. The
condemnation of *The Marrow*, however, continued to rankle.
Boston spent four laborious years in his study in Ettrick
Manse preparing a new edition with copious and learned
notes which he published in 1726. No official notice was taken
of it, and in that year the second Simson case brought Hadow
and the Marrow men into the same camp.

This time Simson was accused of teaching Arianism after
the fashion of Samuel Clarke, whose treatise on *The Scripture
Doctrine of the Trinity* was creating a stir in England. Simson's
process continued for four years. Two years were occupied
with minute investigations carried out by a special committee which included among its members four senators of
the College of Justice. Simson was repeatedly interviewed
and some of his students were interrogated. The committee
reported to the assembly of 1728, when there was a tremendous debate lasting for several days and ranging over the
most abstruse points of Trinitarian theology and the canon
law affecting heretics. So far as learning is concerned the
Supreme Court proved itself to be adequately equipped.
Again Simson protested that he held no opinion contrary to
the *Confession of Faith*, but admitted that in certain matters
not defined in the *Confession* he had used certain ambiguous
phrases. If these were deemed to be heretical he professed
himself willing to withdraw them. But his attitude to his
inquisitors had not been co-operative or even respectful.
Many now clamoured for his deposition, but the assembly
was divided and resolved to send the record of the case to
presbyteries for their considered views. The presbyteries were
almost unanimously unfavourable, and the assembly of 1729
finally decided to suspend Simson indefinitely from teaching
without, however, deposing him or depriving him of his
chair. Thomas Boston alone dissented from this judgement as
derogatory to the Divinity of Christ, but was prevailed upon
not to insist on his dissent being recorded. Simson continued
until his death ten years later to enjoy his position and

emoluments as professor, all the while preserving a discreet silence.

Throughout these doctrinal controversies, bitter as they were, all parties had professed to contend for strict confessional orthodoxy. The Seceders, however, in their judicial testimony described the condemnation of *The Marrow* and the leniency shown to Professor Simson as signs of grave defection from the truth on the part of the Church, aggravated in their eyes by the easy dismissal of charges of heresy brought against Professor Campbell of St. Andrews in 1736 and Professor Leechman of Glasgow in 1743. Both of these were in fact Apologists of the eighteenth-century type and their use of the current apologetic arguments aroused suspicion of rationalism. The Seceders attributed the lack of severity to the fact that too many of the old episcopal conformists had been admitted into the ministry. In reality it was a sign that a new generation had sprung up that had had no experience of the Covenanting struggles, and in the enjoyment of Hanoverian security and growing prosperity was coming to dislike 'enthusiasm', that deadly sin of the eighteenth century. One of Campbell's incriminated publications was a discourse entitled 'The Apostles no Enthusiasts'. Moreover, the violent language used by the extremists gave offence. Two parties were forming in the Church, the Moderates who made their influence felt from 1752 onwards and the Evangelicals or Popular party (from their opposition to patronage) called also by their opponents the Zealots or High-flyers.

The latter probably embraced the bulk of the ministers, at least up to the middle of the century even after the Secession had drawn off many of the hot-heads. The Evangelicals predominated in several important presbyteries and synods and certainly had the esteem and support of the mass of the common people. There were some outstanding men among them. There was John Willison (b. 1680), one of the ministers of Dundee from 1716 to 1750 whose writings remained for long, together with Boston's *Fourfold State*, the favourite religious literature among the people of Scotland. Willison's theological and ecclesiastical position was exactly similar to that of Thomas Boston. He sympathized deeply with all the contendings of the Seceders, but he could not contemplate schism and worked hard for reconciliation. His warm evangelical witness is said to have kept Dundee from being a fruitful field for the Secession during his lifetime. He was also the chief opponent of his co-presbyter, John Glas of Tealing, who had come to the conclusion that the Church ought to be a purely spiritual society having no connexion with the State, and that therefore the idea of a national Church, so dear to Willison, was sinful. Glas became the founder of the little sect of Glassites, later known as Sandemanians. There was Alexander Webster (b. 1707), son of James Webster who first challenged Simson and brother-in-law of Ebenezer Erskine, from 1737 to 1784 minister of the Tolbooth Church, Edinburgh, the best attended church in the town. His congregation was devoted to him, and as he had married a lady of good family and some means he cut a good figure in the social life of Edinburgh and was noted for his wit and even for his convivial habits, 'a love of claret not being reckoned in those days a sin in Scotland' as Alexander Carlyle, Webster's critic, notes sarcastically. During the Forty-Five when Edinburgh was in the hands of the rebels Webster courageously preached against the rebellion. He inaugurated the fund for the widows and orphans of ministers, and had much to do with the planning of Edinburgh's new town. There was John Maclaurin (b. 1693), one of the most popular ministers of Glasgow from 1723 to 1754, a renowned preacher and theologian, and competitor with Leechman for the chair of divinity in Glasgow. His brother Colin was a brilliant professor of mathematics in Edinburgh. Above all there was John Erskine (b. 1721), minister of Greyfriars Church, Edinburgh, from 1767 to 1803, respected by everyone as scholar, preacher, and saint. It was he who first pled the cause of foreign missions on the floor of the assembly.

Here must be mentioned one who was no leader but a simple and earnest parish minister, William McCulloch, minister of Cambuslang 1731-71. It was under his ministry that there occurred in 1742 the revival known as the 'Cambuslang Wark'. Some earnest souls among his parishioners had instituted a praying society and they asked the minister to help them by giving a week-night lecture once a week. This developed into a series of nightly services at which McCulloch was assisted by his friends. Soon people were awakened to an acute sense of sin. Signs of deep emotion expressing itself in bodily agitation were witnessed, and the fame of the movement attracted crowds from far and near. Willison, Webster, and Maclaurin with many others came to assist, including the English evangelist George Whitefield whose impassioned oratory swayed a multitude estimated at 30,000. This was the high-water mark of the revival, and the excitement gradually subsided. In many cases the effect was short-lived, but there is ample evidence that a considerable number of persons had been permanently influenced for good. Ministers of the Evangelical party hailed the Cambuslang Revival as the work of God's spirit, but the Seceders and the Cameronians denounced it as a delusion of the devil. No good thing could come out of the Establishment. What perhaps angered them most was the fact that Whitefield, a prelatic priest of the Church of England, had been allowed to take part in it.

George Whitefield was at this time at the height of his powers as a preacher both in England and America. The Associate Presbytery of the Seceders had invited him to come to Scotland in the hope that he would strengthen their cause. But they expected him to renounce his prelatic ordination, embrace Presbyterianism and the Covenants, or at least confine his preaching to their own meeting houses. Sorrowfully he had to part company with them and carry on as he had opportunity his itinerant evangelism. Between 1741 and 1768 he paid fourteen visits to Scotland, and everywhere, in Edinburgh, Glasgow, Dundee, Aberdeen, he was welcomed by evangelical ministers into their homes and pulpits. We have seen the part he took at Cambuslang. The ecclesiastical divisions he found in Scotland were a great grief to him and by his gracious Christian behaviour he did something to assuage their bitterness. After his visit to Dundee Willison wrote of him, 'God, by owning him so wonderfully, is pleased to give a rebuke to our intemperate bigotry and party zeal.'

Against the advice of Whitefield John Wesley also made

U

Scotland part of his mission field, visiting it no less than twenty-two times between 1751 and 1790. He came in the first instance at the invitation of an English colonel commanding a regiment of dragoons stationed at Musselburgh, but he found a welcome in Glasgow from John Gillies, minister of the College Church (Blackfriars) who braved the prejudice of his people by introducing the innovation of hymn-singing. In 1761 Wesley was likewise welcomed by the ministers of Aberdeen, and later in Inverness and other towns in the north. And yet his mission was less successful in Scotland than it had been in England. In a sense it was less necessary. He himself recognized that in Scotland congregations were not alienated from the gospel as were the urban populations of England, and that this was due to the effectiveness of the Scottish ministry. But, moreover, Wesley was more of an Anglican than was Whitefield, and less sympathetic to Scottish ways. He was twice in Edinburgh during the meetings of the General Assembly, but he could not understand why Whitefield had been so favourably impressed. On one occasion he heard a number of lawyers arguing for and against the translation of a minister, and the case dragged on for five hours which, Wesley comments, could have been settled in five minutes. One of his Edinburgh visits coincided with a Communion Sunday, and after some hesitation he 'judged it best to embrace the opportunity' of communicating in the West Kirk (St. Cuthbert's). He gives an account of the service, at which the communicants were served in relays at tables covered with tablecloths. His comment is, 'How much more simple, as well as more solemn, is the service of the Church of England.' But what militated most against Wesley's work in Scotland was the theological gulf that separated him from his natural allies, the Evangelical ministers. They were like Whitefield strict Calvinists while Wesley was an Arminian and a Universalist. This theological difference threatened for a time to disrupt the Methodist movement in England. It certainly weakened it in Scotland when John Erskine threw the weight of his immense influence into the scales against Wesley. Whitefield had made no attempt to organize his followers, and recognized that there was no need in Scotland for a Calvinistic Methodist connexion as there was in Wales. Wesley on the other hand did organize Methodist societies but they remained small. His influence was the quite general one of preparing the way for the Evangelical revival of the nineteenth century.

During the eighteenth century, however, and especially in the latter half, Moderatism was dominant in the Church. In a sense Carstares might be named as the first 'Moderate' in so far as his aim was to preserve the peace and unity of the Church on a broad basis. His spirit may be seen at work in the increasing impatience shown to over-zealous brethren who were continually on the outlook for doctrinal deviations especially in the universities. But Moderatism had also its roots in the spirit of inquiry and criticism that characterized the Enlightenment, and in the feeling for culture as opposed to 'enthusiasm' in the bad sense in which that word was then used.

By general consent the Apostle of the Enlightenment in Scotland was Francis Hutcheson, professor of moral philosophy in Glasgow, 1730–46. Son of an Irish Presbyterian minister and himself destined for the Irish ministry, he studied in Glasgow 1711–17 where he seems to have been influenced by the ideas of Professor Simson. At all events on his return to Ireland he preached a mild form of Arminianism. As Professor, Hutcheson broke with tradition in his teaching method, for he lectured not in Latin but in English, pacing up and down his rostrum as he eloquently expounded an early form of Utilitarianism and extolled benevolence as the primary virtue. He founded no school, but by popularizing philosophical inquiry he prepared the way for the great argument with Hume out of which arose the Scottish philosophy of Thomas Reid and his followers. Hutcheson was charged with two dangerous heresies; (1) 'that the standard of moral goodness was the promotion of the happiness of others', and (2) 'that we could have a knowledge of good and evil without a knowledge of God', but the case got no farther than the presbytery of Glasgow. It was Hutcheson who by judicious wire pulling secured against much opposition the appointment of William Leechman, minister of Beith, Ayrshire, to the Glasgow chair of divinity in 1743. Leechman, he believed, would 'put a new face upon Theology in Scotland'. Alexander Carlyle who attended Leechman's class 1743–4 praises his course as 'the most instructive set of lectures on theology that had, it was thought, ever been delivered in Scotland'. Hutcheson and Leechman, he tells us, attracted many students to Glasgow. 'A new school was formed in the western provinces of Scotland where the clergy till that period were narrow and bigoted. . . . Though neither of these professors taught any heresy, yet they opened and enlarged the minds of the students, which soon gave them a turn for free enquiry, the result of which was candour and liberality of sentiment.'

Carlyle was a son of the minister of Prestonpans, and naturally attended Edinburgh University. He profited from the teaching of some of the arts professors, but has no good account of the divinity faculty. Goldie (or Gowdie), Professor of divinity, was 'dull and Dutch', and the best that could be said of him was that by having no influence on the minds of his students, he left them to make up their own minds! The professor of ecclesiastical history was Patrick Cumming who was also minister of the Old Kirk, Edinburgh. Of his teaching Carlyle says nothing, but evidently regarded him later as a small-minded and unreliable intriguer, in touch with government officials and influential in the manipulation of Crown patronage. This made him leader of the 'Moderate interest', but it is entirely to the credit of Carlyle and his friends that they proved not susceptible to his 'lures' when he made advances to secure their support. But if the professors were insignificant, there was at Edinburgh a group of fellow students who were destined to wield great influence in the Church. Not the least interesting is Carlyle himself, known from his distinguished appearance and power as a church leader as 'Jupiter' Carlyle. He was minister of Inveresk 1748 to 1805, and in his Autobiography, written towards the end of his long life, he gives a fascinating account of his times and the ideals of the Moderates. There was Hugh Blair, minister of St. Giles from 1758 to 1800, who was also professor of rhetoric and belles lettres at Edinburgh University, whose sermons are perfect examples of Moderate preaching of 'mere morality' in highly cultivated literary form. There was John Home, minister of Athelstaneford 1746–57, author of the tragedy *Douglas*, the production of which in the theatre of Edinburgh created such a storm that Home deemed it advisable to demit his charge. Above all there was William Robertson in whom the ideal of Moderatism was realized.

William Robertson was born in the manse of Borthwick, hard by the ancient castle where lingering memories of Queen Mary stimulated in his father an interest in the history of the ill-fated queen. In 1733 William Robertson, senior, became one of the ministers of Old Greyfriars, Edinburgh, and about that time his son began his studies at Edinburgh University where he was from the first recognized by his fellow students as a leader and a man of great promise. In 1744 he was ordained to Gladsmuir in East Lothian. Almost immediately his labours were interrupted by the news that Prince Charles Edward was marching on Edinburgh. Hastening to the capital he enlisted along with his friends Home and Carlyle in a volunteer corps for its defence. Their military career was short and inglorious for they were disbanded before the Highlanders arrived. Carlyle witnessed the battle of Preston-pans from the safe distance of his father's manse and has left a vivid account of what he saw. Incidentally he tells us that 'many people in East Lothian were Jacobites. . . . The commons in general and two-thirds of the gentry had no aversion to the family of Stuart; and could their religion have been secured would have been very glad to see them on the throne again'. Only the ministers and middling townsfolk were convinced Whigs. Carlyle also had glimpses of the prince in Edinburgh and gives a not unfriendly picture of him, but concludes that his abilities were mediocre and his chance of success small, for his following was attracted by sentiment only and not animated by serious political purpose. When the excitement was over Robertson returned to Gladsmuir where he continued as minister for some fourteen years being then translated to Lady Yester's Church in Edinburgh and promoted in 1761 to Old Greyfriars, his father's old charge. There, strangely enough, he was soon to receive as his colleague the evangelical John Erskine. In spite of being of opposite views theologically and ecclesiastically the personal relations of the colleagues seem to have been amicable. Next year he was appointed principal of Edinburgh University and held both appointments in conjunction till his death in 1793.

Robertson's fame, which was not limited to Scotland, rests chiefly on his historical works. His *History of the Reign of the Emperor Charles V*, published in 1769, won him instant recognition as one of the outstanding historians of his time, comparable with Voltaire, Hume, and Gibbon, all of whom paid tribute to his genius. Even his earliest work, *The History of Scotland during the Reigns of Queen Mary and James VI*, written while he was still at Gladsmuir, created a sensation in London literary circles, where not only his erudition but above all his style was admired. He was among the first of purely Scottish education to reach a wider public, for which the acquisition of literary English was essential, an achievement which must have cost him infinite pains, and in which he had the help of Hugh Blair and David Hume. His treatment of his highly controversial theme was also remarkable, for he contrived to avoid partisanship so successfully that he may be said to have taken all the colour out of the picture. He is conspicuously fair to Queen Mary, and of course a very lukewarm defender of John Knox, who had to wait for Thomas McCrie to reinstate him in the esteem of his countrymen. Robertson's *History* therefore reflects his general 'moderate' outlook. Perhaps his experience as ecclesiastical statesman contributed some insight into the historical problems with which he had to deal in his *Charles V*. For Robertson not only wrote history; he made it, if only in a restricted sphere.

He and his friends first attracted attention in 1751. In spite of repeated injunctions from the Supreme Court the presbytery of Linlithgow refused to induct a presentee to Torphichen in face of the almost unanimous opposition of the people. In the Assembly of 1751, therefore, Home moved and Robertson seconded that the members of the presbytery be suspended for six months. The motion was lost, only eleven voting for it, but Robertson's speech so impressed the assembly that it decided to censure the presbytery. In the following year, as we have seen, the assembly took a much stronger line with the presbytery of Dunfermline on a similar issue, actually deposing one of its ministers, Gillespie of Carnock. Carlyle, who was a member for the first time, in a maiden speech proposed to go farther and depose one or two more, but he cynically informs us that this was a pre-arranged manœuvre to inspire fear in any who might still be inclined to recalcitrance. The leader in this movement for what Carlyle calls 'the restoration of the ancient discipline of the Church' was Robertson. He was not a member of the assembly of 1752, but he appeared at the bar and was heard in defence of a dissent he had entered against a majority decision of the commission earlier in the year in the Dunfermline case. In a carefully drafted document he had set forth his view of the constitution of the Church. It is a society and as such by its very nature it implies an authority to which the judgement of its individual members must be subject. The basic principles of Presbyterianism are the parity of ministers and the subordination of courts. It thus ensures liberty while avoiding anarchy. The judgements of the Supreme Court are not infallible but they must be final, and all ministers at their ordination are required to promise to submit to and concur with the orderly discipline and government of the Church. Moreover, though patronage may be held to be a grievance, so long as it remains the law of the land the Church by law established is bound to obey it. Robertson bases his case on indubitable political principles. If, as many good men felt, these were not really congruous with ecclesiastical government, the reply must be that in no other way could the Presbyterian system be made to work.

To view Presbyterianism merely as a system of 'judicatories', inferior and superior, is to mistake its structure for its essential nature. But structure has its own importance, and as the main function of the General Assembly was at that time to act as a supreme court of law for the whole Church, it was right that its procedure should be as orderly as that of, say, the Court of Session. To that extent Robertson's policy may be justified. He formulated it and defended it in the assembly when he was still a comparatively young obscure country minister, when it was unusual for young men to speak at all because only senior ministers and distinguished elders were apt to catch the moderator's eye. And he steadily pursued it throughout a long period of ascendancy in the Church. From 1762 to 1780 Robertson was the undisputed leader of the moderate party, and in the language of the time had the 'management' or the 'administration' of the Church in his hands. He did not, of course, have any official position in the assembly. Only once was he elected moderator, in 1763, when he had little to do save to draft and sign an address to King George III congratulating him on the birth of his eldest son and on the conclusion of the Seven Years War by a treaty that added to his dominions 'territories more extensive and of greater value than have been acquired by any nation since the division of Europe into great kingdoms and the establishment of a balance of power have put a stop to the rapidity of conquest'. It was noted even by an opponent that he did not owe his power to subservience to any great minister of State, through whom he might have managed the patronage of livings in the gift of the Crown. The Crown patronage he left entirely in the hands of the Duke of Argyll, who used it to appoint 'moderates' to vacant parishes. Robertson's ascendency was due to personal qualities, to his ability, his unquestioned integrity, and especially to his gift of lucid persuasive speech. He would intervene only at the end of a debate, when he would aptly sum up what had been said, and rarely failed to carry the majority with him. But he had also the immense advantage that, as principal of the university, he was elected its representative in the Assembly year by year, whereas other ministers could be members only every fourth or fifth year. In this way he gained an intimate acquaintance with its procedures and experience in guiding it. Moreover he had behind him something in the nature of a party organization. Carlyle tells us that during the meetings of the assembly some ministers and lawyers used to gather to discuss the business to be transacted and adopt a policy with regard to it. He tells us further that at this period young advocates were eager to take part in assembly business 'to display their eloquence and exercise their talents', and that many noblemen and Judges were also regularly members and swelled the numbers of 'the prevailing party'. This goes far to explain the weakness of the Evangelicals in the assembly.

The first principle of the Moderate régime was that the law of patronage must be obeyed regardless of the opposition in the parishes, which was often enough frivolous and partly the result of agitation fomented by the 'Popular party', and likely to die down when it was proved to be futile; regardless also of the spread of disaffection and dissent, which if evil was a necessary evil. To that extent the Moderates were prepared to see the national Church reduced to an Ecclesiastical Establishment.

At the same time it is only fair to recognize that Robertson and his friends sincerely believed that patronage was a good thing for the Church as a means of providing it with a better ministry. Patrons being men of position and education, they held, were better judges of the qualities of ministers than the unlettered folk who formed the bulk of the congregations. Since 1712, it was maintained, a better class of men had entered the ministry to the enhancement of its character and quality. Intellectually this was certainly true. In the so-called Select Club, founded in Edinburgh in 1754, city and country ministers met on equal terms with noblemen, judges, advocates, writers to the signet, professors, medical men, and successful business men, and held their own with them in literary and philosophical discussions. In 1791 Alexander Carlyle could justly claim that there were few branches of literature in which ministers of the Church of Scotland had not excelled, and he enumerates history ancient and modern, philosophy, rhetoric, tragedy, mathematics, even agriculture. He has less to say about theology, but he does mention 'treatises in defence of Christianity' referring no doubt especially to the 'Dissertation on Miracles' in which Dr. George Campbell, Principal of Marischal College, Aberdeen, sought to answer Hume. The Evangelicals might rail at Hume and threaten him with proceedings for his infidelity, but he was on intimate terms with all the leading Moderates, Carlyle included, who defends him against the imputation of atheism!

Another Moderate, Thomas Reid, minister of New Machar, Aberdeenshire, later professor of philosophy in King's College, Aberdeen, and finally professor of moral philosophy in Glasgow, spent a lifetime in elaborating a philosophical escape from Hume's scepticism.

It is questionable whether the attempt to raise the social status of the ministry was equally successful. It was one of the objections urged against Alexander Carlyle when presented to Inveresk that he was too much addicted to the company of his superiors. His *Autobiography* bears that out. He tells us much of his dining and wining with his heritors and of his association with the great, and remarkably little of his relations with his ordinary parishioners. But he was not a sycophant: he enjoyed intelligent cultured conversation and he seems to have been welcomed in circles where it could be had. The interests of the landed gentry and the ministers, however, clashed at one point even when with the help of the Moderate party patrons had come into the exercise of their rights without question. Ministers were poorly paid and their stipends did not rise with the increasing prosperity of the country. Indeed their financial position deteriorated by comparison with that of 'the inferior orders'. Twice an attempt was made to induce the government to legislate for an augmentation of stipends—shortly after the Forty-Five when ministers had declared their loyalty in no uncertain fashion, and again in 1788 when the battle over patronage had been won. On both occasions the attempt failed on account of the determined resistance of the landowners. Carlyle has to lament that he knows very few capable of sharing his vision of an adequately paid clergy admitted to the franchise as freeholders and united with the heritors for the security of the British constitution.

Presbyterianism is the name of a form of church government, and those who contended for it against every other form did so in the belief that it could best secure an effective parochial ministry. The Moderates claimed that by making the system work in an orderly fashion they achieved its purpose. It is not easy to form a just estimate of them as parish ministers. A later generation brought serious charges against them of sloth and negligence, of spiritual deadness, even of immorality and infidelity. No doubt there were individuals guilty of some or all of these faults, but many can be shown to be worthy men though they had nothing of the zeal that marked their critics. In drawing towards the representatives of the new culture and in attempting to align themselves with the aristocracy they may have lost contact with their parishioners, many of whom in the Lowlands resorted to one or other of the seceding bodies. In the Highlands earnest religion, the product of a long struggle against popery and episcopacy, provided somewhat crudely for its own needs apart from the ministers without formally breaking with the national Church until 1843. On the other hand moderate ministers contributed to the spread of enlightenment in their parishes. Dr. Samuel Johnson was constrained to admit that even in remote places he found many of them to be men of good sense, breeding, and learning. Carlyle thought that the temptation to sloth might have been irresistible if he had accepted the first presentation offered to him, namely to Cockburnspath in Berwickshire, for there he would have lacked the stimulus of interesting and intelligent company which was available in Edinburgh and neighbourhood. But the *Diary* of Ridpath of Stitchel, a rural parish in Roxburghshire, shows him to have been not only a literary man, but active not least in the concerns of his parishioners, visiting them assiduously in their troubles and sicknesses. The contribution of the Moderates was to the intellectual and cultural development of Scotland rather than to its evangelization.

In doctrine the Moderates were ostensibly if tepidly orthodox, but theology did not figure among their interests. They did not encourage heresy-hunting, but neither did they promote theological liberalism. One who ventured into heresy in print saved himself only by a timely recantation. One of their leaders, Principal George Hill, of St. Andrews, gave to the Church its standard textbook of Calvinist divinity, which long remained in use. No one questioned, in public at all events, the authority of the Confession of Faith. But in their sermons moderate preachers avoided all reference to the great doctrines of the Church, and to the Reformation doctrines of sin and grace and the Plan of Salvation. They confined themselves to inculcating the moral virtues with illustrations drawn from secular literature even more than from Scripture. Carlyle claims credit for the clergy for their unwearied diligence in teaching 'a rational religion' which he thinks must have contributed in some degree to the advancement of the tranquillity and prosperity of the country. The unwearied diligence is amply evidenced in Ridpath's *Diary*.[1] Ridpath lectured and preached regularly at Stitchel twice every Sunday often for an hour or more, except when he was 'colleaguing' with neighbouring ministers at some Sacramental occasion elsewhere. But it is disconcerting to read in his *Diary* a frequent Saturday entry, after references to much miscellaneous reading and other activity; 'prepared for tomorrow' or 'looked out something for tomorrow'. He gives no indication of the content of his preaching, but it may be assumed to have been that 'rational religion' which evangelicals described as 'cold morality' or 'legalism' without a touch of gospel to stir or comfort souls. If the Moderates took little thought for their sermons, they took even less for the rest of the Sunday services. The Westminster Directory was not followed, and there was no compensating interest in liturgy. The only enrichment of worship during the period was the preparation and, after much hesitation and delay, the authorization in 1781 of the collection of Scripture paraphrases still in use. It was an Evangelical, Gillies of Glasgow, who, following Wesley's visit, attempted unsuccessfully to introduce the singing of hymns.

With regard to the charge of moral laxity brought against the Moderates it probably amounts to little more than that they abandoned the Puritan ways still followed by the old-fashioned. Alexander Carlyle takes to himself a large share of the credit for this progress. He claims to have been the first son of the manse to have had dancing lessons, and the first minister to play cards openly; and he was the chief figure in the celebrated controversy over theatre-going. John Home, minister of Athelstaneford, had written a tragedy, *Douglas*, and encouraged by his friends had had it staged in Edin-

[1] Ed. J. B. Paul, for Scottish History Society, 1922.

burgh's only theatre in the Canongate in 1756. It was an immense success and was attended by many, including judges, who did not usually go to the theatre. A number of ministers also attended mostly from outside Edinburgh, and they made themselves as inconspicuous as possible. Not so Carlyle who occupied a prominent seat in a side-box, and was observed to expel a man beside him who was drunk and disorderly! The presbyteries undertook to reprimand their erring members, and all submitted except the minister of Inveresk who maintained that he had broken no law of the Church. He appealed from his presbytery to the synod which by a majority of three acquitted him, and when the presbytery appealed to the General Assembly the synod's verdict was upheld by 117 votes to 39. The assembly then passed an Act forbidding ministers to countenance the theatre, but the Act remained a dead letter. Home as the chief culprit was proceeded against by his presbytery of Haddington, but demitted his charge before sentence was passed. Fortunately he had many influential friends who found him honourable and lucrative employment in government service, and he was magnanimous enough to bear no grudge. In connexion with this controversy Carlyle claims that the most meritorious service he and his friends rendered to the Church was 'to discriminate the artificial virtues and vices formed by ignorance and superstition from those that are real'. There is certainly something in this distinction, but it may be thought that Carlyle himself all his life merely followed the lead of the fashionable people whose society he loved and at whose moral lapses he closed a charitable eye. If his puritan opponents are 'fanatics and hypocrites' his own ideal differs not at all from that of the 'man of the world'.

Moderatism reached its zenith under the administration of Principal Robertson largely owing to his intellectual distinction and statesmanlike leadership in the General Assembly. It came, therefore, as a shock to his followers when in 1780, while still at the height of his power and influence, he announced his intention to withdraw from active participation in the business of the assembly, giving as his reason a desire to devote himself to his historical labours. That there were

other predisposing considerations is likely enough. In 1778
a Bill to repeal the penal laws against Roman Catholics in
England was introduced into Parliament followed by a Bill
to the same effect applicable to Scotland. Robertson was
whole-heartedly in favour of the Scottish Bill and successfully persuaded the assembly not to oppose it. But widespread
popular indignation was aroused. Protests poured in from all
quarters, and riots occurred in Edinburgh and Glasgow.
Robertson was constrained to admit that he had misjudged
public opinion and advised the withdrawal of the Bill as
inopportune. He presumably acquiesced in a resolution of the
assembly of 1779 expressing their desire that toleration be
extended to Protestants of every denomination, their strongest
disapprobation of the recent riots, but also 'their firm persuasion that a repeal of the penal laws against Papists would
be highly inexpedient dangerous and prejudicial to the best
interests of religion and civil society in this part of the United
Kingdom'. This was Robertson's first failure to carry his
point. Another consideration seems certainly to have weighed
with him. For some time there had been vigorous discussion
in England especially but also in Scotland as to the legitimacy
of creeds and confessions, and an agitation against any demand for compulsory subscription even on the part of the
clergy. Some of Robertson's friends would gladly have seen
the abolition of theological tests and pressed him to take the
matter up. To such a course he declared himself resolutely
opposed. He is said, however, to have predicted that that
would be the next serious problem with which the Church
would be confronted, and with that thorny problem involving statutes and even the Treaty of Union he had no wish to
meddle. The historian's prophecy proved to be quite mistaken.

It may be suggested that Robertson's self-imposed task as
churchman was accomplished by 1780 and that he knew it.
It was to bring the Church to the tranquillity of order conso-
nant with the times. His policy of using the church courts to
enforce obedience to a statute obnoxious to the bulk of the
people at the cost of driving multitudes into dissent, must now
seem harsh. But even the Seceders discovered after much

bitter experience of division and subdivision that a Presbyterian Church could not live by zeal alone. It may indeed be said that Robertson achieved tranquillity only too effectively. The years of his 'administration' show little attempt to increase the spiritual efficiency of the Church at home; and the pronouncements of the assembly on the revolt of the American colonists, which occurred during these years, are lamentably conventional and lacking in understanding of the issue involved. On the other hand it may justly be claimed for Robertson that he saved Presbyterianism in Scotland by making it an orderly and workable system of church government on a national scale, and one which could in other hands become an efficient instrument for the promotion of the Christian good of the nation. After his withdrawal from assembly affairs he continued to be minister of Greyfriars and principal of the university till his death in 1793 when Moderate and Evangelical united in bearing testimony to his kindliness, sincerity of motive, outstanding ability and signal services to the Church.

The removal of Principal Robertson was a blow to the Moderate party for it had no one of comparable authority to replace him in the leadership. His acknowledged successor was George Hill, a young man who had been appointed professor of Greek in St. Andrews University at the age of 22 and had only recently entered the ministry on presentation to the Second Charge of St. Andrews. For some years he had been continuously a member of the assembly and had distinguished himself as a notable champion in debate of the Moderate interest. Intimacy with Henry Dundas, for twenty years the 'uncrowned king of Scotland' and all-powerful manager of government patronage, gave Hill great influence and secured his own promotion in 1788 to the chair of divinity, and in 1791 to the principalship of St. Mary's College, to which in due course was added the First Charge of St. Andrews. As professor of divinity he expounded Calvinism faithfully and lucidly, while warning his students that it was not for use in the pulpit. To one of them, Thomas Chalmers, later to be famous, he conveyed the impression that 'his orthodoxy was formed in conformity to the

Standards rather than as the truth most surely to be believed'. Principal Hill's leadership lasted for some thirty years but was sometimes challenged by members of his own party and the opposing party were growing in numbers and confidence under such notable and trusted leaders as John Erskine of Greyfriars and Sir Henry Moncrieff Wellwood of St. Cuthbert's. Moreover, the closing years of the eighteenth century brought a severe shock to the complacency that had characterized the Moderate régime, and had prevailed generally among the ruling classes in Church and State. The French Revolution shook the political foundations of Europe and propagated subversive republican and free-thinking ideas. Complacency gave place to fear and when war broke out between Britain and revolutionary France patriotism came to the aid of extreme conservatism in its endeavour to suppress every suggestion of change or reform. But change was inevitable, and that Britain was spared violent revolution in the early years of the nineteenth century was in large part due to the revival of Evangelicalism among the people.

III

THE EVANGELICAL REVIVAL

THE revival of Evangelical Christianity in England is associated with the names of the Wesleys and White-field. Their preaching caused multitudes to discover a new warmth of religious experience of which the essence was a quickened sense of sin and a joyful realization of forgiveness through the grace of God in Jesus Christ. Many could point to the day and hour when they had been converted from indifference to lively faith, from moral apathy to earnest endeavour after righteousness, from callous selfishness to care for others in Christian charity. Throughout the eighteenth century the movement gathered momentum in spite of the opposition and contempt of the powerful and the educated. Gradually Methodism detached itself from the Church of England and became a new, zealous, and well-organized denomination. But its evangelical fervour transmitted itself to important circles within the Church of England and the older dissenting bodies. It manifested itself in a new earnestness of preaching and in a long series of Christian humanitarian activities in many of which Anglicans and non-conformists co-operated. About 1780 Robert Raikes started Sunday schools in which the children of the very poor received a simple education mainly but not wholly religious. The modern missionary movement began when by the efforts of William Carey the Baptist Missionary Society was founded, to be followed three years later by the inter-denominational London Missionary Society, and in 1799 by the Church Missionary Society, founded by Charles Simeon and supported by Anglican Evangelicals. In 1804 the British and Foreign Bible Society began its remarkable work. This was again an inter-denominational enterprise aiming at the distribution of the Scriptures in all the languages of the earth. During the period of Enlightenment, Christianity had lost its hold on the masses and was on the defensive in educated circles. Its apologists were neither few nor undistinguished, but what they defended was 'rational religion' rather than the 'peculiar doctrines' of the faith. Now Evangelical Christianity took the offensive. Charles Simeon's long ministry at Cambridge exerted a powerful influence over generations of students, and is still a tradition in the university; and the members of the 'Clapham Sect', a group of wealthy men of good social position, turned their influence in the city and in Parliament to good account. William Wilberforce, for example, a close friend of the younger Pitt, was the tireless and ultimately successful leader of the anti-slavery movement.

Methodism, as we have seen, was for various reasons less conspicuously successful in Scotland than in England. But all through the eighteenth century Scotland had a succession of strongly Calvinist Evangelical ministers. Strangely impotent in the General Assembly they were highly esteemed and beloved by the people, partly because they defended the interests of congregations in the calling of ministers, but also because of their pastoral zeal. They were possibly more numerous in the far north, but were to be found throughout the country and even in some outstanding city churches. They too had moved with the times and could no longer be dismissed with contempt as wild, illiberal, and illiterate. Sir Henry Moncrieff Wellwood of St. Cuthbert's, Edinburgh, friend and biographer of John Erskine, was as presentable a figure socially and intellectually as any Moderate, and excelled most of them in his devotion to the proper functions of the ministry. But in the 1790's the Evangelical movement in Scotland was far behind the corresponding movement in England. The London Missionary Society found unofficial support in Scotland, and some of its early missionaries were Scots. Similar if smaller societies of the same nature came into existence in Edinburgh and Glasgow, but the General Assembly of 1796, in spite of the pleading of John Erskine, and overtures from two synods, refused to countenance support for missionary activity. All it would do was to recommend to all members of the Church in their different stations to use every competent means of promoting within the sphere of their influence, the knowledge of the Gospel and a just sense of the inestimable blessings it conveyed. Simeon of Cambridge visited Scotland in 1796 and was the cause of an awakening in central Perthshire, and Rowland Hill, an eccentric Anglican Evangelical whom no bishop would ordain, preached to great crowds in various places. But he gave a very critical account of the religious condition he found prevailing in Scotland. Certainly the Presbyterian system with its insistence on parochial ministrations did not offer a kindly welcome to itinerant evangelists, even when they were its own children.

Among Simeon's companions on his tour of central Scotland in 1796 was James Haldane, younger brother of Robert Haldane, proprietor of the estate of Airthrey in Stirlingshire. The Haldanes belonged to a pious and well-to-do evangelical family connected with the Church of Scotland. Both had had honourable careers in the navy before evangelism claimed their whole interest. A project for a joint mission in India had to be abandoned, but James discovered a talent for preaching through having been called to take services in a mission hall in the collier village of Gilmerton near Edinburgh. Simeon's example encouraged him to undertake evangelistic journeys throughout the length and breadth of Scotland, in which he preached to vast audiences, distributed tracts and started Sunday schools. At first his practice was to attend the Sunday morning service in the parish church, and later in the day to hold a meeting in the open air at which he attacked the minister of the parish when his doctrine came short of the evangelistic standard. Then with the lavish financial assistance of his brother he built preaching 'Tabernacles' in some of the larger towns, organized a Society for the Propagation of the Gospel at Home, and set up a college for the training of evangelists. In all this the Haldanes were animated solely by devotion to the preaching of the Gospel which they believed to be sadly neglected by the parish ministers generally, not by hostility to the Established Church. Nevertheless it is not surprising that great resentments were aroused.

The matter was brought up in the assembly of 1799 by complaints from all parts of the country, and the assembly

took severe measures in an endeavour to crush the movement. It passed an Act forbidding the admission to a pastoral
charge within the Church of any who had not pursued the
course of study prescribed by the Church for those intending
the ministry, and who had not been licensed by a presbytery
after the prescribed trials, also forbidding ministers to employ
unqualified persons in any services or ordinances of the Church
or to hold 'ministerial communion in any other manner with
such persons'. It further investigated the legal position of
'vagrant teachers and Sunday Schools' and enjoined presbyteries to be diligent in the exercise of their legal power to
supervise all schools within their bounds. Finally it issued
a pastoral admonition signed by the moderator to be read
from every pulpit in the land. The admonition began with
a patriotic reference to the misdeeds of revolutionary France,
with which of course Britain was at the time engaged in the
most perilous war in the history of the two countries. It
warned against books and pamphlets which propagated athe-
istic and seditious opinions; and went on to deplore the
activities of the missionaries of the so-called Society for the
Propagation of the Gospel at Home, who without training
or authorization set up schools and held meetings at which
they censured the doctrine and character of the ministers
and endeavoured to draw away the affections of the people
from their pastors. It reminded the people that the Church
of Scotland had always insisted on an educated and accredited
ministry conforming to established standards of doctrine worship discipline and government, and urged them to remain
loyal to the principles for which their fathers had fought and
suffered. All this must seem to breathe the very spirit of
Moderatism, and yet the assembly's policy was adopted
unanimously, and was also in line with that of the Seceding
Churches. Indeed it represents the general Presbyterian,
churchly, reaction to an evangelism that abandons ecclesiastical standards and methods. If it is to be reproached it must
be on the ground that it was unconstructive. At most the act
against 'vagrant teachers' may be said to be the beginning
of a new interest in education which developed fruitfully
in the first half of the nineteenth century. But there is no

recognition of the fact that it was the Church's own negligence that justified and provided opportunities for the Haldane mission. Hugh Miller shows how in parishes such as Cromarty which enjoyed an Evangelical ministry 'the Haldanites' could not find a footing.[1] The real answer to their challenge was supplied by a new generation of Evangelical ministers, increasing in number and in influence as the new century wore on. By them the main stream of Evangelicalism was retained within the Church of Scotland, and the Congregationalist and Baptist denominations, of which the Haldanes may be said to be the founders, remained relatively small.

Among the men who were to determine the fortunes of the Church in the new age first place must be given to Andrew Mitchell Thomson. Born in 1778, he was ordained in 1802, and, after short ministries successively in Sprouston, near Kelso, the East Parish, Perth, and New Greyfriars, Edinburgh, he was appointed in 1814 first minister of St. George's parish in that city. With that charge his name is chiefly associated. St. George's was one of five new churches erected by the town council between 1784 and 1836 to serve the new town. In its parish the *élite* of Edinburgh's citizens found their homes. It was a surprising appointment for Thomson was well-known as an outspoken Evangelical. But he was also a man of fine literary and musical gifts and immense energy, and before his early death in 1831 he had won for Evangelicalism not only a hearing but also a devoted following in the west end of Edinburgh, the very heart of Moderatism. By means of his magazine, *The Christian Instructor*, which he founded in 1810 and brilliantly edited for twenty years, he provided a religious counterpart to the *Edinburgh Review*, literary, liberal in its outlook on public questions, but definitely Christian Evangelical in character. To his vigorous leadership the growth of the Evangelical party within the Church owed much.

The dominant figure in the movement after Thomson's death was his contemporary, Thomas Chalmers, whom we have already met as an unappreciative student of Dr. Hill in St. Andrews. Born in 1780 and brought up in a strict

[1] *My Schools and Schoolmasters* Ch. xxii (pp. 474 ff. 14th ed.).

Calvinist home Chalmers was sent to the university of St. Andrews at the phenomenally early age of 12, vaguely with a view to his entering the ministry. He soon discovered an aptitude, even a passion, for mathematical studies, and for years his sole ambition was to become a professor of mathematics. Licensed as a preacher at the age of 19, under dispensation on the ground that he was 'a lad of pregnant parts', he spent two sessions in Edinburgh in the study of chemistry and natural philosophy, and was then appointed assistant to the aged and infirm professor of mathematics in St. Andrews, with entire charge of the teaching of the class. In 1803 he was presented to the Fifeshire rural parish of Kilmany, and in 1805 was a candidate for the chair of mathematics in Edinburgh. There were however two senior candidates of great distinction, and the appointment, which lay with the town council of Edinburgh, was the occasion of a fierce controversy between their partisans. On the one hand was John (afterwards Sir John) Leslie, whose claims were supported by many members of the Senatus. On the other hand Dr. Thomas McKnight, minister of the Old Kirk, Edinburgh, who had for some time acted as assistant to the professors of Greek and of natural philosophy, had the support of his Moderate brethren of the presbytery of Edinburgh. They went so far as to seek to disqualify Leslie by bringing a charge of heresy against him and carrying it to the General Assembly. The appointment thus became a party issue in which the Moderates appeared as sticklers for orthodoxy while the Evangelicals took the liberal side, a most remarkable reversal of rôles due largely, it must be admitted, to personal and party loyalties. For the first time the latter carried the day in the assembly. The charge was dismissed, Leslie secured in his chair, and the Moderates were discredited in the eyes of the literary classes with whom they had eagerly and proudly allied themselves in the past. Chalmers was of course precluded from taking any direct part in the controversy itself but was provoked to intervene on a more general issue. In support of Leslie, Professor Playfair had written an open letter to the Lord Provost of Edinburgh in which he alleged not only that there were very few Scottish clergymen eminent in mathematics or natural philosophy, but also that the pursuit of these sciences was incompatible with clerical duties and habits. Stung by this aspersion on the whole body of the clergy Chalmers published an anonymous pamphlet in which he declared that 'after the satisfactory discharge of his parish duties a minister may enjoy five days in the week of uninterrupted leisure, for the prosecution of any science in which his taste may dispose him to engage'. When these words were later quoted against him he handsomely acknowledged his error, but they seem to show that in 1805 he was a Moderate of the Moderates.

Some time in 1811, after a severe and prolonged illness, Chalmers experienced an evangelical conversion which altered his whole outlook on the ministerial vocation. His preaching became more earnest and his attention to his parish more assiduous. The leisure he had once devoted to scientific pursuits was now employed in active furtherance of the causes of foreign missions and of the Bible Society, both in his parish and in the neighbourhood. His increasing fame as a preacher led to his translation in 1815 to the Tron Church, Glasgow, and there for four years he held large congregations spellbound by his magniloquent oratory. Even so he could not be satisfied. The population of Glasgow had grown enormously by the end of the eighteenth century, and the Church had failed to keep pace with it, with the result that it had lost the masses of working people. Moreover in the depression following the Napoleonic War poverty had become a serious problem. In his student days at St. Andrews Chalmers had read Godwin's *Political Justice* but was repelled by its radicalism. On the other hand political economy fascinated him, and while still at Kilmany he wrote a substantial work on the subject. In particular he had given his attention to the question of poor relief and had come to the conclusion that legal assessments for the relief of the poor only increased pauperism by discouraging independence and self-help. He had convinced himself that the old method of relief from church-door collections, if it was controlled by a carefully organized system of parochial visitation, was still the best means of dealing with the problem; and he now conceived a remarkable plan to test his theory in a city parish. The opportunity to do so was lacking in the Tron, which as one of the old city churches had no independence for experiments of the kind he had in mind. Such was the influence Chalmers had gained with Glasgow's leading citizens that he persuaded the town council to erect and endow a new parish, St. John's, in which he would be free to develop his plan. From 1819 to 1823 he laboured abundantly in St. John's, among a teeming population of the poorer sort, preaching, visiting, organizing congregational charity, starting schools and apparently proving his case, though, for reasons which seem obvious enough now, he had no imitators, to his own disappointment. To the end of his days he believed passionately that the parochial system faithfully worked was the solution to Scotland's religious and social problems. Perhaps he was over-optimistic, but his faith did not fail though it was severely tried at the very opening of his ministry in St. John's. In December 1819 a one-day strike was called in Glasgow, in which almost the whole of his parishioners took part, and in the spring of 1820 Glasgow lived in terror of a radical revolution. Chalmers believed that Radicalism was simply an 'aspect of infidelity and irreligion', which he had made it his business to overcome. Like Sir Walter Scott Chalmers was a Tory who looked to a vanished past, in Scott's case the old medieval feudal romantic Scotland, in Chalmers's rural pre-industrial Scotland with its effective parochial system. Yet both also profoundly influenced the future, and Chalmers's work in Glasgow did much to win respect for the Gospel, by revitalizing the Church and arousing its social conscience.

Evangelicals have been commonly reproached for their neglect of learning, even of theological learning. If this reproach was in general merited, Chalmers was a brilliant exception. For all his abounding energy and practical organizing capacity he was at heart a scholar, and his voluminous works on economics, moral and social problems, and theology are unquestionable proof of his mental powers and of the extent of his scholarship. That his reputation was great beyond the confines of his native land is shown by the fact that he was invited to contribute a volume to the series of

Bridgewater treatises, apologetic treatises designed to prove 'the wisdom and benevolence of the Deity as manifested in the works of creation'. To the invitation he responded with his work *On the Adaptation of External Nature to the Moral and Intellectual Constitution of Men*. For this work among others he received the honorary degree of doctor of civil law from the university of Oxford, and in recognition of his contribution to economics he was elected a corresponding member of the Royal Institute of France. His first ambition had been to become a professor of mathematics and the academic life had always great attractions for him. But it came to be valued chiefly as an opportunity to influence the youth of the country and particularly those who intended to enter the Christian ministry. He therefore gladly accepted appointment to the chair of moral philosophy in St. Andrews University when it was offered in 1823. In 1828 he was transferred to the even more congenial chair of divinity in Edinburgh. In this latter position which he held for fifteen years Chalmers exerted his tremendous powers to the full. His teaching inspired a whole generation of younger ministers who regarded him with the utmost veneration, and on the death of Dr. Andrew Thomson in 1831 he became the acknowledged leader of the Evangelical party in the church, and the eloquent spokesman in every cause in which it was concerned. It is time now to look at some of these.

During the eighteenth century the relations of the Church with the universities were extremely close. All university teachers had to accept the Confession of Faith and were consequently to some extent subject to the discipline of the Church. The principals, the professors of divinity, and even professors in other faculties were commonly drawn from the ranks of the ministry. Moreover the operation of patronage made it possible and not uncommon for a principalship or a professorship to be held in conjunction with a pastoral charge, usually but not always in the university town. Some justification for this union of offices may be found in the fact that academic salaries were small and the duties light, and the same might be said of ministerial salaries and of parochial duties at least as understood by the Moderate clergy. By the beginning of the nineteenth century objections to this system began to be raised both from the academic and from the ecclesiastical side. Personal and partisan considerations obscured the deeper issue involved in the Leslie controversy, namely the freedom of the university from church control. We have seen how the insinuation that ministers as a class were unqualified for academic appointments provoked a pungent reply from Thomas Chalmers in his Moderate days. He had himself been taken to task by his presbytery for absenting himself from his parish in order to teach, unofficially, in St. Andrews. After 1811, however, his views completely changed. No one was more outspoken in opposition to the settlement of William Ferrie, professor of civil history in St. Andrews, who in 1813 was presented to the living of Kilconquhar, twelve miles distant from the university. After four years of heated debate throughout the Church all that the assembly could be persuaded to do was to enact in 1817 that no one might hold a professorship along with a pastoral charge unless the latter was situated within the university town or its suburbs. This act was far from satisfying the growing number of people who believed that a city charge was a full-time occupation, and they were deeply shocked when in 1823 Dr. Duncan Macfarlane, principal of Glasgow University, was presented by the Crown to the High Church of Glasgow, the foremost of the city churches; for at that very time Chalmers was demonstrating what a city minister's task really was. The presbytery judged that it was 'inexpedient and incompetent' to induct the presentee, and Macfarlane appealed to the General Assembly of 1824. Chalmers, now professor in St. Andrews, was a member, but his eloquent pleading to have the appeal dismissed was of no avail. By a majority the assembly sustained it. Agitation for the abolition of pluralities continued unabated in the Church until a Royal Commission on the Scottish Universities in 1828 reported that they were 'inexpedient'. It should be added that this decision was welcomed by Chalmers as beneficial to the universities and to learning as well as to the Church. He was eager to see more regular teaching and examining of students in all faculties, and it was due to his insistence that the Church with much hesitation increased its requirements of regular attendance by its own students on university courses particularly in the years devoted to the study of divinity.

One of the most clamant needs of the Church at the beginning of the nineteenth century was church extension particularly in those areas in which in consequence of the Industrial Revolution there had been a vast increase of population. The cities and large towns had always had a certain responsibility in the matter, and the first method of meeting it was to increase the number of ministers serving in the original churches, which thus became collegiate. But this method became inadequate, and a certain number of new churches were built. In Edinburgh, for example, the town council erected five churches for the new town, all of them at least externally impressive from an architectural point of view, as became their situation. They were therefore costly and the council, which retained the patronage, recouped itself by charging high seat rents. In each case a stipend was found for the minister by 'uncollegiating', with the consent of the presbytery, one of the churches in the old town. Thus though the number of churches was increased the number of ministers remained the same when the population was rapidly expanding, and the high charge for sittings made them prohibitive for the poorer section of the community.

There was in addition another, less official, movement of church extension leading to the erection of chapels in various localities. But these raised certain difficulties which have to be understood if we are not to judge unfairly the rather cold welcome offered to such chapels by the church authorities. Sometimes, doubtless, the purpose to be served by a chapel-of-ease was to provide an alternative to the local parish church (short of actual secession from the Church of Scotland) when the minister was unpopular or unacceptable. Moreover church door collections in the parish church were the main source of funds for the relief of the poor, supplemented if necessary by an assessment on the heritors. The latter were accordingly averse to anything that might increase the assessment as the existence of a chapel might do. The General Assembly therefore in 1798 by a majority enacted that the decision to recognize a proposed chapel-of-ease must rest with the assembly itself and not with the presbytery concerned. Regulations were drawn up regarding among other things the qualifications of the minister to be appointed, the amount of stipend to be paid, the security offered for its payment, and the availability of the collections taken for the poor-fund of the parish. The chapel had no area allocated to it as its parish and had no kirk session of its own. Its minister had no seat in the presbytery, and his congregation was subject to the jurisdiction of the kirk session of the parish within which the chapel was situated. Nevertheless chapels-of-ease were erected and won recognition. The earliest to do so was the relief meeting-house in which Thomas Gillespie had ministered after his deposition in 1761. On his death in 1774 the majority of his congregation petitioned the presbytery of Dunfermline to be admitted as a congregation to the Church of Scotland. The petition went to the assembly and in four successive assemblies was the subject of animated debate. At last in 1799 the petition was received and the first chapel-of-ease in the Church of Scotland received a constitution. By 1826 twenty-seven chapels had been recognized, and in addition some forty were in process of erection and endowment as a result of a Parliamentary grant of £100,000 voted in 1824. These last were all in the Highlands and Islands where the parishes were of vast extent. One of them was on the Island of Iona, which for all its historic memories had long been a derelict part of a united parish embracing almost the half of the Island of Mull!

During his ministry in the Tron Church, Glasgow, Chalmers came to realize the magnitude and urgency of the problem of church extension, particularly in the poorer districts of the cities. He was appalled by the spiritual destitution of the masses of the people in his own parish not half of whom, he estimated, had any church connexion whatever. The remedy, he believed, must be sought in making the parochial system really effective in the cities. More churches must be provided, manageable parishes attached to them and their ministry endowed so that seat rents could be, not indeed dispensed with, but kept so low that no one should be unable to afford them by reason of poverty. Chalmers's work in St. John's was meant to be a demonstration of what could and should be done. To the end of his days long after he had ceased to be a parish minister church extension on these lines was his consuming passion, 'the highest object of Christian patriotism'. The Church of Scotland, he believed, was specially called to save the working classes of Scotland from lapsing into heathenism and moral degradation. Only as an instrument of Christian good could he venerate it.

In 1828 the General Assembly took the matter up and appointed a Committee on Church Accommodation which, however, attempted little beyond vainly applying to the government for further aid. The time was hardly propitious. The country was shaken by the violent agitation for parliamentary reform, and the minds of politicians were fully occupied with hopes and fears, until in 1832 the Reform Bill became an Act. Two years later the General Assembly of 1834, in which for the first time the Evangelical party predominated, resolved on a forward movement. The Committee on Church Accommodation was enlarged and its powers extended. Chalmers himself was appointed convener, an office, he said, 'above all others congenial to his taste' and fitted to call out all his energy in an endeavour to realize his ideal on a national scale. An immense activity followed. Appeal was made to individuals and congregations. Church collections were taken, and congregational associations of penny-a-week contributors formed. In 1835 the convener was able to report that £65,000 had been contributed within the year and that 64 new churches were being built. In four years the sum raised was over £200,000 and 200 churches had been erected. Nothing like this had been attempted before, and to Chalmers's indefatigable labours and organizing ability the credit for the success of the scheme was due. He was besides able to fill the new pulpits with earnest preachers, many of them his own pupils. Outstanding among these was Murray McCheyne of St. Peter's, Dundee, who, though he died at the age of 30, exercised while he lived an extraordinary influence as an evangelist and left his name to be a household word for two generations of evangelical Scots.

But how were the new churches to be supported? It was always part of Chalmers's plan that a parochial church should be for the benefit of its parishioners only. They would be expected to pay seat rents to give them a personal interest, but these rents must be kept low so that even the poorest could afford them. An endowment therefore would be necessary to pay the minister's stipend, and to secure this an approach was made once more to the government. A memorandum setting forth the need of church extension and the proposals to meet it was drawn up and submitted, and members of the government publicly expressed sympathy and willingness to help. But before anything could be done, greatly to Chalmers's surprise and chagrin, opposition arose in Scotland, expressed in the first instance by a strongly worded memorial from the Scottish Dissenters who saw in the church extension project an endeavour on the part of the Establishment to counteract their influence. The Whig government of Lord Melbourne, therefore, temporized. A parliamentary commission was appointed to investigate the position in Scotland. In due course it reported on conditions of church accommodation in Edinburgh, Glasgow, and elsewhere and concluded generally that 'the opportunities of public religious worship and the means of religious instruction and pastoral superintendence at present existing and in operation were inadequate'. The government had committed itself to taking some action when the report was received, and now proposed to introduce a Bill to give some aid to rural parishes, but none to the larger towns. As this proved completely unacceptable the Bill was withdrawn.

Chalmers seriously underestimated the strength of the opposition to his plan for further endowments for the Church. The Whigs of the *Edinburgh Review* were contemptuous of the new Evangelical zeal, and found *their* patriotic task in removing the abuses in the country's representative and municipal systems. To the left of them were still more radical reformers who had no use for any Church. Among the industrial workers in the cities there was not only indifference to religion but often active hostility to the Established Church especially. Hugh Miller was saddened to find among the workers in Edinburgh a very different attitude to that to which he had been accustomed in Cromarty, and, though a Liberal in politics, accepted the editorship of the Evangelical newspaper *The Witness* in order to do what he could to win popular support for the cause of which Chalmers was the leader. Like Chalmers he believed that there was in the country no other institution so valuable as the Church, or in which the people of Scotland had so large a stake if they could only be brought to see it. Of all the elements of opposition none so astonished and shocked Chalmers as that which professed to be motivated by religious interests, uniting the groups that now proudly designated themselves 'Dissenters'. His controversy with them left a mark on Scottish religion which has not even yet been wholly erased.

In the main the Dissenters were the children of the Secession of 1733 but they had moved away from the ideas of their ancestors in many respects. The Erskines professed to carry on the covenanting tradition while accepting the Revolution Settlement. They withdrew from the national Church in protest against certain alleged defections from the old ways and appealed 'to the first free faithful and reforming General Assembly of the Church of Scotland'. The movement soon had troubles of its own. In 1747 it was split in two by violent disagreement as to whether it was lawful or sinful for a Seceder to take the oath required of burgesses of certain cities whereby they acknowledged the true religion publicly preached within the realm and authorized by the laws. Those who allowed the lawfulness of the oath, and these included Ebenezer and Ralph Erskine, were excommunicated by the more intransigent party, and two ecclesiastical bodies were organized, popularly known as the Burghers (Associate Synod) and Anti-Burghers (General Associate Synod). In spite of the schism both bodies maintained themselves and grew slowly but steadily at the expense of the national Church, gathering to themselves many who were dissatisfied by the operation of patronage, or by laxity in matters of doctrine and church discipline. Seceders generally were persons of sturdy independent minds, and their congregations were found largely in the rural areas and county towns in the Lowlands. Their ministers were humble men of great seriousness with strong evangelical, presbyterian, even covenanting principles. The Evangelical party in the Church itself deeply lamented the loss of these people, but in course of time the existence of Dissenting congregations was accepted as natural and even beneficial, certainly not dangerous to the Establishment, which could placidly watch them engage in interminable controversies amongst themselves both in their congregations and in their synods. At the turn of the century both branches of the Secession began to develop scruples regarding the section of the Confession of Faith which dealt with the duties of the civil magistrate in ecclesiastical affairs. Both set about revising their Testimonies in order publicly to disavow 'compulsory and persecuting principles', and in both there were conservatives rendering this difficult. When the New Light prevailed (in 1799 among the Burghers, in 1806 among the Anti-Burghers) 'Auld Licht' remnants hived off from both maintaining the traditional positions. The 'Auld Licht' Burghers gravitated towards the Church of Scotland which they joined in 1839. The 'Auld Licht' Anti-Burghers or Constitutionalists continued as the Original Secession Church. Though a small denomination, the latter made a distinctive contribution to Scottish religion, for their first leader was Dr. Thomas McCrie, the historian, who by his biographies of John Knox (1811) and Andrew Melville (1819) created a new interest in the principles of the Scottish Reformation and the Covenanting period which powerfully influenced Chalmers and his friends. On the other hand the New Lichts drew nearer to one another and in 1820 united to form the United Secession Synod with some 280 congregations 'under its inspection'.

As minister of Kilmany Chalmers had in his parish a Burgher congregation with whose minister he was on amicable if not intimate terms. In Glasgow where dissent had not yet become prominent he had his chosen field to himself. Some members of dissenting congregations might have taken part in the 'radical war' but the dissenting churches as a whole had refused to take part in politics. As professor in St. Andrews he exerted himself in opposition to his colleagues to free the students from compulsory attendance in St.

Leonard's parish church, the university church, now the university chapel of St. Salvator, in order to give those of dissenting families liberty to find more evangelical preaching elsewhere. His wife and family commonly attended the independent chapel to which he also went occasionally himself. So far from having any antipathy to Dissenters he valued their contribution to evangelical religion though recognizing its limitations.

It was shortly after his settlement in Edinburgh that Chalmers first came into unsought collision with Dissent. In 1829 the government of the day, forced by threatening events in Ireland, felt constrained to sponsor a Bill for the relief of Roman Catholics. Many both in England and Scotland believed that this would endanger the Protestant Established Churches, and the measure was widely unpopular. Chalmers defended it both at a public meeting in Edinburgh and in the presbytery for the curious reason among others that 'the perfection of an ecclesiastical system' embraced an Establishment on the one hand, and free unrestricted Dissenterism on the other! To Andrew Marshall, Secession minister in Kirkintilloch, however, the emancipation of Roman Catholics appeared to be the first step towards the re-establishment of the Roman Church by the State. In a sermon published under the title *Ecclesiastical Establishments Considered* he attacked all Establishments as unscriptural, unjust, and destructive of the true mission of the Church. The Church should be maintained, and its mission to the world supported solely by the liberality of its faithful people. Thus the practice of the dissenting churches was elevated into the Voluntary principle. Marshall himself was an inveterate controversialist whose pertinacity in heresy-hunting kept his own denomination in theological turmoil for years. But in his assertion of Voluntaryism he had most of his own people with him, and he could appeal to a much wider public where hostility to the Church was rife. For a decade therefore there raged the fiercest controversy the Church had known since the days of the Covenant. A Voluntary Church Association was confronted with an Association for Promoting the Interests of the Church of Scotland, each with its own magazine. Pamphlets

Y

were written, sermons preached, and public meetings held, and the language of vituperation and vilification exhausted on both sides. In the dust of battle most of the combatants must appear to us today to have forgotten the interests of the Gospel itself, and to have been blinded to the deeper issues involved. To his credit Chalmers lost neither his head nor his temper. Voluntaryism meant the denial of his ideal means of achieving the Christian good of Scotland, 'the dearest object of his existence', but in the main he kept aloof from the actual controversy. He made no reference to Marshall in a sermon he preached in which he dealt with some of his arguments. In his Lectures on the *Establishment and Extension of National Churches*, delivered in London in 1838 in defence of the Church of England which felt itself to be in a plight even more parlous than that in which the Church of Scotland found itself, he expounded once more and at greater length the policy which he had long before adopted and never abandoned. The only defence of Establishments is to make them effective instruments for their purpose of evangelism.

In one particular episode in the controversy, however, Chalmers did figure conspicuously. The ministers of the burgh churches in Edinburgh derived their stipends from an old assessment on certain properties in the city known as the annuity tax. Its incidence was universally admitted to be inequitable and proposals were made from time to time to rectify this. But there were those who wished to have it abolished altogether as a matter of principle. Taking the law into their own hands they withheld payment, and the authorities had to resort to prosecutions and even to distraint of goods. In 1833 there were as many as 846 prosecutions, and one of the outstanding Dissenting ministers went to prison rather than pay the small sum due, winning popular applause and bringing odium on the ministers of the city churches which personally they had done nothing to deserve. Chalmers clearly felt that this was a mean and dishonourable course of conduct against which he protested strongly and with dignity. Towards the end of the year the new town council took office, elected, in accordance with the provisions of the Scottish Burgh Reform Act, by householders entitled to vote in parliamentary elections, and including therefore both dissenters and radicals. The council at once sought a solution of the annuity tax controversy and entered into negotiations with the presbytery with a view to an agreed scheme. But agreement could hardly be expected when the council asked (1) that the number of city ministers be reduced from 18 to 13, by uncollegiating five churches in the old town and (2) that the primary source of stipend should be the seat rents eked out if necessary by a subsidy from the town. Both these demands struck directly at Chalmers's ideal and he attacked them fiercely. At that moment he had in hand a plan for a new church with a minister to work in the destitute area of the Cowgate and hoped that the town council would take it over. By his advice the presbytery rejected the proposals, although it seems to have concurred later in the uncollegiating of the city charges one by one. Not until 1860 was the annuity tax abolished or rather compounded for by the council.

Then came the appeal for parliamentary endowment of new church extension charges, and the memorial of the Dissenters in opposition. It is indeed a very extreme not to say malicious document. It asserted that while 'the avowed object of Dr. Chalmers's scheme is the supplying with religious instruction those of our countrymen who are destitute of it, the scarcely concealed design of this measure is the annihilation of dissent'. It is true that Chalmers, while acknowledging that the Dissenters did an essential service in providing opportunities for religious instruction in the places where they had congregations and churches, always insisted that Voluntaryism was impotent to overtake the whole task of evangelism. It could supply religious instruction where there was a demand for it, but the demand for the Gospel was not universal. It is also true that in his stirring appeal to the Church to support church extension he could say 'In proportion to our success shall we earn for the cause of religious establishments the friendship of the wise and the good, the support of every honest and enlightened patriot.' Nevertheless it was unworthy to insinuate that the annihilation of dissent was any part of his design. Much worse was the sneer

that 'to provide church-accommodation as the means of reclaiming the avowedly irreligious, vicious persons and crimi-
nals from their evil courses would betray a lamentable degree
of ignorance of human nature'. The report of the commissioners dealt entirely with church accommodation and made
it clear that in Edinburgh and Glasgow both the Established
Church and the Dissenters had accommodation to spare while
yet there were multitudes who attended no church. It may
be admitted that in commending his scheme in terms of additional 'accommodation' for religious instruction Chalmers
stressed too much the merely mechanical aspect of it; but in
his heart there glowed the fire of true and eager evangelism,
and his urgent plea for church extension in fact roused the
Church of Scotland from its long period of slumber. Chalmers
entered the ministry at a time when it stood lower in public
esteem than at any period before or since. To him more
than to any other is due its steady recovery of influence and
esteem throughout the nineteenth century.

The Evangelical movement concerned itself chiefly with
practical matters and little with theology. It was of course
theologically conservative, but so in a sense was Moderatism.
The difference between the two parties lay in the aim, manner,
and content of their preaching. Moderates were content to
teach the commonplaces of natural or rational theology
and to inculcate the prudential virtues. Evangelicals laid
emphasis on the great Christian doctrines of sin, grace and
redemption, and their aim was to awaken in their hearers
a deeper personal religious experience. Both parties alike
acknowledged the authority of the Westminster Confession as
the standard of the Church's doctrine. Now that Confession
is a noble and carefully balanced exposition of the Christian
faith in the terms of scholastic Calvinism, and for that reason
was apt to prove something of a strait-waistcoat for eager
souls who believed that personal religion was of greater
importance than the niceties of correct dogmatic definition.
So the Marrow Men had found it to be, and they were
condemned for deviations of which they were themselves
unconscious. After a century of almost untroubled orthodoxy
the Church of Scotland found itself compelled once more to

condemn in the name of its Confession a number of large-hearted men whose evangelical passion led them to break away from the strict letter of the Confessional position. In the proceedings taken against Edward Irving and John Mc-Leod Campbell Evangelicals and Moderates were united.

Edward Irving was a truly tragic figure. Born in 1792 of humble parents in Annan, Dumfriesshire, he struggled through an arts course at Edinburgh University not without distinction, and thereafter maintained himself as a school-master first at Haddington and then at Kirkcaldy while pre-paring for licence as a preacher. In 1819 he eagerly accepted appointment as assistant to Dr. Chalmers in St. John's Church, Glasgow, and for nearly three years he took his full share in the work of the parish. If somewhat uncouth in the pulpit he was popular with the people, associating with them 'as man with man or friend with friend, a soother of distress, a brother of the youth, an encourager of the children, and often a listener to the wisdom of the aged'. In the bitter year 1820, though no radical, he had nothing to fear from any-one, for all trusted him and loved him for his open sincerity. For Chalmers he had unbounded admiration as a man of 'transcendent genius' giving himself to the task of maintain-ing and furthering the 'spiritual economy of Scotland'. But it would be difficult to imagine two men more completely different in temperament. Irving was unconventional, simple, generous, sensitive, exuberant, and eccentric. Intensely loyal to the Church of Scotland as 'a free plebeian Church which never pined till she began to be patronised', he had also a high sense of personal mission to meet the moral and religious needs of the age by 'a new natural style of preaching' that would proclaim a more magnanimous form of Christianity than that in vogue. A scorner of patronage and ecclesiastical intrigue, he found no one to present him to a parish in his native land, and was fain in 1822 to accept the call of a small Scots congregation in London. There his new style of preach-ing at once attracted attention and his church was crowded with the most eminent people in the metropolis. A larger one had to be built for him in 1824, the National Scotch church, it was called, in Regent Square. Dr. Chalmers came to preach at its opening, but now he began to find his old assistant too much for him. He could not understand his intimacy with Coleridge! And Irving's long-drawn-out eloquence in sermon and prayer made him impatient. Had the plaudits of London society turned the head of the Scotch preacher? Or was it domestic sorrow, the loss of three dearly loved children in infancy, that drove him to an interest in Prophecy and the Second Coming of Christ? In 1828 he visited his native land and preached to gigantic congregations in Annan, Edinburgh, Kirkcaldy, and elsewhere. But already rumours were abroad that he was preaching unsound doctrine with regard to the human nature of the Saviour, and on a second visit in the following year he found the Edinburgh pulpits denied to him. Then came the scandal of his allowing persons claiming 'the gift of tongues' to exercise it in his London church, which alienated his congregation and led to his ejection from the Church by the presbytery of London. In 1831 the General Assembly took note that he taught that Christ in the Incarnation had assumed man's fallen sinful nature, and instructed the presbytery of Annan as the presbytery which had ordained him to bring him to trial on a charge of heresy. Never surely was a small country presbytery confronted with a more awesome task. It met in open court in Annan parish church with some 1,800 persons looking on. For two hours Irving maintained the truth of his doctrine with a torrent of impassioned oratory addressed as much to the public present as to the presbytery. It must have taken courage in such circumstances to condemn Annan's most illustrious son, but all the ministers in turn pronounced the libel proven. Among them was one minister of real distinction, Henry Duncan of Ruthwell, founder of savings banks, restorer of the famous Ruthwell Cross, a man of extensive culture and a noted evangelical, who confessed that conscience alone drove him to the most painful judgement of his life. It only remained for the moderator to pronounce the solemn sentence of deposition. Edward Irving is now chiefly remembered for the part he played in the foundation of the Catholic Apostolic Church. But it was a small part and his connexion with the new denomination was very brief for he

died in 1834 in the 43rd year of his age. The Church of
Scotland must bear some of the responsibility for the extravagances of his later years for it was her inhospitality and lack
of sympathy that drove him, her devoted and gifted son, to
keep strange company. It may now be conceded that what
in his teaching appeared as heresy to most good men in his
day was in fact a groping for a profounder view of the true
full and real humanity of the Man of Sorrows.

The assembly of 1831 which animadverted on the teaching
of Edward Irving had also to deal with a charge of heresy
brought against John McLeod Campbell. These two men
during a brief acquaintance had been drawn to one another
by mutual esteem, and Campbell's condemnation provoked
Irving to proclaim the assembly to have been 'a wicked synagogue of Satan'. There is nothing to show that Campbell in
any way approved his friend's later doings. Indeed beyond
the fact that both shared a passionate desire for a deeper
humaner understanding of Christianity there was little resemblance between the stormy prophet and the pastor-
theologian. Brought up in an Argyllshire manse McLeod
Campbell was in due course (1825) presented by the then
Duke of Argyll to the beautiful parish of Rhu on the shores of
the Gareloch. From the beginning of his ministry he took a
high view of his responsibilities towards his people. He determined therefore to hold aloof from ecclesiastical politics
and from both the contending parties, and to devote himself
exclusively to his pulpit and pastoral work. As a result of his
own intense study of Scripture he soon became dissatisfied
with the effect of the current religious teaching upon the
people, especially the more serious minded among them.
They were taught that their salvation depended upon believing in Christ and in being good. But their faith, while real so
far as it went, came short of full assurance of God's love for
them and for all men 'irrespective of what they are', and
therefore brought no peace or joy in believing or in endeavour
after a holy life. Saving faith means simple acceptance of the
fact revealed in Christ that God had once for all manifested
his love towards all men. Contemplation of that given ob-
jective fact would give the believer confidence 'that God is

able to make him what He wills him to be'. He would be
delivered from all anxiety as to his spiritual 'state' such as
had tormented Thomas Boston and many earnest Christians
since. The burden of Campbell's preaching now became Universal Atonement through Christ, pardon for sins freely
offered to all men as the ground of Assurance without which
there is no saving faith. He did not directly reject the doctrine of Election, though he realized that it was in part
responsible for the doubts and anxieties of earnest Christians,
and more and more came to find it logically irreconcilable
with active evangelism. But as his doctrine seemed implicitly
to deny Election, Evangelicals were offended for they were
strict Calvinists. On the other hand Moderates sensed 'fanaticism' in the word Assurance, which also smacked of Antinomianism for which *The Marrow* had been condemned in
1720.

Rhu was then as now a holiday resort and visitors carried
reports of what was being taught there to Glasgow where it
encountered much opposition. In Edinburgh the redoubtable
Andrew Thomson preached in St. George's a series of sermons subsequently published in a volume *The Doctrine of
Universal Pardon Considered and Refuted* (1830). Libelled for
heresy before the presbytery of Dumbarton, Campbell was
found guilty of entertaining and promulgating 'the doctrine
of universal atonement and pardon through the death of
Christ, and also the doctrine that assurance is of the essence
of faith and necessary to salvation'. The case went by appeal
to the synod and finally to the assembly which, in spite of
a petition in his favour signed by nearly all his parishioners
and a moving appeal from his own father, resolved by 119
votes to 6 to depose him from the ministry. Characteristically
he received the sentence without bitterness. A congregation
gathered round him in Glasgow to which he ministered until
failing health compelled him to retire to Rosneath on the
Gareloch opposite his old parish where he died in 1872. He
is now remembered for his book on *The Nature of the Atonement*, a sincere book, whether his theory is approved or not,
and Scotland's greatest contribution to theology.

Irving (apart from his later enthusiasms) and McLeod

Campbell must be accounted genuine products of the Evangelical revival, and yet it was the Evangelicals who were specially involved in their condemnation. Andrew Thomson had done much to arouse hostility to the 'Row heresy'. The attitude of Chalmers is more puzzling. With Irving's eccentricities he had long lost patience, but he was curiously detached in the Rhu case. He was not a member of the 1831 assembly and it is impossible to know what advice he gave to members who consulted him on the matter. He retained a high regard for Erskine of Linlathen who was certainly a supporter of McLeod Campbell, and he seems to have admitted that the latter's deviation from orthodoxy was microscopic. But Evangelicals were not in general theologians, and it was natural enough that they should suspect, ignorantly it may be and unreasoningly, any who questioned or seemed to question the Church's confessional position. The Secession Church too had similar difficulties. James Morrison of Kilmarnock was cast out because as an Evangelical he denied the doctrine of Election, and John Brown, an eminent scholar and leader in the United Secession, was for years subjected to charges of unorthodoxy on the doctrine of the Atonement. McLeod Campbell lived long enough to see and rejoice in what may be called a liberalizing of Scottish theology without abandonment of its evangelical warmth.

IV

THE DISRUPTION

AFTER two years of violent agitation throughout the country the Reform Bill passed into law on 4 June 1832. Many good people believed that a deadly blow had been struck at the well-being and constitutional stability of the nation. The authors of the measure on the other hand were satisfied that by a timely and moderate concession to popular demands revolution had been averted. But there were many who regarded it as merely the first step towards more drastic change. Certainly it was a turning-point in the history of Britain inaugurating an age of reform in which all aspects of the national life were involved. Nowhere was there more enthusiasm for the Bill or a more vociferous welcome for its passing than in Scotland where interest in politics, dormant since the Union of 1707, had been reawakened. There were of course opponents. Sir Walter Scott died in September 1832 lamenting that the Scotland he loved and had idealized had passed irrevocably away. Thomas Chalmers also reflected sadly that the new interest in secular politics meant the frustration of his dream of a political economy based on religious individualism.

Among the institutions that felt themselves threatened by the extension of the franchise were the Established Churches of England and Scotland, for parliamentary reform had put increased political influence into the hands of dissenters and of rationalists hostile to all religion. To many English churchmen the position of their church seemed desperate. 'The Church as it now stands', wrote Thomas Arnold, 'no human power can save.' Unquestionably the Church of England offered a vulnerable target to its enemies. Its great wealth was inequitably and inefficiently distributed, and to it clung hoary abuses which the Reformation had not swept away. In these circumstances some anxious churchmen invited Thomas Chalmers to deliver a course of lectures in London in defence of the idea of church establishments. His eloquent pleading was admired and perhaps had its effect. The Church of England was saved in spite of itself by a parliamentary reformation which removed many of the glaring scandals in its administration and thereby increased its efficiency. A very different line was taken by the Oxford Movement which began with Keble's famous Assize sermon on national apostasy, an attack on the very idea of State intervention in church affairs, and went on to claim spiritual freedom for the Church as a society deriving its authority from the primitive apostolical Church and not from Acts of Parliament. But if the original inspiration of the movement was anti-erastian its suspected Rome-ward tendency alarmed the public and the politicians, and made them unsympathetic to the equally anti-erastian though otherwise utterly contrasting movement that developed contemporaneously in Scotland. Dr. Thomas Chalmers and Dr. Edward B. Pusey were alike champions of the spiritual freedom of the Church, but here the resemblance ends except that both were regarded with extreme disfavour in high political circles. We have seen how the Evangelical party in the Church of Scotland had been increasing in numbers and influence since the beginning of the century, and how, when its hopes for a revived national Church looked like being realised, the dissenters launched their attack on ecclesiastical establishments in general.

A compulsory support of religious institutions is inconsistent with the nature of religion, the spirit of the Gospel, the express appointment of Jesus Christ, and the civil rights of man, its tendency as exhibited by its effects is to secularise religion, promote hypocrisy, perpetuate error, produce infidelity, destroy the unity and purity of the Church, and disturb the peace and order of civil society.

Moderates and Evangelicals alike rallied to the defence of the Church, but the latter most keenly resented this sweeping condemnation of their most cherished convictions. The Voluntary Controversy was well under way when the Reform Act seemed to bring disestablishment within the bounds of possibility, unless something could be done and done quickly to popularize the Church itself. The Evangelicals had, of course, been also the 'popular' party because they championed the rights of congregations in connexion with the appointment of their ministers, when the nominees of the patron gave dissatisfaction, i.e. they were non-intrusionists. But not all of them now objected to patronage as such. Chalmers believed that a good use might be made of patronage to secure an effective ministry. He realized the danger of unbridled popular liberty of choice, for he was no democrat. But the interests of patrons were not always those of evangelical religion, and in general patrons belonged to the opponents of reform. This made them more than ever unpopular, and in their unpopularity the Church undoubtedly shared. In the existing state of political feeling the question of patronage therefore acquired a new urgency.

The assembly of 1832 met in May just before the Reform Bill reached the Statute Book, and it elected Dr. Thomas Chalmers, its most distinguished member, to the Moderatorial chair. No reference was made to the impending legislation though many of those present must have regarded it as ominous. But the popular demand for the Bill may have been partly responsible for the fact that overtures were submitted from three synods and eight presbyteries calling attention to the evils of patronage and asking for remedy. After long debate the assembly by a majority of 46 rejected a motion to remit the matter to a committee for consideration and report to next assembly. It was declared to be unnecessary and inexpedient to raise the question at that time. The presbyteries were not content to let it rest there. It soon became apparent that a greater number of overtures would be made to the assembly of 1833. The leaders of the two great parties had therefore to make up their minds as to the policy they would adopt.

Chalmers was in favour of hastening slowly, using the powers he believed the Church already possessed. As early as 1813 he had stressed the power of the church judicatories to reject a presentee judged unsuitable by his circumstances (in this case the holding of a university chair) for a particular charge, and dismissed as unthinkable the suggestion that a court of law might hold a presentee entitled to the benefice if the Church refused to induct him to the pastoral charge. 'The stipend is the minister's, and the minister is he, and only he, who comes in with the sanction of the Church judicatories.' He never doubted that the church courts had the ultimate power to decide whether, viewing all the circumstances of the case, it was for the Christian good of the people that a particular presentee should be inducted to a particular charge. The rights of patrons were obviously not absolute. A patron could only present one who held the Church's licence, and over the training of students for licence the Church had complete control. Moreover it was not disputed that the Church could by prohibiting pluralities still further curtail the rights of patrons; and a presentation required to be sustained by a presbytery, which then took the steps necessary for the admission of the presentee. But what of the rights of congregations in the settlement of ministers? By the parliamentary Act of 1690 abolishing patronage the right of congregations to object to a minister nominated by the heritors and elders had been recognized, as well as the right of the presbytery to judge of the objections; and the Act of 1712 restoring the right of nomination to patrons had not explicitly denied the rights of congregations to object and of presbyteries to adjudicate. Throughout the eighteenth century it was usual for the presbytery to require a presentee to preach in the Church to which he had been presented, and then to give members of the congregation an opportunity to sign a call in his favour which, at his induction, he was asked to accept. Under the Moderate régime less and less importance had been attached to the call. It was sustained provided one or two signatures appeared upon it, but though reduced to a mere formality even a Moderate-dominated General Assembly in 1790 refused to abolish outright this vestige of popular rights. The problem in 1833, as Chalmers saw it, was 'as to the best way of restoring significance and effect to this now antiquated but still venerable form'.

Chalmers's own idea was that the church courts themselves should reverse the policy by which the call had been denuded of significance and insist that a sufficient number of signatures would henceforth be held to be necessary to validate a call. But many insisted that such a course would be too slow, while others feared that it would bring about a collision with patrons, which they desired to avoid. Few of the responsible church leaders desired the abolition of patronage, which could only be accomplished by a parliamentary Act; and an appeal to Parliament in 1833 might have had undesirable consequences. A different and rather surprising course was agreed upon. Instead of declaring that a call to be valid must contain a substantial if necessarily indeterminate number of signatures, the Church should assume the concurrence of the parishioners in a ministerial appointment unless a majority of them expressed disapproval. 'A majority of dissentient voices should lay a veto on every presentation.' Chalmers himself moved a motion to this effect in the assembly where in spite of his eloquent pleading it was lost by twelve votes, and a motion from the Moderate side was carried allowing for dissents providing they were specific and were substantiated.

Even so the synods and presbyteries were dissatisfied, and the matter was again raised by overtures in the General Assembly of 1834. Chalmers was not a member but the motion that had been defeated in the previous assembly was with little alteration moved again, this time by Lord Moncrieff, one of the judges of the Court of Session and an earnest evangelical churchman. As it was to become of momentous importance its terms must be quoted in full.

The General Assembly having maturely considered the overtures do declare that it is a fundamental law of this Church that no pastor shall be intruded on any congregation contrary to the will of the people; and that, in order to carry this principle into full effect, the Presbyteries of the Church shall be instructed that if in the moderating in a call to a vacant pastoral charge the major part of the male heads of families, members of the vacant congregation and in full communion with the Church, shall disapprove of the person in whose favour the call is proposed to be moderated in, such disapproval shall be deemed sufficient ground for the Presbytery rejecting such person and he shall be rejected accordingly, and due notice thereof forthwith given to all concerned; . . . and further declare that no person shall be held entitled to disapprove . . . who shall refuse, if required solemnly, to declare in the presence of the Presbytery that he is actuated by no factious or malicious motive, but solely by a conscientious regard to the spiritual interests of himself or the congregation.

In 1834 for the first time the Evangelical party predominated in the assembly, and this extraordinary motion was carried by a majority of 46. One hundred and thirty-eight voted for a counter-motion requiring objections to a ministerial settlement to be specific and given in in writing, so that the presbytery might adjudicate upon them, all parties being given full opportunity to be heard. Of these 138 no fewer than 105 asked that their dissent should be recorded. Nevertheless the triumphant majority determined without delay to put the resolution into effect. Before it could be finally enacted it had to receive the consent of the majority of the presbyteries under the Barrier Act, but the assembly resolved to make it at once an Interim Act and gave its approval to a long series of regulations for the guidance of presbyteries in operating the veto. These, too, were ordered to be sent down under the Barrier Act.

The enthusiasm for the Veto Act is hard to understand. Its declaration against intrusion would be generally welcome both to those who wanted an all-out attack on patronage and to those who recognized that patrons of late had been more considerate of the wishes of congregations. The sponsors of the veto frankly admitted that its object was to curb abuses of patronage, not to abolish it. They abandoned the attempt to restore significance to the call because they believed there was a simpler way within the existing law of giving some recognition to popular rights. The idea of limiting responsibility to 'the heads of families' may well betray a patriarchal if not an anti-democratic attitude; but even if 'heads of families' may be supposed to be the wiser and more responsible section of a congregation, the proposed safeguard against factious and malicious motives must be pronounced naïve. Moreover to give to a majority of heads of families the power to veto a presentee without reasons stated was to deprive presbyteries of the judicial function that was legally theirs, and had been frequently exercised without being strictly defined. It must be supposed that the evangelical majority in the assembly were happy in the thought that the Church itself at last was doing something to meet an ancient grievance.

It was this assembly that determined on a more vigorous policy in the matter of church extension and appointed Chalmers convener of a strengthened committee to promote it. Moreover, still further to encourage the movement it passed a Chapels Act, whereby all existing chapels-of-ease and those to be erected were recognized as parish churches *quoad sacra*.[1] Parochial bounds were to be assigned to them, kirk sessions constituted, and their ministers were to have full standing as ministers and to be enrolled as members in the church courts. This Act gave an impetus to the cause of church extension which hitherto it had lacked and had something to do with the success which attended Chalmers's efforts. Whatever doubts may have been in the minds of some shrewd observers, to the majority members of the assembly and to multitudes of sympathizers throughout the country it appeared that a great forward movement had begun; the Church was shaking off its century-old lethargy, and was entering upon a new period of quickened life. So indeed it was, but no one perceived that the way was to lie through ten years of bitter conflict culminating in the largest secession in the history of the Church.

The trouble began with one particular case of the operation of the Veto Act. Within six months of its passing as an Interim Act and before it was made a standing law of the Church the parish of Auchterarder became vacant through the death of its minister. The patron, the Earl of Kinnoul, presented a certain Robert Young, a respectable person and a recent licentiate. By appointment of the presbytery Young preached on two successive Sundays in the parish church. When the presbytery met it was found that only two resident parishioners had signed his call, while 286 male heads of families out of a total of 330 came forward to express disapproval. Young appealed to the synod and then to the General Assembly of 1835, which instructed the presbytery to

---

[1] i.e. for ecclesiastical purposes only, as distinguished from civil or *quoad omnia* parishes.

proceed according to the terms of the Veto Act, now finalized. The presbytery, therefore, rejected the presentee. Young now consulted John Hope, dean of the Faculty of Advocates, an elder of the Church who, as a member of the assembly in 1834, had voted against the veto resolution and tabled a reasoned dissent, and who now made it his mission in life to have its illegality established in the Law Courts. On Hope's advice Young sought from the Court of Session 'declarator' that the presbytery of Auchterarder were 'bound and astricted' to take him on trials and if found qualified in 'literature, life and doctrine' to admit him as minister of Auchterarder irrespective of the veto of the parishioners. Here was seemingly a straightforward test case but one of no ordinary significance. On both sides the most eminent counsel were briefed, and they took ample time and the greatest pains in their preparations, for they were required to review the whole history of the Church since 1560 in its relations with the State and the law. Not till late in November 1837 was the case called in court. For three weeks it was argued with erudition and skill on both sides before the entire bench of judges, thirteen in all, of whom Lord Moncrieff, the mover of the veto motion, was one, while the public looked on with intense interest and excitement. Towards the end of the following February the judges began to deliver their opinions and by a majority of eight to five they found in favour of the pursuer. Judgement was pronounced on 8 March. Virtually the Supreme Court declared that in passing the Veto Act the Church had acted *ultra vires* and that in operating it it infringed the statutory civil rights of patrons and presentees.

Looking back we may be tempted to think that the judgement of the court should have been accepted and another way found to achieve the purpose which the veto was designed to serve. Indeed some of the church leaders including Chalmers were in favour of rescinding the Veto Act. But it was not so simple as that. The dean of faculty in his pleadings, and the majority judges in their opinions had presented a view of the implications of ecclesiastical establishment that was utterly at variance with the Church's Confession of Faith, and challenged the doctrine of the Church's nature which

z

many had cherished. The notion of the Church as an independent spiritual community governed by its own officers and capable of entering into a compact with the State was repudiated. All talk of a power 'to legislate and regulate bestowed on the Church by its great spiritual Head . . . is the most pernicious error by which the blessed truths of Christianity can be perverted'. As a national establishment the Church was judicially declared to be a creation of the State deriving all its powers from specific Acts of Parliament. 'It is wholly of statutory creation, of statutory authority and statutory jurisdiction.' When it was urged that the Church had always claimed an independent spiritual power, and had in fact exercised it, the answer was given that that was in a time of rebellion and confusion now happily long past. Such an interpretation of 'establishment' might have been acceptable to most churchmen in the period of the Moderate ascendency, but in 1838 it could hardly be agreeable to any party within the Church. Not many even in the remnant of the Moderate party could welcome a doctrine which delighted the Voluntaries with whom they had long been in controversy; and the jubilation of the extreme Voluntaries added to the sense of cruel frustration under which the Evangelicals were smarting. Moreover in that very year the second centenary of the National Covenant and the Glasgow Assembly fell to be celebrated. People were eagerly reading the writings of Dr. Thomas McCrie, and the spirit and principles of the Covenanting period were being revived and extolled. Instead, therefore, of repealing the Veto Act the assembly resolved to appeal to the House of Lords, and in the meantime as a counterblast to the Erastianism of the Scottish judges passed a resolution anent the independent jurisdiction of the Church of Scotland, acknowledging the exclusive jurisdiction of the civil courts in regard to the civil rights and emoluments secured by law to the church and its ministers, but claiming for itself a spiritual jurisdiction derived from Jesus Christ, the sole Head of the Church. It declared its readiness 'to assert and at all hazards defend' this spiritual jurisdiction 'by the help and blessing of God who in days of old enabled their fathers, amid manifold persecutions, to maintain a testimony even to the death for Christ's kingdom and crown'. Finally it proclaimed its determination to secure obedience from all its office-bearers.

The appeal to the House of Lords was heard in March 1839 before the Lord Chancellor (Cottenham) an Englishman, and the ex-Lord Chancellor (Brougham) a native of Edinburgh and co-founder of the *Edinburgh Review*, but long resident in London. It was dismissed in words even more contemptuous and galling, especially on the part of Lord Brougham, than any used in Edinburgh. It was now declared that the patrons' rights were absolute, that no objections on the part of parishioners were relevant, and that even presbyteries had no authority to take account, in judging of a presentee, of anything except his professional qualifications 'in life, literature and doctrine'. This was too much for Chalmers. If he had wavered with regard to the veto he was convinced now, and in the assembly of 1839 which met a few weeks after the judgement was delivered, in a passionate speech of three hours' duration he declared that the Church could not submit. He moved that no further resistance should be made to the claim of the patron and the presentee to the benefice of Auchterarder, and that a committee should be appointed to consider how the national establishment and the harmony of Church and State could be preserved, and to confer if necessary with the government. The motion was carried but some who were nominated to serve on the 'Non-Intrusion' Committee refused to do so. For it must be remembered that there was always a very considerable minority who held that the course the prevailing party was pursuing was unwise and disastrous, and some who had hitherto supported it now began to draw back, seeing the hopelessness of defying the law. From this time onwards can be traced the emergence of a middle party, largely evangelical and non-intrusionist in sympathy, but chiefly impressed by the damage that was being done to church life and work by ecclesiastical strife. The middle party never attained great numerical strength, and it was apt to draw to itself the scorn and hatred of the ardent evangelicals, because it appeared to be a camp of deserters from the great cause. It came to be derided as the party of the 'Forty Thieves', but the Church of Scotland would have been fortunate had there been more of them.

While the appeal to the House of Lords was pending the General Assembly and its commission continued to enforce the Veto Act, claiming that ordination to a pastoral charge was a purely spiritual act with which the civil courts had no concern and professing to be willing to surrender the emoluments of the benefice to the patron and his presentee when the latter was rejected. There had been a few instances of such separation of cure and benefice in the eighteenth century, when the stipend was retained by the patron. But in 1838 by a recent Act of Parliament vacant stipend was payable to the ministers' widows' fund, and consequently the Court of Session gave no weight to the Church's plea. The attempt to enforce the Veto Act provided Mr. Hope with new clients, and it is surprising that they were so few. It has been computed that between 1834 and 1839 out of 150 presentations to vacant parishes only ten were vetoed, and of these ten only three or four led to legal action. Two of them attained unhappy notoriety. In the Lethendy case the presbytery of Dunkeld, in obedience to the orders of the assembly and its commission and in defiance of an interdict issued by the Court of Session, ordained a minister to the pastoral charge 'irrespective of the civil benefice attached thereto'. The members of the presbytery were summoned to the bar and publicly censured for breach of interdict and threatened with imprisonment. Much more serious was the Marnoch case. A certain John Edwards, a licentiate of twenty years' standing who had long been a schoolmaster in the neighbourhood, was presented by the patron and vetoed by the great mass of the heads of families. Only one parishioner, the village innkeeper, signed his call. The presbytery of Strathbogie, within whose bounds the parish lay, referred the matter to the assembly of 1838, and was directed to reject the presentee, which it did. The patron then presented another, David Henry, and Edwards obtained from the Court of Session an interdict prohibiting the presbytery from taking Henry on trials. Unlike the presbytery of Dunkeld the presbytery of Strathbogie was by majority 'moderate', it resolved by

seven votes to four that 'the Court of Session having authority
in matters relating to the induction of ministers, and having
interdicted all proceedings on the part of the presbytery;
and it being the duty of the presbytery to submit to their
authority regularly interposed, the presbytery do delay all
procedure until the matter in dispute be legally determined'.
For this resolution which appeared to contradict the last
assembly's declaration of spiritual independence the presbytery were censured and enjoined to take no steps towards the
induction of Edwards. But when the matter in dispute seemed
to have been legally determined by the judgement of the
House of Lords, and the Court of Session issued a declarator
that the presbytery was bound to take Edwards on trials
and, if found qualified, to admit him as minister of Marnoch,
the presbytery in December 1839 sustained the call and appointed his trials. A week later the Commission of Assembly
met and, to prevent further proceedings, suspended the seven
ministers who formed the majority of the presbytery from
their ministerial functions. It appointed a large committee of
distinguished evangelical ministers to co-operate with the
four remaining ministers of the presbytery in discharging
ministerial duties in the parishes of those who had been suspended. The latter sought to defend themselves by securing
interdicts against all who should intrude into their parishes
without their consent, interdicts which the intruders entirely
disregarded and which became the laughing stock of the
populace. Finally on the petition of Edwards the court again
declared the presbytery bound to proceed to his admission,
and on a wintry day in January 1841 five of the seven suspended ministers met in the church of Marnoch and in face
of a hostile crowd ordained and inducted Edwards as minister
of the parish. For this act of insubordination they were deposed
by the assembly of 1841 on the motion of Dr. Chalmers.
Edwards's ordination was declared null and void, and his
certificate of licence was withdrawn. An interdict and suspension of sentence issued by the Court of Session was laid
on the table of the assembly and provoked protest as an un-
warranted encroachment on the Church's jurisdiction.

The story of the Marnoch case is a truly sorry one that can

bring satisfaction to none today. At the time it grieved and shocked many sincere lovers of the Church who belonged to no party in it, while the ribald enjoyed a clever cartoon showing the leading churchmen on both sides boisterously engaged in 'The Reel of Bogie'. The seven deposed ministers refused to obey the sentence of the assembly and in this they were supported and encouraged by prominent members of the Moderate party, even as the four evangelical ministers were supported by the Church's official committee. The Church, or, as we must in fairness say, the 'prevailing party' within it, by its high-handed actions alienated much sympathy in influential circles, and finally destroyed all hope that Parliament would come to its rescue by legislative action. In the eyes of parliamentarians, who were of course mostly Englishmen, it had got into the hands of lawless fanatics. Perhaps we may now admit that it failed to see that Samuel Rutherford's principle of *Lex Rex* was as applicable to ecclesiastical as to royal pretensions. Conscious of a new vitality in itself and encountering unsuspected legal restrictions the Church resented them as encroachments upon its spiritual province. It is interesting to recall the reflections of Lord Cockburn, one of the judges who found in favour of the Church in 1838, as he looked back over the whole conflict.

What I am chiefly sorry for is the Court of Session. . . . The Judges . . . all delivered what each, after due enquiry, honestly believed to be the law. . . . The majority of the Court may have been right at first, and to a certain extent; but they soon got rabid, insomuch that there seemed to be no feeling except that of pleasure at winging Wild-Churchmen. The apology was that they were provoked by their law being defied; but a Court has no right to be provoked.

In August 1842 he notes 'a gush of complaints for breach of interdict' and foresees that 'the chief business of the Court of Session next winter will consist in supporting the Establishment by fining and imprisoning the best men it contains; and that will only promote the repetition of the offence'.

One case of particularly serious import must still be mentioned, for the effect of the judgement was far reaching. In

1839 eleven congregations of the Old Light Burghers were received back into the Church of Scotland. In terms of the Chapels' Act of 1834 their ministers were enrolled as members of the appropriate presbyteries which were instructed to allocate to them territorial areas as their parishes *quoad sacra*. This the presbytery of Irvine proposed to do in the parish of Stewarton, Ayrshire. The patron and a body of heritors protested, and the case was referred to the Commission of Assembly, which ordered the presbytery to proceed but in express words to reserve the rights of heritors and their tenants to all their privileges in the original parish church. In spite of this careful avoidance of what might give rise to civil action the heritors sought and obtained 'suspension and interdict' from the Court of Session, again by a majority of eight to five. The Chapels' Act too was thus declared illegal, and a blow delivered at the church extension movement, which it had done so much to encourage. Further it was declared that presbyteries in which chapel ministers had been enrolled were illegally constituted and their decisions consequently invalid. Thus the Church's discipline since 1834 was called in question, and two ministers deposed for scandals took advantage of the situation to obtain reinstatement. The cup of bitterness was full.

Meantime the so-called Non-Intrusion Committee appointed in 1839 with Chalmers as convener had been busy. On appointment it lost no time in approaching the government, still the Whig government of Lord Melbourne which a few years earlier had refused to aid the church extension scheme. Melbourne, an easy-going, somewhat flippant Whig aristocrat, was little of a reformer. He had no love for radicals and dissenters, but as they supported his party he dared not offend them, and he had conceived a dislike for Chalmers. As before he temporized, holding out vague hopes and then withdrawing them. But there were in both Houses of Parliament friends of the Church of Scotland who would gladly have promoted legislation in the interests of peace. First the Earl of Aberdeen introduced in the House of Lords a Bill to give presbyteries greater powers in judging of objections to presentees, but it did not go far enough in providing security against actions in the civil courts. The Evangelical party, therefore, would not support it. Then the Duke of Argyll proposed what was virtually a legalizing of the Veto Act with minor modifications, and this the Moderate party refused to accept. Finally Sir George Sinclair tried hard to find a compromise in a strengthening of the Aberdeen Bill. But the Marnoch case had now cast its dark shadow, and the friends of the deposed Strathbogie ministers, themselves threatened with church censures, besought the new government to maintain and enforce the law as it stood. In 1841 Melbourne gave place to Sir Robert Peel as prime minister supported by a large Conservative majority in the House of Commons, with Sir James Graham as home secretary, responsible also for Scottish affairs. Both Peel and Graham had once been on friendly terms with Chalmers, but both now felt that the situation in Scotland had got out of hand. In the obviously divided state of opinion in the Church and in the country they were not prepared to take any action.

When the assembly met in May 1842 it found its path bristling with difficulties. Interdicts with penalties threatened against those who broke them challenged its authority. Even its own membership was called in question, when the 'seven' Strathbogie ministers, the deposed majority of the presbytery, produced an interdict against sustaining the commissions of the representatives of the opposing four. Undaunted the assembly held on its way. It sustained the interdicted commissions and protested against the interference of the civil court in the matter. It declared, for the first time in the conflict, 'that patronage is a grievance, has been attended with much injury to the cause of true religion in this Church and Kingdom, is the main cause of the difficulties in which the Church is at present involved and that it ought to be abolished', and appointed a committee to prepare petitions to the two Houses of Parliament and an address to the queen on the subject. In so doing it accepted belatedly the policy which the Veto Act had been frankly designed to avoid, and which in fact was the main cause of the Church's immediate difficulties. Finally it adopted a lengthy resolution which was to become famous as the Claim, Declaration and Protest anent the Encroachments of the Court of Session, or more simply the Claim of Right. Taking its stand on statements in the Westminster Confession regarding the Sole Headship of Christ over His Church and the independent jurisdiction in matters spiritual, derived from Christ, of the Church's officers, the Claim of Right goes on to quote parliamentary Acts recognizing and ratifying that jurisdiction, and particularly the Act of 1690 abolishing in Scotland the royal supremacy in spiritual and ecclesiastical causes. It skirts rather lightly round Queen Anne's Patronage Act, and sets over against it declarations of the Church both earlier and later against the intrusion of a pastor on an unwilling congregation. It lists the recent actions of the Court of Session which

have invaded the jurisdiction and encroached upon the spiritual privileges of the Courts of this Church. Therefore the General Assembly, while recognising the absolute jurisdiction of the Civil Courts in relation to all the temporalities conferred by the State upon the Church, claim as of right freely to possess and enjoy the liberties and rights and privileges bestowed on the Church according to law; declare that they cannot in conscience intrude ministers on reclaiming congregations or carry on the government of Christ's Church subject to the coercion attempted by the Court of Session; protest against sentences of the Civil Court in contravention of the Church's liberties, which rather than abandon they will relinquish the privileges of establishment; and call on all Christian people everywhere to note that it is for loyalty to Christ's Kingdom and Crown that the Church of Scotland is obliged to suffer hardship.

That the Claim of Right set forth an essential doctrine of the Church and a fundamental principle of its constitution is indubitable, though both the doctrine and the principle had for a century tended to fall into oblivion, and neither had been explicitly recognized by legislation. How far they were compatible with existing law was clearly for the Law Courts to determine unless and until Parliament altered the law. Within a few months of the close of the assembly a claim for damages against the members of the presbytery of Auchterarder on the part of the patron and presentee was allowed by the Court of Session and, on appeal, by the House of

Lords, Lord Brougham once again distinguishing himself by the sharpness of his condemnation of members of 'corporations' who do not fulfil their known duties.

In such circumstances the resolution against patronage and the Claim of Right could hardly be favourably received by the government, and its answer, delivered by Sir James Graham, was quite uncompromising. Nevertheless one further appeal was made to Parliament, and a Scottish member moved in the Commons that the House go into committee to take into consideration the grievances of which the Church of Scotland complained. Of the Scottish members present and voting 25 were in favour and 12 against, but the motion was lost by an overwhelming majority (March 1843).

During the winter preparations had been going on in Scotland to meet all eventualities. In November a convocation was held in Edinburgh to which ministers of non-intrusionist sympathies were invited, and they assembled in great numbers. The proceedings were in private but it is known that Chalmers was the moving spirit. By his eloquence he aroused an immense wave of enthusiasm that swept away the lingering hesitations of many. Moreover, drawing upon his experience in his church extension campaign he was able to put forward a plan for financing a secession should it have to take place. Resolutions were adopted deploring the encroachments of the civil courts on the spiritual powers of the Church, and declaring that if the State refused remedy conscience demanded the abandonment of the civil advantages of establishment. Thereafter the 'Convocationists' organized a nation-wide propaganda. Public meetings were held in all large towns. Rural parishes were visited by enthusiastic deputations, and when the minister was unsympathetic an endeavour was made to detach his people from him or at least to split his congregation. Local committees were formed, money collected, and at least one church was built in Edinburgh to receive the congregation of St. George's which was pledged to follow its minister, Dr. Candlish, a leading 'Convocationist'.

In spring it became necessary for presbyteries to appoint their commissioners to the ensuing General Assembly. Much depended on their choice, for it was suggested that the Non-Intrusionists, if they had a majority in the assembly, might resolve to put an end to the Church's connexion with the State and even excommunicate all who opposed them. Besides, the final judgement in the Stewarton case had now been pronounced, making illegal all participation of chapel ministers in the proceedings of the church courts. Some presbyteries acted on this ruling. Partly for this reason and partly because the Middle party refused to co-operate with the Non-Intrusionists, when the assembly met it was known that the latter were in a minority for the first time in ten years. What they would do was the subject of excited, sometimes cynical, surmise, and many affected to believe, or perhaps did believe, that the secession if it came would be inconsiderable. This seems to have been the belief of the government. According to custom the retiring moderator, Dr. Welsh, preached at the opening service in St. Giles, and then took the chair in St. Andrews Church where the assembly was to be held. Instead of constituting it, however, he announced that he and others could not regard it as a free assembly, and were resolved to leave it. He then read a protest setting forth his reasons, handed it to the clerk and left the chair and the Church followed by Chalmers and his lieutenants and about 190 ministers and elders.

As soon as Welsh, who wore his Moderator's dress, appeared in the street, and people saw that principle had really triumphed over interest, he and his followers were received with the loudest acclamations. They walked in procession down Hanover Street to Canonmills . . . through an unbroken mass of cheering people and beneath innumerable handkerchiefs waving from the windows. But amidst this exultation there was much sadness and many a tear, many a grave face and fearful thought, for no-one could doubt that it was with sore hearts that these ministers left the Church, and no thinking man could look on the unexampled scene and behold that the temple was rent without pain and sad forebodings.

So wrote Lord Cockburn, adding 'It is the most honourable feat for Scotland that its whole history supplies.' His colleague Lord Jeffrey, on hearing of what had happened, exclaimed

'I'm proud of my country; there is not another country upon earth where such a deed could have been done.'

In Tanfield Hall, Canonmills, the seceding brethren were joined by ministers and elders from all parts of the country and constituted themselves as the first General Assembly of the Church of Scotland Free with Chalmers as moderator. Their work was carried on in an atmosphere of prayerful devotion marked by fervour and religious exaltation. One of their first acts was to prepare a deed of demission whereby the signatories relinquished all the emoluments and privileges they had enjoyed within the Establishment. It was signed by 451 ministers of whom 162 were ministers of the new church extension charges. The willingness of so many to make financial and social sacrifice for the sake of principle created a deep impression and called forth widespread admiration. It also gave them a sense of moral superiority over the 752 ministers who 'stayed in', though it should not be forgotten that many of those also were faithful conscientious men, who dearly loved the Church and grieved to see it rent. They had to suffer loss of friends, division in their congregations, and the contemptuous reproaches of those who held them to be worldly minded hirelings. It has been estimated that the Church as a whole lost about one-third of its membership, in large part its more active membership, and among those who seceded all classes were represented, even nobles and gentry and eminent professional men. In parishes where the minister 'went out' he was commonly followed by the bulk of his congregation, and few congregations can have escaped serious depletion. In the Highlands especially, where up till now dissent had hardly penetrated, practically the entire population forsook the parish churches.

'Never perhaps', writes Principal Cunningham,[1] 'in the history of any Church has so great a voluntary sacrifice been made for so slender a principle—but yet not too slender for the Scottish ecclesiastical conscience to apprehend and exalt into a question of life and death.' It is a superficial judgement comparable to that which would lightly dismiss the Arian controversy—the Christian Church split on a diph-

[1] *Church History of Scotland*, vol. ii, p. 535.

thong! In 1921 the principle of spiritual independence was written into the articles declaratory of the constitution of the Church of Scotland. Assuredly the Disruption itself which at great cost proclaimed that principle has been amply justified. Moreover it is significant that the Scottish Disruption had contemporaneous parallels on the continent of Europe. Seen in this perspective it appears as part of a general struggle for a revival of religion, particularly of evangelical religion, against rationalist and legalist obstacles. In Holland in 1886 Dr. Abraham Kuyper headed an orthodox secession from the theologically liberalizing Dutch National Church. Theological considerations also led in 1849 to a similar secession under the leadership of Merle D'Aubigné from the State Church of Geneva, and to the formation of the Église Reformée Evangélique in opposition to the Église Reformée de France which since Napoleon's time had enjoyed State recognition and support. More closely resembling the Scottish movement were those which in the Canton de Vaud (1845) and the Canton de Neuchâtel (1873), under the leadership of Vinet and Godet respectively, repudiated the intrusion of the State into the Church's domain, and formed Free Evangelical Churches. It is no accident that all these movements took place in lands where Calvinist Churches had been established since the Reformation. Lutheranism knew nothing of *Freikirchentum*, and the idea of setting up a Free Church of England hardly occurred to the Anglo-Catholic Tractarians, though the claims of the Church of Scotland did arouse some interest. The vindication of these claims after long years of dispute has increased among Anglicans an appreciation of the significance of the Scottish Disruption.

The manifold and increasing difficulties which confronted the Church during the Ten Years' Conflict had been welcomed by many outside its pale as discrediting Establishment; and to many within the intransigence of the dominant party appeared to play into the hands of the Church's enemies. They feared that the sun of the Church of Scotland was about to go down for ever. Some sought a haven from strife in the Episcopal Church which was now recovering its influence among the aristocracy and the wealthy, and would probably have been more successful had it not itself been troubled by divisions caused by the beginnings of 'Puseyism'. Lamentable the schism might be because of the bitterness it caused in Scotland for more than a generation, yet it may be claimed that the Disruption did something to save the Church by demonstrating the attachment of the people of Scotland to the idea at least of a national Church. In the first General Assembly of the Free Church Chalmers was at pains to make it clear that the movement was in no sense directed towards Voluntaryism. 'Though we quit the Establishment we go out on the Establishment principle; we quit a vitiated Establishment but would rejoice in returning to a pure one. We are advocates for a national recognition and national support of religion—and we are not voluntaries.' Indeed he maintained that they could more effectively bear witness to this principle because they could do it disinterestedly, taking their stand firmly on the constitution of the Church of Scotland as set forth in the Claim of Right.

The task that he and the assembly set themselves from the start was a gigantic one, nothing less than that of producing a complete and exact replica of the Establishment they had left, relying on the resources which their faithful people would supply. As the 'true' Church of Scotland they would accept a national responsibility. In every parish in the country a Free Church should stand over against the old parish church, manse over against manse, Free Church school over against the parochial school over which the Established Church retained control. They would take charge of the education of their own students in training for the ministry by providing in colleges of their own an even fuller theological curriculum than that available in the universities; and the possibility of at least one Free Church university was envisaged, for in theory until 1853 chairs in all faculties in the universities might only be held by members of the Established Church. Since 1834 amidst the strife of parties successive general assemblies had commended to the liberality of their people certain specific enterprises or schemes of the Church—education, foreign missions, church extension, and aid to colonial

churches to which in 1840 had been added the scheme for the
conversion of the Jews. All these had received support that
steadily increased from year to year. In 1843 the missionaries
and other agents adhered almost unanimously to the Free
Church which without hesitation accepted responsibility for
the carrying on of their work. Chalmers, sanguine as always,
had absolute confidence that the money required would be
forthcoming whether in large contributions from the wealthy
or in small ones from humbler folk. His expectations were
not completely realized, but his appeal met with astonishing
success and from the beginning the Free Church gave to all
Churches a matchless example of Christian liberality, out-
playing the Voluntaries at their own game. Nothing comparable had happened in Scotland since the days of King
David 'the sair sanct', nor indeed could have happened before the Industrial Revolution brought wealth into the hands
of the middle classes.

In fulfilment of this programme obviously the needs of
seceding congregations first demanded attention. There was
no difficulty about ministerial manpower, for the Free Church
had 450 ministers at its disposal and a great number of
probationers, perhaps as many as 200, who adhered to it,
together with 93 divinity students in Edinburgh and a considerable number in the divinity halls of the other universities. But apart from some fifty of the recently constituted
quoad sacra Churches which it was able to retain it had no
churches, manses, or stipends. Wherever its adherents were
sufficiently numerous locally and a site could be obtained,
preferably in close proximity to the old parish church, building started at once, and within one year it was reported that
470 new if usually quite unpretentious churches had been
completed and others were in process of erection, mostly
from local resources. In some districts landowners refused to
grant sites, probably from hostility to the whole non-intrusion
movement, but partly also from unwillingness to see their
servants and tenants embroiled in ecclesiastical disputes that
to themselves were meaningless or odious. The matter was
taken to Parliament and the House of Commons appointed
a committee of inquiry before which Chalmers and others

gave evidence, with such effect that the offending proprietors gave way and legislation was not required. By 1847 the number of congregations worshipping in churches of their own was in excess of 700. Chalmers, it would seem, would gladly have seen these churches endowed, but that was clearly impossible. Instead he worked out a remarkable scheme for a central sustentation fund to which congregations should contribute according to their means, and from which their ministers should receive what he called the equal dividend. Larger and wealthier congregations in addition to their contributions to the central fund would be expected to supplement their own ministers' stipends, but the ministers of the smaller and poorer congregations would be assured at least of a modest competence and would not be wholly at the mercy of their own people. The Free Church was thus more centralized than the other Churches in Scotland, and hoped in this way to overcome some of the real and obvious difficulties of the Voluntary system. It provided a ministry zealous, orthodox, evangelical, narrow and strait-laced perhaps·and self-consciously pietistic, but one that served Scotland well, and did more to enhance the dignity and raise the status of the ministry generally than the alliance with the patrons and the heritors so diligently and subserviently cultivated by Moderates like Alexander Carlyle. The type has completely passed away in our changed times, and the biographies of the Disruption Fathers and their immediate successors present personalities in many cases saintly that now seem strangely remote in their ideas and aspirations. But their spiritual influence in their own day was unquestionably great and good.

As if the provision of churches, manses, and ministers were not a sufficient burden the Free Church found itself confronted with an educational problem. Hitherto responsibility for education had lain with the Church of Scotland. By law parochial schools had to be provided and maintained by the heritors but under the supervision of the Church. In addition there were schools supported by the Society for the Propagation of Christian Knowledge, a church society, and others were built and maintained by private benefactors. It soon appeared that teachers in these schools who adhered to the Free Church were to be dismissed, and something had to be done to employ them. Within a year £52,000 had been raised to build schools and the Church undertook their maintenance. Soon it established two Normal Schools for the training of teachers, one in Edinburgh and one in Glasgow. Grants-in-aid were made from public funds to schools certified as efficient by government inspectors, but in 1869, shortly before the Education (Scotland) Act was passed which took over denominational schools in Scotland into a national system, it was reported in Parliament that the Free Church had 598 schools and had raised for educational purposes since the Disruption not less than £600,000.

From its inception the Free Church recognized the paramount necessity of providing for the education of candidates for the ministry. Strange as it may seem, interest in this question had always been much stronger with the Evangelicals than with the Moderates, and had been a profound concern of Chalmers ever since he became professor of moral philosophy in St. Andrews. He persuaded successive general assemblies to impose on students entering the ministry ever stricter rules of attendance at classes in the Divinity Faculties, and it was with his support that the assembly of 1839 resolved to press for the establishment and endowment of a chair of biblical criticism in each of the universities—an indication that the work of German critical scholarship was becoming known and feared. This project did not materialize till after the Disruption when Edinburgh took the lead in 1846, followed by Aberdeen in 1860, Glasgow in 1861 and St. Andrews perhaps in 1868. Meantime in 1843 the first General Assembly of the Free Church deemed it essential that a theological college should be established immediately at one of the university seats, offering a curriculum at least as complete as that provided at any of the universities. It was natural that Edinburgh should be selected, for there two out of the three professors in the Divinity Faculty, Chalmers and Welsh, had demitted office and were available for teaching, and they had been followed by 93 of their students. A house in George Street was bought and four professors appointed,

A a

Chalmers and Welsh to teach the subjects they had taught
in the university, divinity and church history respectively;
William Cunningham, a younger man who had been a fiery
non-intrusionist, to teach systematic theology; and John Duncan, later famous as 'Rabbi' Duncan, one of the Church's
missionaries to the Jews in Buda Pesth where he had made
several notable converts, to teach Hebrew and Oriental
languages. Classes opened on 1 November 1843 with an en-
rolment of 103 students. This was but a beginning. A professorship of biblical exegesis was added in the following year,
and a proposal to provide preparatory courses in the liberal
arts was actively pursued. By 1845 appointments were made
to chairs of logic, moral philosophy and natural science. This
increase of staff necessitated a more adequate building. In
1846 the foundation stone of the New College was laid by
Dr. Chalmers on a prominent site at the head of the Mound
overlooking the New Town, and on 5 November 1850 the
college was formally opened, having cost for site and building the then enormous sum of nearly £50,000. As if this were
not enough two further colleges were added, not without
controversy, one at Aberdeen in 1853 and another in Glasgow in 1855. When the other, and one might think more
pressing, calls on the liberality of its people are considered,
the erection and endowment of three theological colleges
was an astonishing achievement, but no one could have foreseen the part they were to play in the development of theological thought.

The primary object of the colleges was the training of men
mainly for the Free Church ministry, and for the defence of
the faith against infidelity and heresy. The Church, that is
to say the General Assembly, retained control, appointing
the professors and keeping a watchful eye on their teaching
and administration through a college committee. The closest
possible relationship between Church and theological college
is certainly advantageous for both, theological learning divorced from the believing and worshipping community must
be barren; pursued with intellectual integrity it can preserve
the Church from the dangers of obscurantism. Nevertheless
there have often been periods of strain when ecclesiastical

authority has had to discipline the Doctors of the Church. The Church of the Disruption was proud to be evangelical but it was equally proud to be orthodox in the Calvinist Confessional sense. An unquestioned article of its creed was the supreme authority of the Bible in all matters of faith and morals. But it was born in a time of intellectual ferment. The theory of evolution had just been propounded and the idea of development was affecting men's minds, influencing theological thinking particularly in its application to biblical studies. German critical scholarship was slow in reaching Scotland and when it did it was by no means welcome. Its first representative in a Free Church college was A. B. Davidson who began to teach in New College in 1862 as assistant to 'Rabbi' Duncan, and continued as his successor in the Old Testament chair from 1870 to 1902.

The first sign of a coming storm was an attack made in 1876 on the learned and literary Marcus Dods, then a minister in Glasgow, for in a published sermon he seemed to have denied the inerrancy of Scripture. But the *cause célèbre* was that of William Robertson Smith. Brought up in an ardent Free Church home and educated by his father who had given up much at the Disruption he was the most brilliant student of his time at Aberdeen. Refusing to consider the prospect of an academic career he chose to serve in the ministry of the Free Church and proceeded to study at New College, Edinburgh, where he came under the influence of A. B. Davidson. After a period of study with Wellhausen in Germany he returned home and at the early age of 24 was in 1870 elected to the chair of Old Testament in the Aberdeen College of the Free Church. Trouble began with an article on the Bible contributed by Robertson Smith to the new 1875 (ninth) edition of the *Encyclopaedia Britannica* in which he expounded and partly accepted the Wellhausen hypothesis on the composite nature of the Pentateuch. Evangelicals were deeply shocked and the more vociferous of them started an agitation against the author who showed himself anything but considerate of the wounded feelings of genuinely pious men. The case dragged on for years before the church courts, amid intense interest on the part of the public, and threatened to split the Church in two. Finally in 1881 it was brought to an end by a resolution of the General Assembly moved by Principal Rainy, which concluded:

The General Assembly, having the responsible duty to discharge of overseeing the teaching in the Divinity Halls, while they are sensible of the importance of guarding the due liberty of professors, and encouraging learned and candid research, feel themselves constrained to declare that they no longer consider it safe or advantageous for the Church that Professor Smith should continue to teach in one of her Colleges.

By this decision, which was followed by another terminating Professor Smith's tenure of his chair, the Free Church was saved from disruption. Robertson Smith must be accounted a martyr for the cause of biblical scholarship within his Church. But he had little of the noble spirit of McLeod Campbell. Fortunately he was not called on to suffer long, for soon he was offered and accepted a chair of Arabic in the University of Cambridge. In the course of the debate in the assembly it had been pointed out that the proposed resolution dealt with the heretic but not with the heresy, and in fact it gave some recognition to the liberty of professors within the Church to pursue learned and candid research. The question of the legitimacy of critical biblical and theological scholarship was not indeed finally settled, but never again was it raised in such an acute form. As the older generation of Disruption worthies passed away and younger men took their place the theological climate changed. The traditionalists became a dwindling minority. In 1890 they brought complaints against Marcus Dods who had recently been appointed to the New Testament chair in New College and against Professor A. B. Bruce of Glasgow. Both complaints were dismissed, and the leaders of the Church saw the advisability of making the cause of liberty more secure. After much discussion and controversy the assembly of 1892 with the consent of the majority of the presbyteries adopted a Declaratory Act explaining the Church's attitude to the Confession of Faith, toning down some of the asperities of the latter, recognizing diversity of opinion on such points in the

Confession as do not enter into the substance of the Reformed Faith, and retaining full authority to determine, in any case which may arise, what points fall within this description, and thus to guard against any abuse of liberty to the detriment of sound doctrine or to the injury of the Church's unity and peace. The Declaratory Act was violently assailed by people who regarded it as plain apostasy from Scripture truth and the Disruption testimony, and some of these, two ministers and about 4000 members mainly in the Highlands, seceded to form the Free Presbyterian Church which still exists. But the liberty secured by the Declaratory Act enabled the Free Church colleges to make an outstanding contribution to theological scholarship, and to Scotland's reputation for Christian learning.

The Church of the Disruption took its stand firmly on two principles laid down in the Confession of Faith and re-asserted in the Claim of Right. The first was the independent spiritual jurisdiction of the Church derived from Christ, Sole King and Head of the Church, or, more picturesquely, the Crown Rights of the Redeemer. The second was the right and duty of the 'civil magistrate' to protect and further religion by supporting a national Church, in other words, the Establishment principle. Both of these are deeply embedded in Scottish history. They go back to the Reformation and became prominent in the Covenanting struggle, the ideals of which were being revived and popularized. It was believed that these principles had been recognized by the Revolution Settlement and guaranteed by the Act of Security at the time of the Union. Certainly they had never been seriously called in question until 1838 when the civil courts, it was held, gave a new interpretation of the law and encroached upon the rights and privileges of the Church. The Free Church claimed that it maintained the historic position and testimony of the Church of Scotland, necessarily outside the Establishment unless and until Parliament should put matters right.

In the last assembly of the undivided Church arrangements had been made to celebrate in July 1843 the bicentenary of the Westminster Assembly in co-operation with the other Presbyterian Churches in Scotland which acknowledged the

Westminster standards. The Disruption notwithstanding, the celebration took place. It was ignored by the Established Church which thus allowed the Free Church to take the lead. The keynote of the proceedings, oddly enough in the circumstances, was church union, and Dr. Chalmers in a characteristically exuberant speech made a pronouncement which has a strangely modern ring. He dismissed as inadequate the slogan 'co-operation without incorporation' and offered as a substitute 'co-operation now and this with the view, as soon as may be, to incorporation afterwards'. The immediate outcome was a movement which led to the formation in 1845 of the Evangelical Alliance, aiming at the defence of orthodox Protestantism against Popery, Puseyism, rationalism, and other evils of the time, and bringing together in its meetings Evangelical churchmen from many Churches in Europe and America as well as from Britain. It is the oldest of the existing agencies for fostering inter-Church relations, and in its early days performed a useful function in deepening the spiritual life and widening the horizons of delegates who attended in great numbers. It probably did something to promote the unions of Churches that marked the second half of the nineteenth century in Scotland.

Of the denominations participating in the celebration of 1843 two smaller and more conservative ones, the Original Secession (Old Lights) and the Reformed Presbyterians (Cameronians or Covenanters) soon recognized the Free Church position as akin to their own, and united with the Free Church in 1852 and 1876 respectively. Unhappily in both cases minorities continued in separate existence. More important for the future was the union in 1847 of the United Secession with the Relief Church to form the United Presbyterian Church. Not without difficulty was this union effected for these Churches differed considerably in ethos. The United Secession stemming from the Erskines had shed some of the characteristics of its founders, notably the custom of 'renewing the Covenants', but still retained a certain strictness of ecclesiastical discipline. The Relief Church was more broadly evangelical, laxer in doctrine and discipline, and prided itself on being non-sectarian and non-covenanting. A peculiarity was its doctrine of free and open communion. One of its leading ministers had declared that 'Scotland with all its enjoyment of religious liberty was penetrated to the core by a disastrous schismatic spirit' and that none of the existing systems of church government could be 'clearly established from the Word of God'. Nevertheless both of those Churches had taken part in the Voluntary controversy, and both agreed in repudiating the allegedly persecuting chapter of the Westminster Confession which asserts the religious and ecclesiastical rights and duties of the civil magistrate. With 518 congregations the United Presbyterian Church was almost as strong numerically as the Free Church, but owing to its method of church finance it was confined chiefly to the cities and towns, and was hardly represented in the Highlands where almost the entire population adhered to the Free Church. There were thus two large Presbyterian Churches outside the Established Church and almost equally hostile to it, but for different reasons. The Free Church opposed an Erastian Establishment while the United Presbyterians were opposed to Establishment as such. Could these two Churches amalgamate?

Of such a union there could be little thought while the Free Church was triumphantly consolidating itself and proclaiming itself to be not a seceding or a dissenting body, but a national Church true to the principles of the Church of Scotland. Not until 1863 did it seem that the time had arrived for an approach to union. Movements towards union of Presbyterian Churches in England and Australia, where Scottish divisions had reproduced themselves, prompted to action. In 1863 the United Presbyterian Synod and a few weeks later the Free Church General Assembly appointed strong committees to confer as to the relative position of the Churches and the steps proper to be taken to promote present co-operation and ultimate union. The committees met and resolved to do the work thoroughly. They drew up a programme listing for discussion eleven points on which it was known the Churches diverged in doctrine and practice. These covered a wide range and included the doctrines of the Atonement,

Predestination, and the universality of the offer of the Gospel, religious instruction in State-aided schools, even methods of church finance. But the question that gave the greatest trouble was that of the civil magistrate. One might have expected that a doctrine stated in the terms of the seventeenth century and expressing its ideas would have lost relevance and interest in the nineteenth, or become purely academic. But it must be remembered that many of the members of both committees had taken part in the Voluntary controversy, and that hard and extreme things had been said on both sides. The Voluntaries had not scrupled to appeal to and ally themselves with persons openly declaring themselves hostile to all religion. In the Free Church it was believed that the Voluntaries advocated a purely secular State indifferent to religion, which seemed to be a form of unbelief, certainly contradictory to the traditional view of the State as a Christian power protecting and supporting a National Church. The point was keenly discussed and the divergence of view considerably narrowed when on the part of the Voluntaries it was conceded that the civil magistrate, short of setting up an Established Church, may, as representing the general sense of the Christian community, further the interests of the Christian religion. Agreement was reached in the joint committee but opposition arose in both Churches, and especially in the Free Church. The assembly of 1867 indeed declared that divergence of views on Establishment was no bar to union, but it soon became clear that a substantial minority were opposed to union, and that it included not only the bulk of the Highland ministers and elders, but also a number of estimable persons who had 'come out' in 1843 and for whom the 'principles of the Disruption' were sacrosanct. A violent agitation ensued in which there was even talk of another Disruption, and the union negotiations had to be broken off in 1873.

The way was now open for the United Presbyterian Voluntaries to resume their campaign for disestablishment, led by Dr. John Cairns who had taken a prominent part in the negotiations for union, and represented a mediating form of Voluntaryism. In the Free Church opinion moved in the same direction but more slowly under the guidance of a new leader, Robert Rainy. Son of a Glasgow medical professor and himself a medical student in 1843, Rainy was won for the ministry of the Free Church by the events of that year. After a theological course under Chalmers and his colleagues in Edinburgh, he was minister successively in Huntly, Aberdeenshire, and in Edinburgh, and was appointed professor of church history in New College in 1862, becoming principal in 1874. He had served on the Union Committee as a comparatively junior member, but in 1867 he was called upon at a few minutes' notice to move the critical motion just referred to, and from that day until his death in 1906 he was the unquestioned leader of the great majority in his Church, if also hated and feared by the minority within it. For throughout the period of his ascendancy the Free Church was bitterly divided on a variety of issues, theological and ecclesiastical, for which the Disruption naturally had provided no answer. His position was often one of extreme difficulty and delicacy, and as ecclesiastical statesman he could hardly have avoided giving on occasion the impression of being an opportunist. It was he who brought the Free Church to declare for disestablishment.

In 1869, when as a result of the Second Reform Bill a Liberal government was in office with W. E. Gladstone at its head, the General Assembly of the Established Church resolved to petition Parliament for the ending of patronage. A deputation waited on the prime minister who with his eye on Scottish supporters of his party received it unfavourably. Not until Disraeli and the Conservatives came into power could the Patronage Act be passed (1874) which gave to congregations of the Church of Scotland the right to elect their ministers. There is no doubt that many in the Church hoped and believed that the Act would make the way open for Free Church people to return to the Establishment. Perhaps some did. In any case the Free Church took alarm, and appointed a 'Church and State' committee with Rainy as convener to watch over its interests, and to keep touch with the politicians. Gladstone in opposition had spoken against the Bill in 1874, and the Liberal party began in 1877 to speak as if it might take up disestablishment in Scotland 'if Scotch opinion, or even Scotch Liberal opinion' was fully formed on the question. Then came the general election of 1880 with the Midlothian campaign that returned Gladstone to power with a sweeping majority, but with many problems to face that put disestablishment in the background. Rainy therefore joined with Cairns in a vigorous campaign to keep it before the public mind, and they succeeded so far that the Scottish Liberal party adopted it as part of their policy in the election of 1885. But disappointment awaited them, for Gladstone in the interests of his party in England refused to take the matter up as an urgent one. In the new Parliament the balance of power was in the hands of Parnell with whom Gladstone came to terms on a measure of Irish home rule. This split the Liberal party irretrievably, and from 1886 under strong Conservative governments disestablishment was a lost cause, revived half-heartedly during the brief Liberal administration of 1892–5. Not in that way was the Scottish church question to be settled.

Co-operation in the disestablishment campaign did something to bring the United Presbyterian and the Free Churches together, but there were other factors at work. The Churches obviously had much in common in doctrine, worship, and church government. In both the younger generation was in revolt against the Calvinism or hyper-Calvinism of an earlier age, a revolt which found expression in doctrinal Declaratory Acts. A reverent biblical criticism was producing a new attitude towards the Scriptures, and an apologetic and philosophical theology was taking the place of dogmatics. On the other hand both Churches had been deeply stirred by the evangelism of D. L. Moody and Ira Sankey from 1874 onwards. Improvements in public worship were making themselves felt, by the introduction of instrumental music in churches and by the use of hymns in addition to the metrical Psalms. When in 1893 the Free Church celebrated the Jubilee of the Disruption and in 1897 the United Presbyterians similarly celebrated the union of the Secession and the Relief, messages of cordial good will were exchanged and the time seemed to many to have come to resume the project of union abandoned with regret in 1873. The first step was taken in 1896 by the United Presbyterian synod which declared its readiness to unite with the Free Church and further that incorporating union alone was adequate. Rainy, however, knowing the feeling still existing in some quarters in the Free Church was inclined to caution, and persuaded the assembly to delay its decision for a year. In 1897 the project was entered upon in earnest. The questions which had protracted the earlier negotiations now presented no difficulty which, it was hoped, could not be met by a slightly modified formula to be signed by ministers and office-bearers by which they pledged their adherence to the fundamental doctrines and principles of the Church. This was accepted by both Churches in 1898. But again opposition arose in the Free Church, this time largely confined to the Highland area, where the extremists who had seceded in 1892 exercised a certain indirect influence. Again there was talk of secession and threat of legal proceedings in respect of the property of the Free Church. Opinions were obtained from three eminent counsel two of which were entirely encouraging to the Union leaders, and, after unavailing attempts to conciliate the dissidents, the Union was effected in October 1900. The United Free Church then formed gathered into one great river the streams of dissatisfaction that had since the Revolution Settlement at various times and for various reasons flowed out of the Church by law established.

It has been claimed as a merit of Presbyterianism that, while not strictly speaking democratic, it nevertheless provides for a wide diffusion of interest in church affairs. For this there is a price to be paid. Scottish church unions have rarely taken place without leaving remnants outside. The Union of 1900 was no exception. Some twenty to thirty ministers of the Free Church and a considerable body of its people, chiefly in the Highlands, refused to enter the Union. This group comprised those who had always regarded with suspicion and hostility any tendency to theological liberalism or innovation in worship. They now claimed to be the true heirs of the Church of the Disruption, loyal to its fundamental principles from which the majority of their brethren had departed. In uniting with a professedly Voluntary Church they had abandoned 'the establishment principle'; and in passing the Declaratory Act of 1892 they had taken authority to modify the Confession of Faith, particularly in the article of Predestination. The sincerity of the minority's devotion to Calvinist orthodoxy is not in doubt, and it is but just to assume that this was their chief motive in going to law to have it declared that they alone were entitled to the name and properties of the Free Church. Their petition was dismissed in the Court of Session first by the Lord Ordinary and then on appeal by the Inner House. It was now taken to the House of Lords where it was heard, finally, in June 1904 before seven judges of whom only one was Scots, a disadvantage perhaps in view of the nature of the case. It was not as in 1838 a matter of the interpretation of certain statutes. This time the judges were called upon to interpret purely ecclesiastical documents including the Westminster Confession at its most recondite point and even to evaluate the constitutional importance of Chalmers's moderatorial address in 1843! Was the Free Church from the beginning an association for certain purposes holding its properties in trust and therefore bound by the terms of the original 'prospectus' like a joint-stock company? By a majority of five to two the court pronounced in favour of the appellants, thus declaring them to be the legal owners of all the properties belonging to the Free Church before the Union—churches, manses, colleges, missionary properties at home and abroad, together with all endowments for their upkeep. Never did a legal judgement create a more preposterous situation, for it was obvious that the victors in the suit could not possibly use or administer the properties declared to be theirs. It was necessary for the government to intervene and in 1905 by an Act of Parliament a commission was appointed with powers to allocate the disputed properties between parties according to certain rules laid down in the Act. The Free Church remnant was treated fairly or even generously, and has maintained itself as an independent body to this day. Indeed it is the dominant Church in parts of the north-west of Scotland and in some of the islands.

The great church case attracted much attention and aroused

interest. In Scotland, in the first place, it may be said to have done more than anything else to cement and solidify the Union of 1900. Moreover it taught churchmen that the Disruption after all had not guaranteed the Church's freedom as had been supposed. It could not by Declaratory Acts free itself from challenge at law. In 1905 the United Free Church Assembly in view of the imminent intervention of the government, and before the terms of the government's Bill were known, unanimously reasserted the Church's 'independent and exclusive jurisdiction and power of legislating in all matters of doctrine worship discipline and government', her 'sole and exclusive right through her courts to alter, change, add to or modify her constitution and laws, subordinate standards and formulas, to determine and declare what these are, and to unite with other Christian Churches'. Equally important or even more important was the effect of the church case on political thought. F. W. Maitland said of the judgement that 'the cold hand of the Law fell on the living body of the Church with a resounding slap'. And there began to dawn on politicians and lawyers the idea of the Church, not as a mercantile trust, but as a living, growing organism, for which spiritual freedom was the breath of life. So the way was prepared for the legislation of 1921, the late but full fruition of the fundamental principle of the Disruption.

V

RECOVERY IN THE ESTABLISHED CHURCH

B Y the Disruption of 1843 the Established Church, if not as yet the idea of an Establishment, suffered a severe blow that many thought must be mortal. Those who 'went out' were completely confident that they took with them all of the Church of Scotland that was earnest, devoted, and spiritually effective, and that they had left behind, in the Erastian Establishment, nothing but a lifeless and useless shell. There was much of course to encourage such views, but they proved to be mistaken. We have now to note the slow, gradual, but distinct recovery of the national Church.

Until the day on which the secession took place there was much speculation as to how large it might prove to be. Actually one-third—about 150—members of the assembly withdrew protesting that owing to the encroachments of the civil courts it was not and could not be 'a free and lawful Assembly of the Church of Scotland'. Those who remained and witnessed the remarkable scene were differently affected. Most of them very likely belonged to the old Moderate school and some, at least, professed satisfaction in being rid of 'the pestilent fellows' who had carried matters with a high hand for ten years. But there were others who were deeply grieved by what had taken place. Some had been personal friends of Chalmers and all had admired him as the chief ornament of the Church, and the inspiring leader in the forward movement in church activity in which they had taken part. Up to a point they sympathized with the principles of those who went out, if not with their methods, but they could not bring themselves to leave the kirk whose traditions meant much to them, and in which they had found ample opportunities of Christian service. Such men spoke fondly of 'our National Zion', and to them the Disruption was a disaster that perplexed and dismayed them.

When the last of the seceders had gone the assembly was duly constituted and Dr. Duncan Macfarlane, principal of Glasgow

University and minister of the High Church of Glasgow, was elected to the moderatorial chair. He was the most venerable and respected person present, and of course a leading Moderate. The queen's letter to the assembly conveyed by her High Commissioner, the Marquis of Bute, was then read. It contained the familiar declaration of the queen's intention to maintain Presbyterian church government in Scotland, but went on to point out that the privileges of Establishment were conferred by statute, and that it became churchmen to obey the law. But it also held out hopes that Parliament would assist in clearing up doubts 'with respect to the right construction of the statutes relating to the admission of ministers' and in passing legislation 'for the purpose of securing to the people the full privilege of objecting and to the Church judicatories the exclusive right of judgment'. Dr. George Cook resumed the position of leader of the House which he had lost since 1833 and secured the adoption of a reactionary policy though not without protests, dissents, and countermotions from a group of fifteen representatives of the evangelical Middle party who were hopelessly outnumbered. Cook had now the support of a new man, James Robertson, minister of Ellon, Aberdeenshire, who had established a reputation in his presbytery and synod as a wise and trusted counsellor. Robertson might be called a Constitutionalist rather than a Moderate. He had always been opposed to the veto because he believed the Church had constitutional powers to deal with abuses of patronage, which he did not doubt were evils. He had held ministerial communion with the Strathbogie ministers for which he had been suspended from his judicial functions in the church courts. But he had been an ardent supporter of Chalmers in church extension and of Duff in the India mission scheme, and had been deeply influenced by both, especially the latter. Robertson saw clearly that the first thing to be done was to extricate the Church from the thicket of Interdicts in which it was entangled, and he believed the best way to do this was to treat the Veto Act and the Chapels Act as if they had never been passed. These Acts were discarded without being explicitly repealed, and the deposition of the Strathbogie 'Seven' was treated as null and void. Robertson had the confidence of Lord Aberdeen and was ready to take the hint contained in the Queen's letter and to approach Parliament for remedial legislation. The only occasion on which the assembly forgot its depression was when Robertson advocated amid applause the maintenance of the Church's mission in India.

Amidst our wranglings of late years I have often felt those days on which the reports of the various schemes connected with the Church were read, to be among the happiest days of my life. And I have felt while such reports were being discussed, that we were in very truth occupied in the proper business of a Christian Church. . . . If the time should ever come when the Church of Scotland loses its missionary spirit then indeed will its death-knell be rung.

The General Assembly of the Established Church was not to relapse into the mere 'Supreme Court' of Moderate times but was to be the focus of the Church's activities at home and abroad. Genuinely Christian schemes or enterprises must replace 'cases' as the main topics for its consideration and decision.

This interest in the schemes of the Church was a sign that the spirit of the past few years was not wholly extinct. And there was another sign. Since 1834 it had become customary for each assembly to send a pastoral address to its 'faithful people' reminding them of their religious duties. The chief part in drafting these had been taken by the assembly clerk, Dr. John Lee, principal of the University of Edinburgh, the most erudite scholar in many fields, and one of the most respected men of his time. For these pastoral addresses he was praised as their author by Thomas Chalmers who on other matters did not see eye to eye with him. The assembly of 1843 resolved to follow the custom and once again Dr. Lee was the draftsman. He drew up a clear and non-polemical statement of the case for remaining within the Establishment and continuing the good work of the Church of Scotland.

In the country generally the situation was far from hopeless. It is true the Church had lost more than one-third of its ministers including many of the most active and zealous. In the northern counties of Ross, Sutherland, and Caithness, practically all 'went out' followed by their congregations. But 752 ministers 'stayed in' and where a minister had proved himself faithful and popular the bulk of his elders and people 'stayed in' too, and resented the virulent propaganda carried on against him. The 'Auld Kirk' was found to have a greater hold over many of its people than had been supposed, and to some extent this was strengthened by the secession. Robertson's parish of Ellon, for example, proved to be a sterile field for the Free Kirk. From other parishes there are reports of its failure to draw away the people in great numbers. But most congregations suffered diminution especially where the minister had himself been careless or ineffective in his pulpit or pastoral duties. It has been estimated that the Church lost not more than one-third of its members, but these had been doubtless its most zealous supporters. As a rule—but there were notable exceptions—the aristocracy and the heritors, when Presbyterian, 'stayed in' and sometimes showed considerable hostility to the Free Church, even refusing building sites. And of course the churches, manses, and stipends were available as before. The chief difficulty was the filling of the 451 vacancies caused by the Disruption, and these included important charges. In Edinburgh, for example, the two colleagues who ministered in the High Church of St. Giles demitted office, both outstanding men, and with them went nearly all the ministers of the burgh churches. The Glasgow churches suffered nearly as much. Ministers of proved ability and character were in great demand. One of them refused five offers of presentation to desirable vacant charges before he found one which he was willing to accept. Some sought a change for reasons of ambition, others in order to escape from the results of the schism in their parishes and the pain of broken pastoral relationships. But the dearth of ministers was a severe handicap to the Church. It could still call on a remarkable number of probationers mostly employed as schoolmasters, but some of these were 'stickit ministers' not likely in normal circumstances to have secured a presentation to any parish. Not all of them proved satisfactory and their weaknesses were exposed to the fiercest criticism when their predecessors continued, as they usually did, to minister in their parishes. There was a real danger that the Church might be unable to hold even those who had not been swept out of it by the wave of enthusiasm in 1843.

In the hope of preventing further secession Lord Aberdeen reintroduced in slightly modified form the Bill he had sponsored in 1840 and withdrawn when it was pronounced unacceptable by the non-intrusionists. At that time Dr. Cook and his party had approved the Bill, but they disliked it and now only with hesitation acquiesced in a petition from the Church in favour of it. It proposed to give to the communicant members of a vacant parish the right to bring forward in writing objections of any kind whatever against a presentee, of which objections the presbytery should be sole judge with authority to decide whether or not to proceed to a settlement, subject to appeal to the superior courts of the Church. This well-intentioned Bill became law in the summer of 1843 and very soon it became apparent that Dr. Cook's misgivings were not without justification. The right of objection was freely exercised. Complaints were expressed of the coldness, formality, incomprehensibility, and unedifying nature of the pulpit ministrations of presentees, their poor or unpleasing voices, their reputation for laziness; in the case of one of them his 'exuberance of animal spirits'! It would be wrong to suppose that the objections offered were as frivolous as they may appear to us now. Some are obviously sincere and testify to a high ideal of the Christian ministry in the minds of simple people, but it must have been hard indeed to deal with them in such a way as to do justice to all parties and at the same time to give them satisfaction. The well-known essayist A. K. H. B. (A. K. H. Boyd, minister of St. Andrews) wittily remarked that in contrast to 'the priest-ridden people' of Ireland, in Scotland there was a 'people-ridden clergy'. Between 1843 and 1869 there were no fewer than sixty-one cases of disputed settlements involving expense and consuming the time of the presbyteries and other church judicatories, and doing infinite harm to the peace of congregations. It became obvious that something must be done to remedy this evil and many churchmen began to consider the possibility of having patronage abolished altogether. The matter came before the assembly of 1866 on an overture from the presbytery of Edinburgh, and a committee of inquiry was appointed, but not until 1869 was it resolved by majority to petition Parliament to end patronage.

We have seen how the leaders of the Free Church, then engaged in negotiations for union with the United Presbyterians, suspected that the anti-patronage move was a design to lure back into the Establishment members of the Free Church who were opposed to union with Voluntaries. Perhaps it was unfortunate that the Established Church spokesmen too often coupled the demand for the removal of patronage with the vision of the reunion of Scottish Presbyterianism. But only excessive touchiness caused by the delicate phase reached in their own union project could have suggested to the Free Church leaders the suspicion of a deep-laid conspiracy against their Church. They took no official steps to oppose the petition of the Church of Scotland, but in other ways they let their hostility to it be known, so that the prime minister, Gladstone, greatly to the disappointment of some in his own Liberal party, politely rebuffed the deputation that waited on him. It was evident that nothing was to be expected from a High Anglican exponent of the Nonconformist conscience. The Conservatives who came into power in 1874 were more sympathetic. In that year a Bill carefully drawn up with the aid and advice of leading churchmen was passed into law with Liberal support in both Houses of Parliament and in spite of an extraordinary outburst on the part of Gladstone. It declared that 'the right of electing and appointing ministers is vested in the congregation', communicants and adherents, and that the power to regulate procedure and the final and conclusive right to decide all questions as to the appointment of ministers belongs to the church courts. The rights of patrons were extinguished, and an agreed sum by way of compensation was to be paid to private patrons who claimed it. At last the positive principle enunciated in the Books of Discipline and in Acts of Assembly was conceded, not merely the negative principle of non-intrusion. There were those in the Church even in 1874 who dreaded the democratization implied in the Anti-patronage Act, though apart from all other considerations it might appear to be a fitting consequence of the successive extensions of the political franchise since 1832. It is true that popular election no more than patronage can guarantee the appointment of the ideal minister to any charge. But popular election in spite of theoretical defects and occasional failings in practice has certainly worked more smoothly than the system which preceded it, and has had no ill effects on the character or status of the ministry, rather the reverse. There can be no doubt that an ancient root of bitterness had been removed and that the Church was greatly strengthened.

Another problem that faced the Church in 1843 was that of church extension. Chalmers's campaign had resulted in the erection of some two hundred chapels in necessitous areas in town and country, but the attempt of the Church to give to their ministers the powers and status of parish ministers had been declared by the Court of Session to be *ultra vires*. In 1843 of the chapel ministers, 117 adhered to the Free Church, taking with them the bulk of their congregations. But the buildings were legally decerned to be the property of the Church of Scotland. In time ministers were found and congregations gathered, but not before Parliament had passed an Act piloted by Sir James Graham giving to the Church wider powers to erect new parishes *quoad sacra* without reference to patrons or heritors. In effect all that the Chapels Act of 1834 was designed to accomplish was now made legally possible, but in order to give permanence to a proposed new parish it was stipulated that an endowment of £120 per annum must be secured before it could be erected. Chalmers failed to get funds from the government for the endowment of churches in 1836. Much less could government aid be looked for in 1843. The Church itself must find the necessary money. Fortunately there was a man who saw in this necessity an opportunity to rally the Church to a great enterprise. In 1844 James Robertson left his parish of Ellon to become professor of ecclesiastical history in the University of Edinburgh. As the depleted Divinity Hall filled up again with students, some of them later to become distinguished, Robertson exercised over them a strong influence more by his earnestness, sincerity and single-minded devotion to duty than by his historical learning. He held before them a high ideal of the Christian ministry. But his greatest contribution to the recovery of the Church was his unwearied leadership in the cause of endowment, which seemed to him to be at that time the most urgent task laid upon the Church. In the spirit of Chalmers he pleaded the need to provide gospel ordinances for those who for lack of them were in danger of becoming spiritually destitute. It was a duty of Christian patriotism to seek the moral and religious good of the whole nation, not simply sectarian advantage. To many the raising of the necessary money at such a time and for such a purpose seemed a hopeless undertaking, and Robertson had to contend with the apathy, ridicule, and even worse, of many of his ministerial brethren, but he went on patiently, laboriously, and magnanimously, sending out appeal after appeal to all classes. Between 1846 when he became convener of the Endowment Committee and his death in 1860, sixty parishes *quoad sacra* had been added to the agencies of the Church of Scotland, and almost as many more were on the point of securing the statutory endowment. The total sum subscribed fell little short of £400,000; and that achievement was largely due to Robertson's passionate faith in the vital importance of his scheme and his persevering unselfish labours in furthering it. He had aimed at adding 150 new parishes to the Church of Scotland within his own lifetime. If he failed to reach his goal, the work he inaugurated and inspired went on after he was gone and by the end of the nineteenth century more than 400 *quoad sacra* parishes had been erected.

By his urgency in pressing the endowment scheme Robertson did much to awaken in a deeply discouraged Church a belief in its future usefulness and a sense of its continuing mission as the national Church. In 1845 a young man who after four years in an Ayrshire parish had become minister of Dalkeith in succession to one who had joined the Free Church wrote in his journal:

It is notorious to every honest man that we have received a terrible shock by the Secession ... the best ministers, and the best portion

of our people have gone. . . . The 'moderate' congregations
will soon make 'moderate' ministers. The tone will be insensibly
lowered. We have many raw recruits but they are thinking more
of the drawing room papers and the fiars prices than of the Church.
We have no *heads* to direct us; not one commanding mind, not
one trumpet voice to speak to men's inner being and compel them
to hear. There are, I doubt not, many who would do right if
they knew what was right to do. Like some regiments during the
war we have gone into battle with our full complement of men,
and the slaughter has been so great that ensigns have come out
majors and field officers, with rank and uniform, but without
talent or experience.

It would be absurd to suggest that Robertson was the trum-
pet-voiced leader desiderated by Norman MacLeod. He was
no inspired or inspiring orator, but he loved his Church and
spent himself in her service, refusing to despair. To him more
than to any other belongs the credit for the recovery of the
Church that was apparent by 1860.

It is possible that Norman MacLeod paints too doleful a
picture of the state of the Church in 1845. His exuberant
Highland temperament was doubtless chafed by the policy
then prevailing of a return to the untroubled days of old and
the complacency manifest even in the attempt to maintain
the missionary work of the Church. He was one of the first to
throw himself whole-heartedly into the endowment scheme.
There were some older men who like himself had witnessed
the Disruption scene with dismay but most of them now held
aloof from the assembly, in which they could do little, and
occupied themselves with parish work. Nevertheless recruits
for the ministry soon began to include men of real distinction
who in time were to raise its repute both at home and abroad.
Many of them were to become professors in the theological
faculties and some principals of their universities, but they
all began their ecclesiastical careers as parish ministers, often
in country parishes, and most of them continued to take an
active part in the affairs of the Church and particularly in
the General Assembly, where their leadership in varied fields
of activity was invaluable. Even after pluralities were abolished
the connexion of the theological professoriate with the Church

and ministry remained close and intimate. In a Church without bishops and cathedral dignitaries a large share of leadership inevitably falls to its professors.

One of the earliest accessions was A. K. H. Boyd. Son of a Glasgow minister, he had first contemplated a legal career at the English Bar, but he returned to be a country minister for nearly twenty years before being appointed in 1865 to the first charge in St. Andrews. He was more of a literary figure than a churchman. John Caird was ordained in 1845 and served in four charges before being appointed professor of divinity in Glasgow in 1862 and principal of the university in 1873. Caird held aloof from all ecclesiastical strife, but he was reckoned to be the greatest Scottish preacher of his age. John Tulloch was ordained in 1845 and became principal of St. Mary's College, St. Andrews, in 1854. For long he was a dominant figure in the General Assembly, a liberal in theology and in politics, and a favourite with Queen Victoria. In the principalship he was succeeded by John Cunningham, an older man, who had been present at some of the stormy debates in the assembly during the Ten Years Conflict and as minister of Crieff from 1845 to 1886 had written his well-known *Church History of Scotland*. As colleague in the chair of church history he had Alexander Ferrier Mitchell, ordained to Dunnichen, Angus, in 1847, an acknowledged authority on the Westminster Assembly and its standards. The next decade brought its equally distinguished new men—James Macgregor, ordained in 1855, a fiery Celtic preacher who made his influence felt in the west and in the east and finished his career as minister of St. Cuthbert's, Edinburgh; John Marshall Lang, ordained in 1856, who filled distinguished charges before becoming principal of the University of Aberdeen in 1900; Archibald Hamilton Charteris, ordained 1858, professor of biblical criticism in the University of Edinburgh 1868–98, pupil and biographer of James Robertson and inheritor of his eager energetic churchmanship; Robert Flint, ordained 1859, professor of divinity in Edinburgh 1876–1903, a theologian of world-wide repute; and Robert Herbert Story who succeeded his father as minister of Rosneath in 1860, becoming professor of ecclesiastical history in Glasgow in 1886 and principal of the university in 1898 in succession to Caird, a redoubtable churchman of strong personality and impressive appearance, for many years the most influential leader in the General Assembly.

Of all the men who laboured for the recovery of the Church of Scotland in its years of difficulty none was more conspicuous than Norman MacLeod himself. His family came from the island of Skye. His grandfather and uncle in succession served the parish of Morven, Argyllshire, for the astonishing period of 107 years, from 1775 to 1882, keeping the people loyal to the Church of Scotland by their devoted labours. His father held charges in the Lowlands, and in 1835 became minister of the newly constituted Gaelic chapel in Glasgow, the chief gathering place for Highlanders in the city. Next year, though a chapel minister, he was elected moderator of the General Assembly. His son Norman was not a Gaelic speaker but he was a true Highlander steeped in the beauty, the poetry, and the sentiment of the west Highland coast. For a time he studied in Edinburgh under Chalmers and became an ardent admirer, and it was Chalmers who recommended him for appointment to his first charge, Loudoun, Ayrshire. Here the young Norman was confronted for the first time with the infidelity and coarseness of life of an industrial community and set himself by word and example to reclaim the people. To a remarkable degree he won their confidence and respect. The Disruption appeared to him an unmitigated calamity destructive of all his hopes, for though sympathetic to the Evangelical party he could not bring himself to abandon the Church of his fathers within which he saw opportunity for active evangelism. In 1844 he removed to Dalkeith, but despairing of his Church he sought and for some years found spiritual strength and comfort in the Evangelical alliance. In 1851 he was appointed minister of the Barony parish, Glasgow, and there for twenty-three years he carried on a remarkable ministry, the like of which had not been known in Glasgow since the days when Chalmers had charge of St. John's. His simple direct style of preaching attracted crowds to his church, and his large-hearted humanity and genial magnetic personality made him a popular hero with his working-class parishioners, who spoke of him as 'our Norman'. He now began to take an active part in the church courts, and spoke out against the unyielding conservatism of the prevailing party which was interested above all else in preserving old privileges of the Establishment. Firm believer in an Established Church though he was, he could write 'We must give up the Church of the past and have as our motto the Church of the future'. He startled the presbytery of Glasgow with a violent attack on the traditional Scottish Sabbath or at least on its traditional basis in the Fourth Commandment, and narrowly escaped being libelled for heresy. His theological views were more and more influenced by his cousin and dearest friend, John McLeod Campbell, in the direction of a broad evangelicalism which ran counter to the orthodoxy of the day. But in spite of the suspicions and criticisms of the conservatives in the Church and outside it his work and his repute gained for the Church of Scotland a popularity with all classes as great as it had ever enjoyed.

A Church which could attract into its ministry so many able men of varied gifts was assuredly not dead, and was not likely to continue long in the doldrums. The Disruption had put the Moderates in power once more, but the reign of stagnant tranquillity did not last. The first indication that it was drawing to a close was a contest for the moderatorial chair in 1849 which resulted in the election of Dr. Alexander Lockhart Simpson, minister of Kirknewton, who after having studied for the secession ministry joined the Church of Scotland and was a prominent member of the evangelical Middle party during the Ten Years Conflict. According to Lord Cockburn the Moderates could only muster an ineffective group of twenty in the assembly of 1853. That must have been accidental for they were still strong enough ten years later to check the movement for the abolition of patronage. On the other hand there was a growing orthodox evangelical party that could assert itself on occasion as for example in opposition to the liberalism of Norman MacLeod. But the old party divisions tended to be blurred as new problems arose that had to be faced and as a new church life developed to meet the needs of the time. The Disruption hastened if it did not cause the loss to the Church of some provinces over which it had exercised control. It was obvious that church door collections in the parish churches could no longer suffice for the relief of poverty and by a Poor Law Amendment Act of 1845, poor relief was entrusted to public bodies with the right to impose assessments on property holders. This was a departure from the system which might once have been beneficent, but which was long known to have become inadequate in spite of Chalmers's eloquent defence of it. In 1853 theological tests for university professors in other than divinity faculties were abolished in spite of the fact that they had been imposed under one of the 'entrenched clauses' of the Treaty of Union; and this link between church and university was broken. More serious was the nationalization of elementary schools for which the Church had long had a responsibility. In 1872 the management of the nation's schools was entrusted to elected school boards which, however, were to provide religious instruction according 'to use and wont', for all children except those whose parents objected. For the retention of a period of religious instruction the Church had to fight hard, but in this it had the co-operation of the Free Church whose schools were also taken into the national system. Thus direct control of education came to an end, but in most places religious instruction continued to be given as before and good relations with the Church preserved. If these changes involved loss of influence the loss was abundantly made good by the gains brought about by these reforms, and the Church was freed to devote itself to other tasks which it soon found to its hand.

Theological issues had little or nothing to do with the Disruption or indeed with any of the secessions from the Established Church. All Presbyterians accepted the Westminster Confession which in 1690 on the demand of their ancestors had been declared by law to be the doctrinal standard of the Church. It had also been secured that all ministers, elders, and university professors should be required to assent to it as the confession of their own faith. The Moderates were often doubtless lukewarm with regard to its doctrines but they were officially orthodox. It was the Evangelicals who took the leading part in the condemnation of Edward Irving and John McLeod Campbell, but the Moderates showed no sign of opposition at that point. In 1843 most of the Evangelicals went out to form the Free Church which ardently maintained confessional Calvinist Orthodoxy. But those who remained in the Establishment did so too. Story of Rosneath, a non-party man who defended McLeod Campbell against his assailants, seems to hint that a charge of 'Rowism' would have been dangerous in the Established Church even after 1843. But soon a change came as English Broad Churchmen such as F. D. Maurice, Charles Kingsley, and Dean Stanley began to exercise an influence in Scotland too. Increasing knowledge of Darwinism, biblical and historical criticism, and German theology all helped to propagate what Newman called 'Liberalism' or 'the antidogmatic principle', to his mind the greatest evil of his time. The first Scottish Broad Churchman of note was John Tulloch, principal of St. Mary's College, St. Andrews, who taught a mild liberalism. John Caird in Glasgow was more philosophical and represented a right-wing Hegelianism. Norman MacLeod after he went to Glasgow became the popularizer of the teaching of his cousin, McLeod Campbell, whose famous book *The Nature of the Atonement* was published in 1856, and created, some thought, 'a brighter, clearer, theological atmosphere purged of Calvinistic gloom'. Even Edward Irving received recognition though much later, when in 1892 Charteris as moderator of the General Assembly unveiled a statue of him in the market square of his native Annan, and paid tribute to his great powers with but brief reference to his 'generous errors'. Charteris could do this all the more easily as he was not regarded as belonging to the Broad Church or Latitudinarian group. For it must be said that this group though distinguished was not large or popular, and attracted to itself a good deal of criticism and even vituperation from more conservative members and ministers. Perhaps the most influential theologian of the time as he was certainly the most erudite was Robert Flint, professor of divinity in Edinburgh University 1876–1903. He was no Latitudinarian, but one who sought to gather 'all the relevant data whether derived from Ethnic Religions, Natural Theology, Science or the Christian Revelation' and to build them into a systematic theology. His apologetic works, *Theism* and *Anti-theistic Theories*, were widely read. Through his many pupils he made a lasting impression upon his Church.

The existence of heterodox Broad Churchmen in the Established Church was put forward by the carefully orthodox John Cairns as one of the reasons for its disestablishment. He held that all its ministers and professors were bound by law and contract to teach the doctrines of the *Confession of Faith*. By failing to do so they broke the contract which should therefore be ended. On the other side it was replied that Establishment secured a measure of liberty for the individual conscience which otherwise would be subjected to the tyranny of majorities in church courts. There was one instance of an able and popular minister of the Free Church who for certain utterances was libelled by his presbytery and censured, and who with his congregation sought and received asylum within the Established Church, which was at least free from heresy-hunting. But of course the relation of a Church as a corporate body to its historic Confession must be a tormenting one, particularly when its Confession is so full and precise as that of the Westminster Divines. The United Presbyterian Church in 1879 and the Free Church in 1892 passed Declaratory Acts modifying their official attitude on certain points. In both Churches there was long and difficult and even acrimonious debate, and from the latter a secession took place though not so large as might have been expected. Even so it was later to be declared by the House of Lords that the Free Church had not in law the freedom it claimed. For many years the question of the Church's relation to its Confession was before the Established Assembly. Some would have had a simpler Confession drawn up anew, but that course commended itself to few. The method of a Declaratory Act was authoritatively declared to be outwith the powers of the assembly, and an approach to Parliament seemed inadvisable. The simplest if not the most satisfactory way seemed to be a modification of the formula of subscription, but even this was believed to require parliamentary sanction. In 1904 the opportunity came. It was evident that Parliament must intervene to rectify the intolerable situation created by the legal decision awarding the properties of the Free Church to the small minority that had refused to unite with the United Presbyterians and claimed to be the Free Church. A Bill was framed for this purpose and to it was added a clause giving the Established Church power to amend the formula under which its ministers and office-bearers should subscribe the *Confession of Faith*. The Churches (Scotland) Act was passed in 1905, and in 1910 after the usual procedure a new formula was authorized. 'I hereby subscribe the Confession of Faith, declaring that I accept it as the Confession of this Church, and that I believe the fundamental doctrines of the Christian Faith contained therein.' To many men of unquestioned integrity this formula has given intellectual relief, but to some scrupulous minds it has appeared somewhat evasive and equivocal. It is hard to see how better provision can be made for general acceptance of the historic faith of the Church while leaving room for the personal faith of individuals. Perhaps the best that can be done has been accomplished in the articles declaratory of the constitution of the Church of Scotland in matters spiritual, drawn up by the Church, recognized by Parliament in 1921 and enacted by the General Assembly in 1926, and now constitutional in the Church of Scotland. Article V claims for the Church

the inherent right, free from interference by civil authority, but under the safeguards for deliberate action and legislation provided by the Church itself to frame or adopt its subordinate standards, to declare the sense in which it understands its Confession of Faith, to modify the forms of expression therein, or to formulate other doctrinal statements, and to define the relation thereto of its office-bearers and members, but always in agreement with the Word of God and the fundamental doctrines of the Christian Faith contained in the said Confession, of which agreement the Church shall be sole judge, and with due regard to liberty of opinion in points which do not enter into the substance of the Faith.

Essentially this has been the claim of the Church of Scotland since the *Scots Confession* was presented to Parliament in 1560, amplified, and made explicit in the light of much bitter experience. Scripture truth, the witness of history, the continuing life and thought of the Church and the liberty of the individual conscience all alike are given their place, perhaps their due place. Scottish Presbyterianism in fact throughout its history has been fortunate in that while it has had within it theological 'liberals' and 'conservatives', neither have been extreme. Only in the Free Church was this divergence a serious matter leading to schisms of no great size in 1892 and 1900.

The weakest element in Scottish Presbyterianism, it has been often said, is the bareness and even the crudeness of its public worship. The ill-fated attempt of Charles I to impose his Prayer Book on the Scottish Church left behind it a strong aversion to anything in the nature of a uniform liturgy, which has endured to the present day. Even the Westminster Directory, adopted by the General Assembly in 1649 as a guide to ministers in the conduct of public worship, fell into desuetude after 1690. Individual ministers were left to their own devices and resources, and were restrained only by a traditional but high and exacting conception of the minister's function as preacher of the Word, dispenser of the Sacraments, and leader in common prayer. The didactic element was dominant and tended to reduce to a minimum those elements in worship that are usually regarded as more properly worshipful. Chalmers pleaded for church extension and Robertson for endowment in order to provide religious *instruction* for the masses of the people who were in danger of lapsing into infidelity for lack of it. Evidently they regarded instruction as practically synonymous with public worship. Moreover the effectiveness of a minister's labours must have depended wholly upon his spiritual and intellectual gifts, upon his earnestness. Where there was shallowness or lack of zeal there would be coldness and deadness in his sermons and prayers. New life came with the evangelical revival but unhappily much of it was lost to the parish churches at the Disruption. The Disruption had, of course, nothing to do with forms of worship, which remained unchanged. But new forces soon began to compel attention to the necessity of improving them. Among these new forces was a general advance in culture, refinement and taste. Closer contact with England consequent on the opening up of railway communication would have an effect. There was a growing tendency among the nobility and the wealthy, especially when they had been educated in England, to prefer the Anglican service to that prevailing in their own land. But this last consideration could also act in a contrary direction by arousing suspicion of any apparent aping of Anglican ways which 'Puseyism' did not make more popular. The Scottish Churches were in fact slow to respond to the inevitable demands of the time, and it is not surprising that it was the Established Church which took the lead here. In 1859 it appointed a committee on aids to devotion which, however, could not move faster than opinion in successive general assemblies would allow. For by 1859 the whole question of innovations had become acutely controversial.

It seems that the controversy was started by what we would now regard as a perfectly innocuous sermon preached in 1857 by Marshall Lang, minister of the East Church, Aberdeen, a young man of 23, who pointed out the appropriateness of standing to sing in Church. The traditional 'postures' had been to stand at prayer and sit during the praise. Lang was censured by his presbytery, and refused to appeal to a higher court though urged to do so by Robert Lee who was soon to be the central figure in the controversy. As a student at St. Andrews Lee had carried off all the academic honours and was ordained in 1833 to a chapel in Arbroath. Three years later he was presented to Campsie near Glasgow where he remained till 1843. During the Ten Years Conflict he took little interest in the great question agitating the Church. On one occasion he voted with the non-intrusionists but, as he put it, he was 'no scruple-monger' and was averse to schism. The Disruption caused a vacancy in Old Greyfriars, Edinburgh, to which Lee was appointed, and in 1847 while continuing in his charge he was elected first occupant of the newly erected chair of biblical criticism in the university. His colleagues were 'the dear old Principal' Lee who had taken charge of the chair of divinity demitted by Chalmers, and James Robertson in the chair of ecclesiastical history. He was, therefore, doubtless the brightest of the professors, original and provocative and typically 'anti-Free-Kirk'. But he was also unpopular with his co-presbyters for his liberalism and for his somewhat aggressive championship of causes to which they were resolutely opposed, pluralities, for example, abolition of theological tests for university professors and the secularization of elementary education. In 1845 his church of Old Greyfriars was gutted by fire, and owing to obstruction in the town council it was not restored till 1857. During that period his congregation shared with another the use of the Tolbooth church. He had therefore ample time to meditate on a *Reform of the Church in Worship, Government and Doctrine*. Not until 1864 did he publish his volume with that title but treating only of worship. When, however, in 1857 his church was reopened he had already in print a book of *Prayers for Public Worship* which he proceeded to use. The congregation was invited to stand to sing and kneel for prayer and to take part in the service by audible responses. These innovations, introduced in a church closely associated with the signing of the National Covenant, aroused a storm of protest, and the assembly of 1858 ordered the presbytery of Edinburgh to institute an inquiry. As a result Lee's practices were condemned by a small majority. He appealed to the General Assembly of 1859 which contented itself with forbidding him to read prayers from a printed book! A member of the assembly describes his attitude as 'very insolent and offensive', and this doubtless prejudiced many against him. He persevered, however, with his innovations except that the printed book was not used again until 1863. More trouble arose over the introduction of a harmonium later replaced by an organ, and the Greyfriars case dragged on till Lee's death in 1868.

Robert Lee may be regarded as a martyr to the cause of improvement of the forms of public worship. Certainly he was its protagonist who dared to challenge opposition. Others who were prepared to proceed more slowly with the consent of their people usually encountered less difficulty, for where the peace and harmony of a congregation was undisturbed the church courts were unwilling to intervene. Clearly changes were taking place all over the country, affecting the other Presbyterian Churches too. Services became more orderly and reverent. Opposition to the introduction of organs died down. Church praise was enriched by the use of hymns in addition to Metrical Psalms and Paraphrases, after 1870 when the first edition of the Scottish Hymnal was authorized by the General Assembly. And a new interest in church buildings and furnishings was aroused. The foundation of the Church Service Society in 1865 greatly contributed to promote these changes. Its object was to study 'the Liturgies— ancient and modern—of the Christian Church with a view to the preparation and publication of forms of Prayer for Public Worship, and services for the Administration of the Sacraments, the Celebration of Marriage and the Burial of the Dead'. The society disclaimed any desire to impose a uniform liturgy on the Church or to discourage the use of free prayer. Nevertheless it aroused much suspicion and received no official recognition from the Church. On the other hand it attracted into its membership a large number of ministers and elders of very diverse views united only in a common interest in the seemly conduct of worship. Through its *Euchologion* or *Book of Common Order*, first published in 1867, it has greatly influenced the practice of ministers, even, in many cases, those who were antipathetic to the purposes for which the society was formed. In a special sense and within its own chosen limits the society may be credited with having brought about a renascence of worship.

A striking illustration of the changed attitude in matters of public worship can be seen in the restoration of St. Giles. The vast building had since the Reformation come to be divided so as to house as many as four congregations, an arrangement for which at least it should be said that it made it possible for the preachers to be heard by the people. What had been the choir in pre-Reformation times formed the High Kirk or parish church of the city and was attended by the Lords of Session and other leading citizens, and by the town council on civic occasions. William Chambers, the famous publisher, who had been Lord Provost from 1865 to 1869, on demitting office conceived the idea of so restoring it as to make it worthy of its function in the civic life. Galleries were removed. The pews were renewed and suitable seats for the judges and the magistrates were provided together with a highly ornamental royal pew, and a new carved stone pulpit. All this was carried out by Chambers and a committee of citizens with support from the general public, and the High Kirk was reopened in 1873. Six years later Chambers undertook at his own expense the restoration of another part of the building which had just been vacated by the extinguished Old Kirk congregation. Finally the congregation occupying the nave removed to a new church built to receive it, and the way was open to complete the reconstruction and restoration of the ancient fane. William Chambers lived to know that his purpose had been accomplished, but he died three days before the High Kirk of St. Giles, sometimes but less appropriately styled St. Giles' Cathedral, was opened for worship with stately ceremonial in May 1883. The original St. Giles was not intended for Reformed worship and the motive in its restoration was chiefly the provision of a dignified and worthy building for services on civic and national occasions. Not all Scottish worshippers would feel at home there, but the fact that most of them regard it with patriotic pride as Scotland's own great church shows how far they have travelled since the days of Robert Lee.

Another aspect of the recovery of the national Church is closely associated with the name of Archibald Hamilton Charteris. As a divinity student in Edinburgh Charteris was specially attracted to the indefatigable James Robertson, 'the faithful Churchman' whose life he wrote. During three successful pastorates, two in country parishes and one in Glasgow, he came to be known as representative of the theologically conservative and evangelical school of thought within the Church. He was more sympathetic than many of his brethren towards other denominations and more ready to co-operate with them in breaking down old barriers. He was

early among the spokesmen for the abolition of patronage,
genuinely and honourably hoping thus to further Presbyterian
reunion, and when Moody and Sankey came to Edinburgh
he was one of the few ministers of the Established Church
who eagerly supported their mission. His appointment by the
Crown to succeed Robert Lee in the chair of biblical criticism
in Edinburgh University was the occasion of adverse criticism on the part of churchmen of liberal views who would
have preferred the brilliant but erratic Robert Wallace.
Wallace in fact was soon afterwards appointed to the chair
of ecclesiastical history, but after a few years he resigned to
become editor of the *Scotsman,* and ended his career as a
Liberal M.P. Charteris remained a loyal and devoted churchman. As professor he took a deep interest in his students,
especially in their training for the pastoral ministry. Under
his guidance and with his encouragement they took part in
home mission work in the derelict Tolbooth parish until a
new congregation was formed.

It was on the motion of Charteris that the assembly of 1869
appointed a committee on Christian life and work, and over
it he presided as convener until 1894. As originally conceived
the purpose of the committee was to inquire as to the progress of Christian work throughout the country and the best
means of promoting evangelical efforts under the aegis of the
ministers and office-bearers of the Church. The inquiry was
conducted by means of questionnaires sent to ministers inviting them to report on work done in their parishes and to
send in suggestions as to what might further be done. Naturally enough there was a good deal of apathy and even resentment against what was called an inquisitive meddling with
the affairs of parish ministers presumably doing their duty
faithfully. Moreover the word evangelism, which is now entirely honourable, was then associated with revivalism with
which many, for good reasons and for bad, had no sympathy.
Repeated attempts were made to discredit the committee and
bring its labours to an end. But Charteris was not to be discouraged. 'The gentlest man in the Assembly' disarmed his
critics, and he had the support of some of the most influential
leaders in the Church, notably Norman MacLeod.

For some ten years the work of the committee was mainly of an exploratory nature in an endeavour to survey the whole field of the parochial ministry, and its questionnaires stimulated thought and discussion as to the means to make it effective. Attention was early directed to the vexed question of presbyterial superintendence, once a serious affair before privy censures became a dead letter, and a beginning was made towards giving it some reality. On the other hand as a result of suggestions received the committee initiated action of the most varied kind. Ministers of remote parishes, particularly in the Highlands and Islands, were strengthened and encouraged by deputations in which some of the outstanding figures in the Church took part. Mission weeks were arranged in parishes which desired them, and were conducted by missioners specially chosen for their evangelistic gifts and experience. Spiritual and social and physical care was provided for the migratory fisher folk who followed the herring shoals from the Hebrides to Shetland and down the east coast to Yarmouth; and something was done also in an attempt to reach farm servants. For the first time the Church of Scotland bestirred itself in the work of evangelism. Not less important were the committee's efforts to encourage church life in the local congregations. In some parishes it found Sunday morning fellowships existing to bring young men together for prayer and Bible study. In 1884 a plan was launched to unite existing fellowships in a nation-wide organization, the Young Men's Guild, with an annual conference attended by delegates from all over the country. The plan was immediately successful. Branches multiplied and developed various activities. Bible study was not neglected and a series of guild textbooks was prepared to meet a felt need. Social work was also undertaken, and in 1889 John A. Graham started his great work in Kalimpong as the guild missionary to the heathen. At home by creating an informed interest in Christian doctrine and service, the guild proved a training ground for many who afterwards became ministers or elders in the Church. Unhappily it hardly survived the 1914–18 War, and the youth fellowships of today do not quite supply its place. More enduring was the organization of women's work in the Church by the foundation of the Woman's Guild in 1887. Few congregations are without a local branch, through which interest is maintained in the general work of the Church at home and abroad. Remarkable also was the revival of the ancient order of deaconesses in which suitable women were solemnly set apart for special service, training being provided in the Deaconess House in Edinburgh, and for those requiring nursing training in the Deaconess Hospital built and equipped entirely by the Church. One other venture of Charteris and his committee may be mentioned. In 1879 began the issue of *Life and Work*, a monthly magazine of a literary and religious nature which also brought information regarding the work of the Church in all fields into the homes of its people.

For years Charteris had to contend with complacency, indifference, incredulity, and even hostility, but he held on his way with quiet and ever hopeful tenacity. His achievement is not so striking as that of those who chose to labour in more public ways, but perhaps to no one does the Church of Scotland owe a greater debt for the recovery of vitality, both local and national, of a sense of evangelical mission, of devoted and purposeful activity in the service of the Kingdom of God.

VI

MOVEMENTS TOWARDS REUNION

THE Ten Years Conflict culminating in the Disruption caused a deep cleavage in the ecclesiastical life of Scotland marked by extraordinary bitterness. It would serve no good purpose to repeat the hard things that were said on both sides. Personal friendships were sundered. The ministers of the two Churches kept rigidly apart and did all in their power to instil into their congregations feelings of enmity. Officially the Churches refused any kind of mutual recognition. In the Established Church the Act of 1799 prohibiting ministerial communion, i.e. exchange of pulpits and other services with those of other denominations, repealed in 1842, came into force again automatically in 1843 and was not seriously modified for twenty years. Dr. Chalmers died while the assembly was sitting in 1847 and no reference was made to the event or to his life-long services to the Church. The bicentenary of the Westminster Assembly and the tercentenary of the Reformation did not serve to bridge the gulf. Only in the Evangelical Alliance was there a common meeting ground for such as cared to take part in its conferences.

Nevertheless there were always some in the Auld Kirk who sincerely longed for reunion and were willing to go far in an effort to achieve it. They began to make themselves heard from 1866 onwards, and their influence grew. Of these men—'profoundly in earnest'—the outstanding leaders were Charteris and Professor Mitchell of St. Andrews. They threw themselves eagerly into the movement for the abolition of patronage in the hope that the removal of this stumbling block would be a first step towards union; and they were disappointed to find their motives misunderstood and misinterpreted. Their design was represented to be to disrupt the Free Church when its union negotiations with the United Presbyterians had revealed the existence of a considerable 'constitutionalist' element that would have nothing to do with

Voluntaries. In spite of all discouragements they persuaded the General Assembly in 1870 to agree 'to record their deep sense of the manifold evils arising from the ecclesiastical divisions of Scotland . . . and . . . their hearty willingness and desire to take all possible steps consistently with the principles on which this Church is founded to promote the reunion of Churches having a common origin, adhering to the same confession of faith and the same system of government and worship'. A committee was appointed to consider the matter and report to next assembly. Nothing came of this at the time for the patronage question claimed all attention. In 1872 Rainy carried in the Free Church Assembly a motion to the effect that 'the proposals on the part of the Established Church with a view to the alteration of the law of Patronage do not affect the grounds of separation which rendered the Disruption necessary and are not fitted to bring about a union of Scottish Presbyterianism'. Moreover he used his influence privately with Gladstone to ensure that the proposals would be rejected, and he declared openly that as an individual his conviction was growing day by day that the only solution of the divisions of the Scottish Church was disestablishment. Two years later patronage was abolished and Rainy joined Dr. John Cairns in a campaign for disestablishment, which he pronounced to be a necessary preliminary to church union in Scotland. To understand that implausible statement it must be remembered that 'the principle of Establishment', tenaciously held by a section in the Free Church, had just wrecked the hopeful prospect of union with the United Presbyterians. For the eradication of that principle the destruction of the existing Establishment might well seem a necessary preliminary. And, of course, the Established Church not only was erastian in its constitution but also harboured and encouraged latitudinarian doctrine and ritualistic practices!

Rainy and Cairns were of course Liberals in politics but they were also entirely sincere in holding that disestablishment would promote the Christian good of Scotland and even Presbyterian reunion. The same idea more obviously mixed with party politics appears in an address presented to Gladstone on the eve of the general election of 1886 and signed by 1,475 'Liberal clergy of Scotland' of all the dissenting Churches. They point out that the Church of Christ in Scotland was broken in pieces, implore the illustrious leader of the Liberal party to make an end of this religious scandal and political injustice and pledge themselves to do all in their power to support him in carrying into law this indispensable measure of Liberal and enlightened statesmanship. Politics and religion are notoriously hard to keep separate, but it may be felt that politics is more evident than religion in this address. Certainly church union has no place in it. Disestablishment may or may not have been a religious issue but it was undeniably a political question upon which appeal to the electorate was clearly in order. But it had to be decided by the electorate not of Scotland only, but of England and Ireland as well. The Liberal party in Scotland gave it its blessing, but Gladstone was not prepared to jeopardize policies he held to be more urgent by giving it first place in his programme. He won the election of 1886 but within two months of assuming the reins of government he split his party on the question of home rule for Ireland, and disestablishment that seemed imminent ceased to be a danger, though it continued to be agitated until 1907.

Within the Established Church the disestablishment campaign naturally enough caused alarm and resentment. A church interests committee vigorously took up the defence of the Church and enlisted the services of all its notable men to address public meetings and write pamphlets. They claimed that the historic national Church was no mere survival which had outlived its usefulness, that it was still necessary if religious ordinances were to be provided for the whole nation, and that its very existence was the symbol of a continuing sense of God's sovereignty over the nation. They even entered the political arena and sought to prevent the return of parliamentary candidates pledged to disestablishment. A gigantic petition signed by 688,000 persons was sent in to Parliament, which at least showed that Scotland though mainly Liberal in politics was not solidly in favour of this particular part of the Liberal programme. Perhaps from the political side the greatest harm to the disestablishment cause was done by its more radical champions whose almost vindictive proposals for the complete extinction of the Church of Scotland disgusted all but the most rabid of its enemies.

In spite of the resentments caused by the bitter strife the question of union was not put aside, and attempts were made again and again to bring together men of good will. In 1878 the abortive appeal of 1870 was renewed and this time was conveyed officially to the dissenting Churches with the request that they would enter into frank and friendly conference 'as to the causes which at present prevent them from sharing the trust now reposed in this Church alone'. The Free Church replied cordially approving the communication and the courteous and considerate manner of the approach, but taking its stand on the Claim of Right of 1842 and declaring its inability to support the maintenance of the existing establishment as at present constituted. It agreed however with the Established Church in the desire to maintain inviolate the principle of the national recognition of the Christian religion. The United Presbyterian Church was more curt. 'In an equally frank and friendly manner', the synod declared, 'that in accordance with the principles and history of this Church it is impossible for this Synod to contemplate sharing with the Established Church the trust reposed in it by the State.' There the matter rested for a time. It was raised again in 1886. In that year, encouraged by the unanimous resolutions passed at many public meetings in favour of the reunion of Scottish Presbyterians on the basis of a National Establishment of Religion, the General Assembly resolved to renew their approach to the other Churches with a view to promoting co-operation and reunion, consistently with the maintenance of Establishment and the sacredness of the ancient endowments. When the Free Church declared that it could only 'enter into conference with a sister Church on a matter which so intimately concerns the Christian interests of the whole community' if Establishment and Endowment could be questions open for discussion, and the United Presbyterians reasserted their absolute opposition to both, the matter was dropped once more.

There were, however, in all the Churches men who, though

they might differ on the Church and State issue, were
thoroughly in earnest about the paramount need for reunion.
In 1894 and 1895 private and unofficial conferences were
held in which eighteen representatives, ministerial and lay,
from each of the Churches took part, with opportunity 'to
talk unreservedly of the Union of the three Churches'. Memo-
randa and counter-memoranda were submitted and discussed with complete frankness and in a friendly, one might
say also, an academic atmosphere. A wide range of agreement was reached. It was agreed, for example, that 'Religion
ought to be acknowledged by the State in its constitution,
legislation and conduct.' The State should 'recognise the
Church of Christ as a Divine institution and the chief means
for the promotion of righteousness and godliness' and should
'respect its true spiritual independence', provide 'facilities
for the religious education of the young and promote measures
for the moral and social improvement of the people'. So the
idea of a secular State was dismissed, and the principle of the
national recognition of the Christian religion accepted. There
remained of course the question of Establishment and on this
agreement could not be reached, but the disputants came to
understand one another better and to respect one another
more. It may fairly be claimed that the gulf that had separated them had been considerably narrowed, possibly even
that the dispute had been reduced to one about words and
definitions. Some felt that the way had been opened for
further clarification and advance. Among the statements submitted not the least interesting was one signed by eight laymen of the dissenting Churches in which they say:

In our opinion Disestablishment by Act of Parliament would
not end in Union but, on the contrary, lead to further estrangement, and possibly to more divisions among the Churches. We
therefore earnestly urge that the proposals by the brethren of the
Established Church should be more fully formulated by them in
order to receive the consideration of the Conference. If they are
set aside, we shall leave the Conference with the feeling that these
brethren have made an endeavour to bring about a reconciliation
of existing difficulties which has not been seconded. . . . We
express the hope that the pending conflict in the Courts of the

several Churches on this question of Disestablishment may cease as being, in our opinion, one outwith their sphere.

The signatories to this statement spoke for a growing volume of lay opinion in all the Churches.

These conferences were purely informal. Those taking part in them formed an impressive group which, however, did not include some of the most influential leaders in the Church. Principal Rainy, for example, held aloof as did Principal Hutton, successor to John Cairns as head of the United Presbyterian Divinity Hall, and spokesman of the extreme Voluntaries in his Church. So likewise did Professor Story, later principal of Glasgow University, moderator of the General Assembly of the Church of Scotland in 1894, whom many regarded as the ablest and strongest leader in the Church and who made no secret of his dislike of dissenters. He and John Macleod of Govan, the moving spirit in the Scottish Church Society, founded in 1892 to promote high church or 'Scoto-Catholic' principles, persuaded the assembly of 1896 to withdraw from co-operation with the other Churches in producing a common Hymn Book, the Church Hymnary. This decision was reversed in the following year, but bitter things had been said on both sides. And in 1897 the negotiations began which led in 1900 to the Union of the Free and United Presbyterian Churches. It could plausibly be alleged that the main object of the union was to strengthen the cause of disestablishment. At all events the United Free Church continued to press for it. In 1907 it approached the new Liberal government of Sir Henry Campbell-Bannerman to that end, and the action was justified on the ground that 'It is an intolerable thing that an alien institution like the State should be suffered permanently to disrupt and keep asunder two great bodies of Scottish Christians, comprising between them the vast bulk of the population'. Truly a paradoxical way of putting the case!

It was clear that public opinion in Scotland was moving in another direction, particularly within the Established Church. The assembly of 1908 issued an invitation to the United Free Church 'to confer in a friendly and generous spirit on the present ecclesiastical situation in Scotland, and to consider

how a larger measure of Christian fellowship and co-operation could be brought about so as to prepare the way for
union for which so many were hoping and praying'. The reply
of the United Free Church was again cordial but, as in 1886,
it asked that the conference should be without restriction,
and that was accepted. For the Established Church that was
a novel and momentous decision; the 'Establishment principle' which had hitherto been regarded as sacrosanct was
now to be discussed as an open question. Both assemblies,
accordingly, in 1909 appointed large and representative committees 'to enter into unrestricted conference on the existing
ecclesiastical situation and on the main causes which keep
the Churches apart'. John White was chosen to be clerk of
the Church of Scotland Committee. To his breadth of vision,
clarity of mind, and indomitable will is due the ultimate
success of this venture of faith.

White's labours were long and arduous. For the first year
little progress was made except in breaking down barriers of
suspicion and mutual mistrust. But something was done to
bring home to the mind of both Churches the clamant call
for closer union if the religious needs of the Scottish people
were to be adequately met. In 1911, however, White was able
to present to the assembly a forward-looking report. Suggestions were made of a course of action the Church might take
in order to meet the complaint that its existing constitution
was inconsistent with the principle of spiritual freedom. It
was proposed that the Church might approach Parliament
with a request (1) for the rescinding of certain clauses in the
ancient statutes on which the legal judgements that forced
on the Disruption had been based, and (2) for a Declaratory
Act recognizing that the powers she claimed in matters spiritual were inherent in the Church as a Church of Christ. It was
believed that this would avoid the danger alleged to lurk in
the old statutory connexion of the Church with the State and
the no less serious danger into which the Free Church had
fallen in 1904 of being in the eyes of the law simply a voluntary association based on contract. The boldness of this proposal greatly impressed the United Free Church. How bold
it was will be realized when it is remembered that the govern-

ment of the day was a Liberal government supported by a large majority sympathetic to Disestablishment. The assembly nevertheless received the report and encouraged its committee to consider the matter further. A memorandum was therefore prepared giving an outline of a Bill that Parliament might be asked to enact, and in 1913 the committee was instructed to produce draft articles of a constitution embodying the spiritual powers claimed to be inherent in the Church.

Already opposition began to be heard. Were not White and his committee giving everything away in order to conciliate the other Church? In abandoning the time-honoured expression 'The Church by law established' had they not thrown overboard all the advantages implied in establishment, substituting for the historic statutory connexion of Church and State a vague and nebulous recognition of the Church by the State? When the constitutional articles came to be drafted two groups presented difficulty. A small group of 'Scoto-Catholics' insisted that the articles must contain an explicit and unalterable statement of the orthodox faith as set forth in the ancient creeds, and they carried their insistence to the point of obstruction. They were supported by others whose objection was rather to the unlimited 'spiritual freedom' in matters of church government being claimed for the Church, in reality for the church courts. The majority of the committee persevered and submitted draft articles to the assembly of 1914, to which the minority likewise submitted a separate report. Both documents were ordered to be sent down to presbyteries informally for criticism and comment, but before they could be dealt with the outbreak of war turned men's minds to other thoughts and cares. Not until the spring of 1918 were discussions resumed and the old oppositions reappeared. But the war years had made church union more than ever necessary, and when in 1919 the articles as completed were sent down to presbyteries for approval or rejection they received almost unanimous approval. In the United Free Church they were also approved as a solution of the problem of spiritual freedom, though not without a considerable number of dissentients. The way seemed now to be open for an approach to the legislature, and in July 1921 the

British Parliament without a division passed an Enabling Act recognizing the right of the Church of Scotland to adopt the articles as a statement of its basic constitution. In so doing the 'civil magistrate' for the first time since the Reformation acknowledged in the fullest sense the freedom of a Church in matters affecting its own spiritual life and work.

Though drawn up in modern times for a specific purpose the articles express the essential and historic witness of Scottish Presbyterianism from the beginning, and form its distinctive contribution to the solution of a problem by no means confined to Scotland. As they have attracted considerable interest in other Churches, some account of them must be given. The Church of Scotland claims to be part of the Holy Catholic or Universal Church. It holds the orthodox doctrines of the Trinity and the Incarnation, and receives the Word of God contained in the Scriptures of the Old and New Testaments as the supreme rule of faith and life. It adheres to the Scottish Reformation, is in historical continuity with the Church as reformed in 1560 and secured in the Treaty of Union of 1707, 'As a National Church representative of the Christian Faith of the Scottish people it acknowledges its distinctive call and duty to bring the ordinances of religion to the people in every parish of Scotland through a territorial ministry.' Its government is Presbyterian, and its subordinate standards of faith, worship, government, and discipline are those drawn up by the Westminster Assembly 'as these have been or may be interpreted or modified by Acts of the General Assembly or by consuetude'. It has received from the Lord Jesus Christ its Divine King and Head and from Him alone the right and power, subject to no civil authority, to legislate and to adjudicate finally in all matters of doctrine, worship, government, and discipline in the Church. It acknowledges the divine appointment and authority of the civil magistrate within his own sphere, maintains its historic testimony to the duty of the nation in its corporate capacity to render homage to God, to acknowledge the Lord Jesus Christ to be King over the nations, to obey His laws, to reverence His ordinances, to honour His Church, and to promote in all appropriate ways the Kingdom of God. It recognizes its obligation to seek

and promote union with other Churches in which it finds
the Word to be purely preached, the sacraments administered
according to Christ's ordinance, and discipline rightly exercised. Finally it has the right to interpret modify or add to
these articles subject to the safeguards for deliberate action
and legislation provided by the Church itself. The only freedom that Andrew Melville could have asked for in addition
would be freedom to require the civil magistrate to compel
all his subjects to obey the judgements of the church courts!

There still remained the troublesome problem of the
Church's ancient patrimony, its churches, manses, glebes,
teinds, and other statutory revenues and claims, which had
been formerly the subject of much dispute. In the United
Free Church it had come to be widely though not universally
accepted that the ecclesiastical endowments should not be
secularised but should be conserved for religious purposes but
it was insisted that these properties should be vested in the
Church in such a way that it had full control over them. To
transfer them to a central body of church trustees proved to be
a highly complex business. Agreement as to their valuation
and conveyance had to be reached with interested parties,
particularly the heritors or landowners of Scotland who paid
the teind-stipends and had certain statutory responsibilities
for the maintenance of the churches and manses. Not until
1924 was a 'Church of Scotland Properties and Endowments
Bill' ready to be introduced into Parliament. Vigorous opposition was encountered, but at last in May 1925 the Bill
became law, and the Church entered into full and free
possession of its properties. In the following year it ratified
the articles and enacted them as its constitution, and the
final stage in the long-drawn-out procedure towards union
could be entered upon. A basis and plan of union was prepared, setting out the substantial agreement between the
Churches as regards doctrine, worship, government, and discipline as vouched for in their historic documents from the
Reformation down to the articles of 1926, and outlining a
scheme for combining the various agencies through which
they had carried on their work. After full and prolonged discussion in assemblies and presbyteries the basis and plan was

approved in May 1929 and in October of that year the two
assemblies became one and the Church of Scotland was reunited. Unhappily but inevitably there was a minority in the
United Free Church of those who could not forget old slogans
and resolved to continue in separate existence, but this time
there was no appeal to the law courts.

It was often asked while the Union was approaching whether
the United Church would be an established or a disestab-
lished Church, and the only possible answer was that it would
be neither, or perhaps that the question had little significance.
In the articles and in the basis and plan of union both words
are avoided as outmoded. The expression 'The Church as by
law established' is not of ecclesiastical provenance. It was a
novelty in 1690, and the Church was not happy about it as
it seemed to deny to it its true nature. The Cameronians made
use of it as a reproach against those who accepted the Revolution Settlement which tacitly jettisoned the principles of the
Reformation and the Covenants, principles which in practice if not in theory subordinated the civil to the ecclesiastical
power. Samuel Rutherford's *Lex Rex* asserted the supremacy
of law over the king, but said nothing of its supremacy over
the Church. Post-Revolution laws, e.g. demanding oaths of
allegiance, legalizing toleration, and restoring patronage, were
resented and resisted for a time as infringing the Church's
rights. It was not until the second half of the eighteenth
century, during the Moderate ascendancy, that Establishment by law came to be regarded as not only advantageous
but also honourable, indeed as the Church's sheet anchor.
Even the Evangelicals were satisfied until the judgements of
the Court of Session revealed the danger that laws once intended to protect the Church could be so interpreted as to
limit and hamper it in its efforts to grapple earnestly with the
demands of a changed situation. They declared the actions
of the court to be encroachments on the spiritual liberties of
the Church. In forming the Free Church they thought of
themselves as the true Church of Scotland and of those who
remained as clinging to a mere legal establishment without
spiritual significance of any kind. The unexpected recovery
of church life and vitality within the Establishment led to an

increasing sense that establishment was an unfair advantage
enjoyed by a rival Church whose privileged position was
moreover a denial of religious equality. Hence the demand
for disestablishment and disendowment. On the other hand,
to the leaders of the Established Church establishment and
endowment appeared to be the indispensable means by which
the Church might fulfil its responsible task on a nation-wide
scale, and so be a truly national Church. If, however, the
expression 'The Church by law established' seemed to carry
with it a slur on the Church's character and mission as the
Church of Scotland, few can now regret that it has fallen into
desuetude, and become as meaningless to most people as the
controversies which it engendered. But the ideal of a national
Church both representing and fostering the Christian faith
of the whole people, an ideal which in spite of all division
was common to all Presbyterians, was in a manner realized.
Into the reunited Church in 1929 were gathered the great
majority of Presbyterians, forming rather more than four-
fifths of the church-going Protestant population of the country.
It is true there were still outstanding five small Presbyterian
denominations historically interesting as maintaining old
testimonies hardly relevant in the modern world. There were
also Congregationalists, Baptists, Methodists, and of course
the Scottish Episcopal Church with claims to represent the
pre-Revolution Church of Scotland. The chief rival was the
Roman Catholic Church consisting largely of Irish immigrants
settled in the industrial areas and increasing rapidly in numbers and consequently in political influence. In numbers alone
the Church of Scotland in 1929 might justifiably regard itself as the Church of the Scottish people. With a history
reaching back to the days before the Union with England
some have found it a national asset of great value. More important, however, is the fact of its acknowledged responsibility for the spiritual life of Scotland. Since the days of
Thomas Chalmers the needs of the unchurched masses have
been laid upon the conscience of the Church of Scotland,
and the realization of the stupendous task of evangelizing
the whole people was one of the most powerful motives for
the Union of the Churches.

PART V

THE CHURCH OF SCOTLAND
SINCE 1929

THE CHURCH OF SCOTLAND SINCE
1929

THE driving force behind the Union movement was a growing sense shared by forward-looking people of the magnitude and urgency of the task confronting the Christian Church generally, and, in Scotland particularly the two great Presbyterian Churches which between them embraced the bulk of the professing Christian population. Hardly distinguishable in doctrine, worship, government, and discipline, they were further alike in acknowledging responsibility for what Chalmers called 'the Christian good of Scotland' and in earnestly striving to promote it. Could they not more effectively and less wastefully meet their responsibility by ceasing to be rivals and by working together for the common end? It was hoped that the achievement of union would of itself give an added spiritual stimulus to the good work at home and abroad which they had undertaken in separation, and that the voice of a united Church would have greater weight in the affairs of the nation at a time when politics was beginning to extend its range to include social and economic questions, and the Welfare State was coming within sight. Some will say now that these hopes were over-sanguine. It is still too soon to judge. It took twenty years to remove an obstacle to union that had become somewhat doctrinaire and insubstantial. Real and practical difficulties must inevitably have emerged in uniting two active Churches long accustomed to separate vigorous existence and supported by strong loyalties, even prejudices, on the part of their people. At least a generation of peaceful development might have been required to complete the necessary adjustments. This was not to be granted. The Union was hardly ten years old when the Second World War broke out which was to shake to their foundations the political, social, and economic structures of the world. In view of that calamity and the tragic years of doubt, fear, and anxiety that have ensued it may now appear that the union did not come a moment too soon. In this final chapter an attempt will be made to show briefly how the Church of Scotland has during these last thirty years endeavoured to fulfil its Christ-given mission.

The uniting Churches had, of course, the same system of church government by kirk session, presbyteries, synods, and General Assembly with only trifling diversities of procedure so that the coalescence of their church courts was easily and happily accomplished. Both Churches also had roughly parallel 'schemes' supported by the whole membership and managed by central committees. These too were amalgamated with little difficulty. But two troublesome problems had to be faced immediately. One was purely financial. The Church Property and Endowments Act affecting some 900 parishes mainly in rural areas relieved the heritors of responsibility for the upkeep of the churches and manses. They had to hand them over in a state of 'tenantable repair', but as they were usually old buildings their maintenance in future would obviously become expensive. Moreover, the Church attempted to get congregations which had never needed to do so before to contribute to their minister's stipend. It has been a common complaint that the Church is always begging for money but certainly financial concern became more evident than it had been in the pre-union Established Church. The 'Maintenance of the Ministry' that is, of the ordinances of religion, in rural parishes has consequently become a major problem.

Even more serious was the problem of readjustment of agencies. Denominational rivalries of an earlier time resulted in the setting up of competing churches even in small communities. There might be two or even three in villages and small towns, each with its minister and a congregation deeply attached to it by powerful sentiment. Obviously after the union many of these local churches would become redundant, and adjustment would be necessary. But it is one thing to unite denominations, and quite another to unite congregations which are proud of their traditions and tenacious of their rights. And Presbyterianism has always fostered strong congregational life. It is easy to be critical of parochialism or congregationalism in this sense and to demand thorough rationalization. But grave spiritual damage may be done if this problem is not handled with patience, sympathy, and Christian insight. These virtues have commonly had their reward. Some 700 local unions have been effected over the years but the process has been necessarily slow and is not yet completed.

Bound up with the problem of readjustment is that of ministerial manpower which for a long time has given cause for anxiety. Up to 1914 both Churches had little difficulty in securing an adequate supply of candidates for the ministry able and willing to undertake the long course of training required of them, which included three years study in arts and three or even four in divinity. It was not unusual to find two scholarly men faithfully ministering to quite small congregations in a Scottish rural parish. After the First World War, however, the number of candidates for the ministry began to be insufficient and the problem has become increasingly acute in recent years, in spite of the institution of shortened or modified courses for selected men of maturer years. Other professions, it is true, similarly complain of shortages, so that shortage of ministers may not be due entirely to the lack of material and financial inducements. Doubtless the work of the ministry today is more exacting than ever it was. The Church still gets a share of able and earnest men from the universities, though not in sufficient numbers to realize the ideal it has cherished since the Reformation of a well-qualified minister in every parish.

Since the days of Thomas Chalmers church extension has had a high priority among the schemes or enterprises of the Church. After the First World War it took on both a new shape and a new urgency. It was not so much that population was expanding as that it was being displaced. In the cities and large towns people were being moved out from the centre to new housing areas on the outskirts. This movement was vastly accelerated after the Second World War when enormous new towns or rather new amorphous communities spread rapidly over what had been the countryside, with little of community spirit and only incipient community institutions. In all more than a million people were thus affected. Some of these people might have a connexion with a central Church and might desire to maintain it. But many more had none or next to none, and their removal to new surroundings might be expected to make them more open to church influences if only there was a church in their midst. Something had been done by the Churches in separation to meet this need, but the Union made possible an appeal of nation-wide scope. John White, 'the architect of union', was the man to make it, and into it he threw all his abounding energy. In 1933, though the time was one of economic depression, he launched an appeal for £180,000, an impossibly large sum as many told him, but by 1936 it had been obtained. Some forty new churches were completed or in process of erection when the outbreak of the Second World War brought the movement to a standstill. With the return of peace and the vast expansion of the new housing areas the problem became correspondingly more acute. Now it was not merely a question of money, but sites were hard to obtain and labour and materials were severely restricted for a time. Work was, however, resumed in 1948, and an appeal made to the Church for the gigantic sum of £1,000,000. Dr. George MacLeod has courageously accepted the task of raising it. The church extension project is in every way the most fruitful form of the Church's mission to the nation. The new congregations formed draw their membership in large part from people who had lapsed or were tending to lapse from all connexion with the Church. They are composed to a large extent of young people, children, young adults, and young parents and are in consequence full of hopefulness and liveliness, and offer to ministers both opportunity and challenge which are often felt to be lacking in the older charges. It should also be said that the new churches are designed and furnished to be in keeping architecturally and ecclesiastically with the new age, to be worthy sanctuaries for the worship of God.

Meantime the Church has not forgotten its more normal territorial mission. At the Union it was hoped to revitalize the parochial system which in the large towns at all events had been little regarded. To each church was now assigned a manageable area as its parish for the spiritual supervision of which it was responsible. The minister, elders, and church workers were encouraged to undertake the systematic visitation of all the homes in the parish, and in this way contact was made with people who often welcomed and valued it. Moreover the word evangelism is now in good repute and is foremost among the interests of the Church. A special evangelist (under that title) devotes himself wholly to this work, studying its methods and organizing and guiding teams of workers to help him in campaigns in town and country, even into the far north-west. Close and understanding relations with trade unions and labour organizations are fostered and arrangements are made for the appointment of ministers to act as chaplains in factories and industrial works. On a wider scale the Forward Movement of 1931 was designed to further the ideals and keep bright the hopes that the Union had brought forth; and the oddly named 'Tell Scotland Movement', inaugurated in 1952, seeks to engage every member of the Church in an evangelism which is not of an occasional nature but is 'a continuing engagement at every level with the whole life of man'. Of this a notable development is that of 'Kirk Weeks', largely lay movements. It is certain, in spite of the doubts of some, that the Church did gain from the All Scotland Crusade of Billy Graham. Never in its history has there been more of the missionary spirit in the Church expressing itself in active churchly evangelism.

Reference must here be made to a special form of evangelism carried on by the Iona community which the brilliant gifts and forceful personality of its founder have made famous in every part of the world. Dr. George MacLeod comes of a family which for several generations has given ministers of great distinction to the Church. His grandfather was the 'Norman of the Barony' of whom we have heard so much. After a short ministry in St. Cuthbert's, Edinburgh, George MacLeod went to the huge industrial parish of Govan near Glasgow when the depression was at its worst; and he had already established himself as a radio preacher of rare power. In 1938, impatient with the ordinary ecclesiastical procedures, he conceived a highly original plan to supplement the training received by students for the ministry in the divinity halls by providing them with an opportunity to learn 'the technique of fellowship', and so to fit them 'to present to the modern day the active and latent vitality of Presbyterianism', especially in the new housing areas where church extension charges were being formed. A company of licentiates and craftsmen would live together for three months in summer in the island of Iona as a community in work and worship. The licentiates would engage to serve for two winters as assistants to ministers working in busy parishes before seeking charges of their own. Part of the plan was the restoration of the monastic buildings on Iona which since 1900 were under the guardianship of the Church of Scotland. While this project appealed to a romantic interest as recalling the life and labours of St. Columba, in many it created suspicions that were increased by certain not obviously Presbyterian emphases in theology, worship, and even in politics. The General Assembly of 1938 gave its blessing to what it regarded as a private experimental venture outside the normal working of the Church. Only after some rather painful tensions was the community accepted in 1949 as an official enterprise under the jurisdiction of the assembly. Its strength still lies in the personality of its leader, but with a growing membership and a powerful appeal to young people through largely attended conferences in Iona, its witness to Christian faith and life is already important and may be expected to increase.

In addition to its primary task of evangelism and in supplement of it the Church of Scotland carries on an expanding social service. Before the State assumed responsibility for the poor and unfortunate they had been the special care of the Church. Dr. Chalmers's famous social experiment in Glasgow was an attempt to prove that, given adequate organization, the Church could meet its obligations to the poor without recourse to legal assessments, of which, he believed, the inevitable consequence was pauperization. The Disruption put an end to such ideas, and State action has more and more replaced action by the Church and charitable societies, until today the Welfare State appears to look after its citizens from the cradle to the grave. But even the Welfare State with its abundant resources is unable to provide for every kind of personal need, and there is abundant scope still for Christian compassion. Since 1904 the pre-union Church of Scotland had a social work committee which opened institutions to help certain classes of needy persons. Today the social service of the Church is the largest and most varied organization of the kind in Scotland, and perhaps the most generally popular of its schemes. It provides homes for children orphaned or otherwise deprived of normal home life, hostels for working lads and young women far from home, institutions for the after-care of delinquents, and more recently Eventide Homes for aged persons. In all these ways the Church endeavours to show the tenderness and helpfulness and pity that are enjoined on His disciples by her Lord.

A Scotch presbytery, according to James VI, we may remember, 'agreeth with monarchy as God and the Devil. There Jack and Tom and Will and Dick shall meet and censure me and my Council.' 'Preaching to the times' was certainly a favourite and characteristic activity of Scottish ministers in the earlier Presbyterian periods. The Union of 1707 removed government to far-off Westminster and the Church of Scotland gradually abandoned the practice and came to share the political apathy of the people. In the nineteenth century when Presbyterianism was seriously and sharply divided attention was concentrated mainly upon issues domestic to the Churches and upon the question of ecclesiastical establishments. A new period of interest in public questions may be said to have begun during the First World War. In 1916 the Established Church appointed a commission to consider the moral and spiritual issues of the war, and its studies led it to raise the question of industrial unrest and social justice. In 1919 therefore a standing committee on Church and nation was set up with a very wide remit. Similar steps had been taken by the United Free Church, and in 1929 an enlarged committee was instructed 'to watch over developments of the Nation's life in which moral and spiritual considerations specially arise, and to consider what action the Church from time to time may be advised to take to further the highest interests of the people'. The Church was thus entering upon a very wide range of questions of general public interest. The committee's business was to study these, report upon them and formulate deliverances which the General Assembly might be asked to adopt. Among the topics dealt with at various times have been pacifism and the doctrine of the just war; atomic warfare and the hydrogen bomb; international relations and the cold war; refugees; questions of colonial policy, colour bar, the rights of colonial peoples and Central African Federation; Christianity and Communism; industrial relations; housing and health; marriage, divorce, and remarriage of divorced persons; broadcasting and television; rural depopulation in the Highlands and Lowlands of Scotland and other matters peculiarly affecting Scottish life and interests; betting and gambling and Lord's Day observance. Obviously some of these topics are highly controversial, and raise the whole issue of the wisdom and value of ecclesiastical pronouncements on matters of public policy. But the debates in the assembly to which they have given rise have often been of a high order, and as fully reported in the press have aroused widespread interest. The complaint is sometimes heard that the assembly with more than 1,600 members, ministers and elders in equal numbers, has become too large and unwieldy to work efficiently as a Supreme Court or as an administrative body, but it has acquired a new significance in the national life, and its deliverances are studied with care and respect by government departments, sometimes not without effect on policy. In this connexion some reference however brief must be made to the work of a special commission of which Dr. John Baillie was convener, appointed in 1940 in the dark days of the Second World War 'for the Interpretation of God's Will in the Present Crisis'. Its reports were submitted to successive general assemblies from 1941 to 1945 and were eagerly studied not only in Scotland but also in England and farther afield. They offered a searching and penetrating review of the nature and mission of the Universal Church in relation to the political, social, industrial, and educational aspects of modern civilization and to world evangelization, and they made clear what the situation implied in duty and opportunity for the Church of Scotland in particular. The recommendations of the commission were not all accepted by the Church to the disappointment of many thoughtful people, but a clearer vision of its evangelical and social task was presented to the Church as a whole.

The Union of 1929 took place exactly 100 years after the first foreign missionary of the Church of Scotland, Alexander Duff, had started work in India. During the century the divided Church had maintained and expanded the work then begun, and in time new Mission fields were opened in Africa, China, and elsewhere. Calcutta, Bombay, Madras, Kalimpong, Darjeeling, Blantyre (Nyasaland), Livingstonia, Lovedale, Calabar, the Gold Coast (Ghana) were familiar names in many a Scottish home, and Robert Laws, Donald Fraser, Alexander Hetherwick, and John A. Graham—not to mention Mary Slessor of Calabar—were heroes to the generation that accomplished the union. Indeed their devoted labours did much to make union possible and inevitable, for on the mission fields close and intimate co-operation was natural and necessary. The reunited Church was therefore a deeply committed missionary Church with responsibilities towards Christian communities growing up in many lands. But already the missionary situation was changing radically. The high-water mark of nineteenth-century missionary enterprise may be said to have been reached in 1910 when the World Missionary Conference was held in Edinburgh attended by delegates from nearly all the Protestant Churches and missionary societies in the world. Its purpose was to take stock of the missionary achievement and to promote fraternal co-operation between missionary agencies. The keynote was hope that the world might be won for Christ within a generation. Instead there came the First World War followed speedily by the Second, so that twice almost all humanity was drawn into ruinous strife that threatened civilization. It is true that the world has increasingly become one neighbourhood, but its racial and national cleavages have become deeper, and the contrast between the material standards of life in the rich and the poor nations more glaring. Once it could be said that the missionary expansion of Christianity went hand in hand with the imperial expansion of the Western nations. Today the slightest suggestion of 'imperialism', if it be only the offer of conditional technical or financial aid to undeveloped peoples, is an insuperable obstacle. In China missionary work has had to cease. Nevertheless possibly even in China and certainly elsewhere Christianity has taken root in the mission fields and 'younger Churches' have arisen conscious of their responsibility for their continuing life in free fellowship with the older Churches whose tutelage they are outgrowing. To work in equal partnership with these is now the aim of the Church's Foreign Mission Committee, and this idea appeals to the generation now entering the service of the Church, who readily offer for work abroad. Upwards of 300 missionaries are at present at work in eighteen different fields, and it has been truly said that 'the missionary enterprise of the Church stands now on the threshold of a period likely to be marked by unprecedented opportunity and very peculiar difficulty', in both respects not dissimilar from the situation that confronts the Church's mission at home, and in some ways more exhilarating.

The Scottish Presbyterian Churches were never completely isolated from the sister and daughter Churches of the Reformed tradition in Europe and America, but the formation of the Presbyterian Alliance in 1875 enabled them to realize more clearly that they belonged to a family of Churches of common origin, structure, and confession, comparable in numbers and influence with other denominations which about the same time were founding organizations on an international scale. It was, however, chiefly through their missionary activities that they were drawn into a still wider fellowship. The Ecumenical Movement, the most impressive event in recent church history, may be said to have originated in the World Missionary Conference, Edinburgh, 1910. From that conference came the International Missionary Council whose meetings at Jerusalem (1928) and Tambaram (1938) marked stages in a growing awareness of the urgency of the missionary task in an increasingly threatening world-situation, and of the need for Christian unity if the task was to be hopefully carried on. At Tambaram representatives of the younger Churches declared their passionate longing for visible and organic union, and appealed to the older Churches to take this matter seriously to heart. Not until 1947 after prolonged discussion was it possible to inaugurate the Church of South India embracing Anglicans, Presbyterians, Congregationalists, and Methodists, with a Church of Scotland missionary, Lesslie Newbigin, as one of its bishops. In the older Churches progress was necessarily even slower. But out of the Edinburgh Conference there also emerged the Movement of *Faith and Order* which after much preparatory work held its first conference in 1927 in Lausanne at which delegates from the Greek Orthodox Churches for the first time met representatives from the Protestant Churches of the West and engaged with them in frank and serious discussion. Meantime another movement sponsored by Archbishop Söderblom of Uppsala gathered a World Conference on *Life and Work* in Stockholm in 1925 to consider common modes of Christian social action. Further conferences on Faith and Order and Life and Work were held in 1937 in Edinburgh and Oxford respectively, and it was resolved to combine the two movements in a World Council of Churches, the formation of which was delayed by the war until 1948 when it was completed at Amsterdam. In all these movements towards church unity the Church of Scotland has been deeply involved. Some of its theologians have taken a prominent part in them, but it can hardly be claimed that the Ecumenical Movement has as yet made a notable impact on the general membership of the Church. The same may possibly be true of other Churches, but there are perhaps special reasons why it should be so in Scotland where since 1929 the Church of Scotland has embraced the bulk of the Protestant population, and ecclesiastical disunity is, generally speaking, less noticeable than for example in England and still more in the U.S.A.

It must, moreover, be frankly admitted that in Scotland the movement towards organic unity encounters one of the thorniest problems raised in the whole ecumenical discussion, for Scotland has witnessed the classical struggle, in political fact no less than in ecclesiastical theory, of presbytery and episcopacy; and in the Scottish Episcopal Church, in spite of its Scottish heritage, Anglicanism is met with in its most uncompromising form. Of fraternal feeling, spiritual unity, and even co-operation there is no lack. The Lambeth appeal for unity issued in 1920 was welcomed with complete and warm cordiality by both the Churches, but not until their contemplated union had taken place could action be taken. Conversations were, however, begun in 1932 and in 1934 a joint report was made of things believed in common and of things that might be undertaken in common. Both in England and in Scotland the report received a cool reception and there the matter rested for a time. A new start was made in 1949 and in 1957 another joint report, commonly called 'The Bishops' Report', was published. Unhappily it was treated by many in Scotland as an attempt to thrust bishops upon the Kirk, and has been rather summarily dealt with in the presbyteries, while Anglicans have said little. On the surface it has appeared that Presbyterians were giving away everything and Anglicans nothing, though it was hoped that the question was being approached in a new way and not in a bargaining spirit. It may be that in time both Anglicans and Presbyterians may come to realize that the ineffectiveness of their witness is due in no small part to mechanical defects in the organization of their ministries, in other words the imperfect adaptation of their inherited order to the vastly changed conditions in which they now find themselves.

The Church in Scotland has had a long and turbulent history since the time when Ninian and Columba and the shadowy Celtic saints first planted Christianity in this land. Through the many changes that have taken place it seems impossible to trace institutional continuity, though continuous witness to the Gospel there has been. Only since the Revolution Settlement of 1690 has the course been a straightforward one. From that time the distinctive features of the Church of Scotland as it is known today are discernible, though only after much contention and schism have its principles been at last vindicated, in a Church at once national and free, a Church and not a sect, acknowledging Christ as its only King and Head, and seeking to advance His Kingdom both at home and abroad. Firmly based on local congregational life, it is also closely knit into a whole through its graded church courts in which at every level elders of the people share equally with ministers in all decisions as to policy and administration. It has maintained a high ideal of parochial ministry whereby the faith has been kept, the Gospel preached, and the people schooled in Bible truth. It has won and in large part retained the affection of the Scottish people, even when so many of them sit somewhat loosely to its ordinances. Moreover its tradition has been enriched by the devotion of brave, good, and sincere men and women who have left behind a heritage not to be lightly surrendered but rather to be conserved and increased and used in a new age of unexampled difficulty but also of splendid opportunity.

E e

SELECT BIBLIOGRAPHY

General

Standard Histories of Scotland by J. HILL BURTON (1870); A. LANG
(1907); P. HUME BROWN (1909).
R. L. MACKIE, *A Short History of Scotland* (1931).
W. CROFT DICKINSON and GORDON DONALDSON, *Source Book of Scottish
History* (3 vols., 1950–4).
JOHN CUNNINGHAM, *Church History of Scotland* (1882).
GEORGE GRUB, *An Ecclesiastical History of Scotland* (1861).
A. BELLESHEIM, *History of the Catholic Church of Scotland* (1887). Trans-
lated by Hunter Blair.
A. R. MACEWEN, *History of the Church in Scotland (to 1560)* (1913).
JOHN A. DUKE, *History of the Church of Scotland to the Reformation* (1937).
HEW SCOTT, *Fasti Ecclesiae Scoticanae* (new edition, 8 vols., 1915–50).

Part I

R. G. COLLINGWOOD, *Roman Britain* (vol. i of the Oxford History of
England, 1937).
WILLIAM REEVES, *Life of Saint Columba* (Historians of Scotland, vol. vi,
1874).
LOUIS GOUGAUD, *Christianity in Celtic Lands* (1932).
JOHN A. DUKE, *The Columban Church* (1932).
DOUGLAS SIMPSON, *The Historical St. Columba* (1927).

Part II

JOHN DOWDEN, *The Mediæval Church in Scotland* (1910).
G. G. COULTON, *The Scottish Abbeys and Social Life* (1937).
D. PATRICK, *The Statutes of the Scottish Church* (1907).
ARCHBISHOP HAMILTON, *Catechism* (ed. T. G. Law, 1884).
D. A. EASSON, *The Mediæval Religious Houses of Scotland* (1957).
P. LORIMER, *Patrick Hamilton* (1857).
ALEXANDER MYLN, *Lives of the Bishops of Dunkeld* (ed. C. Innes for Banna-
tyne Club, 1831).
HECTOR BOECE, *Lives of the Bishops of Aberdeen* (ed. J. Moir for New Spald-
ing Club, 1894).

Part III

JOHN KNOX, *History of the Reformation* (ed. W. Croft Dickinson, 1949).
(Contains in appendices *The Scots Confession* and *First Book of Disci-
pline*).
THOMAS LEISHMAN, *Liturgy of John Knox* (*Book of Common Order*).
P. HUME BROWN, *John Knox* (1895).
THOMAS MCCRIE, *Life of John Knox* (1811); *Life of Andrew Melville* (1819).

A. F. MITCHELL, *The Westminster Assembly* (1890).
R. L. ORR, *Alexander Henderson* (1919).
JOHN BUCHAN, *Montrose* (1928).
E. A. KNOX, *Robert Leighton* (1930).
W. LAW MATHIESON, *Politics and Religion in Scotland 1550–1695* (1902).

Part IV

R. H. STORY, *William Carstares* (1874).
THOMAS BOSTON, *Memoirs* (1776).
—— *Human Nature in its Fourfold State* (1720).
A. R. MACEWEN, *The Erskines* (1900).
—— *Life and Letters of Dr. John Cairns* (1895).
ALEXANDER CARLYLE, *Autobiography* (ed. J. Hill Burton, 1866).
DONALD CAMPBELL, *Memorials of John McLeod Campbell* (1877).
WILLIAM HANNA, *Memoir of Thomas Chalmers* (4 vols., 1849–52).
R. H. STORY, *Life of Robert Story of Rosneath* (1862).
—— *Life and Remains of Robert Lee* (1870).
P. CARNEGIE SIMPSON, *Life of Principal Rainy* (2 vols., 1909).
H. GREY GRAHAM, *The Social Life of Scotland in the Eighteenth Century* (1900).
J. R. FLEMING, *A History of the Church in Scotland 1843–1929* (2 vols., 1927, 1933).

Part V

G. D. HENDERSON, *Heritage* (1930).
AUGUSTUS MUIR, *John White* (1958).
Reports of Commission for the Interpretation of God's Will in the Present Crisis (1945).

KINGS OF SCOTS TO THE UNION
OF THE CROWNS

Duncan I, 1034–40

Macbeth, 1040–57

Malcolm III (Canmore), 1058–93, m. Margaret

Edgar, 1097–1107   Alexander I, 1107–24   David, 1124–53

Prince Henry

Malcolm IV,   William the Lion, 1165–1214   David, Earl of
1153–65   Huntingdon

Alexander II, 1214–49

Alexander III, 1249–86

Queen of Norway

Margaret, Maid of Norway, 1286–90

John Balliol, 1292–6

Robert I (Bruce), 1306–29

Marjory, m. Robert II (Stewart), 1371–90   David II, 1329–71

Robert III, 1390–1406

James I, 1406–37

James II, 1437–60

James III, 1460–88

James IV, 1488–1513

James V, 1513–42

Mary Queen of Scots, 1542–67

James VI, 1567–1625

INDEX

Note. Dates given in the index are inserted as a matter of convenience, to show the period of the person concerned or to distinguish namesakes: their accuracy is not guaranteed, early and medieval dates being often uncertain; *c.* = circa (about), d. = died; pairs of dates are those of reign or office, *not* birth and death.